INSIGHT

SPAIN

www.insightguides.com/Spain

⊙ Walking Eye App

YOUR FREE DESTINATION CONTENT AND EBOOK AVAILABLE THROUGH THE WALKING EYE APP

Your guide now includes a free eBook and destination content for your chosen destination, all for the same great price as before. Simply download the Walking Eye App from the App Store or Google Play to access your free eBook and destination content.

HOW THE WALKING EYE APP WORKS

Through the Walking Eye App, you can purchase a range of eBooks and destination content. However, when you buy this book, you can download the corresponding eBook and destination content for free. Just see below in the grey panels where to find your free content and then scan the QR code at the bottom of this page.

Destinations: Download your corresponding essential destination content from here, featuring recommended sights and attractions, restaurants, hotels and an A–Z of practical information, all for free. Other destinations are available for purchase.

Ships: Interested in ship reviews? Find independent reviews of river and ocean ships in this section, all available for purchase.

eBooks: You can download your free accompanying digital version of this guide here. You will also find a whole range of other eBooks, all available for purchase.

Free access to travel-related blog articles about different destinations, updated on a daily basis.

HOW THE DESTINATION CONTENT WORKS

Each destination includes a short introduction, an A–Z of practical information and recommended points of interest, split into 4 different categories:

- Highlights
- Accommodation
- Eating out
- What to do

You can view the location of every point of interest and save it by adding it to your Favourites. In the 'Around Me' section you can view all the points of interest within 5km.

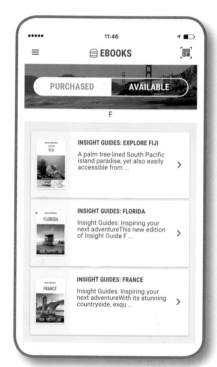

HOW THE EBOOKS WORK

The eBooks are provided in EPUB file format. Please note that you will need an eBook reader installed on your device to open the file. Many devices come with this as standard, but you may still need to install one manually from Google Play.

The eBook content is identical to the content in the printed guide.

HOW TO DOWNLOAD THE WALKING EYE APP

1. Download the Walking Eye App from the App Store or Google Play.
2. Open the app and select the scanning function from the main menu.
3. Scan the QR code on this page – you will then be asked a security question to verify ownership of the book.
4. Once this has been verified, you will see your eBook and destination content in the purchased ebook and destination sections, where you will be able to download them.

Other destination apps and eBooks are available for purchase separately or are free with the purchase of the Insight Guide book.

Contents

Introduction

The Best of Spain 6
Bienvenidos 19
The Spanish People 21

History

Decisive Dates 26
From Prehistory to the
    Visigoth Conquest 31
Muslim Spain 39
The Age of Empire 47
The Civil War and the Franco
    Regime 55
Democracy and Autonomy 63

Features

Spanish Painting 73
Flamenco 81
The Bulls 88
Outdoor Activities 93
Food and Wine 99
Wildlife 105

Insights

PHOTO FEATURES

Fiestas 86
Castilian Castles 160
Granada's Gardens 214
Antoni Gaudí's Vision 266
The Guggenheim in Bilbao 316

MINI FEATURES

Spain's Gypsies 25
Regional Autonomy 69
Spanish Wine 103
Café Life 137
Holy Week 197
The Santiago Legend 336
Inspirational Island 362

Places

Introduction 117
Madrid 123
Madrid Province 139
Castilla y León 147
Castilla-La Mancha 163
Extremadura 173
Seville 187
Córdoba 199
Granada 207
Andalusia 217
Valencia and Murcia 231
Barcelona 251
Catalonia 269
Aragón 283
Navarre and La Rioja 293
The Basque Country 305
Cantabria and Asturias 319
Galicia 329
The Canary Islands 345
The Balearic Islands 357

Travel Tips

TRANSPORT

Getting There 374
  By Air 374
  By Rail 374
  By Road 374
  By Sea 374
Getting Around......................374
  Airport Transfer................374
  Madrid Transport..............375
  By Air 376
  By Rail 376
  By Bus 376
  By Road 377
  By Sea 377

A – Z

Accommodation 378
Admission Charges 378
Budgeting for Your Trip 378
Climate.................................378
Crime and Security 379
Customs Regulations............379
Disabled Travellers 379
Electricity 379
Embassies and Consulates ..379

Entry Regulations 379
Festivals...............................380
Gay and Lesbian
  Travellers.........................380
Health and Medical Care 380
Internet 381
Lost Property.........................381
Media 381
Money 381
Opening Hours......................382
Postal Services 382
Religious Services 382
Student Travellers.................382
Telephones 382
Tourist Information 382
Tour Operators 384
Websites 384
Weights and Measures 384

LANGUAGE 385

FURTHER READING 389

Maps

Spain 118
Madrid...................................120

Madrid Province 140
Castilla y León.......................148
Segovia 158
Castilla-La Mancha 164
Toledo....................................167
Extremadura 174
Seville....................................190
Córdoba 202
Granada 208
Andalusia 220
Valencia 232
Valencia and Murcia..............239
Barcelona...............................248
Costa Brava 270
Catalonia................................272
Aragón...................................286
Basque Country, Navarre
  and Rioja............................306
Cantabria and
  Asturias.............................320
Galicia 332
Canary Islands.......................346
Balearic Islands.....................358
Inside front cover Spain
Inside back cover Barcelona
  and Madrid Metro maps

THE BEST OF SPAIN: TOP ATTRACTIONS

From art and architecture to fiestas and flamenco, here is a rundown of Spain's most spectacular attractions.

△ **Alhambra**. Part forbidding fortress, part ornately decorated palace, part complex of secretive pleasure gardens, this masterpiece overlooking the city of Granada is one of the wonders of Spain, and the world. See page 209.

△ **Prado, Reina Sofía and Thyssen-Bornemisza**. Madrid's three great galleries are all within walking distance of each other. Between them they comprise one of the world's greatest collections of art. See pages 126, 128 and 127.

▽ **Barcelona**. The unmistakable architectural creations of Antoni Gaudí draw visitors to this exciting Mediterranean city. His as yet unfinished masterpiece is the extraordinary church of the Sagrada Família. See page 266.

△ **Córdoba**. A forest of pillars and horseshoe arches, the Mezquita (mosque) here testifies to the magnificence and architectural genius of the Muslim civilisation that ruled Spain in the Middle Ages. See page 201.

△ **The costas**. These are a paradise for water sports. There's good scuba diving off the Costa Brava, and Tarifa, looking across the straits to north Africa, is Europe's windsurfing capital. See page 221.

▷ **Alcázar**. Central Spain is a land of castles – hence its historic name of Castile. The most spectacular of them is the ship-shaped Alcázar at Segovia, more fantasy than defence. See page 159.

△ **Santiago de Compostela**. A famous medieval route of pilgrimage crosses the whole of northern Spain linking up Romanesque and Gothic churches until it culminates in this massive, 13th-century cathedral. See page 333.

▽ **El Teide**. Volcanic activity has shaped and continued to shape the subtropical Canary Islands in the Atlantic. The centre of Tenerife is dominated by this peak and its surrounding national park. See page 352.

△ **Guggenheim Museum**. The creation of Frank Gehry's futuristic, titanium-clad building has transformed the formerly industrial, steel-making Basque city of Bilbao into one of Europe's most lively cultural destinations. See page 316.

▽ **Flamenco**. The fiery, foot-tapping, hand-clapping rhythm of Spain is provided by flamenco: a form of music, song and dance combining a variety of influences but always fuelled by strong emotion. See page 81.

THE BEST OF SPAIN: EDITOR'S CHOICE

Spain is an extraordinarily varied country for the visitor. Here are our recommendations for what to see and do, from the most dramatic landscapes and best resorts to the finest art collections and family attractions.

Ría de Corcubión, Galicia.

BEST LANDSCAPES

Rias Baixas (Galicia). Indented Atlantic coastline of estuaries, beaches, woods and islands and pretty villages. Also a good place to eat seafood and drink white wines. See page 338.

Picos de Europa (Cantabria/Asturias). An attractive mountain range with easy access from the north coast. The highlight is the Fuente Dé cable car. See page 323.

Serra de Tramuntana, Mallorca. Spectacular mountain range hovering over the island's west coast. A high-level road provides one of Europe's most breathtaking drives. See page 363.

Las Alpujarras, Granada province (Andalusia). Pretty valleys on the south side of the Sierra Nevada, their slopes dotted with delightful villages. A great area for walking. See page 229.

El Teide, Tenerife. Volcanic peak with cable-car ride almost to the top. See page 352.

Costa Brava (Catalonia). Spain's most attractive strip of coastline: from Lloret de Mar to Pals, a rugged succession of cliffs and coves concealing a handful of traditional fishing villages and secluded beaches. See page 269.

FAVOURITE FIESTAS

Carnival (February/March). A revelrous start to Lent which is celebrated all over but at its best in Santa Cruz de Tenerife and Cádiz.

Las Fallas Valencia (week leading up to 19 March). Noisy spectacle in which towering papier-mâché monuments are burnt in the streets.

Semana Santa (Easter Week). Celebrated everywhere but at its most sensual in Seville, where religious sculptures are paraded through the streets.

April Fair Seville (April). A colourful and lively week-long celebration of Andalusian culture, with horses and carriages, gaudy dresses, flamenco music and fino sherry.

Los Sanfermines Pamplona (6–14 July). World famous because of its dare-devil early-morning bull running.

Moors and Christians Alcoi near Alicante (April). Mock medieval pageantry with costumed armies fighting symbolic battles to commemorate the Reconquest.

Sant Joan Ciutadella, Menorca (24 June). Elegantly dressed riders put their horses through a series of ritualised medieval games.

El Rocio (May/June). A colourful mass pilgrimage to El Rocio on the edge of Doñana National Park.

BEST ALL-ROUND RESORTS

Barcelona. It's only a short hop across the harbour from the medieval Gothic Quarter to a string of seven beaches. See page 251.
San Sebastián. A perfect horseshoe bay of sand forms the centrepiece of Spain's most stately summer resort. See page 307.
Cádiz. Ancient Atlantic seaport of narrow streets built on an isthmus, with beaches to choose from on three sides. See page 219.
Las Palmas de Gran Canaria. A city with a handsome old colonial quarter and various museums complement one of the Canary Islands' most popular beaches, the Playa de las Canteras. See page 346.
Palma de Mallorca. The capital city of an island best known for its package holidays is rich in sights, including Arab baths, a Gothic cathedral and a castle. See page 359.
Valencia. The city centre, packed with monuments and museums, is only a tram ride from the beach. Close by, too, is the City of Arts and Sciences. See page 231.

Santillana del Mar.

Barceloneta beach, Barcelona.

ONLY IN SPAIN

Tapas. Found all over Spain, these little food dishes are perfect with a glass of chilled beer. See page 102.
Torre de Hércules. The world's only Roman-era lighthouse can be found in A Coruña (Galicia). See page 331.
Castells. Catalonia's human towers, built during festivals, are now on Unesco's list of Intangible Cultural Heritage. See page 277.
Iberian Lynx. This indigenous wild cat has been saved from extinction thanks to conservation programmes in Doñana National Park and Jaén's Sierra de Andújar. See page 106.
Don Quijote. Traces of Spanish literature's most famous character can be found in Castilla La Mancha. See page 163.
Valle de los Caídos. The burial place of General Franco is an imposing reminder of the Civil War. See page 143.

PICTURESQUE PUEBLOS

The White Towns of Andalusia (Cádiz and Málaga). An infinity of pretty, compact towns scattered across the hillsides of the south, the best of them being Ronda, which stands astride a gorge. See page 223.
Baeza and Úbeda (Jaén). Two harmonious towns packed with Renaissance architecture in the midst of endless olive groves. See page 228.
La Orotava (Tenerife). Elegant colonial mansions with wooden balconies and inner courtyards lining narrow cobbled streets. See page 352.
Dalt Vila, Eivissa (Ibiza). The island capital's upper town is a historic citadel overlooking the harbour. Within the walls you will find a cobbled maze packed with whitewashed houses. See page 370.
Santillana del Mar (Cantabria). A perfectly preserved medieval town of gold-coloured stone houses, cobbled streets, farmyards and patrician mansions. A delight to stroll around. See page 322.
Morella (Castellón). Mountain town of handsome Gothic mansions, surrounded by a ring of walls. See page 238.
Alcalá del Júcar (Albacete). Spectacularly sited in a gorge with some of its houses excavated deep into the rock of a river meander. See page 170.

Jamón, jamón!

Royal Andalusian School of Equestrian Art, Jerez de la Frontera.

Fundació Joan Miró.

BEST ART COLLECTIONS

Museo de Bellas Artes. Located in an old convent in Seville, this museum features masterpieces by Zurbarán, Murillo, Goya, El Greco and Velázquez. See page 196.

Museo Nacional del Prado. This Madrid gallery is one of the great art museums of the world. See page 126.

Museo Nacional Centro de Arte Reina Sofía. The national modern art collection in Madrid includes Picasso's *Guernica*. See page 128.

Museo Thyssen-Bornemisza. Stunning privately assembled collection, in Madrid. See page 127.

Teatre-Museu Dalí. See the strange world of Salvador Dalí in the town of his birth, Figueres (see page 273). His former home is in the beautiful coastal town of Cadaqués. See page 274.

Museu Picasso. Visit both this one in Barcelona (see page 255) and the Museo Picasso in Málaga. See page 225.

Museo de Arte Abstracto. A gallery of abstract paintings in a house overhanging a precipice in Cuenca. See page 171.

Fundació Joan Miró (Barcelona). Collection of paintings, sculptures and drawings by the master of modern art. See page 264.

SPAIN FOR FAMILIES

These attractions are popular with children, though not all will suit every age group.

Waterparks. Open from May or June to September. These are mainly on the coast – there is one within easy reach of every major resort – but there are also five around Madrid. See www.aquopolis.es for details.

Theme parks. Two of the biggest, and suited to a whole day out, are Port Aventura on the Costa Daurada and Parque Warner outside Madrid.

Zoos and aquariums. There are zoos and aquariums in or around most cities. Jerez de la Frontera and Barcelona have Spain's best zoos. See pages 219 and 259.

Cable cars. Two of the best rides are up the Rock of Gibraltar and to the heights of the Picos de Europa from Fuente Dé in Cantabria. See pages 223 and 324.

Shows. The Real Escuela Andaluza del Arte Ecuestre at Jerez is famous for its dancing horses. See page 219.

Hiking in the Parque Nacional de Ordesa.

BEST NATIONAL PARKS

Parque Nacional de Ordesa, Huesca (Aragón). The most dramatic scenery of the high Pyrenees offering a range of marked walks from the easy to the extreme. See page 290.
Parque Nacional de Doñana, Huelva and Seville provinces (Andalusia). Protected wetlands and dunes with rare wildlife which can be seen on a guided 4x4 excursion. See page 217.
Parque Nacional de Garajonay, La Gomera (Canary Islands). Home to the Alto de Garajonay, La Gomera's highest peak – 1,487m (4,878ft). See page 353.
Parc Nacional d'Aigüestortes i Estany de Sant Maruici, Catalonia. Very popular with hikers, with a backdrop of snowcapped peaks, lakes and valleys. See page 276.
Parque Nacional de la Caldera de Taburiente, La Palma. Breathtaking scenery. The giant crater has been colonised by nature into a green, fertile valley. See page 353.

On the green at Valderrama Golf Course, Málaga.

Tibidabo theme park, Barcelona.

BEST OUTDOOR ACTIVITIES

Hiking. One of Spain's most spectacular walking destinations is the Serra de Tramuntana, now a World Heritage Site, on Mallorca. See page 363.
Cycling. The Camino del Cid, following the footsteps of El Cid from Burgos to Valencia, is a popular long-distance cycling route. See page 95.
Skiing. Spain offers some great skiing, including Sierra Nevada – Europe's most southerly ski resort. See page 229.
Surfing. The best place to head is the Basque coast, home of the renowned Mundaka wave. See page 93.
Windsurfing. Fuerteventura and Tarifa offer world-class windsurfing conditions – and plenty of tuition. See page 349.

MONEY-SAVING TIPS

Menú del Día. The cheapest eating option is always the set meal *(menú del día)* which most restaurants – even expensive ones – will offer at weekday lunch times and sometimes in the evenings and at weekends.
Rural hotels. Spain has a glut of exquisite small rural hotels that often offer very low prices outside peak seasons.

Shopping. Street markets are the cheapest places to shop for food, clothes and everyday items. In the countryside, look out for roadside farms selling produce direct.
Tourist cards. The largest, most visited cities, such as Madrid, Barcelona and Seville, offer cards which are valid on public transport and give free or reduced admission to a variety of monuments.

Fiestas. Between Easter and the end of September there is almost always a fiesta going on somewhere in Spain offering free entertainment.
Free admission. Many museums and art galleries have a time when admission is free. We provide this information in the opening times for each attraction when this is the case. You can also ask in the tourist office at the beginning of your stay.

Coastline along the Rías Baixas, Galicia.

Toledo, Castilla-La Mancha.

Inside the Mezquita (mosque) in Córdoba.

PARA GLORIA DE LAS ARTES
Y ORNATO DE LA CAPITAL
ERIGIO
ISABEL SEGUNDA
ESTE MONUMENTO

BIENVENIDOS

You can visit Spain for its impressive buildings and
museums, its immense landscapes or abundant
wildlife. But in the end it is the Spaniards' spirit
that makes the biggest impact.

Family fun on the Costa Brava.

S pain. To the ancient Greeks, it was the land where Hercules' golden apples grew; to the Arabs, it was the ground floor of heaven; to writers such as George Orwell and Ernest Hemingway, it was an arena where history skittered between heroic feats and tragedy, and bullfighters flirted with death in the work of an afternoon. Few other places so dramatically stimulate the imagination. Isolated from the rest of Europe behind the Pyrenees, Spain was, for a long time, a mysterious, half-mythical country better known for fictional inhabitants – Don Juan, Don Quixote and Carmen – than its real ones.

Spain has changed beyond recognition since the demise of the *ancien régime* of General Franco in 1975. It has become a mainstream Western European country (although, like the other Mediterranean countries, it has had its fair share of problems since 2008). In the process of transition, the old clichés and the rough charm which so delighted early visitors have been mainly consigned to history. In their place, Spain has vastly improved transport networks, an incredible choice of hotels and restaurants (San Sebastián is a hotspot), and an increasing respect for its national heritage, both manmade and natural. Some of its cities, such as Barcelona, Bilbao and Madrid, are recognised the world over for their cultural riches; Ibiza is Europe's foremost clubbing destination, while the international jetset make a beeline for Marbella and Mallorca.

Flamenco in Seville.

Some things, however, have not changed, and your trip will have a couple of constants. One is light: the sunshine Northern Europeans flock to bask in, the burnished red-gold that suffuses whole cities, the lunar contrasts of sun and shadow, the light El Greco, Velázquez and Picasso saw and painted by.

The other is the tremendous vitality and sociability of the people, which is observed in the busy cafés and strolling Sunday-evening crowds, in exuberant fiesta celebrations, and in the dignified courtesy of almost any stranger you ask for directions.

Puerto Marina, Málaga.

THE SPANISH PEOPLE

Spanish society has evolved rapidly over the past
30 years, and its traditional values are being
increasingly questioned by the young generation.

No other European country has changed as
much in living memory as Spain. For 500
years, from its unification in 1492 almost
until the end of the 20th century, Spanish society remained remarkably homogeneous in its
ethnicity, religion and culture. But when Franco
died in 1975 people were ready for change. Since
then three powerful, long-pent-up forces – the
demands for devolution and personal freedom,
and the influence of other countries – have been
sending shockwaves through the country, with
their long-term consequences yet unknown.

> Most of Spain's 47 million inhabitants live in
> a few densely populated cities, and her long
> reaches of unfarmed, uninhabited terrain
> enhance a sense of vastness and solitude.
> Spanish people tend to speak of Europe as if
> it were elsewhere.

Children by the Puerta del Puente, Córdoba.

Reawakening of the regions

The first of these forces is regionalism, which
has fought for centuries with the imperialist and
Francoist dream of creating 'one Spain'. As part of
the settlement that transformed dictatorship into
democracy, demands for regional autonomy were
assuaged with a federal constitution (see page
66) which has led to much more than political
devolution. The promotion of regional languages
to joint-official status with Spanish in their respective regions has weakened the already vague defi-
nition of 'Spanishness'. Many people in the Basque
Country and Catalonia wouldn't describe themselves as Spanish except in the most reluctant and
half-hearted of senses. Only support for Spain's
football team in international competitions seems
capable of awakening any sense of national pride.

Force of freedom

The second force that drives the new Spain is
the demand for personal freedom. Freedom
in the political sense was won during the
re-establishment of democracy, and this led
to a 'permissive' reaction against 40 years of
repression. The big loser has been the Catholic Church, which threw its lot in with Franco
but which is marginalised under the secular
constitution. Nevertheless, the Church still
has power and prestige in modern Spain,
even though its role is being redefined. When
questioned, 76 percent of Spaniards regularly
tell pollsters they are Catholics, but only a
small minority attend Mass. The best the
Church can do is try to reassert its influence

through the education system, although its involvement here is highly controversial.

If the Church has been the loser in the social shake-up, women have been the victors. Many have seized the chance offered by new times to pursue careers or enjoy easier lives of consumerism rather than be domestic slaves to their husbands and families as their mothers were. As a result, the birth rate has slumped from over three babies on average per woman in the 1970s to less than one and a half today – one of the lowest rates in the world.

Skateboard and scooter tricks in Parc Diagonal Mar, Barcelona.

Influences from abroad

The third and arguably most influential force that has been reshaping Spanish society over the last 30 years is an ambition for Spain to be on a par with its European neighbours. When World War II ended and Europe began to work together and reconstruct, Spain was cut off behind the Pyrenees with its own anachronistic breed of Fascism. With Franco out of the way there was a lot of diplomatic catching up to do, and on 1 January 1986 Spain underwent a quiet revolution when it joined the EC (now the EU). European money provided the country with the modern transport and communication structure it badly needed, and European membership gave Spaniards a conspicuous shot of self-confidence. Spain not only established the same standard of living as in Britain, France and Germany but, in some ways, surpassed its neighbours – it certainly surpassed its own expectations.

Then things started to unravel during the economic crisis of 2008. In Spain, the fifth largest economy in the EU, it was instigated by the issuing of long-term loans and mortgages followed by the crash of the construction sector. In June 2012 a €100 billion bailout package was agreed by the EU for Spanish banks, several of which had been downgraded to 'junk' status.

During the boom years, Spain had become the glittering prize for the 21st century's migrants, the itinerant poor of North and Central Africa, Latin America and Eastern Europe who saw the country as a privileged society with wealth to spare. However since 2008, while many migrants have stayed in Spain due to considerably better living conditions than in their own countries, many have left due to the lack of jobs.

Tourism too was initially affected but overseas visitors are now returning to the Iberian shores since many of the 'cheaper' destinations, like Turkey, North Africa and the Middle East, have experienced political instability in recent years.

The generation gap

Spain may have undergone a badly needed transformation, but there may yet be a social price to pay. The changes have caused a yawning gulf to open up between the generations.

While people past retirement age remember the hardships of Spain after the Civil War, and anyone over the age of 50 remembers the humiliation of living in a Spain cut off from the rest of Europe by its dictatorship, the younger generation has never known anything but democracy and freedom and they take both for granted. They have grown up unquestioningly accepting the values of the consumer society which amount to *'casa, coche, ropa y copa'* (flat, car, clothes and drinks). However, things have been changing since 2008. Just as their grandparents travelled abroad as economic migrants or political exiles, today's young people are increasingly moving overseas in search of work – almost 500,000 left Spain in between 2009 and 2015 due to the high rate of unemployment and lack of opportunities.

The combination of more women working, the reduced birth rate and a younger generation driven by individualism rather than duty has put pressure on the family, which has always been the linchpin of society. Spaniards of all ages remain attached to their families yet the pressures of the economic crisis have led to a considerable amount of family breakdown. But children are still adored, and old people are respected, although now increasingly consigned to retirement homes rather than looked after by their busy families.

Language and culture

Despite all the changes that are taking place, there are still some constants which hold society together and give Spanish people their

Spaniards adore television and guzzle an endless amount of 'reality TV.'

Territory

For all the protestations of Basque and Catalan nationalists, the territory of Spain is another unifying force. To the north, the Iberian peninsula is all but cut off by the Pyrenees – in 400km (250 miles) there are only five main roads across the mountains, and most traffic is squeezed through narrow passes at either end. To the south, a narrow but strategic strait forms an abrupt bound-

Locals catch up on Explanada de España, Alicante.

identity. Chief of these is their language, which is more widely spoken in the world than ever before (thanks, partly, to the growth in the Hispanic population of the US) and more fashionable to learn now than French. Despite the emphasis given to regional languages, Spanish remains the lingua franca, and a whole culture goes with it which is barely perceived by the anglophone world. Spanish has a rich backlist of classic literature and a thriving contemporary publishing industry. Arguably, the art form of the moment is cinema, with Pedro Almodóvar as its unofficial ambassador making films about the undiluted, melodramatic passions which he sees as the timeless mark of the Spanish character. On a more pedestrian level, most

ary between the developed and developing worlds, and Africa, a neighbour with whom Spain is reluctant to be associated too closely, is just 16km (10 miles) away.

Spaniards have always been notoriously loyal to their localities, but one tangible benefit of the new prosperity has been a growth in domestic travel. Whereas people were once inclined to shrug off their national heritage, regional cuisines and traditional festivities as just part of the backdrop, now they are realising the intrinsic value of such things.

Daily life

The working day begins at the same time as everywhere else but lasts until 2pm. The long morning allows time to get a lot done, and some people manage to fit an entire working day into it. Lunch is eaten around 3pm, and although not everyone sleeps a siesta after eating, this is generally a moment to rest. The afternoon begins again at 5pm and a night out starts after dinner at 10pm.

The origin of this daily pattern of life becomes obvious if you visit the south in summer. In Andalusia, the heat makes it impossible to get anything done in the middle of the day, and by far the best time to be out on the streets is in the cool air late at night.

Restaurant in Barcelona's La Ribera neighbourhood.

REGIONAL RULE

Scores of rulers have attempted to unify this country of 47 million individualists who speak four languages and seven different dialects. Franco forbade the use in public of any language except Castilian; it is still the country's only official language. The outburst of regionalism after Franco's death was such that today Spanish-speaking people must arm themselves with a dictionary when visiting Catalonia, Galicia, the Basque Country, and parts of Levante and the Balearics, where regional governments promote the local language. But a dictionary is of no use on the island of La Gomera, where some locals still use Silbo Gomero, a whistled language.

Unwritten rules

The gregarious nature of the Spanish has created a society in which solitude and anonymity are little desired and peace and quiet can be hard to find. The country runs on an unspoken agreement to live and let live, as seen by its high level of background noise. Motorbikes without silencers race through village streets at 3am without raising a whisper of complaint, and most bars have a television (sometimes two) permanently on in the background with no one watching.

At home people make as much noise as they want, when they want, as an inalienable right. If you complain about the racket the people in the flat above are making you're likely to invite the pragmatic response: 'We don't like listening to other people's noise either, that's why we bought a top-floor flat. If you don't like it, do the same.'

This attitude is trivial enough when it concerns two neighbours, but in politics it can lead to corruption. In local politics there is often an unspoken assumption that the party which wins the town hall gets to bend the rules to suit it. A councillor or mayor may feel obliged to give jobs and favours to his friends and family, and the press is duly indignant when such things are exposed. But most Spaniards hesitate to pass too strong a judgement, knowing that if they were in the same position they might feel pressured to act in the same way.

Symbolic bulls

The individual's right to do what he or she wants without criticism reaches its most extreme expression in Pamplona's famous bull-run. Across Spain, people watch the *encierro* and its gorings live on television. Suggest that serious injuries inflicted by charging bulls could and should be avoided, if only to make space in hospitals for those who have had accidents through no fault of their own, and you will be regarded with uncomprehending eyes. The answer is not even worth putting into words: if life is reduced to a series of bureaucratic health and safety measures, what point is there in it? If anything can convince the young that there are elements of their Spanish heritage worth hanging on to, it may be precisely such attitudes. For all their affluence, they still come from a country which values socialising in the flesh over electronic connectivity and in which the thrills of life have not yet all been confined to theme parks.

Spain's Gypsies

The Spanish Gypsies, of Hindu descent, migrated out of India into Europe in the 15th century.

George Borrow wrote of the Gypsies, or *gitanos*: 'I felt myself very much more at home with them than with the silent, reserved men of Spain...' When he travelled with them in the 1830s they had been in Spain for over 400 years, yet he found them to be foreigners in their own land, clinging to their language and culture long after they had begun to settle in the 18th century.

Today, nearly two centuries later, the Gypsies still hover on the edges of society. A few may catch the limelight as singing or dance stars, but more often they remain largely invisible in Spanish art, history and literature – Carmen, for example, the heroine of Bizet's opera, was the creation of Frenchman Prosper Mérimée. As one Gypsy patriarch puts it, they are 'one of the most unknown people in the world'.

Who, then, are the Spanish Gypsies or *gitanos*? Of Hindu descent, from Rajasthan in north-western India, they left their homeland for unknown reasons – possibly an invasion – and migrated slowly westwards via Persia to arrive in Spain in the 15th century, bringing with them their language *(caló)*, costume, social laws and large flocks of sheep and goats. Travelling in groups to avoid attack, they worked as blacksmiths, professional musicians, fortune-tellers, horse-dealers and sheep-shearers.

A growing population

Six hundred years later there are an estimated 600,000 Gypsies in Spain, and, with the highest birth rate in Europe, their numbers could double in the next 30 years. Around half live in Andalusia.

Gypsies may be antique- or scrap-dealers, fruit-pickers, market-stall holders, horse-handlers, flamenco musicians, or flower-sellers. In less independent jobs they often disguise their origins for fear of racism. Few have accumulated material wealth, and they are often intensely religious. The Gypsy Holy Week processions are among the most moving in southern Spain, and there have been sweeping conversions to Evangelism in some Gypsy communities. Only a few words of *caló* are sprinkled through their speech, but they remain closely bound by private social rules, family loyalties, patriarchal authority and cultural pride.

The Gypsies' marginalised position is explained by their history in Spain. Relentless persecution from 1499 was aimed at forced assimilation through restricted movement and eradication of their culture. To quote one of a dozen laws, Philip IV's Pragmatic of 1633 banned *gitano* language, costume, music, horse-dealing, possession of weapons, marriage and association in public as well as the use of the

Day of the Gypsy, Pamplona.

word 'Gypsy', on pain of life slavery. Even Charles III's 1783 law granting equal rights of work and residence made Gypsy 'behaviour' punishable by red-hot irons or the death sentence. Settlement and integration finally began in the 18th century in southern towns where the Gypsies had taken on jobs such as blacksmithing. But it was to be a slow process.

Today the Constitution protects the Gypsies' rights, but the exclusion of *gitano* children from schools and housing schemes is an everyday event. In response, the Gypsies have learned to defend their culture not only through Civil Rights movements, but also, with humour, art – and, as in Borrow's time, by keeping a safe distance from Spanish society.

DECISIVE DATES

800,000 BC
Hominids, thought to be the earliest Europeans, live in Sierra de Atapuerca near Burgos.

18,000–14,000 BC
People of the Stone Age Magdelanian culture create the cave paintings at Altamira in northern Spain.

11th–5th century BC
Phoenicians and Greeks land, establishing trading centres and colonies. Invading Celts intermingle with indigenous Iberians.

3rd and 1st century BC
Carthaginians conquer southeast Spain. The capture of Sagunto by the Carthaginian general Hannibal leads to the Second Punic War (218–201 BC). Rome triumphs and begins its 200-year conquest of Spain (Hispania).

1st century AD
Christianity spreads in Spain.

Roman amphitheatre, Tarragona.

Ambassadors' Room in the Alcázar, Seville.

409
Vandals and Barbarians invade from north.

414
Visigoths conquer Swabians and Vandals and establish a monarchy. They rule Spain as a Christian nation for three centuries, with Toledo as their capital. In 589 Roman Catholicism is adopted as Spain's state religion.

711
Battle of Guadalete: Muslims invade and conquer the kingdom. They succeed in capturing most of Spain in two years.

722
Battle of Covadonga won by Christians.

1085
Toledo recaptured by Christians.

The Catholic Monarchs

1474
Isabel, wife of Fernando of Aragón, succeeds Enrique IV of Castile.

1478
The Inquisition introduced by papal bull.

1479
Fernando becomes King of Aragon; Christian Spain is united under one crown.

1483
Torquemada appointed Grand Inquisitor.

1492
The fall of Granada, the last Muslim stronghold, to the Christians completes the Reconquest of Spain from Muslims. Expulsion of all Jews who refuse to be baptised. Christopher Columbus discovers the New World.

1496
Juana, daughter of Isabel and Fernando, marries Felipe, the son of Emperor Maximilian of Austria.

1499
4,000 Muslims baptised at Toledo by order of the Catholic monarchs Fernando and Isabel.

Statue of Cortés in Medellín's town square.

1504

Death of Isabel; Fernando rules in the name of his daughter, Juana La Loca (Jane the mad) and later as regent for his child grandson Carlos.

Habsburg Rule

1516

Fernando dies and his grandson becomes Carlos I of Spain. In 1519 Carlos is elected Holy Roman Emperor Charles V, following the death of Maximilian of Austria.

1519

Hernán Cortés lands in Mexico.

1521–56

Charles wages war five times against the French; prevents advances of François I.

1532

Francisco Pizarro lands in Peru.

1556

Charles V abdicates and Felipe II succeeds to the throne.

1561

Capital moved from Toledo to Madrid, which becomes focus for artistic excellence.

1571

Battle of Lepanto against the Turks gives Spain control over the Mediterranean.

1588

Defeat of the Spanish Armada by English destroys Spain as a sea power.

1598

Felipe II dies. He leaves a huge empire which, despite wealth from the New World, is debt-crippled after 70 years of war and massive building projects.

17th century

Golden age of art and literature continues under Felipe III, Felipe IV and Carlos II, but Spain declines economically and politically.

1609

Expulsion of the Muslims.

1618–48

Thirty Years' War. Treaty of Westphalia recognises the independence of the Netherlands.

1659

Treaty of the Pyrenees ends war with France. Felipe IV's daughter promised in marriage to Louis XIV.

1667–97

Further wars against France.

Bourbon Rule and the War of Independence

1700

Carlos II dies without heir. He wills the crown to Philip of Anjou; this offends Emperor Leopold, who supports the claim of his son, Archduke Charles.

1702–14

War of Spanish Succession brings the Bourbon Felipe V to the throne.

1750–88

Carlos III rules.

1788

Carlos IV ascends throne; a weakling, he allows his wife María Luisa and her favourite, Godoy, to rule.

1793

Louis XIV dies; Spain and France at war.

1804

Napoleon is crowned Emperor; Franco-Spanish *rapprochement*.

1805

Spain helps France in war against England. Battle of Trafalgar was a crushing defeat for Spain and ends Spanish naval power.

Portrait of Felipe II.

María Luisa, wife of Carlos IV.

1808
French occupation of Spain. Napoleon arrests Carlos IV and his son Fernando VII and declares his brother, Joseph, king. The Madrid rising heralds the start of the War of Independence (Peninsular War).

1811
Venezuela declares independence, and is followed by other South American republics.

1814
Fernando, freed by Napoleon, returns to the Spanish throne and reigns as absolute monarch.

War and Peace
1833
Death of Fernando VII. His brother Don Carlos disputes the right to the throne of Fernando's daughter Isabel II, leading to the First Carlist War (1833–39).

1847–49
Second Carlist War.

1872–76
Third Carlist War.

1873
First Spanish Republic declared.

1874
Alfonso XII, son of Isabel, accedes to throne. The Bourbon restoration heralds peace.

1898
Cuban independence at end of Spanish-American War; end of Spanish overseas empire.

Monarchy in Crisis, the Republic and Civil War
1914–18
Spain is neutral during World War I, but faces growing discontent at home.

1923
General Primo de Rivera sets up dictatorship with the king's agreement. Order restored; opposition increases among working classes.

1930
Primo de Rivera goes into exile; replaced by General Berenguer.

1931
Republicans seize power in Catalonia. Second Republic proclaimed.

1933
The Falange group, opposed to regional separation was founded by José Antonio Primo de Rivera; right-wing opposition grows.

1934
Catalonia proclaims its autonomy. Insurrection in the province of Asturias is brutally suppressed.

1936
Left-wing Popular Front wins elections. General Franco leads rebellion from. Civil War swiftly follows.

The Franco Years
1938
Franco becomes head of Nationalist Government.

1939
Nationalist victory in Civil War.

1941
Franco supports Germany in World War II.

'The Battle of Trafalgar' by William Clarkson Stanfield.

Civil War poster.

1953
Spain agrees to US bases in exchange for US$226 million of aid.

1955
Spain is admitted to the United Nations.

1969
Juan Carlos is proclaimed heir to throne.

Democracy, Reform, Modernisation

1975
Franco dies. Juan Carlos becomes king and a democratic state is established.

1977
First free elections in 40 years are held.

1982
Socialists sweep into power in elections.

1986
Spain joins NATO and the EU.

1992
Expo '92 in Seville; Olympics in Barcelona.

1996
Conservatives win elections. José María Aznar becomes prime minister following deal with Catalan and Basque nationalists, who hold balance of power.

1999
ETA's year-long truce ends. Violence resumes.

2000
Partido Popular (PP) win landslide second term.

2002
Euro replaces peseta. Oil spill on northwest coastline.

2004
Ten bombs rip through trains in Madrid, killing 191 – an Islamic group is blamed. The general election is won by socialists (PSOE), led by José Luis Rodriguez Zapatero.

2006
ETA declares a 'permanent' ceasefire in March but breaks it in December with a car bomb outside Madrid airport.

2007
ETA formally ends its 14-month ceasefire.

2008
High-speed AVE rail network connects Barcelona with Madrid. The economic crisis hits.

2009
The Basque Country elects its first non-nationalist government since democracy.

2011
The Partido Popular (PP), led by Mariano Rajoy, wins the general elections. Austerity measures introduced.

2013
Spain has the highest unemployment rate in the European Union (over 27 percent). Corruption scandals undermine mainstream parties.

2014
King Juan Carlos abdicates in favour of his son who reigns as Felipe VI. Non-binding independence referendum in Catalonia.

2015
New political parties, left-wing Podemos and liberal Ciudadanos, make important gains in regional and general elections marking the end of the bipartite system and political stalemate. Catalonian parliament passes a resolution declaring the start of the process of independence.

2016
After the June general election fails to end the political deadlock, in October Mariano Rajoy is finally re-elected prime minister after winning a parliamentary vote.

AVE high-speed railway.

FROM PREHISTORY TO THE VISIGOTH CONQUEST

From the earliest times, foreign invaders came to Iberia.
It was the most advanced of the Roman Empire's
provinces, until it was invaded by the warlike Visigoths.

The land now covered by Spain and Portugal is a portion of the former Hercynian continent, which broke apart at Gibraltar sometime before the last Ice Age. Today the southern tip of the peninsula is 13km (8 miles) from North Africa, but stands somewhat aloof from the main mass of Europe, jutting out into the Atlantic as far west as Ireland, and separated from the rest of the continent by the Pyrenees, whose average height of 1,500 metres (5,000ft) exceeds that of the Alps.

Mountain barriers and few rivers

Within this self-contained fragment of land, two geographical facts have helped to shape Spain's history: the presence of mountains and the absence of rivers. After Switzerland, Spain is Europe's most mountainous country: the average altitude of the peninsula is around 600 metres (2,000ft). Mountains serve as a barrier to both Atlantic and Mediterranean air currents, dividing Spain into distinct climatic

Dolmen Tapias, Valencica de Alcántara.

> The Romans knew the Iberian peninsula as
> Hispania, which is rooted in a Semitic word
> meaning 'remote, hidden'.

regions. To the north, in the shadow of the Pyrenees, are the wettest provinces; the eastern and southern coasts have a Mediterranean climate; the *meseta*, Spain's vast dry central plateau, suffers searing summer heat and long, bitterly cold winters.

The peninsula was named Iberia – Land of Rivers – by tribes who crossed over from North Africa. To those desert people, Spanish rivers must have looked impressive, although

centuries later only two – the Ebro and the Guadalquivir – are still reliably full enough to be used in navigation and irrigation.

Chopped up by high, jagged mountains and lacking any unifying waterways, it was perhaps not surprising that Spain developed as a handful of linguistic and cultural shards.

However, while Iberia's landscape encouraged internal fragmentation, her position at the mouth of the Mediterranean made her a natural destination for a succession of migrants, colonisers and traders.

Continental drifters

First to arrive were hominids who had migrated here from Africa via Egypt. Few remains were left of their passing, but in the 1990s archaeologists unearthed fragments of bone in the limestone caverns of the Sierra de Atapuerca near Burgos. Dated to 800,000 years ago, these are the earliest traces of human beings in Europe. The Atapuerca hominids may have evolved into Neanderthal Man, whose remains have been found in Gibraltar and other locations. Homo sapiens were a later arrival, also making the trek from Africa, probably about 40,000 years ago.

Of the abundant prehistoric remains in Spain, the most remarkable are the caves of Altamira on the northern Atlantic coast. There, Stone Age artists painted bison, stags, horses and wild boars some 14,000 years ago. Bones of the depicted animals found on the floor of the caves imply that the paintings served a ritual purpose to ensure good hunting. But their vividness and baffling technical perfection have made them the first chapter in the history of Spanish art.

Other cave paintings, showing lively stick figures using bows and arrows, have been found near Valencia. Painted between 10,000 and 5,000 years ago, they are similar to African

Iberian metalwork taught the world to perceive gold as valuable.

MYSTERY CITY

The exact location of the city of Tartessos, a thriving port and an important source of trade for the Phoenicians, is not known; however, many important archaeological finds have been unearthed in Huelva. A case has also been made for placing the lost Atlantis near Cádiz. Historians have identified Tartessos as the Tarshish of the Bible, the fabulous source of 'gold and silver, ivory, apes and peacocks', where Jonah was headed when he was swallowed by a whale. According to the Greeks, the city was so refined that its laws were written in verse. The oldest known Iberian texts were written in Tartessian, a syllabic writing system.

paintings of the era, and presage the powerful influence that continent would have over Spanish culture for the next several thousand years.

There are more great prehistoric monuments in the shape of enigmatic structures from the Bronze Age, invariably called dolmens. The largest of them stand outside Antequera, but there are also interesting megaliths dotted around the island of Menorca.

Great waves of immigration occurred around 3000 BC, when the Iberians crossed the Strait of Gibraltar and the Ligurians descended the Pyrenees from Italy. Around 900 BC, the Celts moved into Spain from France and Britain – then, as now, fleeing the northern winters and seeking the sun.

Celt-Iberians

The word Celt-Iberian, a generic term used to describe all of these groups, does not mean that they intermingled much. Territory occupied mainly by the Celts included Asturias, Galicia and Portugal, and the northwestern corner of the peninsula, where numerous forts, or *castros*, have been unearthed. In general, the Celts were known as violent, rustic shepherds who made good mercenaries. Their many and varied contributions to succeeding civilisations on the peninsula included iron implements and trousers.

The Iberians flourished in the south. They lived in walled cities, cremated their dead before burying the ashes, and began exploiting the rich copper deposits around Almería. These people have been characterised as peaceful farmers, who were much more receptive to foreigners and foreign ways than their inland neighbours.

However, the 1st-century Greek geographer Strabo found common traits among all the isolated bands living on the peninsula: hospitality, grand manners, arrogance, indifference to privation and hatred of outside interference in their community affairs. Over the centuries, historians have continued to hold up Strabo's description as a good thumbnail sketch of the Spanish temperament; it still holds good today.

El Dorado

The Iberian skill in metallurgy attracted the attention of trading peoples from all over the eastern Mediterranean; it is thought that early Spanish metalwork such as the treasure at Villena (Alicante) taught the world to perceive gold as valuable. In 1100 BC, Phoenician traders discovered Spain's mineral wealth and set up ports of call along the coast, notably at Gadir (Cádiz), which soon became their most prosperous city. The Phoenicians brought the art of fish-salting, the Punic alphabet and music from Tyre to Spain; they left Cádiz so laden that their ships' barrels and anchors were said to be of solid silver.

Another seafaring nation anxious for trade, the Greeks, chanced upon Spain when a Greek ship was carried by a storm to Tartessos (see page 32). At the time, Tartessos had scarcely been touched by Phoenicians, and the Greeks returned home 'with a profit greater than any Greeks before their day', according to one contemporary chronicler. They began to colonise Iberia in the 7th century BC, at Empúries (Girona) and Mainake in the south.

The Greeks made their own contributions to the culture of the already cosmopolitan coast,

> Greek colonisers introduced the potter's wheel as well as high artistic ideals. Sophisticated Greek ceramic vases were an inspiration to native craftsmen.

The mode of dress of the Lady of Elche blends Iberian and Greek styles.

including wine and a stirring passion for bulls, and had a strong influence on art. The Lady of Elche, a haughty stone statue of an Iberian princess carved by an unknown artist 2,500 years ago, is Spain's beloved example of the fusion of Greek and native Iberian style.

Cádiz became a melting pot of Greeks, Phoenicians and native Iberians, and by the 6th century BC the city had acquired a reputation as a rich and sinful place, with three-storey buildings, millionaires and castanet-clicking dancers.

Spain eventually worked her way into Greek mythology: the golden apples of the Hesperides were said to grow there, and it was one of the labours of Hercules to gather them.

The battle for the peninsula

The future of the Iberian peninsula was to be decided by Carthage and Rome as these two great powers jockeyed for supremacy in the western Mediterranean. Defeated by the Romans in 241 BC during the First Punic War and then driven out of Sicily, the Carthaginians bided their time in their North African base, rebuilding their armies and preparing for war. Carthage made its move into Spain under Hamilcar Barca. With a vastly superior army, Hamilcar took over most of Andalusia. He then proceeded up the Valencian coast, defeating those Iberian settlements foolish enough to oppose him.

To bolster the Carthaginian war machine, native Iberians were either drafted into the army or were forced to work as slaves in the gold and silver mines. Hamilcar set about fortifying Carthage's coastal settlements on the peninsula: Barcelona is named after Hamilcar Barca; the second Carthaginian city became Carthago Nova, today's Cartagena.

After Hamilcar's death, his son Hannibal, steeped in his father's hatred of the Romans, led his 60,000-man army out of Carthago Nova

Mérida's Roman theatre.

THE STUFF OF LEGEND

It took the Romans 200 years to conquer Spain. The most dramatic resistance was by Numancia (Numantia in Celt-Iberian), a city of 4,000 inhabitants near the town of Soria in Castilla y León. A 60,000-strong Roman army took several years to subdue the town, and in the final siege, those who had not perished through disease hurled themselves into the flames of their burning homes rather than submit to Roman rule. This battle was invoked centuries later to spur Spaniards to defend their home against invaders. Artefacts from the site can be seen at the Museo Numantino in Soria; the town's football team is even called CD Numantia.

and headed northwards to the Pyrenees. As he took his troops up the coast, he made alliances with groups of Celts and Iberians who contributed money and manpower to his army. With his now legendary band of war elephants, Hannibal crossed into France, headed over the treacherous Alps and swept down towards Rome from the north. In 216 BC he confronted and routed a far larger Roman army at Cannae.

But total victory was to elude Hannibal; for the next 13 years his troops moved up and down Italy, never able to defeat the Romans once and for all. The Romans captured his brother-in-law, Hasdrubal, and in a morale-crushing gesture tossed his head into Hannibal's camp. Hannibal stayed on in Italy for four more years and was finally forced to return to North Africa in 203 BC. A year later, he was soundly defeated in battle near Carthage.

During this period Rome also had to contend with the Carthaginian base on the Iberian peninsula. In 218 BC, Publius Scipio had landed at Empúries with an expeditionary force. For several years he fought the Carthaginians and finally, in 209 BC, he captured Carthago Nova. But there were more furious battles before Scipio's army overran Gadir (Cádiz) in 206 BC, banishing Carthage for ever.

The Roman conquest

It took the Romans only seven years to subdue Gaul, but the conquest of Hispania (Spain) dragged on for nearly two centuries. The Spanish wars depleted the Roman treasury and forced the army to adopt conscription, because nobody wanted to fight in Spain. The Phoenicians and the Greeks, who came to the peninsula as traders, had found the natives to be courteous, but the invading Carthaginians and Romans encountered ferocious warriors.

The natives, accustomed to the harsh climate and to deprivation, defended their territory desperately. However, Celto-Iberian patriotism did not extend beyond city walls, and tribes often betrayed each other to the Romans. The Iberian lack of unity slowed Rome's conquest, since each Roman victory was simply a triumph over an isolated area.

The last stage of the Roman conquest was the Cantabrian War (29–19 BC). Seven Roman legions were forced to participate, and Augustus himself was called in to lead the final campaign in the Cantabrian mountains. So defiant were the Cantabrians that they continued to struggle against their conquerors even after their leaders had been nailed on crosses by the Romans. Rome finally established *Pax Romana* in 19 BC, under the reign of Augustus.

Life under the Romans

During the rule of Caesar, Latin became the unifying language on the Iberian peninsula and Roman law and customs were quickly adopted.

As the Carthaginians had discovered much earlier, Hispania was rich in mineral wealth, and provided Rome with a seemingly endless supply of gold and silver. Also rich in livestock and agricultural goods, particularly fruit and vegetables, it became one of the wealthiest, and thus most exploited, provinces of the empire.

The extension of citizenship proved decisive in the Romanisation of Spain. At first, only colonists of Roman or Italian origin were granted citizenship. Even though full citizenship was not granted to all Celto-Iberians until the Edict of Vespasian (AD 74), initial attempts to include the native population in the greater Roman Empire went a long way to establish at least the appearance of cultural cohesiveness on the peninsula.

Along with language and customs came religion: Christianity entered Spain in the 1st century AD, during the reign of Nero. It is generally believed (though without foundation)

Mosaics in the Museo de Cáceres, part of the Palacio de las Veletas in Cáceres.

that St Paul visited Spain – possibly Aragón – around AD 63–7, and St James, one of Christ's disciples, is said to have preached the Gospel in Spain. The Roman resistance to Christianity, however, led to the persecution, torture and the eventual martyrdom of many Spaniards.

Early Church history in Spain is full of tales of tortured bodies redeemed by eventual sainthood. The hymns of Prudentius (AD 348–405) bring to light the tortures – no details spared – that these early Christian martyrs endured. Yet despite persecution, Christian communities began to flourish on the peninsula. Spain was predominantly Christian by the time of Constantine's reign (AD 325), but it was only under Theodosius I (AD 379–95) – who was born in Spain – that Christianity became the one accepted religion in the Roman Empire.

The influence of Roman civilisation on the peninsula was enormous, especially in the fields of construction and architecture. Roman aqueducts, bridges, roads and walls still stand throughout Spain. Segovia's two-tiered aqueduct is among the most perfect structures of its kind. Tarragona, just south of Barcelona, still has a three-tiered aqueduct, circus vaults and an amphitheatre. The well-preserved Roman theatre in Mérida is still used for staging classical dramas. Carmona has a Roman cemetery, Cartagena a theatre, and the remains of mausoleums can be found in Fabara (Zaragoza), Jumilla (Murcia), Tarragona and elsewhere.

In literature and philosophy, the Roman occupation gave rise to Spain's Silver Age. Notable figures born in Spain include the Cordoban philosopher Seneca, whose Stoical ideals have had a marked effect on the Spanish character; the agriculturalist Columela; the poets Lucan and Martial; and Quintilian, the master rhetorician who later became the teacher of Pliny and Tacitus. These men were all trained in the Latin schools of rhetoric and spent most of their lives in Rome penning works for Italian audiences.

Vandalism

By the 5th century, the Roman Empire was in decline throughout Southern Europe. The Visigoths, a warlike Germanic race under the leadership of Alaric, crossed the Alps in 401 and nine years later sacked Rome. Tribes of Suebians, Vandals and Alans swept across the Pyrenees into Spain, and proved too numerous for the private armies of Spanish landowners. Notoriously barbaric and ruthless (the word 'vandalism' can be traced to the Vandals), the warriors looted and killed as they went, effectively ending five centuries of prosperous Roman rule.

The occupation of Hispania by these Germanic tribes was almost complete by 415. Alliances were forged and power shared, until the Visigoths invaded from Gaul and established their own dynasty on the peninsula.

Jewel-studded Visigothic crown in beaten gold.

King Leovigild did more than any other Visigothic king to unite the peninsula. Militarily, he subjugated the Basques in the north, conquered the Suebians who had managed to keep an independent kingdom in Galicia, and recovered Baetica (later to become Andalusia) from Byzantine control. He allowed Latin to become the dominant tongue on the peninsula, and for the first time permitted Visigoths and Hispano-Romans to marry. By stressing cultural, geographical and linguistic unity, Leovigild provided Hispania with a sense of national destiny, quite independent from Rome.

Leovigild failed, however, in his attempt to convert the Hispano-Romans to Arianism, a form of natural Christianity that refuted the concept of the Trinity and subordinated the Son to the Father. He was liberal enough to allow

EARLY ANTI-SEMITISM

Blame for plots that threatened the Visigothic monarchy often fell upon the Jews, who had emigrated to Hispania during the reign of Hadrian (AD 117–38). Under Roman rule, Jews had been permitted to move about freely, and they were widely recognised as industrious and intelligent.

The Visigoths, however, compelled them to be baptised or banished. Those who refused conversion – and remained on the peninsula – were tortured and had their property confiscated. No wonder that the Jews of Hispania were among the natives who rallied to the Muslims when they launched their invasion from North Africa in 711.

his son Hermenegild to marry a Christian, but when Hermenegild converted to Christianity and rose up against him, Leovigild sought his revenge. He plundered churches, exacted huge sums of money from wealthy Christians, and sent many who opposed him to their deaths.

When Leovigild died, his son Recared converted to Christianity and became Spain's first Christian king. With the religious issue resolved, Hispano-Romans developed a new, strong loyalty to the Visigothic monarchy. Recared's conversion symbolised the victory of Hispano-Roman civilisation over the barbar-

Decline and fall

When King Witizia assumed the throne in 702, he hoped to sidestep the tradition of the elective monarchy and leave the Crown to his son Akhila; those nobles who opposed him were beaten and punished. But when Witizia died in 710, Akhila was in the north and Roderic, the Duke of Baetica, was acclaimed king instead by the southern Visigoths.

Witizia's family appealed to the Muslims in North Africa for help. Fired by his zeal for the new religion of Mohammed, Tarik ibn Ziyad, the governor of Tangier, agreed to join in the battle.

Visigothic stone carving in the 7th-century church of Quintanilla de las Viñas, near Burgos.

ians, and signalled the start of a new alliance between Church and state on the peninsula that would last, with few interruptions, into the modern age.

Drawing on Roman precedents, the Visigoths introduced a codified law and a workable tax system. But while they spoke Latin and emulated Roman laws, administration, customs and dress, they clung tenaciously to their belief in an elective monarchy. Visigothic society was an assembly of warriors who cherished the right to elect their king and permitted ambitious nobles to aspire to the throne. Smooth transitions to the throne were rare; in the first 300 years of Visigothic rule there were more than 30 kings, many of whom met bloody deaths.

His expeditionary force of around 12,000 troops, the majority of them Berbers, was ferried across the Strait of Gibraltar and poured ashore into southern Spain. King Roderic was routed in the Battle of Guadalete and perished by drowning.

The year was 711 and the Visigoths were without a king; they retreated to Mérida, where they put up a desperate last stand in vain. Tarik should have returned home to North Africa victorious, but he was driven by two overriding desires: to carry his religion into the land of the unconverted and to seize King Solomon's legendary treasure, purported to be in Toledo. The Muslims swept through Spain and by the year 714 they had established control over almost all parts of the peninsula.

*Mihrab inside the Mezquita,
Córdoba.*

MUSLIM SPAIN

The Muslim presence in Spain (al-Andalus) gave rise to a brilliant civilisation. After almost eight centuries, the last bastion fell in the Reconquest, which was both a battle against an invader and a war against Islam.

The Muslim invasion ended the cultural, linguistic and religious unity that the Visigoths had tried to achieve on the peninsula. Yet Muslim values did not flourish exclusively during the years of their occupation of Spain (711–1492).

While Muslims took Seville, Mérida, Toledo and Zaragoza, Visigothic nobles regrouped in the mountains of Asturias. In the same region where 700 years earlier hardy mountaineers had held off Roman legions for 10 years, Pelayo's small Christian force confronted a more powerful invading army. The Muslims could not prise Pelayo's men from their mountain stronghold, and the Christians achieved victory at Covadonga in 722. This triumph marked the start of the *Reconquista* – the Reconquest of Spain – and assumed symbolic proportions; the Christians regarded the victory as proof that God had not abandoned his people after all.

> Under the Umayyad Caliphate, science and culture flourished in Spain. Muslim scholars translated Greek texts, and a library was built in Córdoba which held over 250,000 books.

Islam sweeps north

However, the Muslims, intent on conquering all of Europe, were undeterred by Covadonga. They continued over the Pyrenees into France, until they were stopped at the Battle of Poitiers in 732 by French troops led by Charles Martel, 'Charles the Hammer'. This stunning defeat forced the Muslims to look southwards again and to begin the difficult task of ruling over the people they had just conquered.

Unlike the Romans, who established a link with a strong, centralised government outside

Patio de los Leones in the Alhambra.

the peninsula, the Muslim invaders were only nominally the political and spiritual subjects of the caliph of Damascus, a distant overlord. The conquerors fought each other for control, dividing up the booty.

These early years of Muslim rule were characterised by rebellions and frequent infighting among the individual kingdoms. Moreover, Spain became the nesting ground for new converts to Islam coming over from North Africa. The Berbers, for example, came from Mauretania and, after a generation of being treated like second-class citizens by the Arab nobles, they rose up against them. After years of internecine fighting, a new Muslim governor redivided the conquered lands. The

Berbers were given territory in the Duero River valley but, after years of famine, many returned to North Africa.

Meanwhile Pelayo, followed by his son Favila, set about creating a powerful Christian kingdom in the north. Later, under King Alfonso I (739–57), the Asturians occupied Galicia to the west and Cantabria to the east; under Alfonso II, they moved their capital to Oviedo, where the Asturians tried to restore the institutions of the Visigothic monarchy.

When Charlemagne took control of Pamplona and Catalonia late in the 8th century, he

most cultured cities in the world. At its height in the mid-10th century, Córdoba's population had swelled to more than 300,000, and there were well over 800 mosques to serve the religious needs of the predominantly Islamic population. As the Muslims performed daily ablutions *(wudu)* as part of their religious obligations, some 700 public baths dotted the city.

The caliphs of Córdoba supported all aspects of learning. During the reign of al-Hakem II (961–76), the city library was established and soon held 250,000 volumes. Greek texts, which the Arabs had come across in their triumphant

Alfonso the Wise (1252–84) encouraged scholars to write and paint.

set up the Spanish March *(Marca Hispanica)*, a buffer zone to keep Muslims out. They had no choice but to build their base in the south, in the area now known as Andalusia.

The emirate

In 756, Abd-al-Rahman I, an Umayyad prince, came to power in Córdoba and established an emirate aligned with, but independent of, the main seat of power in Damascus. He proclaimed himself Emir of *al-Andalus* (the Muslim name for Spain), and his ascendancy marked the dawning of the most important and advanced civilisation of the Middle Ages.

Córdoba was at the heart of this Golden Age; it became one of the largest, wealthiest and

march across the Middle East, were also introduced to Europe. The works of Aristotle, Euclid, Hippocrates, Plato and Ptolemy were translated and commented upon by such noted Arabic philosophers as Avicenna and Averroës.

Poets, too, were highly regarded. They also served a political function similar to that of television commentators today. The bloodthirsty al-Mansur was reputedly surrounded by 30 to 40 poets when he marched off to battle. Poetry was written in Castilian, Galician and Hebrew, but the most powerful verse was written in Arabic: with its fondness for metaphor this poetry would influence 15th-century Spanish lyrics and, in the 20th century, the sensuous *casidas* and *gacelas* of García Lorca.

Many phrases of modern Spanish have their roots in Arabic, especially expressions of courtesy: Esta es su casa (This is your house) and Buen provecho (Enjoy your meal).

Arabic influence

More than 4,000 words of Arabic origin are still in use in modern Spanish. Foods introduced by the Muslims – *azúcar* (sugar), *berenjena* (aubergine), *naranja* (orange) and *sandía* (watermelon) – contribute to the daily diets of most

silk-weavers increased its fame as a place where fine garments could be bought. Glass and ceramics factories were built, and the old heavy metal tableware was replaced by glass or glazed pottery. Spaniards journeyed to Córdoba to examine the latest designs by its renowned leatherworkers and silversmiths.

Islamic architecture

But the Muslims left their most indelible stamp upon Spain with their architecture. The solid Romanesque churches of earlier centuries were far surpassed by constructions that

Gunsmiths at the Palace of Alhambra, by Filippo Baratti, 1878.

Spaniards. Also, words connected with administration, irrigation, mathematics, architecture and medicine can be traced back to Arabic.

Córdoba also became the scientific capital of Europe during the Middle Ages. The introduction of Arabic numerals into Spain – far less cumbersome than their Roman counterparts – spurred great advances in mathematics; the Arabs are thought to have invented algebra as well as spherical trigonometry. Astronomers and astrologers were numerous, and there was a significant following for the occult sciences.

New industries flourished in Córdoba. The royal factory of carpets was known throughout Spain, and Córdoba's many wonderful

were lighter, airier and more colourful. The cupola, the horseshoe arch and the slenderest of columns, often of jasper, onyx and marble, were all introduced by the Muslims and can best be appreciated by visiting Córdoba's Mezquita or mosque.

The Jews in Spain

The story of the Islamic occupation would be incomplete without including the illustrious, and eventually tragic, role played by the Jews during this renaissance of culture. Savagely persecuted by the Visigoths, the Jews were held in high esteem by Muslim invaders for their role in bringing the invasion about. Generally speaking, they were protected by both kings and nobles, for whom they worked in administrative posts. Jews were valued as merchants, ambassadors and emissaries, and were taken into the confidence of Muslim and Christian rulers when their own people could not be trusted. Abd-al-Rahman III's minister of finance was a Jew, as was the vizier of the King of Granada in the 11th century.

Because of their honesty, many Jews were used as tax collectors, igniting the hatred of the labouring classes. With the arrival of the Almoravids and the Almohads, fanatical converts to Islam who came from North Africa to reinforce Muslim Spain, the Jews were either expelled to Christian lands or murdered.

Jews fared well especially under the Caliphate of Córdoba. Maimonides, the great Jewish philosopher and author of the *Guide to the Perplexed*, was born in Córdoba and lived there until forced to flee to Egypt during the Almohad invasion. The Talmudic School of Córdoba attracted Jewish thinkers from all over Europe.

Jews were also held in high esteem in the Christian kingdoms; they held positions as royal treasurers and physicians, and the Catholic Monarchs came to depend upon their Jew-

Image from John Skylitzes' 11th-century 'Synopsis of Byzantine History' showing war with the Arabs.

PALACES AND POOLS

As they descended from a desert people and because the Koran required daily ablutions, the Muslims were extremely fond of water. In addition to their public baths, they incorporated fountains and pools into their palaces and villas. This can be best appreciated in Granada's Alhambra and Generalife, the royal summer residence. Built in the 14th and 15th centuries, both these structures combine water and greenery to establish a mood of relaxed splendour. Not only did water have religious significance but it represented power too: the pools and fountains required complicated engineering and a lot of money to construct.

ish subjects for financial and medical advice. Alfonso X (1252–84), the 'Wise King' of Castile and the founder of the University of Salamanca, created a school of translation in Toledo where Christian, Jewish and Islamic scholars worked together. The Bible, the Talmud, the Cabala and the Koran were all translated into Spanish at the king's behest.

Soon, however, the effect of the Crusades, which fanned hatred throughout Europe, was felt in Spain. When outbreaks of plague in 1348 and 1391 resulted in the deaths of hundreds of Christians, Jews were singled out as the cause. Zealous friars stirred up a wave of anti-Semitism which led to the burning of Jewish ghettos and the murder of their inhabitants. In the 14th century, the Valladolid *Ordenamientos* deprived Jewish communities of their financial and juridical autonomy. Expulsion and the Inquisition were yet to come, under Isabel and Fernando.

> *Rodrigo Díaz de Vivar of Burgos battled Christian and Muslim tyrants alike. A man of courage, he was dubbed El Cid, from the Arab Sidi (Lord). The poem El Cantar del Mio Cid immortalised him as a hero of the Reconquest.*

Reconquest

The Reconquest of Spain, which spanned 750 years, was both a battle against an invader and a war against Islam, seen as a heretical religion that did not recognise Christ as the Messiah.

In the later 9th century, Alfonso II (866–911), taking advantage of Muslim infighting, began to colonise the Duero River valley, now abandoned by the retreating Berbers. To the east, he built many fortresses to repel Islamic attacks. These Asturians saw themselves as the heirs of Visigothic power and tradition, responsible for wrenching power from the Muslims.

But when García I moved the Asturian capital from Oviedo to León in 914, the unified Muslims – under the rule of the caliphs of Córdoba – wreaked great destruction upon the Christians.

Al-Mansur came to power in Córdoba in 976 and, to distract the Muslims from his own misrule, led what became almost yearly raids into the five kingdoms of Christian Spain: Asturias, León, Navarre, Aragón and Catalonia. In 985 he burned Barcelona, and its inhabitants were killed or enslaved; three years later, he plundered Burgos and León. When al-Mansur died in battle in 1002, the Christian states counterattacked. Count Ramón Borrell of Barcelona led troops southwards, where they joined rebellious Muslims. However, progress was slow: Córdoba was finally sacked in 1010, precipitating the end of the Caliphate. Meanwhile, Sancho III became King of Navarre (1000–35); by alliance and warfare, he came to rule over Aragón, Castile and the city of León.

Civil wars and the division of territories into splinter states called *taifas* further undermined

Islamic power on the peninsula. The Christian kings played one Muslim ruler off against another. By weakening them in this way, the Castilians were able to retake Toledo, which was widely acknowledged as the capital of Spain, in 1085. This marked the fall of the first Muslim city and allowed the Christian forces to advance south. Meanwhile, the Aragonese won Zaragoza and the Catalans retook Lleida and Tarragona. Later, when the King of Aragón's daughter married Count Ramón Berenguer of Barcelona in 1151, Catalonia and Aragón were united under one ruler.

Statue of El Cid in his home town of Burgos.

Holy wars

But the Muslims were not going to relinquish Spain easily. To counter the growing Christian strength, the Muslim kings sought aid from Morocco. Help came from the Almoravids – 'those vowed to God'– a group of Saharan people who had recently converted to Islam and had conquered much of West Africa.

Under the leadership of Yusuf, the Almoravids brought camels and African guards to carry their weapons. In time, they captured Badajoz, Lisbon, Guadalajara and Zaragoza. Though they were repelled at the gates of Barcelona and held at bay in Toledo, the Almoravids remained in control of their territories for 50 years. By the middle of the 12th century, however, the power of the

Almoravids was collapsing and the Christians regained most of Andalusia. But then, in 1195, the Almohads, a Berber group from Morocco's Atlas mountains, invaded Spain. They defeated and killed the Christian King of Castile at Alarcón and drove thousands of *Mozárabes* (Christians living on Islamic lands) and Jews out of Andalusia.

In response, Pope Innocent III called for a Crusade, and many Christian kingdoms in Europe sent contingents of knights to wage war against the 'infidel'. A furious battle ensued at Las Navas de Tolosa in 1212. Alfonso VIII of Castile united troops from Navarre, Aragón and

were burned, vineyards destroyed, orchards set ablaze; the mosque in Seville was pulverised and only its minaret, the Giralda, was left.

With these Christian victories, Islamic domination in Spain was vastly reduced. By the end of the 13th century, only the provinces of Granada and Málaga and parts of Cádiz and Almería were still in Muslim hands. A Muslim state under Christian protection was set up in Granada; refugees from the rest of Spain settled there under the rule of the Nasrid Dynasty.

Yet, because of partisan politics and feuding, the reunification of Spain was delayed by

Surrender of Granada by Muslims to Catholic kings Ferdinand and Isabelle.

Portugal against the forces of Miramolin, the Almohad leader. Not only did the Christians achieve victory, but they were now poised for attacks on northern Andalusia.

The subjugation of Muslim Spain was to follow quickly. Jaime I, the 'Conqueror King', captured Valencia and the Balearic Islands. Meanwhile, Fernando III, 'the Saint', united Castile and León, thus merging their forces for further attacks. Córdoba surrendered to his troops in 1236, followed by Valencia in 1238. Many other Muslim territories futilely resisted the Christian advance. In 1246, Fernando III laid siege to Jaén, which fell after months of battle. After a siege lasting over 16 months, Seville surrendered in 1248. Many of its houses

150 years. The kings of Spain contested the throne in repeated bloody encounters. Pedro I, 'the Cruel', ruled from 1350 to 1369, leaving a trail of blood, including the murder of family members.

Fernando and Isabel

Early in the 15th century, the Aragonese took control of Catalonia and Valencia, and the House of Castile assumed charge of Murcia and Almería.

Union between these two powerful kingdoms came about in 1474 when Fernando of Aragón married Queen Isabel of Castile. But this was a union of crowns, not kingdoms, for each region maintained its own leadership, government, traditions and rules of succession.

From 1483 to 1497 the Cortes, the assembly of nobles in court, did not convene, and the 'Catholic Monarchs', Fernando and Isabel, put an end to feudalism and established an absolute monarchy. They took over the nobles' privileges and created a new upper middle class.

The Inquisition

In order to achieve Catholic unity, in 1478 Fernando and Isabel obtained a papal bull from Sixtus IV to set up the Sacred Office of the Holy Inquisition. Thousands were condemned and imprisoned or killed; others fled the country.

The Catholic Monarchs, on the advice of Tomás de Torquemada, the first Inquisitor-General and son of a *converso* family, ordered the expulsion of all Jews who refused to be baptised. Some 170,000 Jews were expelled. They went to North Africa, Greece or Turkey. Many of these Sephardic Jews still use their Castilian language, known as *Ladino*, today. Over 300,000 *conversos* remained in Spain. They were treated badly and were required to show the solidity of their new faith, but the Golden Century of Spain would not have been possible without them.

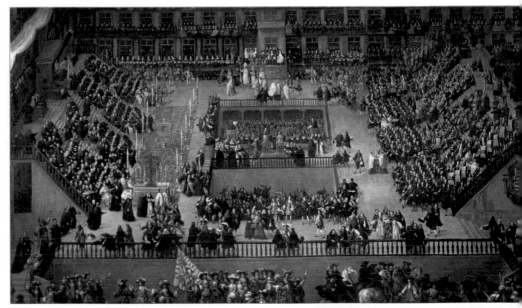

An 'auto-da-fe' (trial) in the Plaza Mayor in Madrid.

Converted Jews could stay only if their conversion was total. Many had posts both in the government and even in the Church itself. In 1483, all Jews were ordered to leave Andalusia and Fernando demanded their expulsion from Zaragoza, but both instructions were largely ignored; it would prove a temporary reprieve.

In the meantime, the troops of the Catholic Monarchs were laying siege to Granada. Ironically, Fernando and Isabel once more sought lands from wealthy Jews to finance the final phase of the *Reconquista*. On 2 January 1492, after 11 years of battle, the Muslim King Boabdil personally surrendered the keys of Granada to Fernando and Isabel.

THE SPANISH INQUISITION

Authorised by a papal bull, the Inquisition was set up in 1480 and its main remit was to try suspected *conversos* – false converts to Catholicism from Jewish and Muslim faiths. The Inquisition used torture to obtain confessions. Defendants were not informed of the charges against them, were denied counsel, and were not allowed to cross-examine hostile witnesses. Those found guilty faced imprisonment, beheading, hanging or burning at the stake. Prior to their deaths, the 'guilty' were subjected to an *auto-da-fé* (act of faith), a religious ceremony including Mass, where they were paraded in public and had their sentences read out.

THE AGE OF EMPIRE

**Freed from the Muslim yoke, Spain looked abroad.
Colonial expansion made it briefly, under the
Habsburg kings, the greatest power on earth.**

Towards the end of the 15th century Portugal was the world maritime power, aggressively exploring the Atlantic coast of Africa and establishing colonies on the Azores and the Cape Verde Islands.

In 1485 Christopher Columbus, a Genoese navigator who had been in the service of Portuguese captains, approached the Catholic Monarchs Fernando and Isabel and asked for financial support to find the shortest westward route to India. He offered them new territories, abundant riches and more souls for God.

Columbus was held off for nearly seven years, but once Granada had been conquered, Spain began to concentrate its resources on overseas exploration.

Spain discovers America

On 12 October 1492, about 70 days after setting sail from Spain, Columbus and his crew landed on the island of San Salvador in the Bahamas. He claimed the new lands for the

The 'invincible' Spanish Armada, destroyed in 1588.

> At the height of the Spanish Empire in the 16th century, Spanish territory in the Americas stretched from Alaska to Patagonia.

Spanish Crown. The papal bull of 1494 ceded much of the New World to Spain, thereby encouraging Fernando and Isabel to finance other expeditions. In time, Spain would conquer huge empires in the Americas, notably in Peru and Mexico.

The Spaniards were driven by two equally powerful desires: to obtain gold, power and land in the Americas; and to convert and "educate" the American Indians. As Castilian money

had financed the voyages, the Crown insisted that it had the right to control all trade with the colonies, and that the *quinto real* – the royal fifth – of all monies should revert to the Crown.

When Isabel died in 1504, her daughter Juana became Queen of Castile. After the sudden death in 1506 of her husband Philip, the Archduke of Austria, she became depressed and was widely judged to be mad – thus her nickname Juana La Loca – and her father, Fernando, took charge of Castile.

Fernando's rule was characterised by a number of struggles in which he tried to consolidate power under the Spanish crown. Aragón held Sicily and Sardinia but, when the French intervened in Italy, Fernando went to battle; victorious, he annexed the kingdom of Naples in 1504 and established Spain as a powerful challenger to French designs on the continent. In 1512, he annexed the kingdom of Navarre, south of the Pyrenees, to Castile. By shrewdly marrying off his children – Catalina (better-known as Catherine of Aragón) to Henry VIII of England, Juana to Philip, the son of Maximilian, Emperor of Austria and Duke of Burgundy, and María to King Manuel of Portugal – Fernando had strengthened Spain's position with several of its European rivals.

A fragment of the Maya Codex.

The Habsburgs

When Fernando died in 1516, the Crown devolved on his grandson Carlos, the son of Juana and Philip. The heir to the Habsburg lands in Austria and southern Germany, Carlos was unattractive, inexperienced and spoke no Spanish. Spain was apprehensive about being ruled by a foreigner. His arrival at Santander in 1517 and his first gestures did not quell fears. The Spanish nobility, especially, resented the king's reliance on his Flemish advisers and his unwillingness to consult with them. One unpopular decision was to appoint his own nephew to the rich, prestigious archbishopric of Toledo. To make matters worse, Carlos tried to levy new taxes on both the

King Felipe II reputedly once said he would prefer not to rule if the alternative was to reign over a nation of heretics.

church and nobility, as well as raise the *alcabala*, or sales tax.

When his grandfather Emperor Maximilian died in 1519, Carlos was elected Holy Roman Emperor as Charles V. But as he set sail for Germany, the Castilians, feeling overtaxed and ignored, rebelled. This was the infamous uprising of the *comuneros* or commoners; led by the town of Toledo, the *comuneros* wanted to dethrone Charles and replace him with Juana La Loca. They also declared that only Castilians should have administrative posts, and that the Cortes (parliament), not the king, had the right to declare war. The nobles vacillated, but when they finally aligned themselves with the court, the army crushed the rebels at the Battle of Villalar in 1521. The *comunero* leaders were executed. The power of the monarchy was restored and Charles V rescinded some of his tax levies.

Charles V's rule coincided with the opening up of the Americas. During his reign, Hernán Cortés conquered the Aztecs and Francisco Pizarro defeated the Incas in Peru; after raiding the treasuries, both conquerors opened huge gold and silver mines in Mexico, Bolivia and Peru. Seville was placed at the centre of the burgeoning metal trade, and in a few years the city doubled in size.

Growing debt

With peace at home and gold flowing across the Atlantic, Spain – now the most powerful country in Europe – became involved in several long and expensive wars abroad. As Charles V defended southern Italy from Turkish incursions, he became embroiled in combat with the Ottoman Empire. He also waged four wars with France, and by the end of his reign he had gone to war with almost every European nation.

Spain was forced to use the gold and silver of the Americas as collateral to secure loans from foreign bankers to finance the wars. As prices shot up, the Crown levied higher taxes and set up price controls. But as the nobles had invested much of their newly acquired wealth in land, jewellery and decorative objects rather than in industry or agriculture, Spain remained economically weak and uncompetitive. It sank deeper into debt while its European rivals developed their industries.

Struggle against heresy

Another of Charles V's struggles was with the Protestant movement. As the ideas of Martin Luther took root in Germany, Switzerland and England, the Pope appealed to Charles to put an end to a heresy which claimed that 'the Pope could not release souls from Purgatory on payment of a fee', and which allowed Christians to communicate directly with God without intermediaries. Charles responded by giving support to Catholic military groups, including St Ignatius Loyola's 'Society of Jesus', which fought for the Papacy. In Spain itself there was a Counter-Reformation in which certain books were prohibited and the popular humanist ideas of Erasmus were considered heretical.

In 1556 Charles V abdicated, retiring to the monastery of Yuste in Extremadura. His brother Fernando was given most of the Habsburg Empire, though he left his Spanish possessions, Flanders and parts of Italy to his son, Felipe II.

Unlike his extrovert father, Felipe was withdrawn, sickly, almost bookish in his imperial pursuits. He dedicated over a decade to building the palace, monastery, retreat and church of El Escorial near Madrid.

Felipe II

As his kingdom was more limited than that of his father, Felipe II generally pursued issues pertinent only to Spain and Catholicism. However, when the Calvinists rebelled in Holland, he had their leader beheaded and many of his followers slaughtered, thus cementing his reputation as a religious fanatic and a merciless king. He even had his own son accused of treason and heresy, and ordered that the Primate of Spain be deposed for having voiced his admiration for Erasmus. Felipe's cruelty was immortalised in both Schiller's *Don Carlos* and Goethe's *Egmont*.

By the 1560s Spain was, despite a surface opulence, in dire financial straits. Its industries were floundering, foreign wars were depleting her treasury and English pirates began hijacking Spanish ships returning with much-needed gold from the Americas. By 1575 Felipe II owed

so much money to foreign banks that he was forced to suspend his debt payments.

But Felipe's aggressive religious principles dominated his economic considerations. He made the Inquisition hunt out the *moriscos*, Spaniards of Islamic ancestry, many of whom had converted to Christianity during Queen Isabel's rule but were still suspected of adhering to the Muslim faith. Spain's best farmers took refuge in the stony mountains of Andalusia until it was safe to return to their lands.

To counter the Turks who from time to time had menaced the Spanish coastline, Felipe II

One of the 'Conquest of Mexico' paintings showing the Spanish conquering the Aztecs.

formed a league with Pope Pius V, Malta and Venice. Under the command of Felipe's brother, John of Austria, the alliance defeated – at great financial cost – the Turks in 1571 at the Bay of Lepanto, near Corinth.

Spain sinks

In Felipe II's struggle with England, however, economics and religion fused: he prepared the Spanish Armada not only because Queen Elizabeth protected the pirates who attacked Spanish galleons, but also because she persecuted English Catholics and had imprisoned his cousin Mary Stuart. But when the 'Invincible Armada' confronted the more manoeuvrable English fleet led by Sir Francis Drake in 1588, Spain lost thousands of sailors and more than half its ships, although it is now believed that it was the English weather rather than military strategy that sunk the Armada. Defeat led Felipe into a long period of indecision and introspection. What was certain was that Elizabeth's victory established English maritime supremacy for decades to come.

Spain was ruled during the 17th century by the last three Habsburg kings. When Felipe III became king in 1598, his kingdom included Spain, Portugal, Flanders, much of central and southern Italy, the Americas from California to Cape Horn and the Philippines. But he was indifferent towards his responsibilities, and left the affairs of state to the Duke of Lerma, who used his position to increase his wealth and to appoint relatives to important administrative posts. In 1609 he advised Felipe III to expel the *moriscos* on religious grounds, but also to break the power of the Valencian nobles. Half a million *moriscos* were forced out, many of whom were among Spain's best farmers.

With silver production down, agriculture in disarray and corruption rife, Spain was drawn

The Royal Palace of La Granja de San Ildefonso.

THE GOLDEN AGE OF SPANISH LITERATURE

Under the Habsburg kings Spain enjoyed its greatest literary flowering. Heralding this golden age was *La Celestina* (1499) by Fernando de Rojas. Written as a play, its sense of time, plot and character development is as modern as Celestina herself, a go-between for illicit lovers.

The poet Garcilaso de la Vega, whose pastoral *Églogas* were published in 1543, revolutionised Spanish poetry with Italian verse forms. Fray Luís de León, imprisoned for five years accused of practising Judaism, wrote mostly prose, but also lyric poetry of great elegance. St Teresa of Ávila wrote with a simplicity and clarity unusual in her time, while the poetry of her disciple, the ascetic St John of the Cross (1542–91), is deeply mystic or lyrically ecstatic. The Baroque poets Luis de Góngora (1561–1625) and Francisco de Quevedo (1580–1645) had contrasting styles: Góngora lush and ornate, Quevedo dry, acerbic, pessimistic.

Of the playwrights, Lope de Vega (1562–1635), founder of Spain's National Theatre, wrote some 1,500 plays (mostly popular comedies), poetry and novels; Pedro Calderón de la Barca (1600–81) is known for his philosophical dramas.

The crowning achievement of the age is the novel *Don Quijote* by Miguel de Cervantes. An instant bestseller when published in 1605, the story of a deluded idealist battling with flawed reality still has a universal appeal.

into conflict with Holland, France and England during the Thirty Years' War. Felipe IV became king in 1621 and political and military reversals during his reign brought the empire to the verge of collapse.

When in 1640 he tried to get the Catalans to pay for the maintenance of Castilian troops, they sought help from the King of France; Felipe backed down, and was forced to grant the Catalans nominal independence.

Later that year the Duke of Braganza proclaimed himself King of Portugal, which signalled that kingdom's final independence. Separatist movements were also under way in Andalusia and Naples. The French defeated the Spanish at Rocroi in 1643, and the Treaty of Westphalia (1648) marked the end of Spain's role as Europe's supreme military power. Military defeats were not the only cause of Spain's demise. Spain failed to use gold and silver from the Americas to build strong industries at home: wool sheared in Spain was sold cheaply to Europe's northern countries, where it was converted into cloth, then resold on the peninsula at exorbitant prices.

Once the *moriscos* were expelled, the best lands were given over to sheep and-cattle grazing; farm goods had to be imported. The church and the nobility were exempted from paying taxes, and so the poorest of merchants and peasants were obliged to support the state. The *escudo*, once accepted as currency throughout Europe, tumbled in value, and Spain was unable to secure foreign loans. As a result, the vast armies of the empire were underfed and underpaid, and morale sank.

Felipe IV died in 1665. He left an economy in shambles to his only son Carlos, a five-year-old who had yet to be weaned. A regency ruled until Carlos II took the throne at 15.

War with France continued for most of his rule, and he was forced to surrender valuable territories in the Peace of Nimega (1678) and Ratisbonne (1684). Carlos died without an heir and left his crown to Philip of Anjou, the grandson of Louis XIV, in the vain hope that he might keep Spain intact from further French incursions.

The Bourbons

Lacking in experience, the newly crowned Felipe V, the first Bourbon, relied on French advisers. Austria, alarmed by the prospect of French hegemony in Europe, declared war on France; Catalonia, Valencia and the Balearic Islands saw an opportunity to oppose Felipe V and accepted Charles, the Archduke of Austria and a Habsburg, as their ruler.

This War of Spanish Succession lasted 13 years and, for the first time since the Reconquest, a foreign enemy marched across Castile. The Treaty of Utrecht (1713) recognised Felipe V as the King of Spain, but exacted a heavy toll on the old Spanish Empire; Flanders and Spain's Italian possessions were lost, and Gibraltar was ceded to the British.

King Felipe V, painted by Hyacinth Rigaud.

The ruling Bourbons embarked on a plan to unify Spain; by diminishing the role of the Church, they hoped to strengthen the power of the state. By the middle of the 18th century, Spain's economy had stabilised; its army and navy had been reconstructed, and new industries, primarily in Catalonia, began to develop.

The Frenchification of Spain, both in customs and thought, was launched. The ruling kings adopted French mannerisms and clothes, believed in the Age of Enlightenment and introduced a more liberal church service. Carlos III (1759–88) was a devout Catholic but, more than that, a believer in an absolute monarchy: at his behest, church burials were forbidden, and the Inquisitor-General was expelled for drafting a bill without the king's authority. In 1766 he ousted the reactionary Jesuit Order from Spain because of what he perceived as their political intrigues. Unfortunately for the Bourbons, the Spanish masses were deeply conservative and suspicious of any attempt to liberalise life.

Spain truly revived under Carlos III. When he first came to Madrid, he was shocked by the squalor of the Spanish capital. During his reign, work on the Royal Palace was completed, and the Prado Museum, originally intended as a science museum, was built. He also built canals,

Ferdinand VII giving an explanation about the Mutiny of Aranjuez before Napoleon and Tayllerand, 1808.

roads and highways. A steady rise in prices brought economic growth and prosperity.

When Louis XVI was guillotined in 1793, the Spanish king Carlos IV – a nephew of the beheaded French monarch – grew frightened of the growing liberalism on his northern border and declared war on the French. Years of war followed: Spain lost.

Napoleon

Carlos IV was a weak-minded and weak-willed ruler. His queen, María Luisa, and her favourite, Godoy – a common soldier who rose to become Prime Minister – actually ran the state. After Napoleon gained control

> *Spanish sea power came to an end when Admiral Lord Nelson defeated the Franco-Spanish fleet off Cape Trafalgar in 1805.*

in France, he turned his eyes towards Spain. On the pretext of going to occupy Portugal, Napoleon brought his imperial army into Spain and lured the royal family to Bayonne for a meeting. By exploiting the factionalism within the Spanish royal family, Napoleon was able to broker an agreement: Carlos abdicated, his son Fernando was banned from Spain and Napoleon gave the Crown to his brother Joseph Bonaparte.

On 2 May 1808, the Spanish peasantry rose up spontaneously in protest; any Frenchman on the Madrid streets became a target. The crack French troops responded swiftly and brutally. Francisco Goya's *The Third of May, 1808* captures in blazing colours the execution of a group of *madrileños* who resisted. Regional uprisings followed, and France found it increasingly difficult to govern Spain. The War of Independence (also known as the Peninsular War) dragged on until Wellington drove the French back across the Pyrenees in 1813.

During these years of war, the liberal Spanish Cortes (parliament) gathered in Cádiz to draft a constitution. In 1812 it was approved, abolishing the Inquisition, censorship and serfdom, and declaring that henceforth the king had to abide by whatever the Cortes decided.

The Carlist Wars

Despite this, Fernando VII took over the throne and was pronounced absolute monarch. He refused to pledge allegiance to the Constitution, re-established the Inquisition, stifled free speech and allowed the Jesuits to return. Seeing no hope for accommodation with his despotic regime, the Spanish provinces in the Americas rebelled and established independence.

Fernando VII turned his back on the three major movements of the 18th century – the Enlightenment, the French Revolution and the Industrial Revolution – and kept Spain apart from the rest of Europe, brooding over its imperial glories and deep religious soul.

When in old age Fernando VII repealed the Salic law limiting royal succession to male heirs in favour of Isabel II, his daughter by his fourth wife, María Cristina, a woman of liberal background, a far-right religious group that was known as the *Apostólicos* rebelled in protest. The conservatives decided to join them and threw their support behind Don Carlos, the king's brother.

The Carlist Wars were actually civil wars between liberals, who believed in constitutional government without Church domination, and conservatives, who favoured an alliance between Church and state. The liberals were most powerful in the urban areas, while the conservative Carlists drew their

sides agreed to adhere to the principle of 'the peaceful rotation of the parties'. The now united troops were sent off to Cuba and the Philippines, where the native populations were demanding independence. The American Civil War inspired an insurrection in Cuba by those seeking the abolition of slavery on the island and independence from Spain. The rebellion failed, but Cuba won a nominal degree of autonomy. In 1895, the Cuban poet and patriot José Martí resumed the struggle for independence and, after his death, the rebellion quickly spread.

Goya's 'The Third of May' immortalises the madrileños who rose up against Napoleon in 1808.

strength from the countryside, particularly in the northern provinces. The clergy supported the Carlists, thereby stoking anticlerical fires: when it was rumoured that clerics had poisoned Madrid's water supply, dozens of nuns were slaughtered.

This internecine struggle continued until Alfonso XII, the son of Isabel II, assumed the throne in 1874, after a brief republic. By signing the Sandhurst Manifesto Alfonso tried to unite all Spaniards: 'Whatever happens I shall not fail to be a good Spaniard, nor, like all my forefathers, a good Catholic, nor, as a man of this century, truly liberal.'

Liberals and conservatives put down their weapons in favour of political debate. Both

Early in 1898 the United States sent the battleship *Maine* to Cuba to protect American interests; whether because of a mine or some mechanical malfunction, the ship exploded in Havana harbour. Public passion in the United States was aroused; believing that Spain had sunk the ship, President McKinley called for an armistice and the immediate release of all imprisoned rebels. Spain refused.

A series of naval battles followed. The US Navy attacked Spanish ships in the Philippines and, in August, Manila surrendered. The Treaty of Paris, signed in December, granted Cuba its independence, ceded Puerto Rico to the United States as indemnity and passed the Philippines to the US for the sum of US$20 million.

THE CIVIL WAR AND THE FRANCO REGIME

A period of instability and polarisation of Spanish politics led to a brief republic, followed by the horrors of civil war and 40 years of dictatorship.

The loss of Cuba marked the end of all Spanish pretensions to being an international power. In response, a group of writers and intellectuals, including Miguel de Unamuno, Antonio Machado and Ramón Marían del Valle Inclán – the 'Generation of '98' – declared that Spain should abandon dreams of world supremacy in favour of a new, modern course. They stressed the need to revitalise the country's agriculture, reform tax structure and extend free public education to all.

It was during this period after the Spanish-American War – referred to as *El Desastre* (The Disaster) – that labour became unionised and radicalised, primarily in the industrial areas of Catalonia. Anarchism, which had attracted a modest following during the 1870s when Bakunin's ideas were introduced, resurfaced more militantly, and in 1902 an anarchist union was formed in Barcelona, which proposed general strikes.

When the liberal leader Sagasta died in 1903, both liberals and conservatives were in disarray. The army, comprising mostly Castilian liberals opposed to the absolutist tendencies of the conservatives, was seen by all Spaniards as the traditional upholder of the existing order. But its defeat by the US in 1898 made it vulnerable to criticism, mainly by the Socialist Party and Catalan autonomists.

The people rise up

When the Spanish army found itself under siege in Morocco in 1909, Catalan reservists were called to report for duty by the ruling conservative regime. The Catalans, however, saw no need to risk their lives by clashing with Berber tribesmen. A general strike was called in Catalonia and during this so-called 'Tragic Week' (*Semana Trágica*), 200 churches and more

King Alfonso XIII and his prime minister, Canalejas, 1910.

than 30 convents were razed by the strikers and, in retaliation, the army shot dozens of strikers and passers-by.

The whole of Spain was temporarily placed under martial law. When a popular Catalan anarchist was unjustly accused and summarily executed for his role in sparking the strikes, mass demonstrations followed. The conservatives were toppled, and the liberal José Canalejas came to power.

Being a liberal in those days simply meant that one believed in parliamentary government, but not necessarily full democracy. By giving the Catalans regional control in education and over public works projects, Canalejas sought to block the growing strength of the anarchists.

He went further by letting the Socialists be part of Spain's municipal governments, and he tried to woo the Far Left by attempting to limit the number of clergy. But when the railway workers went on strike in 1912 he broke the strike militarily, which aroused the hatred of many workers. Later that same year he was assassinated by an anarchist.

When World War I began, Spain declared its neutrality. It was an expedient move; by continuing to trade with Allied and Central powers alike, Spain eliminated its national debt and increased its gold reserves.

Popular feeling against the army was strong. To make things worse, some 15,000 soldiers were killed in Morocco in another attempt to subdue the Muslims. An inquiry into the army's conduct in Morocco brought down the government, and García Prieto, an old monarchist who had become liberalised, came to power.

Terrorism against the Church and the army intensified – the Cardinal-Archbishop of Zaragoza was assassinated – but the government refused to cede to the army's wishes for a sterner crackdown on protesters. In September 1923 the garrison in Barcelona revolted. It was

José Antonio Primo de Rivera, son of General Miguel Primo de Rivera, giving a speech to Falange supporters, 1935.

In 1917 the part-anarchist, part-socialist labour unions called for the first nationwide strike to protest against price increases and Alfonso XIII's appointment of conservatives to the cabinet. The strikes began in Barcelona and Madrid, but soon spread to Bilbao, Seville and Valencia. The economy ground to a halt. The army crushed the strike, killing hundreds of workers.

When the wartime industrial boom came to a sudden end, thousands of workers found themselves without employment. With the success of the Russian Revolution fresh in their minds, the anarchists resumed their struggle in the streets. Military law was once more imposed in Barcelona.

followed by other rebellions throughout the country, and the civilian government collapsed. With the blessing of Alfonso XIII, Miguel Primo de Rivera, the Captain-General of Barcelona, took control of Spain.

Dictatorship

Primo de Rivera immediately suspended the 1876 Constitution and ended parliamentary rule by closing the Cortes. He made plans to restore the traditional forces of order: the army, the Church and the monarchy. He placed the press under strict military censorship, rescinded Catalonia's nominal autonomy and, by favouring the socialists within the trade union movement, neutralised the power of the anarchists.

The Second Republic

The elections of April 1931 were crucial. The leftist parties won overwhelming majorities, and King Alfonso XIII was forced to leave Spain without formally abdicating. The Second Republic was proclaimed on 14 April, and liberal constitutionalists were installed in power. The monarchy had been overthrown without shedding one drop of blood. Briefly, it seemed as if much of Spain – industrialists, intellectuals and workers – had united for the first time.

Yet the constitutionalists were caught in the middle, between a Far Right that clung to its

> By staying neutral during World War I, for a few short years Spain became a kind of Switzerland, where international and financial issues were resolved.

In 1926 Spain signed a treaty of friendship with Italy. Following Mussolini's example, Primo de Rivera set up management and worker councils to resolve labour disputes and to draw up collective contracts. A period of economic expansion followed in which new

Reinforcement Nationalist troops being sent from Seville to Madrid.

railways and roads were built. But this led to huge budget deficits that became all the more critical because of the world depression of 1929. Moreover, Primo de Rivera began meddling in the army's traditional system of promotion and as a result lost much support. Popular feeling against the dictatorship mounted, anarchism resurfaced and there were battles between workers and the police.

In 1930 Primo de Rivera failed to rally the Captains-General behind him: under pressure, Alfonso XIII asked for his resignation. General Berenguer assumed power, but his attempts to return to a rotational constitutional system failed. Berenguer eased censorship, reopened the universities and permitted strikes.

privileges and memories of past glories and the growing anarchist unions that were opposed to any form of government.

When elections were held for parliament in June 1931, the socialists and anarchists were swept into power. Six months later a new constitution was drafted, in which Spain became a 'democratic republic of workers of all classes'. In one fell swoop Spain ceased to be a Catholic country in which the Church was subsidised by the state. War was renounced as an instrument of national policy, civil marriages and divorces were to be permitted without Church sanction and state-supported education was secularised. Spain had made a complete about-face.

Manuel Azaña came to power and set about expelling the Jesuits – who had always been considered a fifth column by the Left for their allegiance to the Pope – and confiscating their property.

Other liberal measures were adopted. The Agrarian Reform Act of 1932 expropriated large estates and compensated their owners by giving them government bonds: these lands were either redistributed to the rural peasantry or reorganised on a socialist/collectivist model. Certain Spanish provinces, including Catalonia and Galicia, were granted semi-autonomy.

one month later more than 1,400 Asturians had been killed and several thousand injured.

When elections were held in 1936, the Left garnered the majority of the vote; though the Right was almost equal in power, the Centre had crumbled. A new wave of church burnings, coupled with new seizures of land by the peasants, followed the elections. Assassinations carried out by both the Right and the Left became the daily fare.

The Spanish Civil War

On 18 July 1936, a rightist revolt was launched: the army, supported by the National Socialist

Republicans readying themselves for an attack, c.1936.

In the 1933 elections, the Right – monarchists, Catholics, and José Primo de Rivera's newly formed Falange Party – achieved a small plurality. A centrist coalition was formed, but it discovered that Spain was now almost irreconcilably split between an organised but divided leftist camp and a rapidly growing right-wing Falange Party modelled on the Fascist parties of Italy and Germany.

The ruling Centre had to contend with the Basques and Catalans, who still sought independence, and peasants and anarchists incensed by the government's decision to halt the expropriation of large estates. The government was further weakened when striking miners in Oviedo, Asturias, rose up against the army. Just

parties of Italy and Germany, decided to seize power and put an end to the Second Republic. The Spanish Civil War had begun.

While the Republicans established their base of support in the urban areas of Madrid and Barcelona and in the provinces of Catalonia, Murcia and Valencia, the Nationalists – as the rebels proudly called themselves – led by General Francisco Franco, moved in from Morocco. They established their control in rural areas and in the more conservative provinces of Andalusia, Old and New Castile and Galicia. As the army (but not the navy), police and the Civil Guard sided with the Nationalists, the Republicans had to improvise a fighting force by arming the workers.

Franco, the former Captain-General of the Canaries, internationalised the conflict: only days after the rebellion began, Italian warplanes were in Morocco and Italian forces had secured the Balearic Islands. The French and the British responded by setting up a Non-Intervention Committee with Italy and Germany that feebly attempted to limit the flow of arms into Spain and thereby contain the conflict. The United States, for its part, also decided to respect the arms embargo and in essence abandoned an ally and a legally elected government.

While the Allies pussyfooted, Germany, Italy

from the start. In terms of military hardware, they were outnumbered by more than ten to one. Some of the fiercest struggles were between the communists, who wanted to establish disciplined cadres, and the anarchists, whose militias were loosely organised guerrilla forces where decisions were made communally. The anarchists gained control in Aragón and Valencia where they set up skeletal governments, burned churches and killed the hated clergy, and collectivised the local factories.

But on the battlefield, the Republicans could never do more than hold off the

The bombing of Barcelona in the Civil War by the Italian Air Force.

and Salazar's Portugal poured arms and munitions into the Nationalist forces. By early 1937 Germany and Italy had recognised the Franco regime, Italian troops had taken part in the capture of Málaga, and German and Italian ships were patrolling Spain's Mediterranean coast.

The Republicans, meanwhile, delivered their gold reserves over to Russia in order to pay for arms and support. In many countries of the world there were calls for volunteers to form International Brigades and come and fight in Spain in defence of the Republic.

Franco's *Reconquista*

The Republicans, who saw themselves as opposing Fascism in Europe, were at a disadvantage

HEROES AND EXILES

Among the heroes of the Civil War were the intellectuals who defended the Second Republic. The Andalusian poet Federico García Lorca was shot by the Fascists in Granada in 1936; his body has never been found (although the search is ongoing). Many writers were killed or imprisoned, but most, including Rafael Alberti, Jorge Guillén, Manuel de Falla and Luis Cernuda, were exiled. Picasso's *Guernica*, inspired by the German bombing of a Basque town, mobilised artists against Franco. The Catalan cellist Pablo Casals refused to perform in Spain as long as Franco lived; he died two years before the dictator so never played in his home country again.

furious Nationalist charges. The most striking Republican victory was in 1938, when they occupied Teruel. Had the Republicans been more united and had they received real support from abroad, the result might have been different. The Nationalists, on the other hand, were well-disciplined and well-armed troops. They were led by experienced generals and had all the necessary material from abroad. Moreover, the Nationalists seemed to be on a holy crusade to crush the infidels. The death knell for the Republicans sounded early in 1939 when Franco's forces, after weeks of

to accede to Franco's demand that Morocco, Tunisia and Algeria be handed over to him, he adopted a course of non-intervention. He did not give German troops permission to pass through Spain in order to attack the British at Gibraltar and, perhaps unbeknown to Hitler, he allowed thousands of Jews safe passage into North Africa as they fled from the Nazis in occupied France. Yet Spain's sympathies were unmistakable. When Germany attacked Russia in 1941, Franco sent a 17,000-man volunteer division (the Blue Division) to fight alongside the Germans.

President Franco with the future King of Spain Juan Carlos de Borbón in 1970.

siege, entered Barcelona. The remaining 250,000 Republicans withdrew, most of them crossing into France.

By 1 April, Franco had entered Madrid and the Civil War was over. In the following months thousands of Republican sympathisers were killed in mass executions, and millions of others were brought in for questioning and jailed.

World War II

Franco attempted to maintain Spain's neutrality during World War II, but his indebtedness to the Axis powers could not be denied. Franco did not want an exhausted Spain, dependent on supplies from other countries, involved once more in war. So when Hitler refused

The Franco era

When World War II drew to a close, the Allies, angered by Franco's role of professed neutrality and responsive to the clamours of thousands of Republican exiles living within their borders, blocked Spain's entrance into the United Nations and NATO and excluded it from the Marshall Plan. Spain, now the only fascist country left in Europe, was isolated by an economic blockade, but survived thanks to huge shipments of meat and grain from Juan Domingo Perón's Argentina.

In 1947 a referendum was held, and the Spaniards, given no other option, voted to establish a Catholic kingdom with the knowledge that Franco would be head of state for life and would choose a successor of royal blood. Domestically, Franco stifled all dissent and ruled, supported by the Church and the army, with an iron hand.

But in 1953 two important agreements were signed that signalled world *rapprochement* with Spain. As the Truman administration was worried about Soviet designs on Europe and North Africa, Spain's wartime role was cast aside, and the United States signed a treaty giving the administration bases on the peninsula in exchange for US$226 million in aid. The second agreement was a concordat signed with the

> Franco lies in the Valley of the Fallen, a mausoleum near Madrid with a 135-metre (450ft) cross, built by Republican prisoners in memory of the half a million people who died in the Civil War.

Pope. Roman Catholicism was recognised as the sole religion of Spain, the Church was given state financial support and the right to control education, Church property was exempted from taxation and all appointments of prelates were to be agreed by the Pope and Franco. The Franco regime had been legitimised.

In 1955 Spain was admitted to the United Nations and its isolation ended. Its economy began to improve due, in large part, to the increase in tourism. As tourist dollars began to reach Spain, Franco earmarked the money for the revitalisation of industry. He also started a huge public works programme that expanded highways, built hydroelectric plants and brought cheap water to the dry central plains.

Middle-class prosperity

Social security was extended to cover all workers, free medical care was offered to those unable to pay for it, and subsidised housing was given to the poor. Education was liberalised, and thousands now had the chance to attend university. A powerful upper middle class of executives, managers and technocrats developed. With a million Spaniards working abroad and sending money home, Spain was prospering.

In order to gain access into the European Common Market, Spain passed the Religious Liberty Act in 1967, which loosened the grip of the Catholic Church on all worship.

A year later, it passed the Press Act, which made some effort to restrict press censorship. In 1969, Juan Carlos, the grandson of Alfonso XIII, was proclaimed heir to the throne. When Franco either retired or died, Juan Carlos de Borbón would become king.

Forty years of Franco

Nearly 40 years of rule under Franco were characterised by order at the expense of freedom. Any protest against the severe restrictions on speech, press and assembly was met sternly. Moreover, the desire of both Basques and Cata-

Headlines announce the death of Franco.

lans to establish linguistic, cultural and financial autonomy through protest, and at times violence, was rapidly crushed.

Most artists and intellectuals within Spain were forced to take an obscurist path. While many writers wrote religious poems and sonnets in the style of Garcilaso de la Vega, others, including Blas de Otero and Dámaso Alonso, expressed thoughts and emotions in print that most Spaniards were afraid even to whisper.

Franco's regime, until his death in 1975, was empowered by the army, the Church and the Falange Party. But as Spain's standard of living rose, a new, more liberal bourgeoisie who weren't haunted by memories of the Civil War came of age.

Inside Madrid's parliament building.

DEMOCRACY AND AUTONOMY

Spain has undergone remarkable changes since General Franco died, pushing ahead with unprecedented political and social reform.

I n 1980, five years after Franco's death, the main concern among Spaniards was the survival of their fragile democracy. In 2000, the 25th anniversary of the dictator's death was barely noticed by most Spaniards, with just a few documentaries on television to mark the occasion. The Spain of the brink of the 21st century was a country Franco would barely have recognised: full membership of the European Union, with an established democracy, a flourishing modern culture and a solid economy, a country where the regional differences Franco strove so hard to suppress were respected and encouraged. But it all started to unravel in 2008.

A new broom

Prince Juan Carlos was crowned King of Spain on 22 November 1975, just two days after Franco died. The young king had been personally educated and trained by Franco. Few Spaniards had much hope that the dictator's chosen heir would be either able or willing to lead the country out of the system that had nurtured him. But they were proved wrong.

> The former Communist Party Secretary-General Santiago Carrillo mistakenly predicted that the new king would be called 'Juan Carlos the Brief'.

The last years of Francoism had given rise to illegal opposition parties whose leaders realised that Franco's end was near. There was the Communist Party (PCE), the most important of all; the Socialist Party (PSOE), which had lain dormant for years and was revived in the early 1970s by the future Prime Minister Felipe

Rally in Barcelona to demand independence for Catalonia, 2015.

González and his young comrades from Seville; the Christian Democrats, Social Democrats, Liberals, Maoists and Marxist-Leninists.

There were also parties on the Right that resisted the move away from Fascism; other conservatives, notably the Popular Alliance (AP), led by the former Francoist Cabinet member Manuel Fraga, saw that they would have to adapt themselves to the new system.

The king's task was to guarantee political stability at a time when inflation was nearly 30 percent, the prisons still held political prisoners, and the armed forces had lost their leader.

Three weeks after assuming the throne, Juan Carlos charged the last Francoist president, Carlos

Arias Navarro, with forming a new government. Arias lasted until July 1976, when the king surprised everyone by appointing Adolfo Suárez, the former head of the Falange, the only political party allowed under Franco, as the country's new Prime Minister. The king, Suárez and Santiago

> In the late 1990s Spain's birth rate plummeted to one of the lowest anywhere in the world: an average of 1.16 children per woman aged between 15 and 49.

Lieutenant-Colonel Antonio Tejero Molina attempts a military coup in Parliament in 1981.

Carrillo, the Secretary-General of the Communist Party, are the three men generally credited with bringing about Spain's political transition.

Democracy returns

In December 1976 Spaniards participated in the first democratic poll since 1936. The 'Political Reform Referendum', which was overwhelmingly approved, set the wheels in motion for the first post-Franco general elections in June 1977.

One of the first tests of Suárez's experiment came in April, when the PCE was made legal. The Minister of the Navy resigned in protest and the first sabre-rattling could be heard. It would not be the last time that the military threatened to take things into their own hands. Suárez was Prime Minister, but did not belong to any political party that could return him to power. So he created the Union of the Democratic Centre (UCD), a hotchpotch of centrist parties that won 27 percent of the vote.

On 12 December 1978, Spanish voters approved the new Constitution, which had already been passed by Parliament. The abstention rate was 33 percent, and in the Basque Country, the negative votes plus the abstentions were higher than the affirmative votes, indicative of home-rule sentiments in northern Spain.

Attempted coup

In January 1981, Suárez resigned as party chief and Prime Minister. On 23 February 1981, before Leopoldo Calvo-Sotelo could be invested as the country's new head of government, a group of over 300 Civil Guards and military men, led by Lieutenant-Colonel Antonio Tejero Molina, burst into Parliament and tried to stage a military coup d'état. At the same time, an army general declared a state of emergency in Valencia and tanks began rolling down the city streets. Around six hours after the coup began, King Juan Carlos appeared on television and ordered the insurgents to desist. Twelve hours later they surrendered.

Calvo-Sotelo was invested on 25 February, and two days later an estimated 1 million Spaniards participated in a demonstration in Madrid in support of democracy. The inherently unstable UCD was back in power, but its days were numbered. In October 1982 the PSOE swept into power with an overall majority – the first time since 1936 that socialists were in the government and the first time ever that an all-socialist government ruled Spain. The conservative Popular Coalition shot up to 106 seats from the nine it had before. The bipartisan system was taking shape.

The most pressing question following the death of Franco was whether there should be rupture or reform. Was there to be a clean break with the former regime and the monarchy Franco imposed, or was there to be a gradual adaptation to modern democracy?

Spain joins Europe

King Juan Carlos was initially rejected by many in the anti-Franco opposition who saw him as a continuation of the dictatorship. They wanted to return to the Republican system that had been violently abolished with the Civil War.

These same sectors demanded that full-scale purges take place in the police, the armed forces and the judiciary once Franco had died. None of this happened, and they ended up accepting a slower reform as they saw the king was serious when he said he was the 'King of all Spaniards' and not just of the victors of the Civil War.

The Left and the Right both moderated their position, thus guaranteeing the stability of the new democracy. One of the most important tasks facing the Spanish government was the re-establishment of Spain as a member of the international community of nations after many

but its violations of democratic principles were an obstacle to its entry. After the restoration of constitutional government, Spain finally took its place as a member on 1 January 1986.

Economic crisis

While Spain was trying to regain its footing politically, it also had an economic crisis to face up to. The country was saddled with an over-bureaucratic and paternalistic economy that had grown up in isolation over 40 years. It lacked flexibility, and when protectionist measures were dropped, business automatically suffered.

Juan Carlos I, King of Spain, and his wife Queen Sofia, 1982.

years of political isolation. After the Civil War, nearly all the world's countries had ceased diplomatic relations with Spain.

Immediately after Franco's death, this situation was reversed. In 1975, only one head of state visited the country. By 1986, however, 29 heads of state had come, an indication of the degree to which Spain had gained equal standing with the rest of the world's industrialised countries.

By far the most important sign of Spain's desire to become 'part of Europe' was its stepped-up campaign to join the European Community (now the European Union), a process which was completed in 1992, and its entry into NATO, the North Atlantic defence alliance. Spain had tried on and off over a 20-year period to join the EU,

The restructuring of key industries caused the loss of more than 65,000 jobs in the early 1980s. By far the most serious economic problem facing Spanish society was unemployment.

By the early 1990s the number of people who were out of work had reached 3 million, and the numbers continued to rise. This dramatic figure would signify social chaos in most other countries. However, the strong family structure in Spain, combined with the fact that an estimated 20 percent of the GNP was being produced on the black market, provided a cushion against soaring unemployment.

Gradually, as Spain brought its economy into line with those of other European nations in the 1990s, the unemployment rate was reduced by half.

The crash course in political affairs was mirrored, in an even more visible way, by the changes in social questions that affect Spaniards' daily lives. Education, the Church, family life, culture and social services – none of these emerged from the post-Franco transition unscathed.

As the conservative laws regarding divorce, birth control, abortion, homosexuality and adultery were gradually relaxed during the centrist and socialist administrations, social behaviour began to resemble that of other European countries. The women's movement was launched in December 1975 and its first campaigns were largely concerned with the demand for birth control, a divorce law and an abortion law.

Spain reinvented in 1992

In 1992, a much-modernised Spain was revealed to the world. Three of the country's greatest cities played host to the world: the first Universal Exposition in over 20 years took place in Seville, the Olympic Games came to Barcelona and Madrid was the EU's Capital of Culture.

Madrid's Palacio de Linares was superbly refurbished and became a centre for Latin

Expo 1992 in Seville.

CONSTITUTIONAL RIGHTS

Under the terms of the 1978 Constitution, Spain was divided up into 17 'autonomous communities'" or regions: Madrid, Castilla y León, Castilla-La Mancha, Extremadura, Granada, Andalusia, Valencia, Murcia, Catalonia, Aragón, the Basque Country, Navarre, La Rioja, Cantabria, Asturias, Galicia, the Canary Islands and the Balearic Islands. These regions were granted varying degrees of autonomy, but all had their own government and president. The country's first constitution had been passed in 1812 in Cádiz, which gave powers of veto to the king, Ferdinand VII, who used them to prevent the government from performing effectively.

American culture, and there were major improvements to the city's museums.

It was also the 500th anniversary of Columbus's exploratory voyage to the New World. Expo '92 was timed to begin and end on the same days as that historic journey, and had as its theme 'the Age of Discovery'. Millions visited the Exposition site, and Expo also had an ambitious arts programme.

The Alta Velocidad Española (AVE), a high-speed train linking Madrid with Seville (in 2.5 hours), was built in time for Expo '92.

Expo '92 brought a new energy and stimulus to southern Spain, and helped to put Seville back on its feet. Andalusia was transformed from one of the most isolated into one of the most accessible areas of the country.

Similarly, Barcelona used the Olympics to revamp itself. An ambitious urban renewal project became a reality, opening up the city to the sea, getting rid of slums and creating beaches where previously there had been industrial wasteland. It gained a remodelled airport, a new ring road, and new telecommunications systems.

The honeymoon is over

The celebrations of 1992 were followed by the need to face up to the reality of a slowdown in the world economy. This coincided with the loss of credibility of the PSOE, which had governed the country since 1982 amid a series of corruption scandals. Party sympathisers convicted for their financial shenanigans included the governor of the Bank of Spain and the civilian head of the Civil Guard. Members of the government were also linked to GAL, a shady hit squad set up to fight a dirty war against ETA terrorists but which ended up kidnapping or murdering people who had nothing to do with the Basque separatist movement.

All this led to the Socialist Party's defeat in the 1996 general election. The Partido Popular (PP), headed by José María Aznar, won a relative majority, and were able to govern with the support of the Catalan regionalist parties. Spain's economy was once again on an upturn. In order to be among the first countries to adopt the euro, sustained economic growth, along with reduced inflation, unemployment and interest rates, was required. Spain passed the test, and the euro was adopted at a trade level in 1999.

In 2000, Aznar won a second term in office, this time with an absolute majority. The government was widely criticised for its handling of environmental disasters such as industrial pollution in the Doñana national park in 1999 and the *Prestige* oil tanker spilling its cargo of crude oil off the coast of Galicia in 2002. The National Water Plan to divert the natural course of the River Ebro to supply arid areas also met with fierce public disapproval, while Prime Minister Aznar's staunch allegiance to the US in the Iraq War provoked a nationwide outcry.

Terror in Madrid

On 11 March 2004, 10 bombs ripped through three commuter trains in central Madrid, killing almost 200 people and injuring a further 1,800. Prime Minister Aznar immediately blamed ETA although initial evidence pointed towards the work of terrorists inspired by al-Qaeda; but no

link to the terrorist organisation has ever been proved and in 2007 a Moroccan national was convicted of the attacks. An estimated 90 percent of Spaniards had been against their country's involvement in the war in Iraq. Spain's Socialist Party, PSOE, under José Luis Rodríguez Zapatero, claimed that the PP blamed ETA rather than Al-Qaeda so that the attacks would not be seen as a direct result of Spain sending troops to Iraq. Unfortunately for the PP, the Madrid attacks happened three days before the general election; PSOE won and one of Zapatero's first decisions was to withdraw Spanish troops from Iraq.

Opposition leader Mariano Rajoy heading his party's campaign 'Yes to Europe' in 2005, before Spain held a referendum on the EU Constitutional Treaty.

'La Crisis'

The 2008 international credit crunch hit Spain hard because the economy had for decades been buoyed up by a construction boom fuelled by domestic and foreign investment. This had created thousands of jobs and attracted legions of migrant workers, both legal and illegal, from Africa, South America and Eastern Europe into a country which had hitherto had a history of emigration rather than immigration.

Zapatero was re-elected in the spring of 2008. His government did not shy away from controversial policies, including giving marriage rights to same sex couples in the face of strong opposition from the Catholic Church and dealing with the unfinished business of the Civil War by opening graves where atrocities were committed so that the families of victims could at last know what happened to their loved ones. That democracy, still only 30 years old, could deal with such potentially explosive issues in a peaceful, constitutional way was a sign of how far Spain had travelled.

However, PSOE were late in recognising the economic crisis and in the 2011 general elections, the PP were voted in under the leadership of Mariano Rajoy. Almost immediately, the

King Felipe VI and Queen Letizia.

party launched a range of austerity measures, one of whose aims was to reduce unemployment by raising the retirement age from 65 to 67 and overhauling employment laws (making them less favourable to workers); cuts in public administration were also implemented. Once the property bubble burst, a few hundred thousand people lost their homes, unable to afford their mortgage repayments; this caused widespread outcry and even more public anger. The Spanish were not impressed and two grassroots movements, Democracia Real YA (Real Democracy Now) and Juventud Sin Futuro (Youth Without a Future), disillusioned by the economy and politics, organised demonstrations around the country via social media and

inspired the 'Occupy' protests in other countries in the process. Adding to the mix, the so called Indignados Movement (also known as the 15M Movement) held countrywide protests against the government's austerity measures and widespread political corruption, and calling for the end of bipartisanship and a devolution of power to the Spanish people.

In spite of the cuts, Spain still has one of the highest unemployment rates in Europe: hovering around 20 percent and more than 40 percent of young people are without jobs. At the time of writing there is light at the end of the tunnel, with the country achieving a robust 3.2 percent GDP growth in 2015. Like many other European countries, alleged corruption has been rearing its head among the ruling class. In 2013 Prime Minister Rajoy was accused of receiving illegal payments, which led to calls for his resignation. The same year Juan Carlos I's own daughter Cristina and her husband were investigated for embezzlement of public funds and tax evasion (in 2016 they await the verdict of their trial and have been stripped of their titles of Duchess and Duke of Palma). Even the king himself lost popularity with his people in the wake of his elephant hunting in Botswana and an alleged relationship with a German aristocrat. As a result of these scandals and ill health, in 2014 Juan Carlos abdicated in favour of his son Felipe to 'save' the monarchy. The new king Felipe VI has endeavoured to repair the tarnished image of the royal family, but the process will certainly take time.

Growing disillusion with the political establishment led to the creation of new political parties, including the left-wing Podemos and the liberal Ciudadanos, which made great gains in regional, municipal and general elections. Their rise to prominence weakened the two traditional parties – the centre-right PP and the left-wing PSOE – and the two-party rule in the country was effectively ended after the general elections in December 2015.

This very proud nation came a long way from the difficult times of the Franco era to create a country with an envious way of life, only to have it cruelly snatched away again in 2008, like the other Mediterranean countries, due to living beyond its means. Recovery now beckons and one thing is for certain: the spirit of the Spaniards has certainly helped them to find a way out of another troubled time.

Regional Autonomy

Some of Spain's 17 autonomous regions are fiercely independent – both in their thinking and in their relative freedom from interference by central government.

For 500 years, successive rulers of Spain from the Catholic Monarchs, Fernando and Isabel, to General Franco did their best to turn the country into a unified, homogenised and centralised state, but the truth is that it has never been a harmonious whole, always an amalgam of cohabiting parts.

The inescapably federal nature of Spain was finally recognised in the Constitution passed during the transition to democracy after Franco's death.

Since then the country has been formally divided into 17 *comunidades autónomas* (self-governing regions), each of which exercises a variety of state functions, including the provision of social services, health care and education, planning, the promotion of the arts and tourism, and the raising of some taxes.

This arrangement was the only way to appease the two 'historic nations' of northern Spain, the Basque Country and Catalonia, each of which believes it has a non-negotiable claim to be regarded as a state in its own right, even if history has left it nominally, and reluctantly, beholden to Madrid. Each of these states-within-a-state has its own language, history, cohesive culture and, more importantly, a prosperous, industrialised economy. They are both treated as constitutionally special cases with slightly stronger power than the other regions.

Calls for independence

Although there is pressure from some quarters within the Basque Country and Catalonia to go the whole way and secede from Spain, most Basques and many Catalans see independence as unsustainable, unnecessary and ultimately undesirable; however, Catalonia held a non-binding referendum on the subject in 2014 which resulted in an 80-per-cent vote for independence. It is not hard to argue that in both cases the economy has been built on 'exporting' goods to the rest of Spain while relying on migrant labour from poorer regions. A cynic might ask whether Barcelona FC would be quite as successful if it were confined to a Catalan football

league, and whether Barcelona itself would be as culturally influential if its large publishing houses catered solely for a Catalan market. Nevertheless, the Catalan nationalist movement is pushing hard for separation from Spain, and in 2015 the regional parliament in Barcelona passed a motion triggering the official process of independence.

Calls for independence have historically been most vociferous in the Basque Country, where a terrorist organisation, ETA, saw itself at war with the colonialist state of Spain. In 2011, ETA declared a definitive end to violent activity – a ceasefire considered by all to be irreversible.

Pro-independence rally in Barcelona.

The other *comunidades* of Spain were only created to balance the autonomy given to the Basque Country and Catalonia. Three of them have a strong identity mainly because they have their own languages (in official use, along with Spanish): Galicia, Valencia (properly called the Comunidad Valenciana) and the Balearic Islands.

The other regions are more or less artificial groupings: Castilla y León (the largest region), Castilla-La Mancha, Extremadura, Andalusia, Aragón and La Rioja (the smallest region). A 17th region, the Canary Islands, is a remnant of colonialism far removed geographically and climatically from the mainland. Two other territories, the North African enclaves of Ceuta and Melilla, are not *comunidades autónomas* but, like the Canaries, are considered an integral part of Spain.

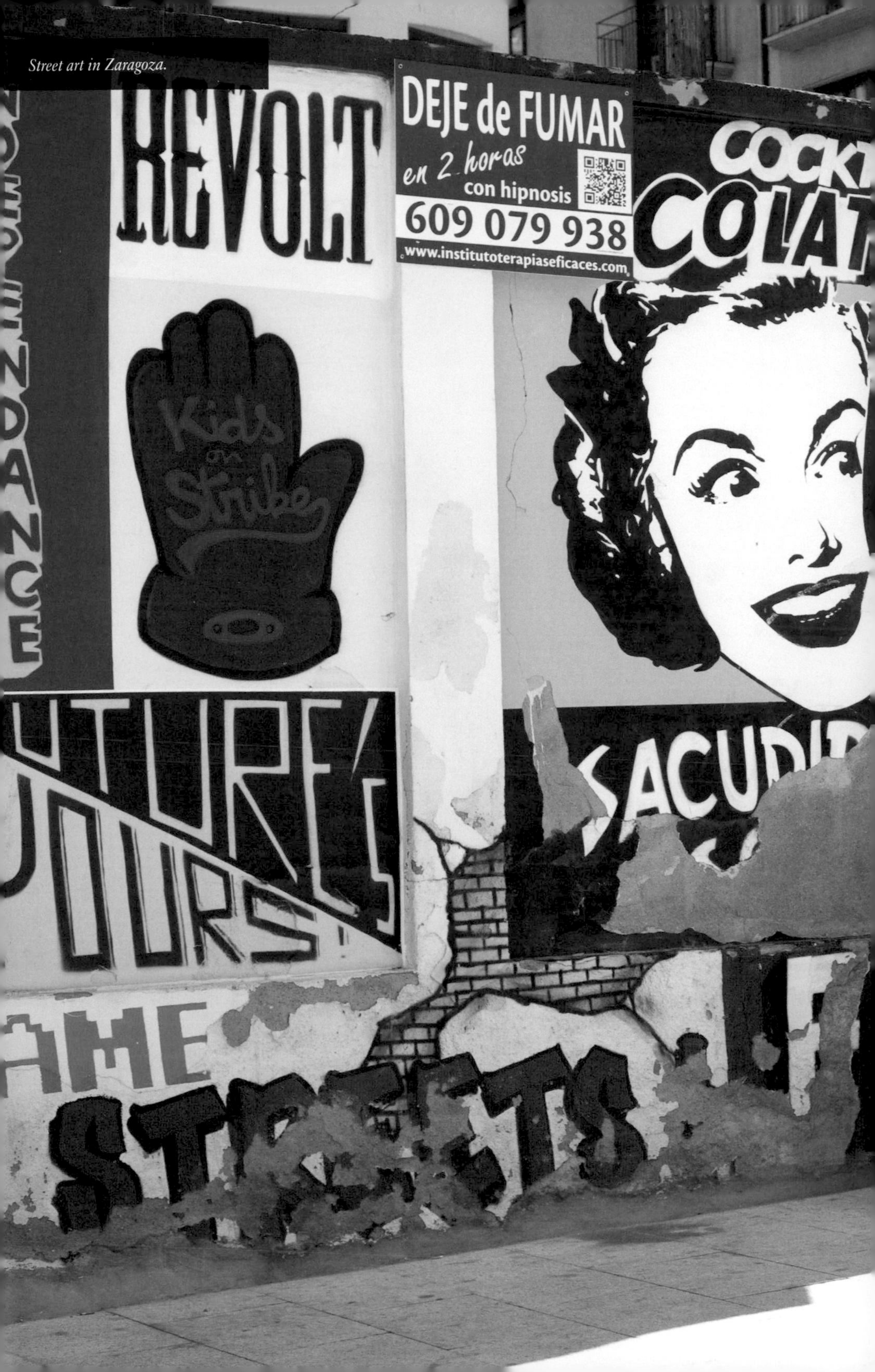

Street art in Zaragoza.

El Greco's 'Gentleman with his hand on his chest'.

SPANISH PAINTING

From the early cave paintings to Picasso's *Guernica*,
there is one characteristic above all others that
distinguishes Spanish art: heightened realism.

When Pablo Picasso visited the famous cave at Altamira (Cantabria) in the 1920s, Spanish art seemed to have come full circle. Picasso looked up with admiration at the 14,000-year-old work of his anonymous forerunner, which seemed so strikingly modern in its vigour, intensity and eye for detail, and remarked: 'After Altamira, all is decadence.'

Spain's prehistoric art stands apart from the story of Spanish painting because of its inscrutability. No one knows why Stone Age man crawled down dank passages to scrawl on inaccessible cave roofs, or what the paintings were meant to say, but it is possible that the motivation was the same as that which would inspire Spanish art from its re-emergence after the Roman occupation until the arrival of Picasso and the other moderns, that is to say religion.

The majority of Spanish masterpieces were commissioned by the Church, court and higher aristocracy for Spanish eyes only and meant to induce lingering contemplation on subjects such as Christ's Passion, the lives of the saints, the nobility of earthly portrait sitters and the omnipotence of the Church.

Medieval art

In the Middle Ages, pilgrims' trails and trade routes brought the stylistic influences of French and Italian, Netherlandish and German, Near Eastern and North African art into Spain's ecclesiastical network. All artists patronised by the Church were affected by these. Thus, the decorative figures and rich colours of medieval wall paintings are also found in illuminated manuscripts in the libraries of León cathedral, El Escorial and other cathedrals and museums.

One of the most surprising ensembles of rediscovered early medieval mural paintings is

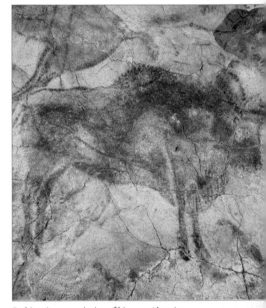

Prehistoric cave painting of bison at Altamira.

in the little pre-Romanesque church known as 'Santullano' (or San Julián de los Prados) in Oviedo, built in the early 9th century. Mosaics from Roman villas have been excavated near Oviedo, and Roman wall paintings similar to those preserved at Pompeii in Italy inspired the trompe l'oeil decoration of this Asturian church.

In León, south of Oviedo, the mid-11th-century Panteón de los Reyes, a royal crypt adjoining the Colegiata de San Isidro, has unusually well-preserved wall paintings dating from 1175. León is on a pilgrimage trail to Santiago de Compostela, so it is possible that French artists painted the relatively naturalistic Christ in Majesty and scenes from the New Testament. But one of them, in which the angle appears to the shepherds, is often cited as an example of Spanish realism. Ordinary details such as a shepherd feeding his dog are found in the sacred art of other European schools, too; but in the frequency with which they occur in Spanish art, many people read a special Spanish sense of the dignity of everyday life.

Catalan Romanesque

Catalonia was the most important centre for Romanesque painting in Spain, and there are many superb examples in the Museu Nacional

anecdotal detail can be seen in the fresco in which Lazarus, propped on his crutch, is licked by an ecstatic dog.

Foreign influences

During the 14th and 15th centuries, the technical breakthroughs of the increasingly realistic Northern European and northern Italian schools profoundly affected Spanish painting. It is unclear how many Spanish artists visited Italy or the Netherlands, but in a fresco cycle by the Catalan Ferrer Bassa, who is thought to have studied in Italy, there are squared, three-

12th-century altar frontal from the town of La Seu d'Urgell.

d'Art de Catalunya in Barcelona, where the frescoes are displayed in rooms emulating the shapes of the churches from which they have been taken. The Moors, who entered Spain from North Africa in the 8th century, had reinforced the Spanish artists' flair for flat, linear, brightly coloured stylisation.

However, the oriental gift for pattern also wafted across the Mediterranean via Italy from Byzantium. The Catalan Romanesque style, in particular, shows the Byzantine influence. Its ritualistic figures are almost expressionless, even when they undergo horrifying martyrdoms. Some of the finest paintings in this style come from the Pyrenean church of Sant Clement in Taüll, Lérida, dedicated in 1123. Spanish

dimensional figures and striking narrative scenes strongly reminiscent of Giotto.

In the late 14th century, an International Gothic style spread from the Burgundian and French courts. Integrating the Flemish artists' careful drawing in meticulous detail and the Italo-Byzantine love of pattern and colour, the style was characterised by courtly elegance and a new interest in individual psychology.

A superb example is the Flemish painter Rogier van der Weyden's *Deposition* in the Prado, an altarpiece of around 1435 that came into the Spanish royal collection in the 16th century. Lluis Borrassa's altarpiece of Santa Clara in Barcelona (*c.*1412) is a Catalan version of this International Gothic style.

The altarpiece was the most important commission for the artist of the *Reconquista*. In this lively period, Spanish fresco painting eventually died out, and the altar frontal was then replaced by the *retablo*, which was stretched out to become a wall of panels that climbed up to fill and tower over the east end of the church.

Hispano-Flemish

From around 1440 Flemish influence came to dominate Spanish painting. Lluis Dalmau, a Catalan, went to study in Bruges and, returning to Barcelona, passed on his training to the younger Jaime Huguet. The *Virgen des Concellers*, Dalmau's impressive altarpiece in Barcelona, has a Spanish Virgin and Child on a Gothic throne in a Flemish landscape. A panel by Huguet in the same museum contains charming Spanish anecdotal details: votive offerings hanging over the corpse of the miracle-working St Vincent, and a tiny devil escaping from the mouth of one of the cured.

The Hispano-Flemish style peaked at the centralising, art-collecting court of the Catholic Monarchs Fernando and Isabel from the mid-15th and into the 16th century. Flemish or Flemish-trained artists painted his portrait (now at Windsor Castle) and hers (now in the Royal Palace, Madrid). Fernando Gallego (*Piedad* in the Prado), the outstanding Castilian master of this style, combined the decorativeness of International Gothic with the monumentality that had been developing since Giotto.

The Renaissance

From the early 16th century a new wave of Italian influence brought the High Renaissance style to Spain. The collecting fever of the monarchy begun by Charles V, who befriended Titian, meant that Spanish painting was exposed to wider influences and lost much of its provincial character. Felipe II moved Spain's capital from Toledo to Madrid, giving the country's artistic life a focus. A great patron of art, he also imported several Italian artists to decorate his palace at the Escorial, which consequently became a training school for Spanish painters.

But the pagan classical ideals of the Italian Renaissance were not initially in tune with the prevailing ethos of priest-ridden Spain, and religious subjects continued to predominate. The Church and the Inquisition militated against the portrayal of idealised nudes and mythological subjects. Similarly, High Renaissance perspective, brought to Spain by Felipe IV, was attempted by only a few Spanish artists.

Felipe II's Escorial project attracted the great Mannerist painter, El Greco, who travelled from Italy to Spain hoping to find employment. But his weird, hovering, Byzantine figures wiped with eerie bluish light did not appeal to Felipe, who had expected something very different from a pupil of Titian. Fortunately, El Greco's portraits and religious subjects commanded

'*Consecration of Saint Augustine*' by Jaume Huguet.

an audience elsewhere in Spain. His portraits reveal an unexpected realism: in *The Gentleman with a Hand on His Chest* the dark background emphasises the man's facial features and aristocratic fingers.

In his altarpieces for Toledo's churches, El Greco displayed his own brand of piety and a streak of mysticism. The Inquisition was ambivalent about religious ecstasy, but the number of contemporaneous copies of his work attest to his popularity.

The Golden Age

The 17th century was a Golden Age for Spanish painting. The era was dominated by three painters from Seville: Francisco

Zurbarán, Bartolomé Esteban Murillo and Diego Velázquez; and José de Ribera, a Spaniard who worked in the Spanish kingdom of Naples. Although the range of acceptable subject matter broadened to include history and mythology, religious subjects remained the most important. Paintings had to conform to Counter-Reformation ideals, which decreed that the visual arts should give clear, straightforward expositions of religious subjects to act as an aid to devotion.

This aim is most clearly realised in the work of Zurbarán, whose series of paintings

Still life and Velázquez

The 17th century was also a time when the Spanish love of naturalism culminated in a flowering of still-life painting. Unlike Flemish examples, Spanish still lifes are often spare compositions: a few fruits, vegetables or pots arranged with austere simplicity. Lovingly delineated still-life details are often inserted into narrative paintings. This is true of the type of painting known as *bodegones* – genre scenes set in a kitchen or tavern. No one painted these with more assurance than Velázquez, whose *Old Woman Frying Eggs*

'The Drinkers' by Velázquez shows the artist's realism, sympathy and insight.

featuring a single figure – usually a saint or monk – in meditation are stark, uncompromising images with violent contrasts of dark and light. Ribera also delighted in painting scenes of bloody martyrdom with the energy and verve of Caravaggio. Murillo's soft-edged treatment of religious themes was more in tune with popular taste, and his compositions were distributed in print form among the middle classes. Favoured subjects were the Immaculate Conception, the Holy Family and the Madonna and Child. Modern taste favours Murillo's pictures of children and beggars in which the vivacity of the subject is tempered by an unsentimental rendering of the reality of their circumstances.

(National Gallery of Scotland, Edinburgh) is a prime example.

Velázquez enjoyed a successful career, becoming Felipe IV's favourite painter at the age of 24. His sitters ranged from the king to the court dwarves. Pope Innocent said of his portrait by the artist that it was 'troppo vero' – too truthful. *Las Meninas*, in the Prado, records one of the royal family's visits to Velázquez's studio in the Alcázar. The bold technique, the sense of depth created by the figures in the mirror and, above all, the spontaneous snapshot quality of the royal portrait, have made this picture a masterpiece of world art.

Apart from *bodegones* and portraits, Velázquez made a few excursions into other fields. His monumental *Surrender of Breda* in the Prado is inspired by Rubens. Painted for Felipe IV's court theatre, Buen Retiro, it re-creates a gesture of magnanimity on the part of the victor and vanquished after the Spanish siege against the Dutch stronghold a few kilometres north of Rubens's studio in Antwerp. Velázquez's *Rokeby Venus*, one of the few paintings of the nude in Spanish art, shows his awareness of the work of Titian, who popularised the subject of Venus gazing at herself in a mirror attended by Cupid.

Goya probably took his cue from this canvas, which belonged to his patron the Duchess of

by the French troops when they occupied Spain in the Peninsular War. This darker tendency culminated in the late 'black' paintings now in the Prado, originally painted directly on the walls of his home, in which the myth of Saturn, the symbol of death and destruction, constantly recurs.

Goya was an isolated figure of genius in the 18th century, and there was no Spanish painter of comparable stature in the following century. Yet it was then that Spanish art began to be appreciated in Europe: the French Impressionists were stunned by the realism and expressive paint-handling of Velázquez and Goya.

Painting of Charles IV of Spain and his family by Goya, 1801.

Alba, when he came to paint his *Naked Maja* 150 years later.

Like Velázquez, Goya was a court painter, and his portraits of the royal family are suffused with an astonishing realism: Ernest Hemingway claimed that he 'painted his spittle into every face' in his portrait of the degenerate *Family of Charles IV* in the Prado.

Goya's realism could also descend to the horrific: following a severe illness that left him profoundly deaf, a darker and highly original side emerged in his work. He produced a series of etchings, *Los Caprichos* (Caprices), which took a satirical look at the follies and inadequacies of humanity; a second series of engravings, *The Disasters of War*, depicted atrocities committed

ART OF THE MOMENT

Spain holds its contemporary art in high regard, and there's no shortage of small galleries, bars and artists' workshops where you can see for yourself what's being produced. More established places to look for the major trends are the country's top galleries, which include the Guggenheim in Bilbao, the Valencian Institute of Modern Art (IVAM) in Valencia, and the Atlantic Centre for Modern Art (CAAM) in Las Palmas de Gran Canaria. However, the economic crisis is affecting the art world too: in 2013 it was announced that a new gallery planned for Santiago de Compostela, to rival the Guggenheim, will now not be built due to spiralling costs.

The 20th century

The 20th century gave rise to several giants of Spanish painting, including Pablo Picasso, who, like many modern Spanish artists, spent most of his career outside Spain.

Along with fellow Cubist painter Juan Gris, he spent his formative years in Paris, and most of the rest of his life in France. But his work retained its Spanish roots. As Gertrude Stein put it, he 'had in him not only Spanish painting but Spanish Cubism, which is the daily life of Spain'. His famous painting *Guernica* was inspired by his distress at the bombing of a

Drawing of Picasso aged 20 by Ramón Casas.

The strong graphic quality of Miró's work, together with its inherent wit, led the Spanish National Tourist Office to ask him to design their publicity.

town during the Spanish Civil War. Barcelona's Picasso Museum has an unrivalled collection of his early works.

Salvador Dalí, too, lived most of his life in exile, in Paris and the US, and there is a Dalí museum at his birthplace, Figueres. A Catalan like Miró, he took up the thread of realism, but turned it to Surrealist ends, to produce what he called 'hand-painted dream photographs'.

Joan Miró, on the other hand, after an initial period in Paris, lived in and around his native Barcelona before moving to Mallorca. His Surrealism was of an entirely different complexion to Dalí's, based on imagination rather than external reality, blending Primitivism, personal

The influences of Spanish cave drawings, early Christian church murals, Goya and Velázquez and the subject of the bullfight, all find their way into Picasso's work.

mythology and abstraction. The graphic quality of his work is inspired by the rhythmic forms of traditional Catalan art. The Miró Foundation in Barcelona houses many of his works.

Antoni Tàpies, Spain's most important postwar painter, was a member of the Dau al Set collective; he developed a distinct abstract style in the 1950s, using mixed media to produce works of startling originality.

From the 1950s to the mid-1970s much of Spanish art was directed against Fascism, the oligarchy and, later, consumer culture. Antonio Saura's violent monochromatic pieces were attacks on the Church and the repression of the individual. Art collectives Equipo Realidad and Equipo Crónica, and painters Eduardo Arroyo, Juan Genovés and Antonio López, used realism or Pop Art to make ironic social comment.

From Velázquez to Almodóvar

Since the death of Franco and the advent of democracy, Spanish painting has sought new directions by consciously referring to earlier traditions. Soledad Sevilla and Pablo Palazuelos, for instance, both found inspiration from Velázquez. Some artists have made alliances with other media, especially installation, computer technology and cinema, the art form of the moment – Mariano Dis Berlin, for example, formed a mutually creative partnership with the idiosyncratic and hugely successful filmmaker Pedro Almodóvar.

Meanwhile, other painters are forging their own styles from their own times and immediate surroundings, such as Miquel Barceló of Felanitx, Mallorca, who has won international acclaim for his realist, abstract and expressionist works.

*Flamenco dance is essentially an
individual art.*

FLAMENCO

The jazz genius Miles Davis said: 'Sometimes, when I hear flamenco, I fall on my knees.' Andalusia's passionate musical genre is keeping a new generation of fans on their feet.

In recent decades, flamenco has proved its power to move audiences the world over, yet its musical complexities, lyrics and emotional depth are rarely understood. So what is it in flamenco that communicates so directly with musicians and audiences from so many varied cultures?

A music and a way of life

Although deeply rooted in southern Spanish folklore, flamenco is now a complex intertwined art form. Its song, music and dance have each developed separately and responded together to changes in the world at large.

In the past 50 years, waves of southern emigration to northern cities and the mushrooming of dance schools all over Spain have left their mark. Yet for all its growing sophistication flamenco remains eminently popular. The majority of its artists and enthusiasts still come from the poorer fringes of society, where life's experiences have taught them to be fiercely independent, proud and sceptical. Above all, they share a profound sense of suffering.

These are the emotions that audiences readily pick up across the divides of culture and language in flamenco. Sparing with words and rich in metaphor, the lyrics strike directly at our feelings. As the American anthropologist William Washabaugh put it, they share 'a rustic poetic style that operates like a psychic key to open up floodgates of passion.'

Ancient art, religious roots

Flamenco's roots lie in the distant past. The hedonistic Tartessans (6th–4th century BC), thought to have come from Africa, were famed for their music and primitive dance. Later, in Roman times, dancing girls from Cádiz were

A Gypsy dancer entertaining the crowds in a 19th-century tavern.

shipped off to the imperial capital where they earned a reputation for rhythmic virtuosity and sensuality verging on the lascivious. The melancholic scales of Greek music are also a base element of flamenco.

Other elements entered during the Muslim centuries. Fragments of Jewish religious song survive in the *saetas* sung during Holy Week processions, and 11th-century *andalusí* music shaped folk dances such as the *fandango, jarcha* and *zambra*, which provided flamenco's formal framework. *Ziriab*, a music that originated from the Damascan Caliphate, may be the source of flamenco's use of repetition to build to a cathartic emotional climax. One

Arabic account tells of a fish-seller driven to such a state of ecstatic frenzy by *ziriab* that he ripped open his shirt, just as Gypsy flamenco audiences once did in moments of uncontrollable emotion.

After the fall of Granada to the Christian Kings in 1492, the plaintive sounds of Gregorian plainsong – derived from Visigothic Byzantine chants – filtered right through the Spanish folk tradition. Singer Enrique el Mellizo created one flamenco song style after sitting outside Cádiz cathedral and listening to the monks singing Mass.

> During the 1950s, romance song forms preserved by a few Gypsy families, who had handed them down by word of mouth, resurfaced in Cádiz Bay.

markets, they sang for money, using the lyrics of Castilian Renaissance romances.

In the 18th century, as the persecution of the Gypsies became less acute and they began to settle in southern towns, flamenco also took root there. From the 1760s travellers

Flamenco performance in a cave on the Sacromonte hill, Granada.

Gypsy song

Among all these elements, the contribution of the Gypsies (see page 25), who had been professional musicians even before their arrival in Spain in the 15th century, was a vital one. Flamenco was born – alongside bullfighting and banditry – in the rich hybrid culture of the semi-nomadic frontier world they shared with converted Muslims and those who had been left landless by the Reconquest. The word flamenco may have its roots in the Arabic *felagmengu*, meaning wandering peasant.

As the Gypsies learned the structures of southern folk song, they added complex rhythms, expressive vocals and, above all, emotional depth. At *ferias*, cattle fairs and horse

began to chance upon flamenco in Cádiz, Jerez and Seville.

In search of black sounds

Song remains flamenco's essential form of expression. The voices are dark and wailing, hoarse and deep, capturing the pain at the heart of flamenco. When flamenco is good, it is said to pinch the listener. The singers, called *cantaores*, shift from a gravelly whisper to an intense musical shout and slide from top to bottom notes within a few seconds in search of what singer Manuel Torres once called 'black sounds'. But for aficionados, technique is secondary to the singers' courage in pushing their voices and emotions to the limits.

Musical discipline

Behind this apparently uninhibited improvisation is a strict underlying musical discipline: a canon of more than 50 song styles (palos), each defined by a different rhythmic or melodic pattern (compás) and mood. Each style is further subdivided into as many as 30 different variants. Mastery of a handful or spread of these styles is the foundation from which all flamenco artists work. Likewise, the audience's understanding of their subtleties gives a live show its two-way electricity. Hence, so often, a cantaor often introduces each piece by its song style.

Two early styles with Gypsy roots remain fundamental today. One is the seguiriya, the most tragic style of cante jondo, or deep song, which expresses anguish in the face of despair. Its structure illustrates flamenco's rhythmic complexity: each line of its four-line stanzas has seven syllables, except for the third, which has 11, and on to this is grafted a 12-bar rhythm, with the emphasis on the off-beat.

The second early song style widely performed today, the soleá, has generated more variants than any other. It explores themes from the everyday to the dramatic, filtering them through the wisdom and irony of experience.

A third group of song styles, tonás from the forge and prison, is a surviving example of old flamenco song stripped back to its starting point, the naked voice.

Dancing out emotions

Flamenco dance, marked out by its sensuality, is also rooted in a fusion of earlier forms, among them folk dances and courtly boleros. 'The fandango is an excitation to lust when danced by Gypsies,' noted the minutes of Cádiz council in 1761. By 1800 it had found its way from the Gypsy quarters of Cádiz, Jerez, Seville and Granada via taverns and variety theatres to dance academies.

Flamenco dance's energy still pivots on the physical tension between discipline and freedom of movement, evoking a sense of caged desire. In 'pure' flamenco the dancers, or bailaores, do not follow any choreography. Instead, anchored by the rhythmic pattern of each song style, they dance out their emotions, which can produce lightning switches from moments of contained inner absorption to unleashed passages of furious rhythmic stamping called zapateo.

Flamenco dancers have always played with other forms, adapting them freely to reach audiences: operas staged in bullrings around the beginning of the 20th century, Antonio Gadés's film trilogy made in the 1980s, and Joaquín Cortés's spectacular stage musicals in our own time all fall within that tradition.

The cafés cantantes

From 1850 onwards flamenco found its way into wider paying audiences via cafés cantantes, or singing cafés with small stages. In these cafés, performances took their present-day form, with

A poster for the Seville Feria, 1945.

MAJOR FLAMENCO FESTIVALS

Festival de Jerez (Feb–Mar): the sherry town's festival attracts the biggest names in flamenco and holds workshops for novices and experienced dancers. **Festival Suma Flamenco**, Madrid (June): this month-long festival is one of Spain's best. **Potaje Gitano de Utrera** (June), Seville province: Spain's foremost flamenco festival. **Festival de Cante Flamenco**, Moguer (July): song festival. **La Noche Blanco de Flamenco**, Córdoba (July): flamenco outdoors through the night. **Festival Nacional del Cante de las Minas**, La Unión, Murcia (Aug): song contest and galas. **Bienal de Sevilla** (Sept–Oct): month-long festival every two years.

each artist coming forward at various points for solos. Here, too, the guitar finally emerged as an element in its own right. A hybrid of two earlier stringed instruments – one Arab and the other Christian, the first plucked and the second strummed – was initially used as basic accompaniment to dance and song. But simple early technique quickly gave way to more intricate tremolos and arpeggios.

However, virtuosity is second in importance to depth of feeling. A strong rhythmic baseline, warmth of tone and vast array of chords give flamenco guitar its particular human quality.

Listening to compositions by some of the great concert guitarists of different generations – Paco el de Lucena, Javier Molina, Ramón Montoya, Niño Ricardo, Sabicas and Paco de Lucía, to name but a few – it is extraordinary to think that none of them could read music.

As Gypsy and Andalusian folk singers performed alongside one another in the *cafés cantantes*, the crossover of styles gave rise to new song forms which to this day remain the base of flamenco's repertoire. In this way the range gradually widened to include *fandango* variants, such as *malagueñas*, *granaínas*, and the

'Cante', or song, is the heart of flamenco.

SO MANY SONG STYLES

The *cantiñas* of Cádiz province – including *alegrías*, *romeras* and *caracoles* – grew around the Aragonese *jota* brought south by troops during the Napoleonic Wars. *Cantes de ida y vuelta* (round-trip) are folk songs taken to Latin America, or brought back from there, and then flamenco-ised. Other song styles focus on working life: *livianas* and *serranas* reflect the preoccupations of peasant life in the Andalusian sierras, while *cantes mineros* – including *tarantos*, *tarantas* and *mineras* – stem from eastern Andalusia's mining communities in the late 1800s. Two other song forms, *tangos* and *bulerías,* are closely linked to fiestas.

mining songs, which sprung up towards the end of the 19th century.

Into the modern age

Today, a surge of creativity since Franco's death has made flamenco more popular than ever and now it is enjoyed all over Spain. In fact, in 2010 it was added to Unesco's list of Intangible Cultural Heritage. Flamenco exists wherever its artists choose to be. Some aficionados argue, as in the 1920s, that flamenco is a dying art form and that only unpaid flamenco is authentic. But in fact, ever since the early cattle fairs, flamenco's paid artists have also been its creative innovators. This remains true today.

Skilled performers can graft any flamenco style onto bulerías, flamenco's liveliest and most vibrant form: you will often see them in the 'fin de fiesta' at the end of the show.

New dance forms like the *seguiriya*, *martinete* or *rondeña* were created by individual dancers such as Antonio (1921–96). Another important influence was Carmen Amaya (1913–63), whose footwork revolutionised both men's and women's dance. She was captured on film in

over flamenco today. Although there are widely admired singers of great technical breadth and creativity – among them Enrique Morente, Arcángel, Carmen Linares and Mayte Martín – none has acquired the iconic status of Camarón. This is also considered a golden age for guitar. Until his death in 2014, Paco de Lucía, who accompanied Camarón de la Isla, was a towering influence through his search for harmonic range and jazz influences, his innovations, such as the introduction of the *cajón* (sand box), and his respect for the flamenco canon.

Catch one of the nightly flamenco shows in Seville.

Los Tarantos (1962), a Gypsy version of *Romeo and Juliet*. Today's key *bailaores* divide into two groups: those who have moved back to flamenco from Spanish classical companies – like Joaquín Cortés or Antonio Canales – and others, such as Farruquito or Eva Yierbabuena, who have trained and shaped their artistic personalities from within the genre.

Each generation has produced great voices. Antonio Mairena and Fosforito marked the revival of unadorned Gypsy and *payo* (non-Gypsy) styles in the 1950s, and in the following generation Camarón de la Isla took *cante jondo* to a far wider Spanish and international audience than ever before. His early death, at the age of 42, casts a huge shadow

A flamenco evening

Live flamenco today is shaped not only by the artists, but also by its performance spaces. Open-air festivals in Andalusian town plazas, in bullrings and stadiums are now on the wane as flamenco wins itself a niche in theatres, jazz clubs and concert halls. Inevitably, perhaps, in some of these new spaces, especially the large ones with large sound systems, part of the essentially improvisational spirit is lost.

In this sense, flamenco remains at its best in intimate spaces in late-night sessions. Yet for all the changes flamenco goes through, its essence as a vehicle for deep emotions does not change. As long as there is love and despair, innocence and loss, there will be flamenco.

FIESTAS

Spain celebrates the great feast days of the Catholic Church and other special days of the year with an unbridled intensity and passion.

Even the tiniest village in Spain downs tools for at least one fiesta a year in honour of its patron saint. Whether it is a day of communal pilgrimage (*romería*) to a shrine or a week of parades, a fiesta offers a chance to dress up in colourful costume, dance through the night, let off firecrackers or run with bulls. Ranging from exuberant fun to solemn acts of worship or pagan fertility rites, Spanish fiestas have one thing in common: there is rarely a boring moment for spectators.

The most bizarre rituals have a distinctly medieval flavour, but many Spanish fiestas are pure Baroque in their excess and ostentation. The greatest number of celebrations take place at Epiphany (the arrival of the Three Kings on 6 January), at Carnival (in February or March), during Easter Week (March or April), on the first few days of May, at Whitsun and Corpus Christi (in May or June), on Midsummer Eve, also called St John's Night (23–4 June), and around the feast of the Assumption (15 August). In recent years, two festivals have been added to Unesco's list of Intangible Cultural Heritage – the Festival of the Patios in Córdoba and La Mare de Déu de la Salut in Algemesí in Valencia.

Spain's biggest Carnival is held in Santa Cruz de Tenerife in the Canary Islands which is distinguished by its processions of revellers in flamboyant if not outrageous costumes.

The five-year-old 'anxeneta' crowning a five-storey or higher 'castell' is the most breathtaking moment of a fiesta.

Processions of hooded penitents can be seen in towns and cities all over Spain during Holy Week, the week leading up to Easter Sunday. The robes were widely used in the medieval period, meaning penitents could demonstrate their penance while hiding their identity.

Hundreds of papier-mâché monuments (fallas) are filled with fireworks and set alight at midnight in Valencia on 19 March, the feast of St Joseph.

Parade of carriages during Seville's spring fair.

SEVILLE'S FAMOUS FERIA

Seville's springtime fair may have started off in the 19th century as a gathering of farmers and businessmen, but it has since evolved into a gigantic party with no other purpose than pleasure. For six days and nights, running from Monday to Sunday in April or May, the purpose-built fairground on the far bank of the river, made up of over 1,000 *casetas* (booths, both corporate and private), reverberates to the sound of Seville's flamenco-related music, the *sevillana*. Here, Seville's 'high society' entertains its guests until the early hours: eating tapas, dancing and drinking sherry.

Both men and women dress for the occasion – the former in distinctive suits and *cordobés* hats, the latter in stunning, brilliantly coloured, flamenco-style dresses – and parade up and down on horseback or seated in horse-drawn carriages. Bullfights in Seville's Plaza de la Maestranza are also an essential ingredient of the week's celebrations. To stay in Seville during the world-famous feria, much loved by Ernest Hemingway, it is necessary to book accommodation months in advance. Many other towns in Andalusia hold smaller but similar fairs.

...ocession of the Virgin heading to the Cathedral during Holy ...eek in Seville.

...ll de Gitanes performance during the festa major in Sitges.

The San Fermín festa in Pamplona sees the running of the bulls.

THE BULLS

The majority of Spaniards never attend bullfights, but most argue that they are an ingrained part of Spanish culture that should be allowed to exist.

First-time visitors to Spain are likely to approach the whole idea of bullfighting with varying mixtures of excitement, fascination, apprehension and possibly revulsion. Sitting in the stands and waiting for the initial pageantry to begin, one knows instinctively that what is about to happen is not a sport. Spanish newspapers categorise the *corrida de toros* as a spectacle; ardent *corrida* advocates fiercely defend its artistic nature, and bullfighting has left its mark on painting, sculpture, music, dance and literature.

The toro bravo

Spain's brave fighting bull is a fierce, untamed animal, whose bloodlines and pedigrees have been protected over the centuries in order to maintain its purity and the characteristics that make it both fundamental to and particularly apt for the *corrida de toros*.

The fighting bull is not trained to charge; this herbivorous creature is born with the tendency

Poster at the Plaza de Toros bullring in Pamplona.

> It is a fallacy that bulls charge only red. Bulls are colour-blind, but they have an innate tendency to attack anything that moves.

to attack anything that moves or challenges its predominance. Pampered as a valuable thoroughbred, the *toro bravo* enjoys four to five years of splendour in the grass before it is faced with the ultimate test, its appearance in the arena.

The first man to turn bullfighting into a profession was the Ronda carpenter Francisco Romero, but it was his grandson, the great Pedro Romero, who is considered the father of modern bullfighting.

With the *muleta* (the red cloth draped over a metre-long stick) in his left hand and the sword in his right, Pedro Romero manoeuvred the animal until it was in position for placing the sword. He killed more than 5,600 bulls between 1771 and 1799 without suffering so much as a scratch. No matador since has matched his feat in terms of physical immunity.

This, then, was *toreo* in its most rudimentary form; the object of the 'show' was to kill the bull. Today, many intricate and artistic manoeuvres have been created with the cape and *muleta*, and the bullfighter is no longer merely a *matador* (killer); he is a *torero*, who expresses his sentiments and artistic ability through the art of challenging and dominating an intimidating beast.

Bulls have inspired countless writers and artists, including Hemingway and Picasso. The poet Federico García Lorca called the bulls 'Spain's greatest vital and poetic treasure'.

Though some view it as an unnecessarily cruel slaughter, others see in the bullfight a dramatic dance between man in all his elegant cognisance and the bull in all its natural, earthy fierceness and brutality.

Death in the afternoon

The *corrida* commences with the pageantry of the *paseíllo* or entrance parade in which the *alguacilillos*, the mounted constables in 16th-century attire, lead the march of the bullfighters into the ring to the tune of the *paso doble*.

The *alguacilillos* are followed into the arena or *ruedo* by the three matadors who precede in turn the three rows of their respective *cuadrillas* or teams. Each matador has in his service three *banderilleros*; their role is to assist him in the handling of the bull by using the cape and also in the placing of the *banderillas*, the 60cm (2ft) crêpe-paper-decorated darts.

These *banderilleros* were, in their day, aspiring matadors, though probably few progressed beyond the novice stage to the *alternativa*. This is the ceremony in which a veteran matador symbolically cedes the tools of the trade – the *muleta* and sword – to the neophyte, endowing him with the right to kill fully grown bulls and to hold the coveted title of *Matador de Toros*.

The three rows of *banderilleros* are followed by the mounted picadors. Each matador has two in his employ, one to stab each of his bulls. The *paseíllo* is completed with the no less pompous entrance of the more mundane bullring employees who will have to put in an appearance in the arena: the *monosabios*, who guide the picadors' horses, the *mulilleros*, who handle the mule team that drags out the dead bull, and the *areneros*, who tidy up the sand afterwards.

Once everyone has taken his respective post, the president of the *corrida* pulls out his white handkerchief to signal the entrance of the first bull into the ring. This marks the initiation of the first *tercio* (third) of this live drama.

The bull comes charging into the arena through the *toril* gate, which communicates directly with the *chiqueros* – the individual pens where the bulls have been enclosed since the morning's *sorteo* (draw). He is greeted by a *banderillero*, magenta and gold *capote* (cape) in hand, or by an extremely eager matador.

The fight begins

The *torero* effects some initial cape passes or lances directed to either of the bull's horns in order to determine the animal's natural tendencies: whether it favours one horn over the other, has a long smooth charge or swerves about rapidly, whether it sees well, and if it is strong.

As soon as the matador feels confident about

Bullfighter Juan José Padilla, who made a comeback after being gored in the head during a fight.

the bull's condition, he proceeds to perform the most classic and fundamental of the passes, the *verónica*. A tandem of *verónicas* is linked together as the matador leads the bull gradually towards the centre of the ring. The series is concluded with a *media verónica* (half-turn) in which the bull is abruptly brought about, giving the matador sufficient time and space in which to withdraw from the bull's path.

At this point, the picadors make their entrance, the least understood and appreciated aspect of the *corrida*. The picadors have a three-fold purpose. First, they prepare the animal for the culmination of the matador's work, the *faena*. In order for the bull to be able to follow the cape smoothly it must be slowed down, but not excessively, and its head must be lowered. To achieve this they goad the bull with lances to weaken its shoulder muscles.

The picador must also try to correct any defects in the bull's charge, such as a tendency to hook to the right or swing up its horns at the end of each pass, which could prove fatal to the matador who is unprepared for it. The picador's other important function is to determine the *toro's* bravery, for the bull is just as significant a figure in the bullfight as the matador, and the public calls upon

A matador's 'traje de luz' (suit of lights).

FAMOUS FAMILIES

The two most famous families involved with bullfighting are the Romero and Ordoñez dynasties, both from Ronda. The first of the Romero matadors was Francisco (1700–63), while his grandson Pedro (1754–1839) was the best known and admired for his good looks as well as his skill; Ernest Hemingway named a character after him in his book *The Sun Also Rises*. Hemingway was also inspired by the Ordoñez family: Cayetano (1904–61) was the actual model for 'Pedro Romero', while his son Antonio (1932–98) had his rivalry with his brother-in-law, Luis Miguel Domínguín (1926–96), chronicled in *The Dangerous Summer*. Cayetano's grandsons fight today.

both to perform at their best. Generally three jabs or *puyazos* are administered, depending upon the animal's strength. The first third of this phase is brightened by the alternating participation of the three matadors in a competitive display. With the cape, known as *quites*, each matador is supposed to *quitar* or draw the bull away from the horse and perform any of the many varied cape adornments, such as *verónicas*, *chicuelinas*, *gaoneras*, *navarras* and *delantales*.

The president will use his white handkerchief once again to mark the beginning of the second *tercio*, the *banderillas*. Some matadors are skilled in the placing of their own *banderillas*, but 80 percent of the time the assistants place the darts in the most expedient manner. This *tercio* gives the bull the opportunity to recuperate after its cumbersome struggle with the heavily padded picador's horse.

The moment of truth

The trumpet now sounds for the third and final act of the drama. Armed with his sword and the red serge *muleta*, the matador simultaneously salutes and requests permission from the president to kill the bull.

The right-handed pass or *derechazo*, in which the sword is used to expand the cloth, and the left-handed *natural* are the two fundamental *muleta* passes. More importance is attributed to the *natural*, in which the *muleta* is held in its natural and more diminutive size, with the sword in the right hand. A series of smooth or tempered *naturales* is usually completed with a *remate* pass, the *pase de pecho*, taking the bull from behind the matador and leading it past and off to the right.

The matador has 15 minutes in which to bring about the death of the bull, creating his artistic masterpiece, the *faena*. In order to kill in the *volapié* fashion, the matador positions the bull, raises the sword to shoulder level and moves in to kill, using the *muleta* to guide the dangerous horns past his right hip. He must move with determination and a steady hand to ensure that the sword hits its mark, a 7.5cm (3in) -wide opening just between the shoulder blades. If he misses his target, he will hit bone and the *pinchazo* will not be appreciated by the public.

If the steel *estoque* is not well placed or proves to be insufficient to produce the animal's death, the matador will be obliged to make use of the *descabello*. This is a shorter sword fitted with a crossbar close to the tip. The matador directs the *descabello* to the rachidian bulb at the base of the bull's skull, which produces instant death, if performed correctly. As soon as the bull drops to the ground, the *puntillero* rushes out with the *puntilla* or dagger to administer the *coup de grâce* to prevent any further suffering.

At this point the public displays its approval – or otherwise – of the bullfighter's performance. Under satisfactory circumstances the

Bullfighting today

There are people in Spain who regard bullfighting as an abuse of animal rights and even a national disgrace; but they are few in number. Most Spaniards, while never attending a bullfight themselves, see the Fiesta Nacional as an immutable part of their culture which is beyond all criticism. Although Catalonia became the second region of Spain to ban bullfighting in 2012 (the first was the Canary Islands in 1991), plans are afoot to try and overturn the ban in the national parliament as many people consider the 'sport' an important part of their cultural heritage.

Although a traditional sport, bull fighting is a contentious issue and was banned in Catalonia in 2011.

crowd waves handkerchiefs to request the granting of an ear to the matador.

Nowadays, the *orejas* (ears) and the *rabo* (tail) are symbolic trophies for a good-to-excellent performance. A matador who performs well but experiences difficulty with the sword, for example, might be applauded by the crowd and invited to take a *vuelta* or lap of the ring.

As the bulls share star billing with the matadors, a brave animal that performs well is applauded as it is drawn out of the arena by the mules. It may even be granted its own turn of the ring and, in exceptional cases, a pardon. The trumpet sounds again and it is time for the second bull to emerge from its dark pen into the bright sunlight of the arena.

WHEN TO SEE BULLFIGHTS

The bullfighting season officially opens on 19 March (St Joseph's Day) and ends on 12 October (Hispanic Day in Spain), though fights are frequently held before and after these dates. The audience sits in the *tendidos* (stalls) or the *palcos* (balcony), where the president's box is situated.

Seating is divided into three sections: the expensive shady side, or *sombra*; the cheaper sunny section, or *sol*; and the intermediate *sol y sombra*. The *corrida* generally starts at 5pm. The most famous bullrings in Spain are La Maestranza in Seville, which dates from 1761, the Plaza de Toros de Las Ventas in Madrid and the Plaza de Toros de Ronda.

OUTDOOR ACTIVITIES

Whether you're in search of a new experience or something more thrilling to do than relaxing on a beach, Spain offers a wide choice of sports and pastimes that attract enthusiasts.

With such a great climate, for the most part, and such a diversity of landscapes and coastlines, Spain is hard to beat for outdoor activities. If you're on holiday in a beach resort you can usually find something interesting to do close by – ask at the tourist information office. Alternatively, there are many specialist tour operators who offer all-in trips to Spain organised around a particular interest. If you are already an enthusiast of a particular sport or hobby, you might want to contact the relevant national association for more guidance.

Water sports

The most obvious place for outside activities is in the water. A variety of water sports, including pedalos, kayaks and waterskiing, will be on offer on the beach of any major resort on the Mediterranean coasts. More demanding sea sports are widely available, but if you are seri-

Paddling past Seville's Triana neighbourhood.

> There has been a surge of adventure sports in the Pyrenees in recent years, from white-water rafting to kayaking, and paragliding to bungee jumping: check out www.visitpirineus.com

ous about one of these you'll probably want to head for the prime spot for that activity. For example, the Strait of Gibraltar has been nicknamed 'the wind tunnel', and Tarifa, at the Atlantic entrance to the strait, is renowned as the windsurfing (and kitesurfing) capital of Spain. Another famous spot for windsurfing is El Medano in Tenerife. Surfing purists congregate in Mundaka near Bilbao. The most

challenging waves roll in during the winter months (between September and April), and a wet suit is essential.

The Mediterranean offers some excellent snorkelling and diving, but you have to know where to go. For an introduction, you can't beat a short trip out to the Illes Medes off L'Estartit on the Costa Brava. For scuba diving on the south coast the best place to go is La Herradura near Almuñécar. The Canary Islands also have prodigiously clear waters, and there are companies on all the major islands offering both taster (*bautizo*) courses and excursions for qualified divers.

Spain is also a popular sailing destination because of its innumerable coves (particularly in the Balearic Islands and on the Costa Brava), calm bays and, in the north, river estuaries. In preparation for the America's Cup in 2007, Valencia's port underwent a major redevelopment programme, with a new 700-berth marina and revamped dockside. There are marinas along all the coasts and around the islands, ranging from the humble mooring point to the jet-set community of Puerto Banús near Marbella.

Many of these marinas are home to companies which hire out seagoing sailing boats, for a taste of life on the water.

Hiking by the Cola de Caballo (Horse Tail) waterfall, Parque Nacional de Ordesa.

Walking and trekking

Areas of Spain may be drab and dry, but many parts of the country offer outstanding conditions for walking. Spring and early summer are undoubtedly the best times to go walking, as this is when the landscape is smothered in wild flowers and it is not too hot to be out in the midday sun.

The Mediterranean vegetation burns dry in the heat of July and August, although these are good months to go walking at higher, normally snow-capped altitudes. Autumn and winter are suitable seasons for exploring the countryside near the coasts when the access roads aren't clogged with tourist traffic.

Obvious places to go are the 15 national parks, which are all outstanding areas both for their landscape and wildlife, although sometimes access is restricted to protect rare species. The best parks for the experienced hill-walker are the Picos de Europa, the Sierra Nevada and Ordesa in the Pyrenees.

Spain is crisscrossed by several long-distance (GR) footpaths, including the 1,280km (795-mile) -long GR7 (E4), or 'Mediterranean Arc', which connects the Aegean Sea with the Atlantic Ocean. It is always possible, of course, to walk only a section or two of a GR. The most popular long-distance trek is the medieval pilgrimage route across northern Spain from the French border to Santiago de Compostela (see page 336).

Parques naturales (nature reserves with greater public access than national parks) are good places to look for shorter walking routes designated PR-A, which are normally between 1km (0.5 miles) and 10km (6 miles) long and often conveniently circular so that you return to your starting point. They are graded according to their degree of difficulty, from *baja* (easy) to *muy alta* (physically demanding). Tourist offices and nature reserve visitors' centres will be able to advise on these footpaths and other easy strolls within their localities.

Air sports

Being such a mountainous country, Spain provides many good launch sites for hang-gliding *(ala delta)* and paragliding *(parapente)*, and the centre and south enjoy plenty of clear, calm days. A centre for hang-gliding is Segura de la Sierra in the province of Jaén. Empuriabrava on the Costa Brava, meanwhile, is Spain's de facto skydiving capital, but there is another well-known drop zone near Seville.

Fishing

Spain has few large rivers – but a surprisingly large number of reservoirs – and freshwater fishing is better in the wetter northern parts of the country. The 6,000km (3,700-mile) -long coast, however, provides great variety in sea-fishing in both Atlantic and Mediterranean waters. The licensing system is regionally and locally organised, and the best advice is to ask for help in a local tackle shop – tell them where you want to fish and what you are after and they may help you fill out the application form.

Horse riding

Andalusia is a region particularly associated with horses, and Jerez de la Frontera is the home of the renowned Real Escuela Andaluza de Arte Ecuestre (www.realescuela.org), but there are numerous riding stables all over Spain from which to take an accompanied or unaccompanied tour of the surrounding countryside.

it. Added to this, great stretches of the country are dry and drab, and the road network is sometimes sparse and the signposting poor, forcing cyclists on to busy roads. Perhaps because of this, most Spanish cyclists are weekend racers, and cycle-touring has only recently started gaining in popularity.

However, cycling for health and pleasure is on the increase, and one encouraging trend is the conversion of disused railway lines into *vías verdes* or 'green ways' (see www.viasverdes.com for more details). As well as these, there are a few localised spots where cycling is pleasant

Riding lesson at the Royal Andalusian School of Equestrian Art.

Golf

The Costa del Sol has been dubbed the 'Costa Golf' for its concentration of golf courses. There are other well-known golf courses near Spain's major cities. Almost all of them have 18 holes, and some clubs have more than one course. Most are open to non-members on payment of a green fee, but a few of the most select are for members only. Advance booking is recommended, particularly if you want to play on one of the more prestigious courses.

Cycling

Few parts of Spain are entirely flat, and you have to love hill-climbing to cycle-tour around

ADVICE FOR WALKERS

Wherever you go walking, wear adequate footwear (never sandals), long trousers as protection against the spiky vegetation, and a hat, because the midday sun can be unrelenting. Stick to marked paths within your ability, never walk alone and always make sure someone knows where you have gone and when you expect to be back. Above all, always carry plenty of drinking water: dehydration can be a serious problem. Take the best map you can get hold of. The Centro Nacional de Información Geográfica publishes a useful 1:25,000 series and the Spanish army (Servicio Geográfico del Ejército) publishes a 1:50,000 series.

rather than arduous. If you want true flatlands, the Ebro Delta in Tarragona is a good place to watch birds while you roll through pleasant farm and marshland.

Skiing

The best ski slopes with the most reliable snow are in the central Pyrenees. Baqueira-Beret (Lleida) and Candanchú (Huesca) are two of the most popular resorts.

At the other end of the country is the Sierra Nevada, south of Granada. As Europe's southernmost ski resort it has almost guaranteed sun-

Scuba diving over a coral reef.

shine and a season that lasts until May (with the help of snow cannons). Its base station is at 2,100 metres (6,890ft), and its highest run starts from 3,300 metres (10,800ft). There are other, much smaller, ski resorts, such as those in the Sierra de Guadarrama north of Madrid, but they only come into their own during an exceptionally good, snowy winter.

Tennis

Tennis is extremely popular in the Mediterranean parts of Spain due to the agreeable climate. Many large hotels have their own courts for the use of guests.

Failing that, ask at the tourist information office and you'll usually find a private club or municipal sports centre where you can book a court by the hour.

Spas

Spain's traditional spas are usually tucked away in the hills, on remote winding roads, and take the form of hotels-cum-sanatoriums dishing out medicinal and thermal cures for specific ailments. These days the word 'spa' has been expropriated by luxury hotels offering beauty treatments and self-indulgence to well-heeled clients – not to be scorned if you have got the money and are aware that you are not being offered supposedly therapeutic waters. A recent variation on the health-and-leisure theme is thalassotherapy, a spa treatment using sea water. An enjoyable way to spend an hour or two while on holiday in cities like Granada and Seville is to visit an 'Arab bath' (similar to Turkish baths), with hot and cold rooms, and massages available. It is usually necessary to reserve a session in advance.

Special-interest holidays

Many travel companies, based in Spain and abroad, offer all-in special-interest holidays including flamenco dancing, cookery, painting, photography, yoga and even astronomy. The most popular educational reason to visit Spain is to learn the language, and the best way to find a suitable course is to contact the Instituto Cervantes (www.cervantes.es), an official organisation for the promotion of Spanish culture. When choosing a school, remember that you'll hear less Castilian Spanish spoken in the Basque Country and Catalonia because more and more people in these places are speaking their own regional languages; and that in Andalusia you could pick up a strong southern accent. The purest Castilian is said to be spoken in Old Castile, particularly in the city of Salamanca.

Naturism

Naturists, understandably, shun the north of Spain in favour of the Mediterranean where winter temperatures make it more natural to strip off. Topless sunbathing is normal on many beaches, and most resorts now have at least one beach where naturism is permitted.

Andalusia has two dedicated naturists' colonies: Vera Playa Club and the 'village' of Costa Natura near Estepona.

Fino sherry, Jerez de la Frontera, Andalusia.

FOOD AND WINE

It's simplistic to think of 'Spanish food' – there's a huge
regional diversity, enriched by Roman and Moorish
influences and discoveries from the New World.

S pain is 'the last large European country in
which cuisine *really* varies from province to
province', wrote the French historian Jean-
François Revel in 1982. Travellers in Spain today
will quickly see what he means. The choice in
municipal markets, cake shops, pork butchers and
even lorry-drivers' cafés varies not only between
regions but also between neighbouring towns and
villages. And even within the same town each restaurant or tapas bar has its own specialities.

A jigsaw of cuisines

Spaniards talk proudly of their regional cuisine,
but in reality the map is a far more complicated
jigsaw. Along the coast the cooking of each
region or province splits between *montaña y
mar*, or mountain and sea. Inland there are similar divides between the mountains, river valleys
and plains – and all of these are crisscrossed by
traditional shepherds', muleteers' and harvesters'
routes, which share dishes like *gazpacho* (cold
soup) and *ajo-arriero* (braised salt-cod). Finally
there are a few pockets, such as the Empordá in
Catalonia, El Bierzo in Castilla y León or the
Maestrazgo in the Levante, and cities such as
Segovia, Cuenca or San Sebastián (Donostia),
that have nurtured more of a local gastronomy.

Local flavours were once found at their best in
casas de comida (eating houses), *tascas* (taverns) and
ventas or *posadas* (roadside inns). But today they
are genuinely present in the kitchens of Spain's
top chefs, albeit remixed in avant-garde dishes.
The Basques led the way in the 1970s with *nueva
cocina*, and today an experimental third generation of avant-garde cooks, inspired by the example of Ferran Adrià of the now-closed El Bulli
(Girona) – considered by many chefs and food
critics the best cook in the world – keeps a firm
sense of its roots alongside dazzling creativity.

*The Basques specialise in 'pinchos', which come on a
toothpick, usually on a slice of bread.*

Modern transport networks also shape the
map. Spaniards are happy to pay for the freshest fish, and lorries rush from the seaports to
supply markets across the country within hours
of the catches being landed.

Madrid has the world's second-largest whole-
sale fish market, and its wholesalers and restaurants claim the very best from the Atlantic and
Mediterranean ports.

Moorish and New World flavours

For all the wondrous variety of Iberian cuisine,
it has a certain character that sets it apart. For
example, the influence of French cooking is
hardly felt, as the author Alexandre Dumas noted

to his surprise in the 1840s. Instead, Moorish and New World flavours are close to the surface, and underlying Roman influences are still present.

The impact of the Islamic centuries is most apparent in a crescent swinging south through Valencia, Murcia and Andalusia. Here you will find sweet honey and almond pastries, cumin- and aniseed-spiced breads, and a vast family of rice dishes and iced drinks (*granizadas*).

The food plants brought back from the New World by Columbus and others are staples everywhere. Kidney beans (*alubias*) and potatoes (*patatas*) appear in regional *cocidos* (one-pot stews), while tomatoes and sweet peppers, as well as *pimentón* (paprika), leave fiery red splashes right across Spanish cooking. In the Canary Islands, a stop-off point between Europe and the New World, try *papas arrugadas* – 'wrinkled potatoes' boiled in their skins – served with *mojo rojo*, a spicy red sauce.

Bread and olive oil have accompanied meals since Roman times. Spain is the world's largest olive-oil producer and the range of oils is enormous. Try them in a Mediterranean breakfast, drizzled over toast that has been rubbed with fresh tomato and garlic.

Carving jamón, dry-cured ham from Spain.

STAR-STUDDED RESTAURANTS

The Basque Country has more Michelin stars per capita than Paris, and its most acclaimed restaurants are **Mugaritz** (www.mugaritz.com), **Asador Etxebarri** (asadoretxebarri.com), **Arzak** (www.arzak.info), **Akelarre** (www.akelarre.net), **Azurmendi** (www.azurmendi.biz) and **Martin Berasategui** (www.martinberasategui.com). Catalonia is also a gastronomic hotspot. Carme Ruscalleda is the second woman ever to be awarded three Michelin stars, at **Sant Pau** (www.ruscalleda. com), in Sant Pol. Her son Raül Balam runs the two-star **Moments** at the Barcelona Mandarin Oriental. The three-star **El Celler de Can Roca** in Girona was voted second best restaurant in the world in 2016.

Equally, olive oil runs through Spanish cooking from every region and can be found dressing dishes in both the humblest dining rooms and elegant Michelin-starred restaurants, although consumption has gone down in recent years due to rising prices. With Spaniards getting through an average of over 13 litres (27 pints) a year, the country is one of the bastions of the modern Mediterranean diet, which was added to Unesco's list of Intangible Cultural Heritage in 2010. Other healthy ingredients like garlic and red wine – of which Spaniards each drink an average of over 20 litres (35 pints) a year – follow close behind, making this a place where you can indulge without feeling too sinful.

Around the regions

Spaniards often say that in the country's north-ern regions you live to eat rather than eat to live. For the Basques, food and cooking are a fundamental part of their culture and identity; the table is a gathering place, whether at home, in male gastronomic societies, at restaurants, cooking competitions or open-air communal meals during fiestas. Going out to restaurants is part of the Basque way of life, and there are clusters of Michelin-starred restaurants in San Sebastián and Bilbao.

Further west, Asturians remain true to sturdy

Gazpacho with jamón ibérico and diced cucumber garnish.

Meseta and the Mediterranean

Moving south to the central plateau (*meseta*), dishes take on a decidedly medieval air – wood-roast meat such as milk-fed lamb (*cordero lechal*), messy dishes of tripe (*callos*), Manchego cheese made with sheep's milk, and wonderful garlic soups (*sopas de ajo*) – while those of the Mediterranean seem dis-tinctly contemporary: sun-drenched salads, roasted vegetables (*escalivada*), fish baked in salt or turned into soups, and flat, pizza-like breads. They all make for deliciously healthy eating.

Manchego cheese hails from the La Mancha region and uses sheep's milk.

country dishes like bean stew (*fabada*), caramel-ised rice pudding (*arroz con leche*), more than 40 farmhouse cheeses, and dry cider. Galician cook-ing has cleaner flavours, with excellent beef and a wealth of fish and shellfish, sturdy *empanadas* (meat pies), *lacón con grelos* (boiled ham with turnip greens) and paprika-laced dishes.

The inland cuisines of La Rioja, Navarre and Aragón share the produce of the fertile Ebro valley: peaches and pears preserved in red wine, braised spring vegetables (*menestras*), and sweet and spicy red peppers, which are a key ingredi-ent of *chilindrón* – lamb, poultry or game stew. Red peppers also go into *patatas a la Riojana*, a potato stew, which the French chef Paul Bocuse pronounced a work of art.

Catalan cooking has a literary tradition dat-ing from the 14th century. Classics include *romesco* (almond and pepper sauce) served with fish or grilled spring onions, *zarzuela* (seafood stew) and *escudella* (pot-au-feu). Each of the Balearic Islands has its own specialities: Men-orca is known for its lobster and Mallorca for its spiral *ensaimada* pastries and *tumbet* (ratatouille and potato casserole with meat or fish). Valen-cians are justifiably famous as consummate rice cooks. What we think of as paella is a synthe-sised technicolour caricature of the hundreds of rice dishes on menus in this area – some cooked until dry in the wide flat paella dishes, and oth-ers left wet and soupy in earthenware casseroles.

Valencians are also great makers of ice cream and iced drinks (*granizadas*): the most original of these is *horchata*, a refreshing sweet milk made from tiger-nuts.

The deep south

Andalusia, often much maligned for its food, also has its classics. Its chilled gazpacho soups are a vast extended family. The original Roman white almond soup (*ajo blanco*) is very different from today's better-known tomato gazpacho. This is the home of *pescadito frito* (mixed dry-fried fish), hams and *potajes* or bean stews. In the sierras you

as a lid to keep the dust off a glass of wine. These days every region, town and bar has its own tapas, and the selection of dishes can stretch the entire length of the bar. Seville is the capital of traditional southern tapas, while San Sebastián is the mecca of sophisticated modern ones.

> Native black-hoofed pigs produce the superb but expensive jamón ibérico, known as the king of hams. Other cured hams made from white pigs, called jamón serrano, are less pricey.

Cooking scallops.

may be lucky enough to find one of the ingenious country dishes that tell of a poorer past: *migas*, made from fried breadcrumbs or flour spiced up with bits of meat, fish or fruit, garlic and herbs. Andalusia and neighbouring Extremadura are also the principal producers of *jamón ibérico*, cured ham made from black-hoofed pigs, which graze free-range on a mixture of acorns and chestnuts and thus produce meat with an intensely nutty flavour.

Terrific tapas

Tapas, small snacks that are served with drinks in bars, have progressed a long way from their simple Andalusian origins as a mere mouthful of cured ham or cheese on a saucer which was used

To *tapear* in the Spanish style you have to keep moving from one bar to the next, picking up just a couple of mouthfuls in each place. There are three different portion sizes – *pincho* (bite size), *tapa* (snack) and *ración* (plateful) – and a fork will often come for each person to graze from the same dish. You can order one *tapa* at a time, or, in some places, such as San Sebastián (where tapas are known as *pintxos*), help yourself from the bar, but you never need to pay until the very end of your session. In southern Spain tapas are very often free with drinks. Finally, if you want to blend in with the crowd, remember to drop your olive stones and even your toothpicks on the floor. It is all swept up at the end of the night.

Spanish Wine

In the past 30 years Spain's *bodegas* (wine shops) and vineyards have undergone a quiet revolution.

Investment in state-of-the-art wine pressing machinery, widespread experimental planting of new grape varieties, larger vineyards and, above all, a shift of mindset from quantity to quality mean that right now a lot of very good-quality wine is flowing in Spain's bars and *bodegas*.

People tend to think of Spain as a land of red wines, thanks to the fame of its Riojas, but its very first cultivated vines, perhaps grown as early as Phoenician times, were those used to make Jerez- or Montilla-style wines in the sun-baked South. These unique fortified wines, aged using a complex system of stacked casks, range from deliciously dry, chilled *fino*, swigged all around Andalusia, to dark, syrupy-sweet PX (Pedro Ximénez) wines generally served with desserts.

The many *bodegas* of Jerez are often nick-named the 'cathedrals of wine', and some are open for visiting.

Powerful reds

By contrast, eastern Spain – Catalonia, Valencia and Murcia – is rapidly gaining fame for its big, balsamic red wines. Vines were first planted in Priorato's slaty black hills near Tarragona, by Carthusian monks, and today its steep vineyards produce one of Europe's most powerful and expensive reds.

Other little-known Spanish growing areas that are now producing some great modern reds are Jumilla in Murcia, Somontano in Aragón, and Toro and El Bierzo in Castilla y León. These *denominación de origen protegida* (DOP) areas (equivalent to the French *appellation contrôlée*) will appear on good restaurant wine lists, along with better-known wines from La Rioja, Valdepeñas, Penedés and Ribera del Duero.

Bright whites

The modern, crisp, fruity whites tailor-made for drinking with Spain's wonderful fish and seafood are another discovery to make on the spot. These are generally made from just one variety of grape – Albariño in Galicia and Verdejo in Rueda (Castile León) – and are drunk young. Less well known, but highly rated, are the white wines made with Godello grapes in Valdeorras, also in Galicia, and the Basque Country's Txacoli wines. Demand exceeds supply for nearly all these white wines, and few are shipped abroad, so they are worth exploring.

Sparkling *cava*

Finally, there is *cava*, once called Spanish champagne, which picked up its name from the underground *bodegas* in Catalonia where it was first made in the late 19th century.

Made by exactly the same traditional method as French champagne, it is exceptionally good

Sherry tour around Harveys Bodega in Jerez de la Frontera.

value for two main reasons: the expensive hand-turning of bottles is entirely mechanised here, and the milder climate offers a low risk of lost harvests. However, the best *brut cavas* are now very sought-after and more expensive. Spaniards also enjoy semi-sweet *cavas*, since they very often drink sparkling wine with desserts.

Where, then, is the best place to try these wines? Generally speaking, restaurants offer the best choice. And, if you prefer quantity to quality, the fiestas celebrating the grape harvest in each area are fun to experience. However, it is worth remembering that while Spaniards appreciate good-humoured tipsiness, they don't generally admire or indulge in drunkenness.

Spanish lynx in Parque Natural
Sierra de Andújar, Jaén province.

WILDLIFE

From the high Pyrenees to low-lying marshlands, Spain has many beautiful landscapes inhabited by rare and spectacular species.

Few of the millions of international tourists who crowd the *costas* every year realise that Spain, with its vast areas of unspoilt scenery, is host to a wide range of fascinating wild animals and birds. So extensive is the country's list of rare and exotic creatures that, for some naturalists, Spain is Europe's last Eden. Enthusiasm and concern starts at the top. King Juan Carlos has declared: 'Nature conservation is one of the great public endeavours of our age.'

The country has more than 200 nature reserves, including 15 national parks. The contrast in landscapes they cover is extraordinary. The principal highland parks are the Picos de Europa, the Ordesa and Monte Perdido National Park in the Aragonese Pyrenees, the Aigüestortcs and Sant Maurici Lake National Park in the Catalan Pyrenccs, the Sierra Nevada in Andalusia, and Garajonay, the cloud-forest-capped peaks of La Gomera in the Canary Islands.

In southwest Spain, flanking the estuary of the River Guadalquivir, is the huge wetland area of Doñana National Park. The smaller marshland area of Tablas de Daimiel in La Mancha also supports a wealth of birdlife. At the other end of the scale are the moon-like, parched volcanic peaks of Timanfaya (Lanzarote) and Teide (Tenerife). Two national parks cover the sea bed: the island of Cabrera off Mallorca and the Atlantic islands off Galicia.

Rare species

In all these national parks, and in the many nature reserves around Spain which are administered by regional governments (usually denominated *parques naturales*), wildlife abounds and facilities are provided to give the visitor the best chance of spotting the most interesting species.

Spanish Imperial Eagle.

But for all the special hides, nature trails and information panels, the truth is that you are unlikely to see any of Spain's most distinctive animals in the wild. Hunted for centuries until legislation was passed to protect them, and hedged into ever more reduced habitats by the expansion of the built-up environment, these animals only manage to survive because of conservation programmes, and even then some may be headed for extinction.

Imperial eagle

Even its iconic status as a regal symbol seems unlikely to save one of these endangered species, the imperial eagle, which is now confined to isolated subpopulations in the forests of southwest Spain, and has a remarkable pattern of mating behaviour.

It starts with a series of elegant circlings, with wings and pinions fully extended. After soaring together for a few minutes, one bird takes the initiative and dives at its mate. Male and female then perform a display of aerial swoops and chases. One bird eventually rolls on its back in mid-air and presents its unsheathed talons to the other. Finally, they plunge earthward, interlocked, then level out and fly apart a few hundred metres above ground.

White storks play-fighting in Parque Natural dels Aiguamolls de l'Empordà.

The couple build a large ramshackle nest on top of a cork-oak tree. Two or three eggs produce plump balls of white fluff. At two months, the young eagles, now with cinnamon-brown feathers, learn to soar and to dive at prey. Within a year, the adults are ready to mate again and juveniles are on their own.

Lynx

Perhaps even harder to see, in the southwestern region, is one of the shyest of exclusively Iberian creatures – the Iberian lynx, which has the look of a leopard cub. There are currently 312 wild lynx remaining in Spain, in the Sierra Morena and Doñana National Park in Huelva, and, in spite of a successful conservation programme, the species could still become extinct within 20 years.

The biggest cause for their dwindling numbers was a myxomatosis plague which all but wiped out their main diet, rabbits. The 80 percent reduction in its habitat since 1960 has also contributed to this frightening prospect. In 2002, the World Conservation Union listed the Iberian lynx as a Category One Critical Endangered Species, which means that money was made available for a rescue project. Doñana National Park runs an active breeding programme.

Weighing around 12kg (30lb), it has markings even more pronounced than its cousin, the European lynx. The lynx is king of Spain's wildcats, a family that includes the slender genet, with its characteristic long banded tail.

Fur pattern apart, the lynx is distinguished by large and tapering ears, topped with tufts of black hair. These act as antennae, sensitive to air currents during upwind stalking and to the slightest rustle in the undergrowth. A mottled ochre coat provides the perfect camouflage in sun-dappled vegetation.

So lithe as to appear boneless, the lynx is a nocturnal hunter. An agile tree-climber, it is also an expert swimmer. With eyes that can be green or amber, it has ultrasensitive sight – enabling it to spot its supper at a considerable distance on a moonless night.

Black stork

Relax under an oak in west-central rural Spain and with luck you may hear the unexpected sound above you of a saw cutting wood. Look carefully for the carpenter. It could be a black stork *(Cigüeña negra)*, in Spain from its winter sojourn in Africa. A big bird with jet-black plumage, it returns to the same large, untidy nest every year. Unlike the large white stork visible on bell towers and tall chimneys throughout Spain, the black species prefers elm or oak woods, river cliffs or rocky platforms in the sierras. The *Cigüeña negra* is a solitary bird, flying alone or in small groups during migration.

Averse to using their heavy wings, the storks do plenty of gliding, and need thermal upcurrents to maintain altitude. As there are few thermals over large expanses of water, they seek short crossings, like the Strait of Gibraltar, for their north- and southbound journeys.

The black stork shares a curious habit with its white counterpart. On emerging from the egg, the nestling lays its head on its back and makes rapid snapping movements with its bill to signal it is hungry. Though silent at first (the infant's bill is soft), in this way begins the bird's characteristic clacking. In an adult, what may look like a warning of attack can also signal excitement.

When they are courting, the storks throw their heads back and engage in a riot of mutual bill-clapping. When eggs appear, male and female share responsibility for the hatching and, once chicks emerge – three to five of them – the storks are faithful parents. So much so that if the female dies or is killed, the male will

their long hibernation, a prolonged light sleep on a bed of leaves, during which respiration sinks to five breaths every couple of minutes. Heartbeats slow down, though body temperatures drop by only 10 percent. Females that have given birth lie in the den, making a warm circle for their cubs.

Since 1973 Spanish bears have been legally protected. Hunting or killing carries extremely stiff fines, and possible imprisonment. Occasionally one is killed by a hunter or a farmer, though the kill will be claimed as self-defence or for the protection of lambs.

The Cantabrian mountains are the last refuge of Spain's brown bears; about 200 remain.

remain alone at the nest to guard the eggs and rear the chicks.

Brown bear

One of Spain's most elusive wild animals is the brown bear. Even scientists trying to study them may find only one or two of the shaggy giants (at about 2 metres/7ft tall, they are among the largest land animals). But a shrunken colony of bears *is* there, forced from the foothills to take refuge in forests near the peaks after centuries of persecution by hunting parties.

Once, these bears numbered several hundred. Today around 200 survive in the Cantabrian mountains and the Pyrenees. In winter the bears disappear entirely, holed up in caves for

WHEN TO WATCH NATURE

Spain's mountain parks are snow-filled from mid-November to mid-April, making access difficult. The best time to visit the Ordesa or Picos de Europa national parks is midsummer. Aigüestortes can be visited in May, though the highest peaks will still be avalanche-prone. To see migratory birds, visit the wetlands of Doñana and the Tablas de Daimiel in spring or autumn. May and June are the best months to see Mediterranean wild flowers blooming along the coast. The Serra de Tramuntana on Mallorca has great birdwatching opportunities, including the near-threatened cinerous vulture and red kite, from February to October.

Flamingo

In contrast to the secretive bears, greater flamingos are eminently visible – particularly in the large Fuente de Piedra lagoon north of Antequera, or on the mudflats of the Guadalquivir River estuary in Doñana and the shallow

> Spain is the last European stronghold of the great bustard. This 'goose with eagle's wings' is almost grotesque on the ground, yet spectacular in flight.

coastal lakes, floodwaters and salt marshes of the south – a subtropical climate where there is normally a good food supply of algae, molluscs and crustaceans. The rose-pink and white flamingos, wading or in serried flight, are an ornithological treasure. Their stilt-like legs and long necks allow them to 'graze' the shallow water for nutritious algae.

Totally gregarious, greater flamingos 'talk' to their companions with much trumpeting. They breed in company, building circular, mud-heap nests a few centimetres above brackish water.

In the warm places they favour lies a danger to the flamingo populations: a searing summer will shrink or completely dry up water habitats. Lakes become saltpans, and the birds can breed

there only irregularly. Nevertheless, the saltpans at Torrevieja and Santa Pola on the Alicante coast are visited by a mass of migratory birds during the year.

Great bustard

Turning from one leggy bird to another, on the plains of Spain you may see the fascinating great bustard. Weighing about 12kg (30lb), it has a moustache of white bristles, an ostrich-type head and legs, and barks like a dog when excited. One of the world's largest flying birds, it is legally protected.

Western Spanish ibex in the Gredos Mountains.

The courtship of great bustards, in spring often performed by dozens of birds in open spaces, is quite a spectacle to behold. Uttering gruff barks, the males (or *barbons*) attract the assembled females with displays of their gorgeously striped plumage and fan-tail, and showy and prolonged dancing rituals. After the ball is over, the female seeks long grass or a field of cereals for her nest. The principal enemy to her hatchlings is the raven.

Purple heron

Another striking bird, the Spanish imperial heron is the most exalted of its genus, a dramatic figure with a black crest and long, graceful, boldly striped neck. It nests and breeds in colonies, hidden in beds of dense reeds.

The question arises why this bird, *Ardea purpurea*, with its dark plumage, is 'imperial' in Spain when elsewhere it is simply a purple heron. The answer may lie in subtleties of sheen or colouring, but the Spanish name seems appropriate – one that is very different, moreover, from the truly purple, red-legged, red-billed gallinule. Virtually all that the two have in common is that they are secretive dwellers of the wetlands.

Desman

One of the rarest animals on earth inhabits the high Pyrenees. Related to the mole, the desman is a sightless nocturnal rodent with a long, flattened, red-tipped snout, clawed front feet, large webbed hind feet and a rat-like tail.

Visually unappealing, rarely photographed – and unknown to science before the 19th century – there's nothing like it in the animal kingdom. The local saying is that 'God's hand shook when He created the desman.' An aquatic mammal, it feeds on caddis – the larva of mayfly and stone flies – probing icy river beds with its sensitive proboscis. Water pollution has driven it ever higher into the mountains; for all its unwholesome appearance, the desman can only survive in the purest water.

Bearded vulture

The bearded vulture (or lammergeier) is in decline in part due to shooting by hunters and its unfortunate habit of eating poisoned meat put down by shepherds for wolves. Its diet consists primarily of wild or domestic animal remains. As the garbage collectors of the mountains, these birds play a vital role in the scheme of nature.

Splendid gliders, with a 3-metre (10ft) wingspan, bearded vultures will stay aloft for many hours, scanning the landscape in search of food. Carrion creatures though they are, the birds' flight silhouette is not unlike the falcon's. Lacking the long, bare neck that gives other vultures a repulsive image, the birds in flight are impressive and beautiful.

The bearded vulture supplements its food by a neat trick. Its wings extended – primary feathers outstretched like slim fingers – it will soar high over rocky ground strewn with bones left by predators. Swooping down, it picks up

a bone, then drops it from a height so that the bone cracks, exposing a tasty morsel of marrow. Thus their Spanish name *quebrantahuesos*, or bone-breakers.

Nature made visible

Almost all the animals described previously are only ever seen with great effort, through powerful lenses or as a result of immense good luck, but there is always wildlife close to hand.

Across great swathes of western and central Spain the unmistakable white stork nests happily on top of chimneys and electricity pylons, and its comings and goings are easy to watch

Adult male Great Bustard.

in many towns and cities. In mountains, a common sight is a loose group of griffon vultures wheeling around a lonely crag. Fairly common but spectacular birds in rural scrubland and urban fringes include the hoopoe, the bee-eater and the azure-winged magpie. Magnificent butterflies are drawn to gardens, and the Moorish gecko is often to be found clinging motionless to the wall of a porch. With a facemask and snorkel there is plenty of life to see just below the surface of any rocky part of the coast. Above all, Spain has a magnificent variety of wild flowers, including quantities of aromatic herbs and orchids on Mediterranean hillsides.

Plaza de España, Seville.

Main square illuminated for a fiesta in Cudillero, Asturias.

Garden view from Palacio
Generalife in the Alhambra..

INTRODUCTION

**From the nippy north to the sultry south,
Spain's got snowy mountains, beautiful
beaches and world-class cities.**

*Catedral, Santiago de
Compostela.*

The territory covered by Spain's 17 regions is vast and breathtakingly varied. The country can be divided into four main climatic zones, beginning with the central plateau, or *meseta*, of Castile. At its heart is Madrid, home to the Prado Museum. Castile's great medieval cities offer insights into Iberia's layered cultural history and the stern Catholicism that fuelled its empire. Extremadura, the *meseta* region running southwest to Portugal, is an arid country that has traditionally bred conquistadors and brave fighting bulls.

The second zone is Andalusia, the Spanish South. This is the Spain of legend and travel brochures, with its Muslim architecture and passion for flamenco. In addition to the three great cities of Seville, Córdoba and Granada, Andalusia is sprinkled with lovely white villages. Another highlight is Doñana National Park, a coastal wildlife refuge.

Costa Brava coastline.

On the eastern Mediterranean coast, you'll find that the soil is among the most fertile in Europe. For more than 1,000 years, the Valencian and Murcian market gardens have prospered from agriculture made possible by Muslim irrigation. Tourism, and especially high-rise Benidorm, brings millions of visitors to the Costa Blanca and Costa Daurada.

Finally, the Spanish North keeps the most diverse regional culture and features stunning landscapes. Navarre and Aragón offer rugged Alpine vistas, Romanesque churches and the splendid festivals of San Fermín and El Pilar. The Basque Country, with its lush hills and attractive beaches, is a gastronomic paradise, adjoining the famous vineyards of La Rioja to the south. The two upland regions of the mid-north coast, Cantabria and Asturias, share between them the magnificent wilderness of the Picos de Europa.

Beyond, in the northwest corner of the peninsula, bounded by the Atlantic on two sides, are the green misted landscapes of Galicia, trodden over the centuries by innumerable pilgrims making their way to Santiago de Compostela.

MAR CANTÁBRICO
(BAY OF BISCAY)

Costa Verde
Costa de Cantabria

Cedeira · Ortigueira
A Coruña/ · Ferrol · Ribadeo · Luarca · Avilés · Gijón · Ribadesella · S. Vicente de · Santander · Lare
La Coruña · Betanzos · Xistral · Mondoñedo · la Barquera · Bilb
1033 · Villalba · Tineo · Cangas · Oviedo · 634 · Llanes · Altamira · Cantabria · Bilb
Camariñas · Carballo · A6 · 640 · Asturias · Cantábrica · Picos de Europa · Peña Prieta · Mira
Corcubión · Cordillera · Peña Ubiña · 241 · La Robla · Cervera de · Embalse · de E
Cabo · Noia · Santiago de · Lugo · Villager · 630 · 2536 · Pisuerga · del Ebro · 232
Fisterra · Compostela · Sarria · Villafranca · León · 66 · Cistierna · A67 · Briviesca
Muros · Padrón · Lalín · Monforte · del Bierzo · Almanza · Castrojeriz · E80
Cambados · Galicia · de Lemos · Ponferrada · León · A71 · Sahagún · Osomo · Burgos
Pontevedra · A Rúa · Montes de · La Bañeza · Valencia de · 120 · la Mayor
Vigo · Ourense · Peña Trevinca · La Bañeza · Don Juan · A66 · Sto. Do
Baiona · 2124 · Castrocontrigo · A62 · Palencia · A1 · de Silo
Tui · Miño · Larouco · Benavente · A66 · Palencia · Na
1525 · A52 · Castilla y León · Aranda
Viana · Caldelas · Bragança · Villardefrades · A82 · Valladolid · de Duero
do Castelo · Chaves · Zamora · Tordesillas · E5
Braga · Guimarães · Mirandela · Bermillo · A11 · SPAIN
Póvoa · de Sayago · Coca · Cerezo
de Varzim · Vila Real · Alaejos · A6 · de Abajo · Atie
Porto · Peso da · Embalse de · Salamanca · Segovia · 110
Espinho · Pedroso · Regua · Almendra · Tormes · La Granja de
Ovar · Douro · Fuente de · San Ildefonso
Aveiro · Viseu · Guarda · S. Esteban · E80 · Vecinos · Ávila · Guada
Ílhavo · Ciudad · Fresno · S. Lorenzo · Madrid
PORTUGAL · Rodrigo · Alhándiga · Piedrahíta · de El Escorial · A2
Figueira · Covilhã · 110 · Sierra de Gredos · Madrid · A42
da Foz · Coimbra · Castelo · Bejar · Móstoles · Aranjue
Branco · Perales · 403 · Talavera · Torrijos · Ocaña · Tara
Fátima · del Puerto · Plasencia · de la Reina · A5 · Toledo · AP3
Alcobaça · Tajo · Navalmoral · E90 · Mora · E5 · Temble
Abrantes · Castilla · La
Torres · Santarém · Portalegre · Trujillo · Sierra de Guadalupe · Consuegra · Camp
Vedras · Ponte · Cáceres · Guadalupe · Montes de Toledo · Cript
Alverca do · de Sor · Zorita · Logrosán · P.N. de · 401
Ribatejo · Extremadura · Herrera · Cabañeros · Daimiel
Lisboa · Badajoz · Mérida · del Duque · 430 · Ciudad
E90 · A66 · Agudo · Real · Manza
Setúbal · Redondo · Olivenza · Guadiana · Puebla de · Santa · Almodóvar
Almendralejo · Alcocer · Eufemia · del Campo · Almagro · Valder
Reguengos · Jerez de los · 432 · Campillo · Villanueva · Puertollano · Cambró
de Monsaraz · Caballeros · Zafra · de Llerena · de Córdoba · La · 1068
Sines · Beja · Moura · Fregenal · Azuaga · Peñarroya- · Carolina · A4 · Seg
de la Sierra · Pueblonuevo · Molena · Andújar · Linares
Aljustre · Guadiana · Alanís · Sierra · Andújar · Úbe
Odemira · Cabezas · Aroche · Santa Olalla · Guadalquivir · Montoro · Baeza
Rubias · del Cala · Palma · Córdoba · Jaén
Almodóvar · Puebla de · Valverde · del Río · Andalucía · Baena · Martos
Portimão · Guzmán · del Camino · Niebla · A66 · Carmona · Montilla · Lucena · Alcalá
Lepe · A49 · Marchena · A4 · E5 · la Real
Lagos · Ayamonte · Sevilla · Écija · Estepa · Osuna · Loja · Granada
Cabo de · Faro · Huelva · Los Palacios · Utrera · 384 · A92
São Vicente · Golfo de · y Villafranca · Antequera · Nerja · Motril
Cádiz · Sanlúcar de · Arcos de · Olvera · Málaga · Almuñécar
Barrameda · AP4 · la Frontera · Álora · e
Rota · Jerez de la · Ronda · Málaga · 3481 · s
Cádiz · Frontera · Fuengirola · sie
Vejer de la · AP7 · Marbella
Costa de la Luz · Frontera · Estepona · Costa · d
A48 · San Roque
Algeciras · Gibraltar (UK) · Cabo · Tarifa
Strait of Gibraltar · Ceuta (Spain)

ATLANTIC

OCEAN

N

Spain

0 ——————— 50 km
0 ——————— 50 miles

Mont-de-Marsan
Capbreton
Biarritz
nostia/
Sebastián
Azpeitia
Orthez
Aire
s-l'Adour
Salies
de-Béarn
Cambo
les-Bains
Tarbes
Dax
Auch
Toulouse
Bédarieux
Mazamet
Montpellier
Béziers
Carcassonne
Narbonne
St-Gaudens
Lourdes
Foix
Quillan
Port-Barcarès
teiz/
ria
A 8
A 15
Iruña/
Pamplona
Cauterets
St-Lary-
Soulan
Bagnères-
de-Luchon
Tarascon
Andorra
Font-
Romeu
Perpignan
Port-Vendres
Cadaqués
Navarra
Jaca
Pic de Aneto
3408
ANDORRA
Andorra la Vella
Figueres
Roses
ogroño
Tafalla
Layre
240
Benasque
Campo
138
La Seu
d'Urgell
Berga
Ripoll
Olot
L'Escala
Torroella
de Montgrí
ja
Sos del Rey
Católico
Ejéa de los
Caballeros
Sabinánigo
230
Graus
Tremp
17
Girona
Palamós
Sant Feliu de Guíxols
Andorra
A 68
AP 15
Huesca
14
E9
Vic
E 15
Lloret de Mar
lo
E 808
Tudela
Barbastro
Cataluña
Manresa
Terrassa
Blanes
Tarazona
Monzón
A 23
E7
Montserrat
Igualada
Sabadell
Aragón
A 22
Lleida
Barcelona
Ciria
234
Zaragoza
Fraga
Valafranca
del Penedès
L'Hospitalet
de Llobregat
Calatayud
E 90
AP 2
E 90
A 23
Sitges
azán
A 2
Caspe
Poblet
Reus
chón
Daroca
Herrera
1346
Flix
Móra la
Nova
Tarragona
211
Retuerta
1491
Alcañiz
Cambrils
de Mar
Monreal
del Campo
A 23
Calanda
L'Espina
182
E 15
232
Tortosa
S. Alta
1856
Palomera
1498
Morella
Costa Daurada
Mogorfit
1862
Javalón
1695
Cañada de
Benatanduz
Benicarló
Vinaròs
nca
Teruel
Penyagolosa
1814
Peñíscola
Menorca
Ciutadella
420
Javalambre
2020
AP 7
Onda
Benicàssim
Pollença
Maó/
Mahón
Cuerda
1401
320
Segorbe
Castelló
de la Plana
Port de
Sóller
Inca
Embalse
de Alarcón
Liria
Golfo de
Sagunt/
Sagunto
Mallorca
Manacor
ancha
A 3
Valenciana
A 3
Valencia
Palma de
Mallorca
Campos
A 31
Villanueva
de la Jara
322
Requena
A 7
Valencia
La Roda
Júcar
Almira
Xàtiva/
Játiva
Gandia
Ibiza
S. Antoni
acete
A 31
Almansa
A 35
Dénia
Eivissa
322
Pozo
Cañada
Alcoi/
Alcoy
Xàbia/
Jávea
Formentera
caraz
Villena
Altea
Losa
1038
Tobarra
Hellín
A 31
Elda
A 7
Benidorm
La Vila Joiosa/
Villajoyosa
412
Cieza
Elx/
Elche
Alacant/
Alicante
aravaca
la Cruz
Mula
Segura
Orihuela
AP 7
Murcia
San Javier
car
Vélez
Blanco
A 30
Totana
A 7
Águilas
Lorca
Cartagena
E 15
Cuevas del
Almanzora
A 7
Mojácar
ería
MEDITERRANEAN
SEA

Canary Islands
Alegranza
Graciosa
0   50 km
0   50 miles
ATLANTIC OCEAN
Lanzarote
2426
Santa Cruz
de la Palma
Tenerife
Arrecife
La Palma
3718
Santa Cruz
de Tenerife
Fuerteventura
Puerto del
Rosario
La Gomera
Las Palmas de
Gran Canaria
El Hierro
San Sebastián
de la Gomera
1949
Valverde
Gran Canaria

Madrid

0   200 m
0   200 yds

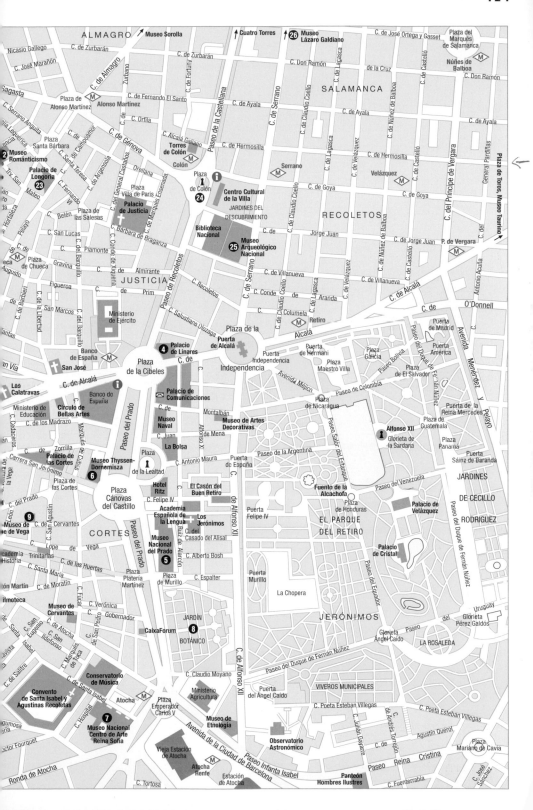

MADRID

The charm of the old quarters, the blue skies and exquisite sierra light, the superb art collections and the vibrancy of the long, long night: these are a few of the attractions of Spain's capital.

Spain's capital city has plenty to offer visitors of all tastes and budgets. World-class art collections in the Museo del Prado, Museo Thyssen-Bornemisza and Museo Nacional Centro de Arte Reina Sofia, Michelin-starred restaurants like El Club Allard and the designer shops of Salamanca cater for those who like the finer things in life. Then there are the historic cafés and bars around Plaza Santa Ana, the breath of fresh air that is the Parque del Retiro and the city's vibrant nightlife, including the happening gay quarter of Chueca. The Plaza Dos de Mayo is a reminder of Madrid's turbulent past.

Think of Paris or Rome, and familiar images spring to mind. But Madrid is more elusive, with an old heart hidden behind its smart new shopping streets. Over the past decades, democracy has brought new dynamism, prosperity and splendid cultural attractions to a city created on the caprice of a king in 1561. Similar to New York, Madrid is a city that never sleeps thanks to its buzzing bars, terrific tapas and eclectic nightlife – from exclusive clubs to corner-café flamenco. Even in difficult times, the locals still know how to enjoy themselves.

The city's evolution

Sixteenth-century Madrid was a placid farming community within sight of the **Sierra de Guadarrama**. The high terrain with its pure water, clear, dry air and dense forests had attracted the Muslims, who built a fort called *Magerit* on a rise over the **Río Manzanares**, just to the south of today's royal palace. It was captured by the Christians in 1083, but the two religions coexisted here in relative tranquillity, remote from the politics of the larger Castilian cities.

When Felipe II proclaimed Madrid the capital against the advice of his father, Charles V (known as King

Main Attractions

Puerta del Sol
Museo del Prado
Museo Reina Sofía
Museo Thyssen-Bornemisza
El Parque del Retiro
Plaza Mayor
Rastro
Palacio Real

Plaza Mayor.

Carlos I within Spain), reluctant courtiers speculated that it was simply because the town was convenient to the building works for his royal palace at El Escorial. Noble houses, convents and monasteries were hastily assembled in order to be near royal influence. As the city grew, living conditions in the sun-baked city became chaotic.

When the Bourbons took over the Crown in the 18th century, they were horrified by the state of the capital. The streets were filthy and crime-ridden; the housing, tightly packed within the city walls, was squalid; the facades of the churches were, in their eyes, lacking in splendour.

Civic improvements weren't always received gratefully by *madrileños*. Carlos III believed that the long capes and broad-brimmed hats worn by Spaniards were conducive to Madrid's many cloak-and-dagger incidents, but his decree that citizens wear European short capes and tricorne hats caused a mutiny which ended in bloodshed. In the early 1800s, Joseph Bonaparte initiated a programme of tree-planting and open spaces, but he had been brought to power by a revolutionary invasion, and his efforts earned him the nickname of '*Rey Plazuelas*' – 'King of Little Plazas'.

By the turn of the 20th century, imposing *Belle Epoque* bank buildings along **Calle de Alcalá** marked the capital's growing financial power. Sweeping boulevards and monumental fountains had given Madrid a truly majestic appearance, yet she could not quite shake off her cow-town reputation. Basque novelist Pío Baroja called Madrid 'an overgrown village of La Mancha'.

Officially, this city of almost 3.2 million inhabitants is still called by its Habsburg title of 'Town and Court', and in spite of a hectic arts scene and an intense nightlife, many find its greatest charm is its mass of old-fashioned quarters or barrios. *Madrileños* are known for being open, unaffected and outspoken, and those very traits have eased the city's rapid political and cultural transformation.

At an altitude of 660 metres (2,165ft), Madrid is the highest capital

Shopping streets off the Puerta del Sol.

in Europe. Pollution from the city's 1.5 million vehicles and the continuing use of coal- and oil-fired heating have made the air rather less champagne-like than it was said to have been in the 19th century, when European princesses often came to Madrid to give birth, but on a clear day the Sierra de Guadarrama still seems within walking distance.

Around Puerta del Sol

At the heart of it all is the **Puerta del Sol** ❶, an oval plaza surrounded by cream-coloured 18th-century buildings. Here you will find Kilometre Zero, a pavement plaque in front of the clock tower, from which all distances are measured; the bronze statue of a bear and a strawberry tree in the plaza is another popular rendezvous point. At midnight on New Year's Eve *madrileños* gather here to eat the traditional 12 grapes, one after each chime of the clock.

Less festive gatherings in the Puerta del Sol included a bloody battle with Napoleon's Egyptian forces, depicted in Goya's *Charge of the Mamelukes*, and an 1830 uprising against Madrid's friars, rumoured to have poisoned the city water supply. The Second Republic was declared here in 1931, and in the 1980s the plaza was the centre of demonstrations against NATO; in 1997 more than 1 million *madrileños* marched here to protest against ETA terrorism; large crowds protested against their government's support for the invasion of Iraq in early 2003 and in the aftermath of the bombings in 2004; in 2011 a sit-in held here to protest against austerity measures started the Indignados social movement.

Feeding into the Puerta del Sol from the north is **Calle de Preciados**, where you'll find lots of shops, including Madrid's largest department store, **El Corte Inglés**. Nearby in Plaza de San Martín, a curious island of peace among the shopping crowds, is the **Monasterio**

de las Descalzas Reales ❷ (www.patrimonionacional.es; Tue–Sat 10am–2pm and 4–6.30pm, Sun and public hols 10am–3pm; free Wed and Thu pm for EU citizens). Founded by Juana, youngest daughter of Carlos I, it remains a working convent, with its own kitchen garden within the walled precinct. It contains a spectacular Baroque staircase and a number of art treasures donated by blue-blooded nuns' families. Many of the works have children as their theme; they represent the triumph of life over death.

Following Calle de Alcalá to the northeast, you will pass the **Real Academia de Bellas Artes de San Fernando** ❸ (www.realacademiabellasartes sanfernando.com; Tue–Sun 10am–3pm for permanent collection). It houses paintings by artists of the Spanish School, including Goya's most famous self-portrait at his easel.

Elegant boulevard

Alcalá ends at the spacious **Plaza de la Cibeles**, graced by a fountain dedicated to Madrid's patron

TIP

If you plan to do a lot of sightseeing, consider buying a Madrid Card, which is valid for 24h, 48h, 72h or 120h. The card gives free and priority access to more than 50 museums, free tours as well as discounts at stores, restaurants and nightclubs. See www.madridcard.com for details.

The Infanta Margarita in Velázquez's 'Las Meninas', housed in the Museo del Prado.

goddess Cybele. The white building opposite resembling a wedding cake is the **Palacio de Cibeles**, the former central post office and now the town hall following a comprehensive refurbishment in 2011, complete with a vast glass-covered patio, an exhibition space (www.centrocentro.org) and rooftop restaurant. On the northeast corner is the aristocratic **Palacio de Linares** ❹ (www.casamerica.es; guided tours in English Sat and Sun 11am–1pm), the palace of a wealthy 19th-century industrialist, which houses a centre for Latin American culture, **Casamérica**. The guided tours reveal fantastic 1870s interiors, the walls groaning with gold leaf, silk and marble, murals and splendid mirrors.

This square stands on Madrid's principal north-south axis. The elegant **Paseo del Prado** runs south from here to Atocha, one of the city's two main train stations. At No. 5 is the **Museo Naval** (www.armada.mde.es/museonaval; Tue–Sun 10am–7pm, Aug until 3pm), the museum of Spain's Navy, which has a fine collection of model ships and antique maps.

To the north is the **Paseo de Recoletos**, a shepherd's track running alongside a small river which was colonised by wealthy families in the 19th century. After the Plaza de Colón comes the Paseo de la Castellana, a broad, prestigious thoroughfare running for over 6km (3.5 miles) to the northern limits of Madrid. It is lined with tower blocks housing banks and other corporations and ends with a cluster of the city's tallest and latest skyscrapers, the Cuatro Torres.

Just before you reach them you pass between two other singular buildings, the Torres Kio (properly called Puerta de Europa) which lean towards each other over the Plaza de Castilla. Nearby is Madrid's other train station, Chamartín.

The Paseo del Prado is invariably busy with sightseers making their way between three world-class art museums which stand conveniently close together. Among them, the **Museo Nacional del Prado** ❺ (www.museodelprado.es; Mon–Sat 10am–8pm, Sun and public hols until 7pm; free Mon–Sat after 6pm, Sun after 5pm) remains

Plaza de la Cibeles.

in a class of its own. Ironically, it was Joseph Bonaparte (elder brother of Napoleon and King of Spain 1808–13) who first proposed a plan to make the royal art collection open to the Spanish public.

Fernando VII completed the project. In 1819 the collection was opened in a building originally designed to hold a natural science museum.

As notions of public morals became more enlightened, pictures such as Titian's *Venus* and Rubens's *Three Graces* were unveiled. Today the museum owns a vast collection, of which 5,000 pieces are on permanent display, here or elsewhere.

On arrival, head for the first floor to see the 17th- and 18th-century Spanish masters. Diego Velázquez (1599–1660), the greatest of Spain's Golden Age artists, produced outstanding royal portraits, notably *Las Meninas* (1656), depicting the Infanta Margarita among her courtiers, and masterful narrative paintings. Also on the first floor are paintings by El Greco (1541–1614) and Francisco de Goya (1746–1828), noted for his brilliantly

unflattering portraits of Carlos IV and family, his early tapestry designs and late 'black' paintings.

Other paintings and drawings by him are on the second floor within the 18th-century European section. The extensive collection of Italian paintings, including works by most of the early Italian masters, is split between the ground floor and first floor, along with early Flemish, Dutch and German masterpieces and medieval Spanish works.

Do not miss the roomful of paintings by Hieronymus Bosch. The museum's annexe, linked to the main building via an underground tunnel and Modernist cube designed by Rafael Moneo, is reserved for temporary exhibitions. Another must-see are the magnificent cast-iron doors by artist Cristina Iglesias on its western facade.

The Thyssen trove

Across the Plaza de Cánovas del Castillo is another extraordinary art collection, the **Museo Thyssen-Bornemisza** ❻ (www.museothyssen.

Museo del Prado.

GOYA

Two Spanish court painters dominate the Prado's collection. One is Velázquez; the other, inspired by his predecessor, is Francisco de Goya, who can be thought of as a forerunner of modern art. Goya's most admired paintings are *The Clothed Maja and The Naked Maja*, the model for which remains a mystery, and *The Third of May*. This latter is an emblematic work of both art and history. It was painted in 1814 but shows events six years earlier when French troops occupying Spain put down an uprising against them by force. Picasso makes reference to the posture of the central figure, hands upraised in a Christ-like posture, in his great anti-war painting *Guernica*. Later Goya took the same theme further in a series of etchings called *The Disasters of War*.

org; Mon noon–4pm, Tue–Sun 10am–7pm; free on Mondays), which has been housed in the Palacio de Villahermosa since 1993.

The lion's share of Baron Hans Heinrich Thyssen-Bornemisza's collection, reckoned the greatest in private hands after that of Britain's Queen Elizabeth II, was bought by the Spanish state for 44,100 million pesetas (£230 million/US$375 million). Spanning the centuries from 1290 to the 1980s, it gives a dazzling overview of medieval northern European paintings, 17th-century Dutch Old Masters, 19th-century North American paintings, and 20th-century Russian Constructivists and German Expressionists.

Guernica

Madrid's other great art museum, just off the bottom end of the Paseo del Prado, near Atocha station, draws a constant crowd to see just one painting, *Guernica*, Picasso's vast painted allegory of the bombing of the Basque town of that name, which, at his request, came to Spain from New York only after democracy was restored. In 1992, amid fierce controversy, the painting was moved to Madrid's showcase for modern art, the **Museo Nacional Centro de Arte Reina Sofía** ❼ (www.museoreinasofia. es; Mon and Wed–Sat 10am–9pm, Sun until 2.30pm), on Calle de Santa Isabel, just off the Paseo del Prado at its southern tip.

The museum is housed in an 18th-century building which was formerly the General Hospital of Madrid and has had its formidable exterior jazzed up by the addition of hi-tech lifts and a new wing designed by Jean-Claude Nouvel. The museum has undergone seemingly endless rehangings.

The collection is currently split into three eras: Utopias and Conflicts (1900–45), Is the War Over? Art in a Divided World (1945–68) and From Revolt to Postmodernity (1962–82). Picasso's *Guernica* is surrounded by the artist's many preparatory sketches, and has a disappointingly cramped wall to itself.

In 2007 a new contemporary art centre opened on the Paseo del Prado, the **CaixaForum** (www.obrasocial.lacaixa. es; daily 10am–8pm). The converted power station, designed by Herzog & de Meuron, features a striking inset glass wall and alongside it is a vegetal wall of tumbling ferns that also serves to insulate the building.

In the park

Behind the Prado is Madrid's extensive pleasureground, **El Parque del Retiro** (daily, summer 6am–midnight, winter until 10pm), which was conceived as an ornamental garden surrounding the royal palace-retreat built to a 17th-century design by Velázquez.

Garden parties and water masquerades reached lascivious heights during the reign of Felipe IV. Fountains, statues, the delicate 19th-century **Palacio de Cristal** (www.museoreinasofia.es; daily Apr–Sept 10am–10pm, Oct till 7pm, Nov–Mar 10am–6pm; free), the original boating lake and the ruined royal

'Brushstroke' by Roy Lichtenstein outside Museo Nacional Centro de Arte Reina Sofía.

porcelain factory still give the Retiro an air of a royal garden; the Centre de Arte Reina Sofía occasionally hosts exhibitions here.

For fresh air between museum visits, the **Real Jardín Botánico** ❽ (www.rjb. csic.es; daily, May–Aug to 10am–9pm, Apr and Sept until 8pm, Mar and Oct until 7pm, Jan–Feb and Nov–Dec until 6pm) is a lovingly groomed oasis just to the south of the Prado. Created in 1774 by Carlos III, it is tranquil and lush, with greenhouses (one full of native desert flora) and a shaded walkway of Spanish vines.

An alternative oasis is Atocha station, where a steamy miniature palm forest is encased in a vast 19th-century glass-and-iron loggia, partly designed by Gustave Eiffel. If you walk through to the neighbouring local station you can access the underground viewing chamber (daily 10am–8pm) of the cylindrical glass monument dedicated to the memory of those who died here on 11 March 2004, when four bombs exploded on commuter trains. The cylinder's plastic inner membrane is engraved with messages left at the station by the public in the days that followed the bombings.

From the Paseo del Prado, literary pilgrims can follow the **Calle de Cervantes** to the **Casa-Museo de Lope de Vega** ❾ at No. 11 (http://casamuseo lopedevega.org; only guided tours Tue–Sun 10am–6pm; booking mandatory; free). Here the great playwright created his most important works. The furnishings and personal effects are not his, but they show how a 17th-century Spanish household might have looked.

Returning to the Puerta del Sol along the Carrera San Jerónimo, you'll pass the parliament building, the **Palacio de las Cortes** (closed to the public). The bronze lions in front are made of melted-down cannons captured in the war with the Moroccans in 1860.

Old Madrid

Madrid's **Plaza Mayor** ❿ or Main Square, west of the Puerta del Sol, is a 17th-century beauty, even if it is no longer the centre of town as it was in ages past, when autos-da-fe, bullfights

Boating lake in Parque del Retiro.

Atocha railway station.

and coronations took place there. The wide, cobbled pedestrian square is a pleasant if pricey spot to have coffee and watch the world go by. Just west of the Plaza Mayor is the **Mercado de San Miguel** (www.mercadodesanmiguel. es), a local market in a lacy early 20th-century ironwork.

Further along Calle Mayor is the **Plaza de la Villa**, a pretty pedestrian square and showcase of Madrid architecture from the 15th to the 17th century. The main attraction is the Baroque Casa de la Villa, or town hall. Also worth noting is the Torre de los Lujanes, with *Mudéjar* arches and a Gothic portal, one of the few examples of 15th-century secular architecture in the capital.

A short walk from here, cutting through the three plazas at the heart of Habsburg Madrid – Cordón, Cruz Verde and Paja – will take you to the **Museo de San Isidoro. Los Origenes de Madrid** (www.madrid.es/museosan isidro; Jul–mid Sept Tue–Fri 10am–2pm, 3–7pm, Sat-Sun 10am–7pm, mid Sept–June Tue–Sun 9.30am–8pm; free) in Plaza de San Andrés. Madrid's

patron saint, San Isidro – beatified jointly with his wife – supposedly lived and worked for the noble Vargas family here. The museum houses local archaeological finds and historical exhibits. To the east of the museum is Calle de la Cava Baja, which has some of the best tapas bars in the city.

On a Sunday morning, head south to the **Colegiata de San Isidro** ⓫ (http://parroquiabuenconsejoysanisidro. blogspot.com; daily for Mass; open 7.30am–1pm, 6–9pm) on Calle de Toledo, the church that for centuries has held the popular status of a cathedral. Its gloomy interior houses the remains of Madrid's peasant patron saint, and a Virgin awarded a field-marshal's sash by Franco. Beyond the church, the **Rastro** (www.elrastro.org), an enormous open-air bazaar, fills Calle Ribera de Curtidores and the surrounding streets for several blocks in all directions on Sunday mornings. Clothes, furniture and animals can all be purchased, as well as specialist items such as rings of skeleton keys, old liquor stills and fascist memorabilia (Beware of pickpockets).

In this hilly quarter, Lavapiés, which was once the Jewish ghetto, Madrid's throaty urban *castizo* accent is at its thickest. At the same time, its cultural diversity has helped it become the city's alternative performing-arts scene.

This is the pulse point of the mid-August Fiesta de la Virgen de la Paloma, when women in colourful kerchiefs and flounced skirts dance through the streets with waistcoated partners to blasts of traditional *chotis* and rock music.

Further west of the Rastro, the neoclassical **Basílica de San Francisco el Grande** ⓬ (Jul–Aug Tue–Sun 10.30am–12.30pm, 5–7pm, Sept–June Tue–Sat 10.30am–12.30pm and 4–6pm) was built on the site of a 13th-century monastery purportedly founded by St Francis during a pilgrimage to Spain. The interior is mostly decorated in florid 19th-century style; one mural shows an apparition of St James in the act of killing Muslims. There is also an early fresco by Goya, which contains a bright-eyed self-portrait.

To the north, alongside the Palacio Real is the **Catedral de Nuestra Señora de la Almudena** ⓭, finally consecrated on 15 June 1993 (www.catedraldelaalmudena.es; daily 9am–8.30pm). The church, a monolithic eyesore, houses the image of Our Lady of the Almudena, patroness of Madrid. Work on the building had started in 1883, but took a century to complete.

Just to the south of the cathedral, the Cuesta de la Vega winds down to the largest surviving stretch of Madrid's Arab 11th-century wall to the Ermita de la Virgen del Puerto.

The Palacio Real

The **Palacio Real** ⓮ (www.patrimonio nacional.es; daily, Apr–Sept 10am–8pm, Oct–Mar until 6pm; free for EU citizens last two hours Mon–Thu) is an opulent 18th-century affair reflecting the French tastes then in vogue. On Christmas Eve 1734, the Habsburg Alcázar burned to the ground, enabling Felipe V to build a palace more suited to the requirements of a Bourbon monarch.

The 18th-century Palacio Real.

Designed by Italian masters Sacchetti and Sabatini, it was so lavish that Napoleon claimed his brother Joseph had better lodgings than his own at the Tuileries in Paris. Inside are the Farmacia Real, with glass cases full of exotic medications, the **Museo de la Real Armería**, containing the swords of Cortés and Fernando the Catholic, and the grand royal apartments. Certain areas of the earlier Habsburg Alcázar and Arab wall east of the palace are being excavated.

Alfonso XIII was the last resident of the palace. The present royal family prefers less elaborate quarters outside town, and the palace is now used only for official functions and events. Below it are the stately 19th-century **Campo del Moro** gardens, entered from the Paseo de la Virgen del Puerto (free).

The **Teatro Real** ⓯ (www.teatro-real.com), opposite the Royal Palace, opened as an opera house in 1850, after 38 years of building work. Legend has it that the cast of one production included live elephants. In October 1997, after lengthy renovations, the building reopened as one of the largest opera houses in Europe.

Plaza de Oriente and Plaza de España

The surrounding streets and **Plaza de Oriente**, laid out as formal gardens around a bronze statue of Felipe IV on horseback, designed by Velázquez and engineered by Galileo, have been pedestrianised, making this a pleasant area to take a stroll.

Just off the northern side of the Plaza sits the **Real Monasterio de la Encarnación** ⓰ (www.patrimonio nacional.es; Tue–Sat 10am–2pm and 4–6.30pm, Sun and public hols 10am–3pm; free for EU citizens Wed–Thu pm), which was once connected to the Royal Palace by a passageway. Apparently the convent was meant to be a refuge for the women of the royal family 'in case of some novelty', as its founder, Queen Margaret of Austria, hinted darkly in a letter. The cloister houses royal portraits, including one of an illegitimate daughter of Felipe IV being received into heaven.

Coffee break in the area near the opera house, Teatro Real.

The church is a splendid example of 18th-century Madrid architecture by Ventura Rodríguez. In the reliquary is a vial of San Pantaleón's blood, which is said to liquefy every year on 27 July.

The centre of the western end of Madrid, at the end of Gran Vía, is the **Plaza de España** ⓱, where larger-than-life bronze statues of Don Quijote and Sancho Panza ride towards the sunset. Just north of the Plaza de España is the **Palacio de Liria** ⓲ (www.fundacioncasadealba.com; visits Fri at 10am, 11am and noon) the magnificent 18th-century home of the Duchess of Alba who, before her death in 2014 aged 88, had more titles than anyone else in the world.

Close by is the **Centro Cultural del Conde Duque** (http://condeduque madrid.cs; Tue–Sat 10am–2pm and 5.30–9pm, Sun 10.30am–2pm), an 18th-century military barracks now housing exhibition rooms around two giant courtyards.

Goya's extraordinary frescoes are a good reason for making a pilgrimage to the Pasco de la Florida to visit the neoclassical **Ermita de San Antonio de la Florida** (http://sanantoniodelaflor-ida.es; Tue–Sun 10am–8pm,; free). In 1798, after completing the frescoed walls and ceiling showing St Anthony raising a murdered man from the dead, Goya was appointed first painter to the court, despite the fact that the fresco's portrayal of street people was a startling departure in church art. Goya died in 1828 and chose to be buried here in front of the altar.

The popularity of the shrine's annual fiesta – St Anthony is the patron saint of disappointed lovers and lost objects – has necessitated the construction of a replica chapel next door.

Other sights in this part of town include the **Templo de Debod** ⓳ (some parts are closed for restoration; Apr–Sept Tue–Fri 10am–2pm and 6–8pm, Sat–Sun 9.30am–8pm, Oct–Mar Tue–Fri 10am–2pm and 4–6pm, Sat–Sun 9.30am–8pm; free), which was given to Spain by Egypt in gratitude for helping with the construction of the Aswan Dam. Originally sited on land flooded by the dam, it was built by the Pharaoh Zakheramon in the

FACT

Malasaña is particularly lively on 2 May when the Fiesta de la Comunidad de Madrid takes place. The festival celebrates the day in 1808 when Napoleon's troops stopped an uprising in the city, in what is now Plaza Dos de Mayo. There is usually live outdoor music and plenty of atmosphere in the bar.

Guarding Palacio Real.

SPAIN'S ROYAL FAMILY

When Juan Carlos came to the throne after General Franco's death, he did so in the uncomfortable knowledge that Spaniards had a well-established tradition of unseating Bourbon monarchs they did not like. His reign was aimed at establishing a monarchy committed to democratic politics. No one can doubt that, against all the odds, he succeeded.

He also helped set the tone of a new Spain free of the formality that constricted his country in the past. His easy-going manner won over many a lifelong republican. A keen sportsman – he sailed for Spain in the 1972 Olympics, finishing 15th, and less popularly, enjoys hunting. Following Juan Carlos's abdication in 2014 due to ill health and the black cloud of corruption scandals hovering over him, the spotlight is now firmly on his son and new king, Felipe VI. Felipe married Letizia Ortiz Rocasolano, a TV presenter, divorcée and popular public figure, in late 2003; they have two daughters, Princess Leonor and Princess Sofia. In 2004, Felipe and his sisters became the first members of the royal family ever to take part in public protest when they joined demonstrations after the Madrid bombings. The new monarch has a difficult task on his hands: repairing the tarnished image of the royal family, whose members (including Felipe's own sister Cristina) have been embroiled in corruption scandals and tax fraud allegations.

Memorial statue and archway in the Plaza Dos de Mayo, commemorating those killed in the 1808 uprising against the French.

The vertical garden on the building next to the CaixaForum.

2nd century BC. This is one of the best spots to watch the city's technicolour autumn sunsets.

Nearby, on Paseo Pintor Rosales, you can board a cable car *(teleférico)* and sail over the **Parque del Oeste** and the Río Manzanares to the **Casa de Campo**, an enormous open space with an amusement park (open late on summer nights), zoo, aquarium and sports pavilion built as part of the city's unsuccessful bids to host the 2012 or 2016 Olympics.

Madrid's rebel roots

Madrid's counterculture centre in the heady late 1970s, after the fall of Franco, was **Malasaña**, between calles San Bernardo and Fuencarral south of Calle Carranza. By day this area is redolent of old Madrid, with local people going about their lives.

A former pharmacy on the corner of calles **San Andrés** and **San Vicente Ferrer** has memorable tiles advertising early 20th-century miracle cures. However, when night falls the neighbourhood changes character. Bars resound with rock 'n' roll, grunge, garage,

hip-hop and jazz, and the streets fill with lively people – both young and old – looking for a good time until the early hours of the morning.

The centre of the neighbourhood, the **Plaza Dos de Mayo** ㉑, was the scene of a fierce battle with Napoleon's forces in 1808; citizens rushed into the streets wielding whatever weapons they could lay their hands on. The casualties were heavy; the archway in the middle of the plaza commemorates those who fell. Some years ago, when plans were made to tear down the old houses and put up new apartment blocks, the neighbours once again mobilised in defence of the barrio. This time Malasaña's bohemian culture was saved, although its nightlife is under pressure. On the corner of the Corredera Bajo de San Pablo, do not miss the richly frescoed 17th-century church of **San Antonio de los Alemanes** (www.realhermandad delrefugio.org; Mon–Sat 10.30am–2pm; daily for Mass).

The **Museo de Historia** ㉑ (www. madrid.es/museodehistoria; Tue–Sun 10am–8pm; free), on nearby Calle Fuencarral, is installed in a former poorhouse with an ornate late Baroque facade. The museum contains exhibits on the history of Madrid from the Palaeolithic period to the present day. Among its attractions are Goya's *Allegory of the City of Madrid*, an exquisite 1830 model of the capital, and early photographs.

The small but interesting **Museo Románticismo** ㉒ (http://en.museoro manticismo.mcu.es; May–Oct Tue–Sat 9.30am–8.30pm, Sun 10am–3pm, Nov–Apr until 6.30pm; free Sat from 2pm), nearby at Calle San Mateo, 13, gives a chance to view a 19th-century interior, preserved by the Marqués de la Vega Inclán, a patron of the arts. Classical music concerts take place here throughout the year and there is a very nice tea room.

While in the area, enthusiasts of Catalan Modernism can gaze in wonder at the **Palacio de Longoria** ㉓ (guided

tours on request; sociosmadrid@sgae.es) on Calle de Fernando VI (at the corner with Calle Pelayo). Designed in 1902 by the architect José Grases Riera, of the Gaudí School, the building is the headquarters of the Society of Authors, who have restored it to its original splendour.

Between here and Gran Vía runs Chueca, another reborn city quarter thriving with art galleries, restaurants, bars, and a cluster of speciality gourmet emporia on Fernando VI; it is also Madrid's gay quarter.

Upmarket Salamanca

A few blocks east, the **Plaza de Colón** ㉔, 'Columbus Square', is graced by a statue of the adventurer on a carved neo-Gothic column erected in 1885. On the other side of the square are four enormous concrete sculptures that resemble large decayed teeth. They, too, commemorate Columbus, with inscriptions describing the 'discovery' of America. At the western end of the square, a giant wave waterfall guards the entrance to the Teatro Fernán Gómez, an arts complex with a theatre, concert hall and exhibition space.

Alongside this plaza is a monolithic structure enclosing the **Biblioteca Nacional** facing west and the **Museo Arqueológico Nacional** ㉕ (www.man.es; Tue–Sat 9.30am–8pm, Sun until 3pm; free Sat after 2pm) facing east. The library, inaugurated in 1892 to mark the 400th anniversary of Columbus's voyage, contains a small exhibitions gallery open to the public (www.bne.es; Tue–Sat 10am–8pm, Sun 10am–2pm; guided tours Mon–Fri at noon, Sat at 11am). The revamped museum showcases the finest archaeological treasures gathered from all over Spain, incuding the mysterious Iberian Lady of Elche, Roman mosaics, a Visigothic crown studded with jewels and two fine carved wooden *Mudéjar* ceilings.

The district of **Salamanca** was constructed in the late 19th century for the Spanish aristocracy who wanted to move away from the noise and congestion of the city centre. The project was bankrolled by the Marqués de Salamanca, who made and lost three

Monument to Miguel de Cervantes Saavedra with bronze sculptures of Don Quixote and Sancho Panza, Plaza de España.

fortunes and whose picaresque business dealings once forced him to flee to France in disguise. Today, however, the neighbourhood is the soul of well-to-do respectability.

Many of the mansions are now foreign embassies. The city's most expensive shopping streets are grouped around **Calle de Serrano**, where French and Italian boutiques are now making room for popular Spanish names such as Camper and Custo.

A quartet of museums

Further north, just before Serrano crosses Calle María de Molina, is a lovely if little-visited museum, the **Museo Lázaro Galdiano** ㉖ (http://flg.es; Wed–Mon 10am–4.30pm, Sun until 3pm; free last hour of the day). The early 20th-century Italianate palace and lush garden was the private residence of a publisher who bequeathed his art collection to the Spanish government in 1948. Medieval enamels, chalices and ceramics are on show alongside paintings from Spanish and Flemish primitives to Constable and Turner.

Gran Vía and Calle Alcalá crossroads.

Close by on the western side of Castellana is another museum full of personality, the **Museo Sorolla** (http://museosorolla.mcu.es; Tue–Sat 9.30am–8pm, Sun 10am–3pm; free Sat 2–8pm and Sun), where the Valencian Impressionist's paintings are on show in his own home.

Two other museums give insights into further aspects of the city's culture. The small **Museo Taurino** (http://lasventastour.com/el-museo-taurino; daily 10am–6pm), part of a tour of the splendid 1930s neo-*Mudéjar* Plaza de Toros or bullring, is worth a visit for those intrigued by bullfighting.

A second museum, to the west, is the **Museo de América** (www.mecd.gob.es/museodeamerica; Avenida de los Reyes Católicos, 6; Sun 10am–3pm, Tue–Wed and Fri–Sat 9.30am–3pm, Thu 9.30am–7pm; free on Sun), just below Moncloa's panoramic lookout tower, the Faro. This excellent museum gives a poignant glimpse into the colonial Latin American cultures that are now, through emigration, enriching Madrid's 21st-century culture.

Café Life

One of the unsung pleasures of the Spanish capital is sitting quietly at a café table observing life.

Most of us think of a café as a place to have a cup of coffee and a sinful pastry. But not so to the Spaniards. To them a café is variously a place to watch the world go by, an academic arena, a setting for cultural input or a therapeutic refuge from the world. The 19th century was the heyday of the Madrid café. The repression inflicted by Franco stifled much of the political and philosophical exchange that was the mainstay of the capital's cafés before the Spanish Civil War; but they at least provided a welcome refuge from the winter cold. As indoor plumbing and central heating became more common in the 1960s and 1970s, the old-world café became almost extinct, but it has made a comeback since the rebirth of democracy.

To experience the Spanish café at its traditional best, visit the **Café de Gijón** (www.cafegijon.com) on the Paseo de Recoletos. More than a century old, this is the grande dame of the city's cafés. The group at the next table may be immersed in a *tertulia* – a lengthy discussion, usually on some artistic or political issue – or simply downing the powerful gin and tonics or a leisurely lunch.

The delightful Art Nouveau decor of **El Espejo** (www. restauranteelespejo.com), also on Recoletos, is deceptive. Its tiled pictures and huge mirrors date from 1978, while the pavilion extension, a seemingly early 20th-century confection of glass and tiles, competing with that of Gijón's close by, appeared only in 1990.

Another new entry in the old style is the **Café de Oriente** (www.cafedeoriente.es), situated opposite the Royal Palace. Draped with plush velvet trimmed with lace, the café specialises in exotic coffees and home-made patisserie.

Something for everyone

In Spain, patronising one café over another is not just a matter of convenience and taste: it is a question of personal conviction and style. There are cafés for the literati, for the film crowd, for the *outré* and progressive. They come together at the **Círculo de Bellas Artes**, near the Puerta del Sol at Alcalá, 42. The café's fabulous interior – columns, chandeliers, lofty painted ceilings and a magnificent sprawling nude as you walk in the door – dates from 1926. There is a €1 admission charge.

Other revered institutions for whiling away a few hours are the lobby café of the **Filmoteca** (Ciné Doré, Santa Isabel, 3), and **Nuevo Café Barbieri** (http://cafebarbieri.es; Ave María, 45), a mirrored Belle Epoque gem.

Late in the evening you can listen to jazz played live in an Art Deco setting at the **Café Central** (www.cafecentralmadrid.com; Plaza del Ángel, 10), catch young singer-songwriters at the quieter **Libertad 8** (http://libertad8cafe.es; Libertad, 8) or pick up on new hip-hop acts and DJs at **Café La Palma** (www.cafelapalma.com; La Palma, 62).

In the summer *madrileños* move outside to cool down at the *terrazas* (terraces), which are usually positioned in breezy spots. Many terrace-cafés change their location from year to year, but you will always find some along the Paseo de Recoletos and Paseo de la Castellana (these are the most upmarket) and more relaxed ones along the Parque del Oeste and at Vistillas, next to the aqueduct.

A final experience not to be missed is a visit to one of the city's *chocolaterías*, such as **San Ginés** (https://chocolateriasangines.com; Pasadizo San Ginés, off Arenal; open all day), where nightbirds spoon up the dark, thick liquid chocolate before dropping into bed.

Jazz musicians at Café Central.

MADRID PROVINCE

Royal palaces, as well as historic towns and villages, lie close to Madrid. El Escorial, Felipe II's monastery-retreat in the foothills of the Sierra de Guadarrama, is the highlight.

Madrid Province is home to some of Spain's finest royal buildings. The jewel in the crown is El Escorial, the once-magnificent home and now burial place of Felipe II. Then there are Felipe's hunting lodges: El Pardo in the heart of the Sierra de Guadarrama mountain range and El Palacio Real in Aranjuez. This region has some lovely old towns too, such as Manzanares el Real, with its fine castle, and Alcalá de Henares, noted for its historic university. The Valle de los Caídos, burial place of General Franco, is a stark reminder of the Civil War.

The 'eighth wonder of the world', a 'monotonous symphony of stone' and an 'architectural nightmare' are just three of the ways that **El Escorial ❶** (www.patrimonionacional.es; Tue–Sun, Apr–Sept 10am–8pm, Oct–Mar until 6pm; free for EU citizens Wed–Thu 5–8pm in Apr–Sept and 3–6pm in Oct–Mar), Felipe II's most enduring legacy to Spain, has been described since it was completed in 1584.

This monastery-palace-mausoleum is in the town of San Lorenzo de El Escorial, an hour from Madrid in the foothills of the **Sierra de Guadarrama**. There are frequent trains from Madrid's Atocha station (line C-8), and a regular bus service from Moncloa station (Autocares Herranz line 664 or 661). If you're driving, take the A-VI and turn left on the M-600.

Manzanares el Real.

The origin of El Escorial was most likely Felipe II's armies' hard-won victory over the French at the Battle of St Quentin, in Flanders. In honour of St Lawrence (San Lorenzo), on whose feast day the battle took place, Felipe decided to build a tribute to the saint. The king sent two architects, two doctors and two stonemasons to seek out a site for the new monastery that was to be neither too hot nor too cold nor too far from the new capital. Astrologers were also consulted to find a suitable meeting place for land and sky.

Main Attractions

Monasterio de El Escorial
Valle de los Caídos
Sierra de Guadarrama
Palacio de El Pardo
Castillo de Manzanares El Real
Universidad de Alcalá de Henares
Plaza Mayor, Chinchón
Palacio Real, Aranjuez

Portrait of Felipe II's favourite daughter, Isabel Clara Eugenia, by Alonso Sánchez Coello.

The stony monarch

Felipe II was an introverted, melancholy, deeply religious and ailing man who wanted a place to retreat from his duties as king of the world's mightiest empire. He wanted to be surrounded by monks, not courtiers, and he conceived El Escorial as a monastery for the Order of Jeronimo monks, as well as a royal residence.

Felipe did not permit anyone to write his biography while he was alive, and instead left it himself, written in stone. The battles he won and lost, the glories and defeats of the empire, the succession of deaths and tragedies around him, and his obsession for learning, art, prayer and order are all reflected in El Escorial. The location of the enormous church in the centre of the complex reflected his belief that all political action should be governed by religious considerations.

Construction began in 1563 and took 21 years to complete. The chief architect was originally Juan Bautista de Toledo, a disciple of Michelangelo, but after he died the task was picked up in 1569 by Juan de Herrera, who is credited with having provided the inspiration for the final design.

The northern and western sides of the monastery are bordered by huge patios, while the southern and eastern sides are the site of gardens with excellent views of the monastery's fields and the countryside beyond. There is a statue of Felipe II there looking out beyond the **Jardín de los Frailes** (The Friars' Garden). Below the garden on the right is the **Galería de los Convalescientes** (Convalescents' Gallery).

Architecture and painting at El Escorial

Visits are unaccompanied, although guides are available. The route starts in two small 'new museums' (**Nuevos Museos**), the first of which explains the building's architectural history through drawings, plans, tools and scale models. Exhibits include machinery dreamed up by Herrera to cope with technical problems.

Flights of stairs then lead up to nine rooms of magnificent 15th- to 17th-century paintings. The range

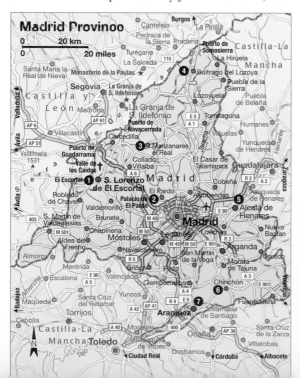

and quality – from Bosch to Veronese, Tintoretto and Van Dyck, as well as the Spanish School – illustrate why the Spanish Habsburgs were the greatest patrons of art of their time. The restored **Sala de Batallas** (Room of Battles) includes scenes from the Azores campaign, the Battle of St Quentin and Juan II's defeat of the Moors at Granada.

The first room of the Habsburg living quarters belonged to Felipe II's favourite daughter, Isabel Clara Eugenia, who took care of him when he was dying. The austerity is broken only by the important collection of paintings and the Talavera ceramic skirting in this section of the palace. The simplicity continues in the Sedan Room, where you will find the unadorned wooden chair in which the king was carried from Madrid after his gout had worsened. In the adjacent Portrait Room are portraits of the Spanish Habsburg dynasty.

A hallway leads on to the Walking Gallery, whose old leaded windows give the best views out over the gardens. The doors, made from 17 different types of wood – surprisingly splendid – were a present from Maximilian of Austria in 1567. These lead through to the Ambassadors' Salon, or waiting room, and, finally, the austerely compact King's Bedroom, adjacent to the main altar of the church, so that Felipe II could hear Mass from his bed. When his gout permitted, he would walk through a small door that leads directly from his room to the church.

Royal remains

One of Felipe II's motivations for building El Escorial was to construct a mausoleum for his father, Emperor Charles V (Carlos I of Spain), whose remains were brought here in 1586. But it was not until the reign of Felipe III, in 1617, that this splendid bronze, marble and jasper **Panteón de los Reyes** (Kings' Pantheon), designed by Gian Battista Genscenzi,

began to be built directly below the main altar of the church. The remains of all the kings of Spain since Carlos I lie here, with the exception of Felipe V, who could not bear the gloom of the place and asked to be buried at Segovia, and Fernando VI, whose tomb is in Madrid.

The queens who produced male heirs are also buried here, while across the way in the 19th-century **Panteón de los Infantes** (Princes' Pantheon) lie the remains of princes, princesses and queens whose children did not succeed to the throne.

Stairs and corridors lead round to the four Chapter Rooms, where the monks once held their meetings. Now the walls are hung with paintings, among them Diego Velázquez's masterpiece, *Joseph's Tunic*, in the first room, and Bosch's *Garden of Pleasures* in the last.

Basílica and biblioteca

While some illustrious visitors have praised the church's perfect grandeur – the French writer Alexandre Dumas referred to the Kings'

Ceiling frescoes at El Escorial.

Courtyard as 'the entrance to eternity' – others have complained about its oppressive size. French writer Théophile Gautier wrote: 'In the El Escorial church one feels so overwhelmed, so crushed, so subordinate to a melancholy and inflexible power that prayer appears to be entirely useless.' The frescoes on the ceilings and along the 43 altars were painted by Spanish and Italian masters. The retable was designed by architect Juan de Herrera himself. On either side of the retable are the royal stalls and the sculpted figures of Carlos I and Felipe II. Don't miss the 16th-century Carrara marble statue, *Christ Crucified*, by Benvenuto Cellini.

El Escorial Biblioteca (library), containing 40,000 volumes and second only in size to that of the Vatican, holds the writings of St Augustine, Alfonso the Wise and Santa Teresa. It has the largest collection of Arabic manuscripts in the world, illuminated hymnals and works of natural history and cartography from the Middle Ages. It is the only library in the world to store its books facing backwards, a measure taken to preserve the ancient parchment.

Pope Gregory XIII ordered the excommunication of anyone who stole a manuscript from here. The ceiling, painted by Tibaldi and his daughter, represents the seven liberal arts: grammar, rhetoric, dialectics, arithmetic, geometry, astronomy and music. At the far end of the hall is the 16th-century **Esfera Armilar** (Armiliary Sphere) showing the solar system according to Ptolemy's theories, that is, with the earth at its centre.

During the reign of the Bourbons, some of the living quarters were converted and two small palaces were built near the monastery to be used as hunting lodges and guesthouses. The **Casita del Príncipe** (the Prince's or Lower Pavilion), around a half-hour's walk down towards the railway station, is a showpiece of Pompeian ceilings, Italian painting, bronze, marble and porcelain. The **Casita del Infante** (Upper Pavilion), located 3km (2 miles) along the road leading to Ávila, is open during summer. Continuing a way along the Ávila road, and then taking a fork to the left, leads to **La Silla de Felipe II** (Philip II's Seat), a group of large boulders on a hill from where the king supposedly gazed out over his monstrous monastery as it was being built.

In the summer months San Lorenzo de El Escorial fills up with *madrileños* escaping the heat of the city. If you stay overnight, you may be lucky enough to catch a play, concert or ballet performance in the **Teatro Real Coliseo**.

North from Madrid

The joy of escaping north from the capital is that the **Sierra de Guadarrama** is almost always in view. The peaks, which reach 2,430 metres (7,972ft) at their highest point, the Peñalara, can be snow-covered until early summer. There are three routes: the A6, which cuts through the mountains by means of a tunnel; the M-607/CL-601, which goes

El Escorial.

via the Navacerrada Pass and is the most picturesque; and the main A1, which goes over the Somosierra Pass towards Burgos.

Just outside the city limits, approximately 15km (9 miles) northwest of central Madrid, is the **Palacio de El Pardo** ❷ (www.patrimonionacional. es; daily, Apr–Sept 10am–8pm, Oct–Mar until 6pm; free for EU citizens Wed–Thu 5–8pm in Apr–Sept and 3–6pm in Oct–Mar), a former royal hunting lodge surrounded by forests of holm oak.

Inside, several hundred tapestries are on display, including some designed by Goya. General Franco made this his residence when governing the country, as did Juan Carlos I for a time.

A little further north and a good place for a picnic stop is the pretty town of **Manzanares el Real** ❸. The 15th-century castle (Tue–Fri 10am–5.30pm, Sat–Sun until 6pm), which dominates the town, is the best-preserved in the province.

Just beyond it is **La Pedriza**, a mountain park with walking trails and climbing routes among its spectacularly formed granite rocks.

The walled town of **Buitrago del Lozoya** ❹ lies just off the A-1 highway about 14km (9 miles) shy of the Somosierra Pass. In the basement of the town hall in the Plaza de Picasso is the charming little **Museo Picasso** (www.madrid.org/museopicasso; Tue–Fri 11am–1.45pm and 4–6pm, Sat 10am–2pm and 4–7pm, Sun 10am–2pm; free). The collection belonged to his barber, who accumulated a private hoard of ceramics, sketches and other small works. To the east, in the wild neighbouring Sierra Negra, are the picturesque slate-built villages of **La Hiruela** and **Puebla de la Sierra**, ideal for visiting (by hire car) if you want to get off the beaten track.

Half an hour's drive west in the green Lozoya valley beside the small town of Rascafríais, the **Monasterio de El Paular** (www.monasteriopaular. com; guided tours only Fri–Wed 11am–1.30pm, 4–6.30pm, winter until 6pm; free Fri 10.15–11am) is a Carthusian monastery dating to the 14th century.

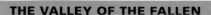

Palacio Real, Aranjuez.

THE VALLEY OF THE FALLEN

Just 13km (8 miles) from El Escorial, on the road back to Madrid from El Escorial, is **Santa Cruz del Valle de los Caídos**, Franco's memorial to those who died in the Civil War and subsequently his own burial place (www.valledeloscaidos.es; Tue–Sun 10am–7pm, until 6pm in winter; free entry for EU citizens Wed–Thu 5–7pm in Apr–Sept and 3–6pm in Oct–Mar). For those without their own vehicle there is a bus to the site that leaves daily from El Escorial (line 660).

A total of 40,000 Republican and Nationalist soldiers lie buried here. Built by Republican prisoners of war between 1940 and 1958, the concrete basilica is a chilling sight, carved several thousand metres into the rock. Opposite Franco's tomb is that of Falange leader José Antonio Primo de Rivera, son of the 1920s dictator Miguel Primo de Rivera, who was killed by the Republicans in 1936. The mosaics in the dome include militaristic details, like a tank, alongside the Apostles. Admirers of Franco still gather here every year on 20 November, the day he died. The tombs lie below a 150-metre (490ft) cross, which can be seen for miles around. In recent years, there have been calls by left-wing politicians to remove Franco's body and bury it elsewhere in order to make the site a monument to those killed in the Civil War. However, since the right-wing PP came into power in 2011 discussions have stopped.

FACT

Miguel de Cervantes Saavedra, the genius in 1 of Spain's Golden Age of literature, is thought to have been born in Alcalá de Henares in 1547, based on church records. He published his masterpiece, *Don Quijote*, in 1605, which brought him acclaim, if not wealth; and died in Madrid in 1616, just 10 days before Shakespeare.

Part of the monastery is a retreat (minimum three-day stay, tel: 682-768 931).

Alcalá de Henares

The old university town of **Alcalá de Henares** ⑤, 35km (20 miles) east of Madrid on the A-2 highway, is well worth visiting for the afternoon. The entrance from Madrid is unpromising, but once you're inside, the charm of its university buildings, convents and churches obliterates that impression.

Founded in 1508 by Cardinal Francisco de Cisneros, the **Universidad** (http://visitasalcala.es; guided tours Mon–Fri 11am–2pm, 4–8pm, Sat–Sun 10am–3pm, 4–8pm) soon rivalled Salamanca as one of the great seats of learning. It was built at the peak of Plateresque, and many of its courtyards and edifices are fine examples of this Renaissance style, so called because it resembles beaten and worked silver. The most exciting is the facade designed by Rodrigo Gil de Hontañón. Allow at least an hour to see the rest of the old town, the highlights of which include the **Catedral**

Stunning interior of El Escorial.

Magistral de los Santos Justo y Pastor (www.catedraldealcala.org).

Alcalá de Henares was also the birthplace of the great writer Miguel de Cervantes; on the corner of Calle Imagen and Calle Mayor is the **Museo Casa Natal de Miguel de Cervantes** (www.museocasanataldecervantes.org; Tue–Sun 10am–6pm; free), which is dedicated to his life.

South from Madrid

Within very easy reach of Madrid, 52km (32 miles) to the southeast, is the picturesque town of **Chinchón** ⑥. It is famous for its splendid and historic, circular **Plaza Mayor**, which has been used for summer bullfights since at least 1502. Bordered on three sides with three storeys of wooden galleries, it is both rustic and elegant. Chinchón's other claim to fame is a strong aniseed drink that takes its name from the town and is drunk all over the country as a bump-start before work. One place to taste it, to have lunch or to stay the night is the **Parador de Chinchón**, set in a former 17th-century convent.

Aranjuez ⑦ lies just off the A-4 highway 45km (27 miles) south of the capital. Sumptuously expanded from the original simple hunting lodge built by Felipe II, the Baroque 18th-century **Palacio Real** (www.patrimonionacional.es; Tue–Sun, Apr–Sept 10am–8pm, Oct–Mar until 6pm; free for EU citizens Wed–Thu 5–8pm in Apr–Sept and 3–6pm in Oct–Mar) was inspired by Versailles and is stuffed with royal portraits, porcelain, stucco and wooden carving.

There are 300 hectares (740 acres) of royal gardens, including the Jardín de la Isla, close to the palace, and the extensive Jardín del Príncipe, with many species of trees. The latter contains two museums: the **Casa de Marinos**, housing former royal riverboats; and the **Casa del Labrador**, a royal pavilion built by Carlos I in 1803 for hunting weekends and court parties.

A bullfight in Chinchón.

Monasterio de la Encarnación, Ávila.

CASTILLA Y LEÓN

The architectural splendours of Salamanca, Segovia, León, Ávila and Burgos give way to timeless mountain scenery and the villages of the vast Castilian plain.

astilla y León is a region with much to offer. Ávila, birthplace of Saint Teresa, has magnificently preserved Roman walls while Salamanca is home to one of the world's oldest and best universities. León, with its ultra-modern Museo de Arte Contemporáneo, and Burgos are both noted for their impressive religious buildings whereas Ciudad Rodrigo was the site of an important battle during the War of Independence. The regional capital, Valladolid, has a lively nightlife and some good museums; it was here that Christopher Columbus died in 1506. Segovia, with its Roman remains and fairytale Alcázar, is a must-see.

The plain-spoken Castilian proverb says 'Wide is Castile.' For centuries Old Castile has been the geographical heart of Spain. Many of the great notions of Spanish history germinated here, including the unification of the medieval Spanish kingdoms and the *Reconquista*. Felipe II chose the dead centre of Castile as the vantage point from which to rule his empire. The empire in turn grew and then gradually disintegrated as a result of the mismanagement and short-sightedness of Castilian governments. This process caused philosopher Ortega y Gasset to lament in 1921 that 'Castile made Spain and Castile has been her undoing.' General Franco increased the

force of the Castilian centrifuge by decreeing that *castellano* was to be the nation's only legal language.

Deadpan and dignified, Castilians themselves often express mixed emotions about their landscape. 'Nine months of winter and three of hell', runs a wry proverb. But spring and autumn are long and richly coloured, with long hours of dramatically beautiful light.

After the democratic government granted autonomous status to Spain's various regions in 1983, Old Castile became the Autonomous Community

Café underneath the arches of the Roman aqueduct, Segovia.

of Castile-León (Castilla y León), a territory covering one-fifth of the nation, or 94,150 sq km (36,350 sq miles), and made up of the provinces of Ávila, Burgos, León, Palencia, Salamanca, Segovia, Soria, Valladolid and Zamora, each with a capital of the same name. The fragrant native scrubland nurturing holm oak, thyme and *jara* (rock rose) of past centuries has in large part been replaced by wheat fields, vineyards and olive groves. Provincial capitals, once medieval cathedral cities, now maintain impressive historic quarters surrounded by modern growth.

Many Castilian villages were built as outposts against the Muslims, and they still have a frontier atmosphere. Some, too, are virtually ghost towns with a steadily declining population, as young people leave to look for work.

Ávila

Sealed within its perfectly preserved medieval walls, **Ávila** ❶ has been compared by poets to both a coffin and a crown. It lies 113km (70 miles) northwest of Madrid. At 1,130 metres (3,710ft), it is the highest city on the peninsula. Hercules was the city's legendary founder, although it is probably older than the Greek invasion of Spain: stone carvings of pigs and bulls found in the area point to a Celt-Iberian

origin. Ávila was passed back and forth between Muslims and Christians until Alfonso VI claimed it definitively in 1090. He promptly transferred his best knights from the northern kingdoms to the city, and they began constructing fortifications. The walls, which average 10 metres (33ft) in height and 3 metres (10ft) in width, have 88 round towers and nine fortified entrances. They stretch round the old city for well over 1km. You can climb them at the city's gates and look out across the surrounding plains (http://muralladeavila.com;, Apr–June and Sept–Oct daily 10am–8pm, Jul–Aug until 9pm, Nov–Mar Tue–Sun until 6pm; free Tue 2–4pm). Alternatively, take the little tourist train (successor to the famous Murallito that ceased operating in 2014), which circumvents the walls in 30 minutes.

Knights and nuns

The city has been a magnet for pilgrims since the late 16th century as the birthplace of Santa Teresa, an outspoken nun who founded a reformed religious Order and wrote about the presence of God in her life in distinctly physical terms.

Teresa de Cepeda y Ahumada was born in 1515 to a noble family with Jewish roots who, possibly to keep their daughter out of the way of the Inquisition, sent her to a convent school. When she left her father's house to enter the Carmelite Order, at her own choice but with misgivings, Teresa wrote: 'I did not think the day of my death would be more upsetting,' but as a nun she thrived. She began to have face-to-face conversations with Christ, beginning with an encounter with the child Jesus on the convent stairs.

Her objections to the opulent lifestyle of the Carmelites spurred her to begin her own Order, the Barefoot Carmelites. Her insistence on austerity made her unpopular with the nuns of her own city, and her unorthodox writings brought the eye of the Inquisition upon her, but she was canonised in 1622, 40 years after her death, and

her personality and austere ideals can be felt throughout the city.

Ávila's **Catedral** (http://catedralavila.vocces.com; Aug Mon–Sat 10.30am–9pm, Sun from 11.30am, June–Jul and Sept–Oct Mon–Fri until 8pm, Sat until 9pm, Sun until 7.30pm, Nov–Mar until 6pm, Sat until 9pm, Sun 5.30pm, but times can vary; free Mon–Tue 9.30–10.30am) is set into the city walls, and has a matching military air. This is the oldest Gothic church in Spain. Inside is the mottled red-and-white stonework characteristic of churches throughout the city. Of particular artistic merit are the choir stalls, by the Dutch artist Cornelius, and the retable, painted with scenes from the life of Christ. Of interest to literary pilgrims is the chapel of San Segundo, where playwright Lope de Vega was chaplain.

Follow **Calle Santo Tomás** southeast to the **Monasterio de Santo Tomás** (www.monasteriosantotomas.com; daily 10.30am–2pm and 5.30–7.30pm, Jul–Aug 10.30am–9pm), which was founded by Fernando and Isabel in 1482. Its adornment includes carvings of pomegranates, or *granadas*, to commemorate

Shrines to Santa Teresa abound in Ávila. Egg-yolk confections called yemas de Santa Teresa are sold as souvenirs.

Ávila's medieval walls.

the recapture of Granada in 1492. The church has a retable considered to be the masterpiece of Pedro Berruguete, depicting the life of St Thomas Aquinas.

Santa Teresa's relics

Enter the town again through **Plaza de Santa Teresa**. The white statue of Santa Teresa was built in honour of the Pope's visit in 1982, at which time she was named Doctor of the Church, the first woman to hold the title. Nearby, the **Convento de Santa Teresa** (www.museosantateresa.com; Tue–Sun, Apr–Oct 10am–2pm and 4–7pm, Nov–Mar 10am–1.30pm and 3.30–5.30pm) is built over the site of her childhood home. Her finger is among the objects on display in the **Convento de San José** (daily 10am–1.30pm and 4–7pm east of the city walls, the first convent she founded. The more appealing relics in this museum include her saddle and her toy drum.

North of the city walls is the **Monasterio de la Encarnación** (May–Sept Mon–Fri 9.30am–1pm and 4–7pm, Sat–Sun from 10am Oct–Apr Mon–Fri 9.30am–1.30pm, 3.30–6pm, Sat–Sun 10am–1pm, 4–6pm), where Teresa

Hiking in the Sierra de Gredos.

spent nearly 30 years. Guided tours take visitors to her cell, and the locutorium where she carried on animated conversations with her confessor and fellow mystic, San Juan de la Cruz.

In her memoirs Teresa describes a scene in which she and 'my brother Juan' became so ecstatic during a theological exchange that they levitated, each on opposite sides of the wooden screen. Today the cloistered nuns at Encarnación still follow Teresa's dictates, and only leave the convent in cases of personal illness, or to vote.

The southern part of Ávila province is traversed by the **Sierra de Gredos ❷**, beloved by *madrileños* for its fresh air and beautiful mountain scenery. A large area is protected as a national park, and was once declared a Royal Hunting Reserve. The Gredos is full of picturesque stone villages, such as **Arenas de San Pedro**, with its 15th-century castle and Gothic bridge, **Mombeltrán** and **El Barco de Ávila**.

Driving north of Ávila, an interesting historical detour is **Madrigal de las Altas Torres**, featuring the ruins of the palace where Queen Isabel the Catholic was born.

Salamanca – seat of learning

The honey-coloured sandstone university town of **Salamanca ❸** 'is the pinnacle; the greatest triumph and honour Spain has ever had; wrote a historian in the 15th-century court of Fernando and Isabel. Salamanca was an important Iberian city 2,000 years before the university was founded in 1218. It was Hannibal's westernmost conquest, and an Islamic town until it was captured by the Christians in 1085. The victors filled the city with churches: San Julián, San Martín, San Benito, San Juan, Santiago, San Cristóbal and the Catedral Vieja all date from a century of feverish Romanesque construction.

Historians suspect that Alfonso IX of León established the university in response to the foundation of one in Palencia by his cousin and rival,

Alfonso VIII of Castile. Salamanca quickly absorbed the latter school, and less than 30 years later the Pope, Alexander IV, proclaimed it one of the four best universities in the world, ranking alongside Oxford, Paris and Bologna.

The Inquisition put an end to the university's reputation as a haven for new ideas and thinkers, and during Felipe II's reign Spanish students were forbidden to study abroad. By the end of the 19th century the colleges were decimated by war and neglect, although the 20th century brought a brief moment of triumph when the philosopher and novelist Miguel de Unamuno became University Rector. Unamuno's *Tragic Sense of Life* is a lucid, poetic exploration of the Spanish soul. Unamuno died disheartened by the atrocities of the Civil War, and the Franco period saw Salamanca, like other Spanish universities, fall into a long sleep. Now, however, it is regaining a vibrant cultural life.

A tour of the university

Salamanca has two universities, but the entrance to the original **Universidad** (http://campus.usal.cs/~museousal; Mon–Sat mid Sept–Mar 10am–7, Apr–mid-Sept 10am–8pm, Sun10am–2pm) can be found in the **Patio de las Escuelas**. The Plateresque facade contains likenesses of the Catholic Monarchs surrounded by a mixture of symbols.

Downstairs there are several historic lecture halls, including the one where Hebrew scholar Fray Luis de León, after five years in the prisons of the Inquisition, began his first lecture with: 'As we were saying yesterday...' Upstairs, the **Library** has over 40,000 rare volumes plus valuable ancient manuscripts. Across the Patio are Plateresque doors leading to the **Escuelas Menores** (primary school). One of the old classrooms (Cielo de Salamanca Mon–Sat 10am–2pm, 4–8pm, Oct–Mar until 7pm) has a ceiling painted with the signs of the zodiac, a reminder that Salamanca once had a Department of Astrology.

The **Plaza de Anaya** is a graceful quadrangle bordered on three sides by university buildings from several cpochs and dominated by the **Catedral Nueva** (New Cathedral; http://catedralsalamanca.org; daily, Apr–Sept 10am–8pm, Oct–Mar 10am–6pm).

Salamanca's Plaza Mayor.

LEARNING SPANISH

Modern Salamanca has built a reputation as the Spanish-teaching capital of the world. Of all the foreigners who come to Spain to learn the language, 16 percent choose to come here – more than anywhere else. Two universities and 22 language schools between them process up to 25,000 foreign students a year. The facilities obviously help but there is another reason for the city's success. It is generally agreed that people in Salamanca speak the clearest and most grammatically correct form of Spanish, which should properly be called Castilian. Elsewhere in Spain, foreign students have to contend with strong accents and regional languages. For information on studying in Salamanca see www.espanolensalamanca.com, www.salamanca-university.org or www.usal.es.

This imposing Gothic church was begun in 1513, when Salamanca's fame was such that the smaller Catedral Vieja would no longer do. It contains a magnificent gate and fine choir stalls.

The **Catedral Vieja** (Old Cathedral; same opening times as the Nueva), which leans against the new one like a chick under the wing of a hen, is a museum. It is the more attractive church of the two, with its Byzantine dome and Romanesque frescoes. In the adjacent cloister is the **Capilla de Santa Bárbara**, where students were quizzed while touching the tomb of a bishop for luck. Exam results were made public, and a crowd of townspeople waited outside to pelt with rubbish those who failed. Those who passed were carried triumphantly around, and painted the word 'Victor' on the university walls in bull's blood.

Franco, who never attended a class here, also painted his 'Victor' on the wall in 1939. Behind the cathedral stands a Modernist mansion, **Casa Lis**, which now houses the **Museo de Art Nouveau y Art Deco** (www.museocasalis.org; Apr–mid-Oct Tue–Sun and Mon in Aug 11am–8pm, mid-Oct–Mar Tue–Fri 11am–7pm, Sat–Sun 11am–8pm; free Thu am).

Many consider Salamanca's graceful **Plaza Mayor** to be the most magnificent in Spain. The square, designed in 1729 by Alberto Churriguera, is bordered by an arcaded walkway lined with fashionable boutiques and delectable pastry shops. A *paseo* (stroll) in the plaza is a tradition beloved by students and locals.

Close to the Plaza Mayor is the odd-looking **Casa de las Conchas**, a noble mansion decorated all over with carved scallop shells, now the regional tourist office with an entrance on Rua Mayor. Following Calle San Pablo from the Plaza Mayor you will come to two gorgeous examples of the Plateresque style: the 16th-century **Convento de las Dueñas** (Mon–Sat 10.30am–12.45pm and 4.30–6.30pm), and the **Monasterio de San Esteban** (www.conventosanesteban.es; daily 10am–2pm and 4–8pm; charge), as delicate as spun sugar. Continue downhill as far as the river and cross over on the **Puente Romano** for a splendid look at the city rising above the bank.

Art aficionados should also make time for the **Domus Artium 2002, DA2** (http://domusartium2002.com; Avenida de la Aldehuela, s/n; Tue–Fri noon–2pm, 5–8pm, Sat–Sun noon–3pm, 5–9pm; free), a contemporary art centre located in the former Salamanca prison.

Historical detours

Southwest of Salamanca, 90km (55 miles) along the A62, stands the handsome town of **Ciudad Rodrigo ❹**. Scene of a famous battle during the War of Independence, when the Duke of Wellington captured the town from French forces, marks of shellfire are still visible on the cathedral belfry. Inside the **Catedral** (www.catedralciudadrodrigo.com; Tue–Sat 11.30am–2pm and 4–7pm, Mon am only, Sun 12.45–2pm and 4–6pm; free entry Sun pm) are cloisters sporting Romanesque capitals and racy choir stalls by Rodrigo

Looking up into the dome of Catedral Nueva, Salamanca.

Alemán. For great views, climb to the top of the tower (Sat–Sun at 1.30pm).

The 14th-century castle overlooking the Río Agueda now houses a pleasant Parador (www.paradores.es), and the old town is crammed with Renaissance palaces and interesting churches, as well as the most unusual **Museo del Orinal** (http://museodelorinal.es), a museum around the theme of chamber pots. Spend time walking the ramparts and wandering the narrow streets around the Plaza Mayor.

To the southwest of the city lies the lovely Sierra de Francia and its villages; elsewhere bulls destined for the *corrida* graze peacefully beneath ilex trees.

Zamora ❺ lies on the banks of the **Río Duero** 60km (37 miles) north of Salamanca by the N-630. The town has a 12th-century **Catedral** (https://catedral dezamora.wordpress.com; daily, May–Sept 10am–8pm, Apr 10am–2pm,5–8pm, Oct–Mar 10am–2pm 4.30–7pm; free Mon pm), which makes it well worth a stop. Its Byzantine dome is a striking addition to the fine Romanesque-Gothic structure.

The cathedral contains a painting of *Christ in Glory* by Fernando Gallego, and 15th-century choir stalls whose carvings are spiced up by lewd satires of monastic life.

Outside the cathedral are the remains of Zamora's walls. Sancho II was treacherously murdered here, and the spot is commemorated by the Postigo de la Traición (Traitor's Gate) in the restored **castillo** (Tue–Sun 10am–2pm and 7–10pm; free). The town also has the region's **Museo Etnográfico** (Tue–Sun 10am–2pm and 4–6.30pm, free), which houses an interesting collection of costumes and artefacts. The **Museo de Semana Santa** (www.museo-etnografico.com; Tue–Sun 10am–2pm and 5–8pm; free Sun pm and Tue–Thu 7–8pm) has objects relating to the Easter festival, for which the town is well known.

From Zamora it is worth making the short drive east to **Toro**, a medieval wine town with fine *Mudéjar*

churches, delicious tapas, and bodegas selling the excellent local wines.

León

Cool, regal **León** ❻ is in many respects a gateway city, with ancient ties both to Castile and to the green regions of Asturias and Galicia to the north. It sits at the base of the Cantabrian Mountains, 314km (195 miles) from Madrid. The city's proudest century was the 10th, when Ordoño II moved his court here. León became a model of reasonable, civilised medieval government, and the assault and burning of the city by the Muslim Almansor in 996 is an event still spoken of with regret. The city was recaptured in the 11th century, and was for a time capital of Spain as well as the seat of the Reconquest.

A visit to León should begin with the **Catedral** (www.catedraldeleon.org; mid Jul–Sept daily 9.30am–8pm, Oct–Apr Mon–Sat 9.30am–1.30pm and 4–7pm, Sun 9.30am–2pm, May–mid-Jul Mon–Fri 9.30am–1.30pm, 4–8pm, Sat 9.30am–noon, 2–6pm, Sun 9.30–11am, 2–8pm, May Sun 9.30–2pm), which has nearly 1,800 sq metres (20,000 sq ft)

Altarpiece in St Stephen's Convent (Convento de San Esteban), Salamanca.

Gaudí's Casa de los Botines in León is now a bank.

TIP

Try to visit León's cathedral at least twice, at different times of the day, to see the effect of the changing light on the coloured glass. Classic Spanish shades of red and yellow predominate, filling the interior with a warm glow.

of magnificent stained-glass windows. Construction was begun in 1258, in the Romanesque style, but the soaring upper portions are Gothic at its best.

Inside are several thousand-year-old sepulchres, including the ornate tomb of Ordoño II. The **Colegiata de San Isidoro** (daily) is a shrine dedicated to San Isidoro of Seville, whose remains were brought here to escape desecration by the Muslims.

Adjacent to the Romanesque and Gothic church is the **Panteón de los Reyes** (www.museosanisidorodeleon.com; 9 Jul–25 Sept Mon–Sat 9am–9pm, Sun 9am–3pm, 26 Sept–Apr Mon–Sat 10am–2pm and 4–7pm, Sun am only, May–8 Jul Mon–Thu 10am–2pm and 4–7pm, Fri–Sat till 8pm, Sun 10am–3pm), which holds the tombs of early royalty of León and Castile. The frescoes in the pantheon are generally described as 'The Sistine Chapel of Romanesque art'. The old city around León's Plaza Mayor, an attractive quarter of winding cobbled streets, has become the domain of the younger crowd, and nearly every block has a bar or pub offering jazz and quirky decor.

A palatial prison

The **Hostal San Marcos** (www.paradores.es), on the **Río Bernesga**, is worth a visit even if you aren't a guest at the five-star Parador inside. It was built in 1168 as a hospital for pilgrims on the road to Santiago.

The ornate Plateresque facade, by Juan de Badajoz, was added in 1513. The hostel became a political prison (the poet Quevedo was the most illustrious guest).

The cloister and sacristy house the **Museo de León** (www.museodeleon.com; Tue–Sat 10am–2pm, Oct–June 4–7pm, Jul–Sept 5–8pm, Sun 10am–2pm; free Sat–Sun). Of particular note are the 11th-century ivory Christ and a 10th-century Mozarabic cross.

The magnificent **Museo de Arte Contemporáneo** (MUSAC; http://musac.es; Tue–Fri 11am–2pm, 5–8pm, Sat–Sun 11am–3pm, 5–9pm; free Tue–Thu 7–8pm, Sun 5–9pm) is northwest of the centre on Avenida de los Reyes Leoneses. The city's latest showcase is housed in a glittering building of steel and coloured glass and has innovative modern-art exhibitions as well as a permanent gallery of Spanish contemporary painters.

West of León, the Roman town of **Astorga** has a huge **Catedral** (www.diocesisastorga.es; Mon–Sat 9–11am, Sun 11am–1pm) with some remarkable features, including an altarpiece from the School of Michelangelo and an interesting museum (Tue–Sat mid Mar–mid Oct 10am–2pm, 4–8pm, winter 11am–2pm, 4–6pm) Even more striking, however, is the **Palacio Episcopal** (Bishop's Palace) designed by Antoní Gaudí. The bizarre edifice caused a great stir when it was built, and the horrified bishop refused to live there. Today it houses the **Museo de los Caminos** (www.diocesisastorga.es; as above), which covers the pilgrimage to Santiago. There are a couple of other interesting museums in the town, including the **Museo Romano** (www.asturica.com; Tue–Sat, 10am–2pm, 4.30–7pm, Sun am only) with finds from the city's Roman past

View over Burgos.

and a 50-metre (165ft)-long prison tunnel; and a chocolate museum (www.museochocolateastorga.com).

Further west from Astorga is **El Bierzo**, a mountainous pocket close to Galicia, with its own hybrid gastronomy and excellent wines. South of the town of **Villafranca del Bierzo** lie the Roman gold mines of **Las Medulas**, now a World Heritage Site set against dramatic bare-rock formations.

Burgos

Situated in the middle of the high plains of Old Castile, **Burgos** ❼ has been a crossroads for a thousand years. Founded in 884 as a fortification against Muslim invaders, it is a relatively young city. Most of the landmarks have to do with its beloved native son, Rodrigo Díaz de Vivar, better known as El Cid. El Cid (from Sidi, Arabic for leader) pursued his own zealous campaign against the Muslims, eventually capturing the city of Valencia in 1094.

Burgos's **Catedral** (www.catedraldeburgos.es; daily, mid-Mar–Oct 9.30am–7.30pm, Nov–mid-Mar 10am–7pm; free Thu 4.30–6.30pm), begun in 1221, was described as 'the work of angels' by Felipe II. Perhaps no other cathedral has so many curios, as well as artistic treasures.

Visitors are usually as anxious to see the marionette clock **Papamoscas** and the life-size Christ made of animal skin and human hair as they are to admire the **Golden Staircase** by Diego de Siloe, the opulent Isabeline **Capilla del Condestable** and the **Capilla de Santa Ana**, with its magnificent retable showing the Virgin's family tree. In the cloister you can see the coffer that El Cid filled with sand to trick Jewish moneylenders (the legend adds that he repaid them with interest). El Cid and his wife are buried in the middle of the cathedral transept.

As an antidote to the still, dark air of the church, cross the Plaza Santa María to the esplanade along the Río Arlanzón. The turreted **Arcos de Santa María** gate was part of the 11th-century city walls

and decorated in the 16th century as a tribute to a visit from Carlos I.

Just west of the city centre, the **Monasterio de Las Huelgas** (www.patrimonionacional.es; Tue–Sat 10am–2pm and 4–6.30pm, Sun 10.30am–3pm; free for EU citizens Tue–Wed pm) is a 12th-century nunnery combining, uniquely, Cistercian, *Mudéjar* and Almohad architecture. Only women from the highest rank of society were admitted. The abbess was second in rank to the Queen of Spain, and it was said that if the Pope were allowed to marry, only the abbess of Las Huelgas would be worthy of the honour.

Statue of El Cid in Burgos.

Around Burgos

The **Cartuja de Miraflores** (www.cartujadeburgos.org; Mon–Sat 10.15am–3pm and 4–6pm, Sun 11am–3pm and 4–6pm; free), less than 3km (2 miles) east of Burgos, was built by Queen Isabel as a memorial to her parents, who are buried here in elaborate tombs. Just 10km (6 miles) southeast of the city is the **Monasterio de San Pedro de Cardeña** (www.monasteriosanpedrodecardena.com; guided tours only Tue–Sat

Arcos de Santa María, one of the gates into Burgos.

FACT

The scenery of flat-topped red hills around Soria is striking. Northwest of the town, tarns such as the beautiful alpine Laguna Negara glisten against the green wooded hills of the Sierra de Urbión, a popular spot for excursions. The large reservoir Embalse de la Cuerda offers water sports of all kinds.

10am–1pm and 4–6pm, Sun 12.15–1pm and 4.15–6pm), from which El Cid went into exile after being banished from Castile by Alfonso VI.

Also just outside Burgos, 15km (9 miles) to the east in the **Sierra de Atapuerca**, is one of Europe's most important archaeological sites, where evidence of the continent's oldest human settlement was found in 1994 within an existing archaeological site. The bones and teeth of 'Homo Antecessor', 80,000 years old, are now housed in a modern museum, the **Museo de la Evolución Humana** (www.museoevolucionhumana.com; Tue–Sun 10am–8pm; free Wed pm, Tue and Thu 7–8pm). The site itself can be visited on interesting guided tours (take walking boots) that must be pre-booked (see museum website).

The province of Burgos is full of villages that strongly evoke the days of chivalry. A detour from the A-I highway takes in two particularly haunting spots. Some 4km (2.5 miles) east of **Quintanilla de las Viñas** is the ruin of a 7th-century Visigothic chapel (Wed–Sun, May–Sept 10am–2pm and

Monasterio de Santo Domingo de Silos.

4–8pm, Oct–Apr 10am–5pm; free), one of the earliest Christian edifices in Spain. Only a square apse and transepts remain of the original church, which can be visited in the company of a guide from the village.

Passing the ruins of the **Monasterio de San Pedro de Arlanza** leads you to the lovely village of **Covarrubias**, with its 10th-century tower where Doña Urraca, one of Spain's most tragic princesses, was imprisoned. The monastery contains the tombs of Doña Urraca's parents. Catching up with the A-I at **Lerma** ⑧ allows a stop at this town rising like a mirage over the Río Arlanza. The grandiose Baroque buildings here were built by the Duke of Lerma in 1605. Lerma's fortress-like appearance is peculiar considering the time it was built, and is testimony to 17th-century Spain's longing for the glory of the Middle Ages.

About 20km (12 miles) southeast of Covarrubias, the **Monasterio de Santo Domingo de Silos** ⑨ (www.abadiadesilos.es; Tue–Sat 10am–1pm and 4.30–6pm, Sun noon–1pm and 4–6pm) is famed for two things: its magnificent 12th-century Romanesque cloister, and its community of Benedictine monks who hit the classical charts in 1994 with their recorded version of Gregorian chant. Visitors can hear live plainsong at the church services (evensong is at 7pm) – a dignified and moving experience. The monks spend the rest of their time gardening, studying and bee-keeping.

There are guided tours of the splendidly carved and tranquil cloisters; don't miss the fascinating old pharmacy, containing gorgeous Talavera jars and antique distilling equipment.

Following the N-234 southeast brings you to the small, friendly provincial capital of **Soria** ⑩, which attracts comparatively few visitors. The **Museo Numantino** (Tue–Sat 10am–2pm and 4–7pm, July–Sept 5–8pm, Sun am only) on Calle El Espolón displays archaeological finds from the Celt-Iberian settlement of Numancia (see page 34), located just north of the town. The ruined **Monasterio de San Juan de Duero** (Tue–Sat 10am–2pm and 4–7pm, July–Sept 5–8pm, Sun am only; free Sat–Sun), built by the Knights Hospitaller, is beside the Río Duero east of the town centre, and has a beautiful, if partially ruined, cloister that reflects *Mudéjar* and Romanesque influences.

Valladolid and Palencia

The N-122 runs southwest of Soria to **Burgo de Osma**, a small town with a splendid cathedral, and then along the Duero valley. At **Aranda** you can visit the underground bodegas, and then drive through the vineyards to the west where Spain's most legendary wine, Vega de Sicilia, is produced. There is a **Museo del Vino** (www.ribiertete. com; Tue–Sun 10.30am–2pm, 5–8pm; charge) in the castle at Peñafiel.

Valladolid **⓫**, home to the regional parliament, was once a medieval court city, but is now a sprawling industrial centre with only an austere cathedral and two fine churches – San Pablo to the north of the centre and its neighbour the Colegio de San Gregorio – as outstanding monuments. The latter houses the excellent **Museo Nacional de Escultura**(http://museoescultura.mcu.es; Tue–Sat 10am–2pm and 4–7.30pm, Sun am only; free Sat pm and Sun), which is a crash course on the Spanish Renaissance. In its bid to improve its cultural standing, the city has also opened museums dedicated to contemporary Spanish art and Christopher Columbus, who died in the city.

Just 45km (28 miles) north is **Palencia**, nicknamed 'the unknown beauty' for its rarely visited but exquisite **Catedral** (http://catedraldepalencia.org; Nov–Apr Mon–Fri 10am–1.30pm, 4–6pm, Sat 10am–1.30pm, 4–5.30pm, Sun 4–7pm, May–Oct Mon–Fri 10am–1.30pm, 4–6pm, 6.35–7.30pm, Sat 10am–2pm, 4–5.30pm, Sun 4.30–8pm; free Tue pm), which is stuffed with medieval art and sculpture, and **Santa Eulalia de Paredes**, a church which keeps the major collection of

locally born artist Pedro Berruguete and other contemporary artists. The town also has some interesting Modernista architecture. It is also worth driving 60km (37 miles) north to visit the museum inside **La Olmeda** (www.villaromanalaolmeda.com; Tue–Sun 10.30am–6.30pm; free Tue from 3pm), one of the province's four exceptionally well-preserved Roman villas.

Segovia

Of all the cities of Castile, **Segovia** **⓬** may be the one whose charms are most evident at first sight. Only 92km (57 miles) from Madrid on the A-6 and AP-61 motorways, Segovia fills up with *madrileños* every weekend, who come to admire the remarkable Roman aqueduct and the fairy-tale castle, and feast on the wood-roast pork and lamb for which the province is famous.

Segovia became important under the Romans, who built the aqueduct in the 1st century AD. The city was long favoured by Castilian royalty, and Isabel the Catholic was proclaimed Queen here in 1474. In 1480 it became the headquarters of the dreaded

View of the Alcázar and Catedral in Segovia.

Building in Segovia's Plaza del Corpus decorated with 'sgraffiti', which involves cutting through a layer of plaster to reveal a different colour underneath.

Inquisitor Torquemada. Economic recession, war and a 1599 plague nearly brought Segovia to ruins, but it rose again under the Bourbons, who built their summer palace at La Granja nearby.

Roman aqueduct

All roads to Segovia lead to the **acueducto A**. One of the largest Roman constructions still standing in Spain, it carried water until the 20th century. Its 165 arches rise as high as 29 metres (96ft) over the **Plaza del Azoguejo**. The huge granite blocks stay in place without mortar, which may have fed the medieval legend that the Devil built the aqueduct in one night. Its future was assured by extensive restoration to the crumbling granite in the 1990s.

From the Plaza del Azoguejo, follow the Calle de Cervantes uphill to the old city, past the **Casa de los Picos B**, (http://easdsegovia.com), a noble house decorated in the 15th century with diamond-shaped blocks of stone. A few steps beyond is the **Plaza de San Martín**, with the beautiful Romanesque **Iglesia de San Martín C** and

a circle of Renaissance mansions. In the middle of the plaza is a statue of Segovian hero Juan Bravo, who led the citizens in their disastrous resistance against the army of Carlos I in 1520.

The **Convento de Corpus Cristi D**, consecrated in 1410, was once the largest synagogue in Segovia. The old Jewish quarter, or *judería*, along Calle San Frutos, still has houses with tiny windows, which allowed the inhabitants ventilation, but not a view of the street.

On **Plaza Mayor** stands the late Gothic **Catedral E** (https://catedralsegovia.wordpress.com; Mon–Sat 9.30am–6pm, Sun 1–6pm, summer daily until 7pm, guided tours of the tower daily at 10.30am, 12.30pm, 4.30pm), designed by Juan Gil de Hontañón and his son Rodrigo. The Isabeline cloister was transplanted here from the old cathedral, which was burned during the insurrection against Carlos I.

Beyond Plaza Mayor is the church of **San Esteban F**, set on a plaza of the same name. It is one of the most beautiful of the 18 Romanesque churches in Segovia.

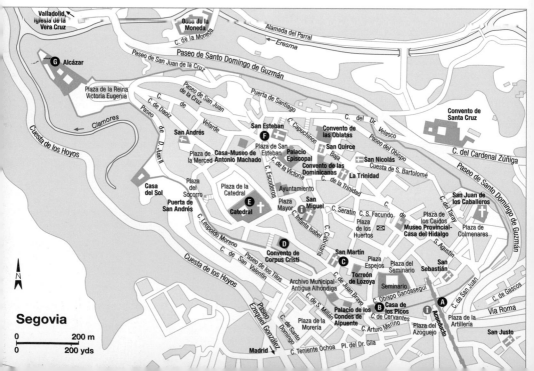

Segovia

0   200 m
0   200 yds

Fairy-tale castle

The **Alcázar** ⑥ (www.alcazardesegovia. com; daily 10am–7.30pm, Oct Sun–Thu until 6.30pm, Fri–Sat until 7.30pm, Nov–Mar until 6.30pm) stands at the western end of the city, the prow of the Segovian ship. Destroyed by fire in the 19th century, its 1882 restoration combines reconstruction of some *Mudéjar* elements with contemporary taste in castles, and the result looks like a child's fantasy. Two of the Alcázar's most interesting rooms are the **Sala de Reyes**, containing wooden carvings of the early Castilian, Leonese and Asturian kings, and the **Sala del Cordón**, decorated with a frieze of the Franciscan cord. According to legend, Alfonso the Wise once ventured the heretical opinion that the earth moved round the sun. A bolt of lightning followed his remark and, terrified, he wore the penitential cord for the rest of his life. The arduous climb up the **Torre de Juan II** is rewarded by sweeping views of the Segovian countryside and the Sierra de Guadarrama.

Look down from here to the **Iglesia de la Vera Cruz** (Wed–Sun 10.30am–1.30pm and 4–7pm, Tue only pm), just outside the walls, a round Templar church.

Little Versailles

The French-style palace of **La Granja de San Ildefonso** ⑬ (www.patrimonio nacional.es; Tue–Sun, Apr–Sept 10am–8pm, Oct–Mar until 6pm; free for EU citizens Wed–Thu Oct–Mar 3–6pm, Apr–Sept 5–8pm) lies 11km (7 miles) southeast of Segovia. It symbolises the vast differences between the Bourbon monarchs who built it and their dour Habsburg predecessors. Felipe V of Bourbon commissioned a palace here suitable for the retirement of an enlightened 18th-century despot.

A team of French and Italian architects built something along the lines of a modest Versailles, the royal residence outside Paris. The palace has a fine collection of Flemish tapestries (one of the most valuable in the world), with the inevitable Spanish touch of a chapel full of saints' bones and teeth. The most splendid part of San Ildefonso, however, are the magnificent, formal gardens, with pools and snow-fed fountains.

The Catedral and facades of houses decorated with sgraffiti in Segovia.

THE MILITARY ORDERS

The Reconquest of Spain provided opportunities for the military orders of knights who combined the skills of soldiering with the religious devotion of a monk. Most famous were the **Knights Templars,** who are believed to have arrived in Spain soon after their order was given official approval by the Church at the Council of Troyes in 1128. When the Templars were dissolved in 1314 many of their possessions were given to another order, the **Knights Hospitallers**, also known as the Knights of Saint John. Later, three home-grown organisations sprang up in Spain: **Calatrava, Alcantara** and **Santiago**. All of these orders were richly rewarded with castles and territories as the Reconquest progressed, but once the Muslims had been defeated their power and properties were gradually subsumed by the monarchy.

CASTILIAN CASTLES

Imperious, impervious, fantastic, steeped in history and dripping with romance – the castles of Spain are the stuff of fairy tales.

Castile is the high, arid heart of Spain, Castilian is the country's spoken language. Both derive their names from *castillo* (castle), the building that for years was the most dominant feature of this part of Spain. Castile was where the first significant advances were made against the Muslims, a Wild West of adventurers and pioneers. Frontiers were marked along the Duero, Arlanzón and Ebro rivers where there were no walled cities, monasteries or manorial estates to run to in times of trouble. Strongholds were established about 100 years after the Muslim conquest, notably under Fernán Gonzáles (910–970), first Count of Castile, and over the next 400 years of fighting, castles appeared all over the countryside.

The Muslims were great castle builders, too; at Berlanga de Duero, they constructed a fortress with a massive curtain wall and drum towers with a commanding view.

As the lands grew safer, castles were adopted as glorified homes. The Fonseca family's Castillo de Coca in Segovia, for example, displays some fine *Mudéjar* military architecture, but it was never intended to be put to the test. As the Muslims were driven out in 1492, castle building was forbidden, but 2,000 had already altered the landscape forever.

The ultimate fairy-tale fortress, Segovia's Alcázar is located on an 80-metre (270ft) rocky outcrop. Originally a Muslim fortre it was later used as a state prison.

The eyries of Castillo de Guadalest have commanding views o the coast needed protection from pirates.

Suits of armour on display in the Alcázar, Segovia.

Restaurant at Parador de Toledo, a manor house converted into a luxury hotel.

ARISTOCRATIC LODGINGS

The picture on the right is of the interior of the Parador at Zamora, a 15th-century castle and former home of the counts of Alba y Aliste on the banks of the Duero. The word parador (from the Arabic *waradah*, meaning 'halting place') had been in use for many centuries before 1928 when the government instigated this chain of state-run hotels in restored historic buildings. Designed to be no more than a day's journey apart, there are around 90 altogether. They are all relatively inexpensive and have a reputation for good service and good food. As a matter of policy, they have always served the best local dishes, and even if you don't stay in one, they are worth a visit for a meal, or just to have a look around.

Peñafiel is one of a number of early Castilian castles built on the banks of the River Duero. It dates from the 10th century, although the walls are mostly 15th-century.

…stle of Berlanga de Duero, in Soria province.

…udéjar castle overlooking the village of Segura de la Sierra, Jaén province.

CASTILLA-LA MANCHA

This region is the quintessential Spain – immense rolling plains studded with windmills and castles fill the landscape, interrupted by olive groves, vineyards and dusty medieval villages.

astilla-La Mancha instantly conjures up one image – Don Quijote, the most famous character in Spanish literature. The region is dotted with the book's associated sites and unforgettable windmills. However, there is much more to interest visitors. The gorgeous historic town of Toledo is forever associated with the painter El Greco while Almagro is home to the oldest theatre in Spain and an important summer drama festival. Alarcón has some fine examples of medieval military architecture and Cuenca is known for its precipitous 'hanging houses' and Museo de Arte Abstracto Español. Kids will love the curious rock formations in the Ciudad Encantada.

Originally part of New Castile, so named when the northern Castilian kings wrested the area from Islamic control in 1085, La Mancha is centred around Toledo, capital of Visigothic Spain and national treasury of art and architecture, and Ciudad Real, whose Don Quijote trail extends from the windmills of Campo de Criptana to the Laguna de Ruidera, bordering Albacete province. All are identifiable in Cervantes's great opus, *Don Quijote de La Mancha*, whose opening line, 'En un lugar de La Mancha de cuyo nombre no quiero acordarme' (In a place of La Mancha, the name of which I do not wish to recall), is the most famous sentence in Spanish letters.

To its northeast are historic Cuenca, with its hanging houses, and Arab-founded Guadalajara, with a *Mudéjar* palace and an impressive pantheon; while to the southeast is Albacete, mainly rebuilt after Civil War ravages.

Picturesque towns and villages fill these varied subprovinces, from Oropesa, Chinchilla and Almagro in the west and south to Pastrana, Brihuega and Sigüenza in the north. Spectacular landscapes – from the wetlands of the Tablas de Daimiel and the peaks of the Sierra de Alcaraz to the forests and

Main Attractions

Mezquita Cristo de la Luz, Toledo
Sinagoga de Santa María la Blanca, Toledo
Museo del Greco, Toledo
Almagro
Alcalá del Júcar
Casas Colgadas, Cuenca
Palacio de los Duques del Infantado, Guadalajara

Cuenca's old town.

*Toledo's imposing
Catedral Primada.*

meadows of the Parque Nacional de Cabañeros and the gorges of the upper Tagus – are abundant and varied; and the medieval castles at Belmonte, Calatrava la Nueva, Alarcón and Almansa are among La Mancha's attractions.

The cultural heart of Spain

Toledo ❶ is both La Mancha's and Spain's historical and cultural heart, former Spanish capital and still the religious seat of the nation. It is known as the city of three cultures due to the influence of its successive Islamic, Hebrew and Christian occupants. A natural fortress occupying high ground with the Río Tajo protecting all but its northern flank, the Roman city of Toletum was founded in AD 192. Little is left of the Roman occupation: a **Circo Romano** off the Avenida de la Reconquista, and a few mosaics and reconstructed buildings.

By the 6th century the Visigoths had set up court in Toledo. In AD 711, the city was taken over by Muslims, and became capital of Christian Spain in 1085 under Alfonso VI. By the 12th century, Toledo was also Spain's most important Jewish centre, with over 12,000 Jewish citizens. During the 13th century under Alfonso X, Toledo became a cultural forum within which Muslims, Jews

and Christians lived in mutual toler-
ance and collaborated in a school of
translators responsible for introducing much Arabic and Greek science
and philosophy into the early Spanish Romance and, from there, into the
budding European Renaissance.

This eclecticism shaped the city's
architecture and art. The Mozarabic
style of architecture was developed
by Christians living under Muslim
domination, while the *Mudéjar* style,
well displayed in the **Taller del Moro**
palace (beautifully restored, but still
closed) behind the cathedral, was the
work of Muslims who remained after
the Reconquest. Less apparent is the
Jewish influence in the city. Of the
ten synagogues, only two survived
the Jewish pogroms. The 1492 expulsion of Muslims and Jews was a blow
to Toledo's fortunes, and in 1561
Felipe II moved the Spanish court to
Madrid to limit Toledo's power. Over
the next 100 years the city's population halved.

Today, Toledo is a small regional
capital (pop. 84,000), but such is its
beauty and history, unusually well
preserved by its sudden economic
decline, which continued until the
early 20th century, that the entire
old city is a national monument and
a World Heritage Site. The city lies
72km (45 miles) south of Madrid. The
neo-*Mudéjar* train station is a good
starting point for a visit. Just outside
the station, the city's patrician profile
rises above the Río Tajo gorge. Cross
the river on the **Puente de Alcántara**
Ⓐ. It was built by the Romans, then
refurbished by the Muslims and the
Christians. On the hill opposite the
city is the **Castillo de San Servando**
(http://juventud.jccm.es/sanservando), built
on the site of a ruined Arab castle and
now a youth hostel.

If you're arriving by bus from
Madrid, the nearest entrance to the
city is by the main **Puerta de Bisagra**,
the most impressive of the nine toll-
collecting gates along the city walls.
On the **Puerta de Cambrón**, built
on the remains of the old Visigothic
gateway at the west end of the city,
you can see the medieval plaque advis-
ing gatekeepers that Toledo residents
need not pay.

*Toledo and the
Río Tajo.*

Churches, synagogues and mosques

Visible from quite a distance on the *meseta*, the massive **Catedral Primada**  (www.catedralprimada.es; Mon–Sat 10am–6.30pm, Sun 2–6.30pm) is testament to Toledo's history as Spain's spiritual capital long after the royal court moved to Madrid. The Goths worshipped on the site before the Muslim invasion, when the church was converted to a mosque. The present Spanish Gothic structure, with five broad naves around a central *coro* (choir), was begun in 1226 and finished 300 years later, during which time *Mudéjar*, Baroque and neoclassical elements were added.

The large polychrome retable depicting the life of Christ; the famously excessive Baroque and neoclassical Transparente altarpiece, built to allow in natural light; the Sacristía (sacristy) with its collection of paintings by El Greco, Titian, Goya and Van Dyck; the sumptuous walnut-and-alabaster choir stalls and *Mudéjar* ceiling in the Sala Capitular (chapterhouse) are just a few of the wealth of details here. There are 22 *capillas* (chapels) around the edge of the cathedral's interior.

Ten minutes' walk from the cathedral, the **Mezquita Cristo de la Luz** ⓒ (www.toledomonumental.com/mezquita. html; daily Mar–mid Oct 10am–6.45pm, mid Oct–Feb until 5.45pm), a church originally built as a mosque, is one of the oldest and loveliest buildings in the city; Alfonso VI held Mass here when he conquered Toledo in 1085. Nearby is the **Puerta del Sol**, the *Mudéjar*-style gate built by the 13th-century Knights Hospitallers.

To get a sense of the unique Visigothic presence in Toledo, visit the **Iglesia de San Román** ⓓ (Tue–Sat 10am–2pm and 4–6.30pm, summer until 7pm, Sun am only; free), where the Visigothic Culture and Councils Museum has been installed. In the museum are illuminated manuscripts and copies of the stunning Visigothic crown jewels.

The major synagogue that survived the 14th-century pogroms is the **Sinagoga de Santa María la Blanca** ⓔ (www.toledomonumental.com/sinagoga. html; daily Mar–mid-Oct 10am–6.45pm, mid Oct–Feb until 5.45pm), on Calle los Reyes Católicos. The most striking features are the capitals, which reflect a Byzantine or Persian influence. The iris, symbol of honesty, and the Star of David play prominent roles in the synagogue's interior ornamentation. Except for the three chapels at the head of the building, added in the 16th century, the synagogue is much as it was before it was converted into a church in the latter half of the 15th century.

The other surviving synagogue is **Sinagoga del Tránsito** ⓕ close by, a simpler, 14th-century structure, with superb Almohad-style plasterwork. Next to it is the **Museo Sefardí** (www.mecd.gob.es/mse fardi; Sun 10am–3pm, Tue–Sat Nov–Feb 9.30am–6pm, Mar–Oct until 7.30pm; free Sat pm and Sun).

The other major Catholic structure is the **Monasterio de San Juan de los Reyes** ⓖ (www.sanjuandelosreyes.org; mid Oct–Feb 10am–5.45pm, Mar–mid Oct until 6.45pm), located in what

Statue of Don Quixote in Toledo.

is left of the *judería*, the old Jewish quarter. The Gothic monastery, with a lovely cloister and church, was built by the Catholic Monarchs.

The **Alcázar ⓗ**, meanwhile, dates to the era of El Cid, and its occupants and purposes have been numerous. Today's building is the result of the work of Spain's finest 16th-century architects, including Juan de Herrera who designed El Escorial, though now heavily restored after Civil War damage; it now houses the **Museo del Ejército** (Military Museum; www.museo.ejercito.es; Thu–Tue 11am–5pm). A lively centre of activity in the city since Arab times is the nearby triangular Plaza de Zocodover ('Zuk-al-Dawad' in Arabic means beast market).

El Greco

Toledo is inextricably associated with the painter Kyriakos Theotokopoulos, known as El Greco and born in Crete in 1541. El Greco lived and worked in Toledo from 1577 until his death in 1614. His paintings are spread throughout the city. One of his masterpieces, *The Burial of the Count of Orgaz*, is in the 14th-century *Mudéjar*-style **Iglesia de Santo Tomé ⓘ** (www.santotome.org; daily 10am–5.45pm, summer until 6.45pm; fee to view El Greco painting via separate entrance) on Calle Santo Tomé. The complexity, the blend of the temporal and spiritual and the inclusion of many supposed portraits, including El Greco's own, are some of the ingredients that make this painting so memorable.

El Greco lived in the Jewish section of the city just behind El Tránsito. His house is no longer standing, but a nearby 16th-century dwelling known as the **Museo del Greco ⓙ** (http://museodelgreco.mcu.es; Tue–Sat 9.30am–7.30pm, Oct–Mar until 6pm, Sun 10am–3pm) contains several of his paintings, including the *View of Toledo* – painted from the north of the city, where the Parador (government-owned hotel) stands today – as well as works by his contemporaries and followers.

The **Museo de Santa Cruz ⓚ** (Tue–Sat 10am–7pm, Sun 10am–2.30pm; free Tue–Sat from 6pm), just off the central plaza, holds fine El Greco paintings as well as several rooms of Toledan crafts. The building is beautiful, particularly its Plateresque entrance and staircase

El Greco's 'St John the Evangelist'. Trained and influenced by Italian masters, El Greco imbued his work with a realism and vigour that makes his paintings seem alive and contemporary even today.

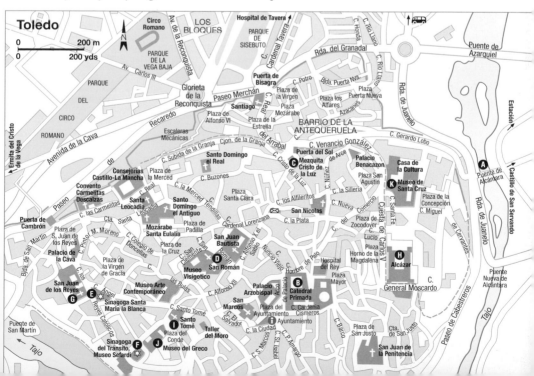

and the *Mudéjar* wooden ceilings. It hosts spectacular special exhibitions and concerts.

Outside the city walls, the 16th-century **Hospital de Tavera** (www.funda cionmedinaceli.org; daily 10am–2.30pm and 3–6.30pm) houses El Greco's *The Holy Family*, *The Baptism of Christ* and several portraits of saints. One of the few Renaissance interiors that has kept intact much of an original art collection, it also has fine paintings by Caravaggio, Titian, Tintoretto, Ribera and Lucas Jordanius. There is a fine Carrara marble tomb by Berruguete of the founder Cardinal Tavera, and a crypt with startlingly effective acoustics. The pharmacy (established 1541; guided tours only) is claimed to be the oldest in Spain.

If you like El Greco and want to see more of his work it is worth viewing five other magnificent paintings by him in the **Hospital de la Caridad** (www.elgrecoillescas.com; guided tours only Mon–Fri 9am–2pm, 4–5.30pm, Sat 9.30am–2.30pm, 4–8pm, Sun 11.30am–2.30pm) in Illescas, a small town just off the A-42 between Madrid and Toledo.

Shop selling swords and other steel, gold and silver items in Toledo.

Around Toledo

Toledo's best-known crafts are the bequest of the Muslim and Jewish legacies: damascene (a type of black enamel inlaid with gold, silver and copper wire), steel knives, swords and the fine ceramic work from nearby **Talavera de la Reina ❷**, one of Toledo's medieval satellite towns. Here, the **Museo de Céramica Ruiz de Luna** (winter Tue–Sat 9.45am– 2pm and 3.45–7pm, Sun 10am– 2.15pm, summer Tue–Fri 9am–3pm, Sat 9.45am–2pm, 3.45–7pm, Sun 10am–2.15pm) near Plaza de San Pedro is the place to view ceramics of all kinds, while the **Ermita de La Virgen del Prado** (daily) has ceramic murals depicting religious themes. Talavera has an old quarter with a 15th-century bridge and Roman ramparts.

The charming town of **Oropesa ❸**, 32km (20 miles) west of Talavera de la Reina on the A-5, is dominated by the 16th-century **Palacio Nuevo** (Tue–Sat 10am–2pm and 4–6pm, Sun only am) or Palacio-Castillo Álvarez de Toledo, part of which is now a Parador (www.

paradores.es). It has other fine medieval and Renaissance buildings and a long tradition of embroidery.

To the south of Talavera and Toledo are the **Montes de Toledo ❹**, a low mountain range stretching west towards Extremadura where some of Spain's largest hunting estates are found.

Along the northern edge of the range is the **Parque Nacional de Cabañeros** (www.magrama.gob.es/es/red-parques-nacionales), consisting of sheep pasture and oak, cork and scrub. You can take a guided tour of the park in a four-wheel-drive vehicle. The wildlife here includes wild boar, red deer and imperial eagles.

Windmills and castles

Consuegra ❺ is known for its windmills, its 13th-century castle and the late-October saffron harvest and fiesta. **Templeque**, a little further north and so named for trembling victims of medieval banditry, is built around one of Spain's most beautiful central squares, a triple-tiered, porticoed gem occasionally used as a bullring.

Southern La Mancha

Approximately 100km (60 miles) south of Toledo on the N-401 is another provincial capital, **Ciudad Real ❻**. It is a largely modern city, but the central streets within the medieval ramparts (accessed via the 14th-century Puerta de Toledo) are bustling. The 13th-century **Iglesia de Santiago** (http://parroquiasantiagoapostolcr.com) and the **Catedral** are the most interesting architectural features.

In the surrounding countryside, some of La Mancha's greatest treasures can be found. The **Parque Nacional Tablas de Daimiel** (www.magrama.gob.es/es/red-parques-nacionales), just northeast, is one of Spain's most important wetlands, a national park on the Río Guadiana and rallying point for migratory waterfowl.

Declared a Historic-Artistic Site, the town of **Almagro ❼**, 24km (15 miles) southeast of Ciudad Real, has the unusual stone Plaza Mayor with wooden porticoes and balconies. At No. 17 is the **Corral de Comedias** (daily; www.corraldecomedias.com), an open-air theatre which is the oldest in Spain.

Houses in Cuenca's old town.

THE QUIJOTE TRAIL

A tour of central La Mancha traces key points from various chapters of Cervantes's most famous novel. A good starting point is the Museo del Quijote (Ronda de Alarcos s/n, Mon–Sat 10am–2pm, 5–8pm, Sun 10am–2pm, Jul–Aug only am) in Ciudad Real, which has a multimedia exhibition on the book. El Toboso, on the AP36N-301 between Albacete and Ocaña, was the village of Dulcinea, Don Quijote's fantasised true love. The Casa de Dulcinea (Tue–Sat, 10am–2pm and 5–7pm, Sun am only), thought to be that of the woman Cervantes had in mind, Dona Ana Martinez Zarco de Morales, has been restored to its 16th-century appearance complete with cellar and mill. The town hall has copies of *Don Quijote* in 36 languages. Puerto Lápice, 20km (12 miles) southeast of Consuegra, has an inn that matches Cervantes's description of the one where Don Quijote officially swore in as a knight errant.

Further east, Campo de Criptana has a fleet of restored hillcrest windmills similar to the ones that made Quijote's day, many of which now contain museums, while Cueva de Montesinos, near San Pedro lake, is the cave in which our hero was treated by Montesinos himself to elegiac visions of other bewitched knights errant and of his beloved Dulcinea. In Argamasilla de Alba is the Cueva de Medrano (now a *casa de cultura*) where Cervantes was imprisoned and started work on *Don Quijote*.

The 13th-century **Castillo de Cala-trava la Nueva** ❽ (www.castillodecala trava.com; Tue–Sun), on the CR-504 about 35km (20 miles) south of Almagro, was founded in 1217 by the Military Order of Calatrava. It was later used as a monastery until it was irreparably cracked by an earthquake in 1802. The triple-naved church has since been restored. It's quite a climb up but the views are worth it.

A curious rural sight just off the A4 highway is **Las Virtudes**, the site of Spain's oldest identified bullring – a picturesque 17th-century galleried corral. These sights and the squat villages of the southern plains are set against the vineyards of the Val-depeñas wine region, the largest in Spain. They have existed since medi-eval times and today, after extensive modernisation, they remain impor-tant to the local economy.

Albacete ❾, at Castilla-La Man-cha's southeastern corner, is a plain town largely rebuilt after the Civil War. In the Parque Abelardo Sánchez, the **Museo Arqueológico Provincial de Albacete** (mid-Sep–Jun Tue–Sat 10am–2pm, 4.30–7pm, Sun am only, Jul–mid-Sept Tue–Sat 10am–2pm, Sun 9.30am–2pm) has some good Iberian and Roman objects. The town has long been a centre for the manufac-ture of knives and daggers. The Museo de la Cuchillería (www.museo-mca.com; Sun am only, Oct–May Tue–Sat 10am–2pm and 5–8pm, June–Sept 10am–2pm and 5.30–8.30pm) on the Plaza de la Catedral documents the history of knife-making in the region.

More attractive are the smaller cas-tle-crowned towns of **Chinchilla de Monte Aragón** and **Almansa** to the east off the A-31. Chinchilla is built around the pretty Plaza Mayor. Here, the 15th-century castle offers sweep-ing views south over the plains to the picturesque **Sierra de Alcaraz**, where the mountain peaks and fertile valleys give way to spectacular gorges and little-explored villages.

The town of **Alcaraz** ❿, with its twin Renaissance towers in the attrac-tive Plaza Mayor, is a good base for exploring this area.

The spectacular village of **Alcalá del Júcar**, 50km (30 miles) northeast of Albacete, juts out over the Júcar gorges, with houses excavated into the limestone. Some of the well-preserved houses even have balconies over the far side, reached via long corridors.

Northeast La Mancha

Nestling to the north in the lower part of Cuenca province, **Alarcón** ⓫ is one of Spain's best examples of medieval military architecture.

Almost completely encircled by the Río Júcar, the triangular castle, now partially converted to a Parador (www. paradores.es), is defended by three ram-parts. A Muslim stronghold, the town was subjected to a nine-month siege in 1184 before succumbing to the Chris-tian conquerors.

Some 55km (34 miles) further north is the provincial capital of **Cuenca** ⓬. The old part of town, with Gothic and Renaissance buildings, lies north of the modern city at the top of a steep hill.

View from Consuegra's fortress.

The **Casas Colgadas** (Hanging Houses) teetering on the edge of the cliff over the Río Huécar are the old town's most emblematic feature. Inside one is the **Museo de Arte Abstracto Español** (www.march.es/arte/cuenca; Tue–Fri 11am–2pm and 4–6pm, Sat until 8pm, Sun am only; free), with a superb collection of abstract art, including works by Chillida, Tàpies, Saura, Zobel, Cuixart, Sempere, Rivera and others. The 18th-century **Plaza Mayor** and the mainly Gothic **Catedral** (www.catedralcuenca.es; daily), built on the site of a mosque between the 12th and 16th centuries, are other key sights. The **Serranía de Cuenca**, to the northeast of the city, whose attractive villages include Beteta and Tragacete, provides a cooling summer antidote to the sun-baked plains.

An unusual sight in this region is the **Ciudad Encantada** (Enchanted City; www.ciudadencantada.es; daily 10am–9pm, Sept until 8.30pm, Oct until 7.30pm, winter 6.30pm), east of Villalba de la Sierra, named for its strange, twisted limestone formations.

Southwest of Cuenca, just off the A-3, are the remains of the Roman settlement of **Segóbriga** ⓭ (www.segobriga.org; Tue–Sun Apr–Sept 10am–3pm, 4–7.30pm, Oct–Mar 10am– 6pm; free Tue and Fri from 4pm). There is a 2,000-seat theatre dating to the 3rd century, which is occasionally used to stage plays.

Nearby is **Uclés**, an austere medieval fortress occupied by the Order of Santiago during the Reconquest, and today a school (daily 10am–8pm, winter until 6pm).

A short drive to the south of Uclés, **Belmonte** ⓮ has a splendidly preserved 15th-century **Castillo** (http://castillodebelmonte.com; June–mid Sept Tue–Sun 10am–2pm and 4.30–8.30pm, mid-Sep–Feb Tue–Fri 10am–2pm, 3.30–5.30pm, Sat–Sun until 6.30pm, Mar–Apr Tue–Sun 10am–2pm, 4–7pm), built by the Marquis of Villena, Juan Pacheco, to defend the domains he is alleged to have accumulated through a series of adroit court intrigues.

In the region's far northeastern corner, **Guadalajara's** ⓯ flamboyant Gothic-*Mudéjar* **Palacio de los Duques del Infantado** (patio Tue–Sun 10am–2pm, 4–8pm, museum Tue–Sat 5–7pm, Sun 10am–2pm; free access to the patio), with its exquisitely carved facade, is the most notable of the city's monuments, which include the Panteón de la Condesa de la Vega del Pozo.

The 12th-century crenellated Romanesque **catedral** (www.lacatedraldesiguenza.com) at nearby **Sigüenza** ⓰ is the site of the strikingly lifelike El Doncel, tomb of Martín Vázquez de Arce, Isabel of Castile's soldier-page (a young knight of the Order of Santiago) who was killed in the taking of Granada in 1486.

La Alcarria, the area east of Guadalajara, has lovely medieval villages such as **Pastrana**, whose Iglesia Colegial (Collegiate Church) contains some fine 15th-century tapestries. **Brihuega**, 30km (18 miles) northeast of Guadalajara, has a picturesque medieval centre notable for its Plaza Mayor, narrow streets and 18th-century cloth factory.

Gothic-style cathedral in Cuenca.

Altar in the church of San
Francisco, Cáceres.

EXTREMADURA

Walk through the honey-coloured old quarter of
an Extremaduran town and step back in time to a
land of conquistador gold and Baroque palaces.

Extremadura is known as 'the land of conquistadors' – both Francisco Pizarro and his cousin Francisco de Orellana were born in Trujillo. Other highlights of the region include the Monasterio de Guadalupe, an important place of pilgrimage for Catholics, and Mérida, with its well-preserved Roman remains including two theatres and floor mosaics. Badajoz and Cáceres are Extremadura's two main towns, each with their own distinctive charm. Plasencia is noted for its cathedral while the Valle de Jerte is famous for its fields of cherry blossom in spring. The Monasterio de Yuste, home of Carlos I, sits in a beautiful location above a lake.

Bordered to the west by Portugal and to the north and south by granite mountain ranges, the expansive plains and hills of Extremadura are sweet with the scent of wild thyme and eucalyptus. Cattle- and sheep-raising are traditional occupations here, while forests of cork and holm-oak provide rooting grounds for the native black pigs that are turned into superb cured hams. A complex network of dams built since the 1960s irrigates newer market gardens and vineyards, and provides water and power to large areas of Spain.

'Land of the conquistadors, land of the gods', is a refrain travellers to this region may hear. You might also come across the apocryphal remark attributed to a French soldier, who declared that Extremaduran cooking made Spain worth invading. *Extremeños* are hospitable, straightforward and independent, the legacy of centuries of poverty and isolation.

Archaeological evidence points to an extensive prehistoric settlement of the area. Mild winters and generally fertile soil made this the site of several Roman towns, most notably Mérida, which became a kind of luxury retirement

Main Attractions

Monasterio de Guadalupe
Teatro Romano, Mérida
Museo Nacional de Arte
    Romano, Mérida
Parque de Monfragüe
Cathedral quarter, Coria
Jewish quarter, Hervás
Jerte valley

In the cloister of Monasterio de Guadalupe, Guadalupe.

colony for distinguished soldiers. Subsequent invasions of Visigoths and Moors disturbed the *Pax Romana*, however, and during the Reconquest the region became a no-man's frontier land between Muslims and Christians. From the 13th century, as the Muslims were driven south, the Christian military religious Orders were granted huge tracts of land to resettle.

An estimated third of the Spaniards who set out to explore and conquer Latin America came from Extremadura; those who survived and triumphed named settlements there and returned to build magnificent palaces in their home towns. Some of the houses are still inhabited by their descendants; others have become hotels or public buildings, or been abandoned to nesting storks.

Guadalupe – Spain's spiritual heart

Monasterio de Guadalupe, Guadalupe.

Perched amid wooded sierras, 214km (133 miles) southwest of Madrid, the town of **Guadalupe ❶** is a striking point of entry to the region. Since the late 13th century, when a shepherd chanced upon a buried image of the Virgin Mary purportedly carved by St Luke, Guadalupe has been an important place of pilgrimage.

Alfonso XI dedicated a battle to this Virgin in 1340; when she brought him victory he ordered the construction of a splendid monastery in which to house her. Christopher Columbus brought the first Amerindians to be baptised to Guadalupe, where the rite was performed at the town fountain in 1496. Over the next few centuries wealthy pilgrims enriched the monastery's Order of Hieronymite monks and donated funds for additions to the original building, which served as a combination palace, church, fortress and royal lodgings (the latter is now converted into a hotel).

By the 15th century the shrine was known as the 'Spanish Vatican' and possessed hospitals, schools of fine arts, grammar and medicine, 30,000 head of cattle and what was possibly the world's best library. Guadalupe was also a renowned centre for the treatment of syphilis, and had a hospital specialising in the 'sweat cure'. The old Hospital San Juan Bautista, with a

graceful 16th-century patio, is now the Parador Zurbarán (www.paradores.es), across the street from the monastery.

Such became the wealth and power of the monastery that a popular refrain went: 'Better than count or duke, to be a monk in Guadalupe.' The place was sacked by the French in 1809, and in 1835, when the Spanish government ordered the sale of monastic property, the Hieronymites fled. Today, however, it is once again become the region's spiritual heart.

The Virgin's treasures

Presently the **Monasterio de Guadalupe** (www.monasterioguadalupe.com; daily 9.30am–1pm and 3.30–6pm) is inhabited by Franciscan monks, who provide both lodging for visitors and a tour of Guadalupe's treasures. A visit begins in the 14th-century Gothic-*Mudéjar* cloister, with its two-tiered horseshoe archways and lovely fountain surrounded by a miniature temple. The old refectory houses a dazzling collection of priests' robes, embroidered with gold threads and encrusted with pearls.

Of further interest is the collection of illuminated choir books, and a room containing the Virgin's own rich wardrobe, necklaces and crowns, given to her by kings, presidents and popes.

The artistic highlight of the tour is the sacristy, which is locally given the grand nickname of the Spanish Sistine Chapel, where portraits of monks by 17th-century master Zurbarán are set against lavishly decorated walls. Finally, up a red marble staircase is the *camarín*, where the Virgin resides. The famous iron grille in the church, entered separately off the plaza, is said to be made from the chains of freed slaves.

The cobbled streets of the town wind among traditional Extremaduran slate houses, their wooden balconies full of potted geraniums. In addition to devotional souvenirs and pottery, you can also take home a bottle of *gloria*, a local drink made from a blend of *aguardiente*, grape juice and herbs.

Crossing the **Sierra de Guadalupe** south takes you through the mountain villages of **Logrosán** and **Zorita**, the former boasting the remains of a pre-Roman town on a nearby hillside. Catch up with the main highway, the A-5, at **Miajadas**.

From there you can take a 28km (17-mile) detour to **Medellín**, birthplace of the conqueror of Mexico, Hernán Cortés. Climb up to the ruined **castle** and survey the **Río Guadiana** shimmering below. The recently excavated roman theatre is now open to visitors (http://medellinsitiohistorico.gobex.es; Wed–Sun 10.30am–1.30pm, 5–8pm, Tue only pm). Medellín is a pleasant, quiet village, noted for its outsize bronze statue of Cortés in the town square – a rare representation, since there are no statues of him in Mexico.

Roman Mérida

Formerly known as Emeritus Augustus, **Mérida ②** lies 127km (79 miles) south of Guadalupe, on a sluggish bend of the Guadiana. Founded in 25 BC, the city became a prosperous capital of the Roman colony of Lusitania,

FACT

In 1531, the Guadalupe Virgin appeared to Mexican peasant Juan Diego, identifying herself as 'Santa Maria de Guadalupe'. More than 100 cities in the New World bear her name, and, today, she is a symbol of hispanidad, drawing thousands of pilgrims every year from the Spanish-speaking world.

Teatro Romano, Mérida.

and Roman ruins are Mérida's pride today. Yet this lovely city, whose buildings and hedges of myrtle and hibiscus give a flavour of the Spanish South, also aspires to modernity. Since becoming capital of the autonomous region in 1981 its skyline has been reshaped by largely brash new development.

But there are modern architectural highlights: Calatrava's sleek Lusitania Bridge and Rafael Moneo's stunning museum are both strokes of genius.

In July and August, Mérida hosts a classical theatre festival, which attracts Spanish and international companies and directors (www.festivaldemerida.es). Performances are held in the **Teatro Romano** (www.consorciomerida.org; daily Apr–Sept 9.30am–9pm, Oct–Mar 9.30am–6.30pm, but check as times vary) and **Anfiteatro** (times as before), which seat 6,000 and 14,000 spectators respectively.

Nearby are the **Circo Romano** (daily Apr–Sept 9.30am–9pm, Oct–Mar 9.30am–2pm, 4–6.30pm), formerly used for chariot races, and the **Casa del Mitreo** (same times as the Circo),

Spanish brotherhoods celebrate 'Semana Santa' (Holy Week) in Cáceres. The robes are a symbol of mourning for Christ.

which was actually a small palace. Of particular interest are the mosaic floors depicting the four seasons, and the remains of a sauna. The **Casa del Anfiteatro** also has exceptionally good mosaics and the remains of some paintings (times as before).

Across the street from the theatres is the brick **Museo Nacional de Arte Romano**, designed by Rafael Moneo, a superb location for the largest collection of Roman artefacts outside Italy (http://museoarteromano.mcu.es; Sun 10am–3pm, Tue–Sat Apr–Sept 9.30am–8pm, Oct–Mar 9.30am–6.30pm; free Sat pm and Sun am). The main hall of the museum, with its high archways and dramatic use of natural light, has the feeling of a cathedral nave, and is an impressive backdrop for the colossal statues.

Two storeys of galleries built around the main hall are dedicated to theme exhibits, such as rare painted friezes, jewellery and glass, replicas of which are on sale.

Many other Roman monuments are dotted around town. The **Arco de Trajano**, just off the Plaza de España,

CONQUERORS OF THE NEW WORLD

The conquistadors of the Americas were not, as they are sometimes depicted, village louts, but often the second or illegitimate sons of aristocrats, with grand surnames and the military training to go with it, but limited expectations in Spain. Hernan Cortés, for example, was the son of a minor nobleman with few prospects, while Francisco Pizarro was the bastard son of another minor aristocrat from Trujillo. Together with his two half-brothers, Pizarro set out to capture the fabled wealth of Peru in 1532. Even in that delirious time the expedition was widely known as *de los locos* – 'of the mad men' – and did not fail to live up to expectations.

During one desperate moment in the jungle, Pizarro drew a line in the sand with the point of his sword and dared his comrades to cross it and head home. All but 13 did. However, the inroads made by those 13 men convinced Carlos I to give Pizarro the ships and armies he so desperately wanted, and with which he was able to conquer the Incas. A few years later, however, Pizarro was assassinated; his body is buried in Lima cathedral. Understandably, the Peruvians are not too fond of him, blaming him for the destruction of their culture, and successfully lobbied for his statue to be removed from Plaza de Armas, Lima's main square, to a less salubrious location in 2004.

dwarfs the narrow street and nearby houses. A short walk away in Calle Romero Leal is the **Templo de Diana** (1st century AD but with Renaissance additions) and the 9th-century riverside **Alcazaba** (same times as Teatro Romano), with ruins inside it. On the edge of town are the **Puente Romano**, with its 60 granite arches (open only for pedestrian traffic), and the **Acueducto de los Milagros** , which until recently brought water to Mérida.

Also worth a look is the 13th-century **Basilica de Santa Eulalia**: the mausoleum of Saint Eulalia is in its Paleochristian crypt.

Around 8km (5 miles) to the northeast of the city, within the lovely wooded **Parque de Cornalvo**, are Europe's oldest working dam and reservoir. They once supplied Roman Mérida with water and still supply local villages.

Badajoz

The capital of Extremadura's southern province, **Badajoz** ❸ is just 6km (3.5 miles) from the Portuguese border. Originally a Roman town named Pax Augustus, it rose to prominence as Batalajoz, capital of a *taifa* (principality), and once dominated half of Portugal, including Lisbon. It was captured from the Muslims in 1229, but its strategic location made it the site of many bloody sieges over the centuries.

In August 1936 it was captured by Nationalist forces, and, in one of the darkest moments of the Civil War, many Republican defenders (possibly several thousand but the exact figure is unknown) were herded into the bullring and shot.

Badajoz's solid post-war appearance today is given limited spark by its monuments. The ramparts of the **Alcazaba**, or Muslim castle, are best approached from the river, not through the old town's poor quarter. It keeps an octagonal tower, the **Espantaperros** (Dog-Frightener), so called because its ancient bell vibrated at a high pitch that terrified dogs. Inside

is a provincial **Museo Arqueológico** (http://museoarqueologicobadajoz.gobex.es; Tue–Sat 9am–3pm, Sun 10am–3pm; free), with interesting displays on local sites that include Cancho Ruano, Spain's only known Tartessian temple, burned down in the 6th century BC.

The city also has two excellent art museums: the **Museo Extremeño e Iberoamericano de Arte Contemporaneo** (MEIAC; www.meiac.es; Tue–Sat 10am–1.30pm and 5–8pm, Sun am only; guided tours Wed at noon; free) is housed in the old prison and is dedicated to Spanish and Latin American contemporary art, and the **Museo de Bellas Artes** (June–Aug Tue–Sat 10am–2pm, 6–8pm, Sun am only, Sep–May Tue–Sun 10am–2pm, Tue–Fri 5–7pm: free) which has works by Zurbarán and Picasso. South of Badajoz is unspoiled countryside dotted with whitewashed towns marked by dramatic military and religious history. **Zafra** is a good base for exploring; it has a magnificent Parador inside the 15th-century palace (www.paradores.es) around which the walled quarter grew. **Olivenza**, to the west, keeps a

San Mateo church, Cáceres city.

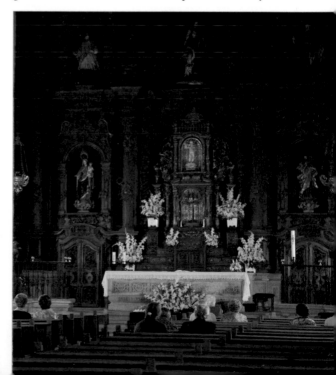

remarkable cluster of monuments built in the Portuguese Manueline style thanks to its long frontier history; it finally became Spanish in 1803.

Jerez de los Caballeros was the seat of the Knights Templar and birthplace of Núñez de Balboa, who 'discovered' the Pacific Ocean. Fountains, churches and heraldic shields are found at every turn in the streets sloping down from the ruined castle.

Cáceres – noblemen's town

Cáceres ❹, capital of the northern Extremaduran province, is a city lifted out of the pages of an illuminated book of chivalry.

Over the centuries, it has been spared the sieges and bombardments that destroyed parts of other Extremaduran cities, a longevity that saw it declared a national monument in 1949. The old city is separated from the new by well-preserved walls and towers originally built in Muslim times.

It is best approached from the **Plaza Mayor**. For the most dramatic ascent, climb the steps leading through the **Arco de la Estrella**.

During the Middle Ages the atmosphere was rather more hectic. When Alfonso IX took the city from the Muslims in 1229, it became the seat of a brotherhood of knights called the Fratres de Cáceres, who eventually became Spain's most noble Order, the Order of Santiago, and a wealthy centre of free trade. At one time there were 300 knights in the city, their palaces just a few steps from one another. Each *solar*, or noble house, had its own defensive tower, and the continual factions and rivalries meant that there was always a small war in progress somewhere around town. In the interests of peace Fernando and Isabel ordered the destruction of most of the towers in 1476, save those belonging to their favourites. Of the few that are left, the most striking is perhaps the **Torre de las Cigüeñas**, or Stork Tower, in the **Plaza San Mateo**.

Directly opposite is the **Palacio de las Veletas**, a Baroque palace built on the site of the Muslim castle. In the basement is an enormous arcaded *aljibe*, or cistern, which looks like a flooded mosque. The palace holds the archaeological and ethnographic sections of the **Museo de Cáceres** (http://museodecaceres.gobex. es; Sun 10am–2.30pm, Tue–Sat mid-Apr–Sept 9am–2.30pm, 5–8.15pm, Oct–mid-Apr 9am–2.30pm and 4–7.15pm; free); displays include artefacts from prehistoric times, Roman coins and local handicrafts and costumes. There are also reproductions of the cave paintings in the nearby caves of **Maltravieso** and contemporary Spanish art on show. Close by is the restored Jewish quarter. To the left of the museum is the church of **San Mateo**, with a beautiful bell tower, and the **Convento de San Pablo**, inhabited by cloistered nuns who sell their famous *yemas* (candied egg yolks) through a screened dumb waiter to avoid showing their faces to the world.

While the old town's palaces range in architectural style from Gothic to Plateresque, they blend harmoniously

Trujillo.

together through their sober grey-gold sandstone and granite facades. Palaces of particular note include the **Casa de los Solís**, with its coat of arms in the shape of a sun, and the **Casa del Mono** (monkey), now a library. **Casa de los Golfines de Arriba**, in calle Olmos, belonged to a family of French knights who were invited here in the 12th century to help fight the Muslims. According to a contemporary chronicler, 'Even the king cannot subject them, though he has tried.' It is believed that the Spanish word *golfo*, meaning 'scoundrel', is derived from this family's surname. It was in this house in 1936 that Franco was declared head of state.

Near the 16th-century cathedral church of **Santa María la Mayor**) are the **Bishop's Palace**, the **Palace of Ovando**, with its lush green patio, and the **Casa Toledo-Moctezuma**, once inhabited by the descendants of the conquistador Juan Cano and Aztec Emperor Moctezuma's daughter and now the repository of the regional archives.

Cradle of conquerors

Crowning a dusty hill surrounded by pastureland, **Trujillo** ❺ is 47km (30 miles) east of Cáceres on the N-521. Its number of extraordinarily beautiful monuments make it well worth a two-day visit. The town's long and dramatic history is said to have begun with its founding by Julius Caesar, but Trujillo's proudest moment was clearly the conquest of Peru by native son Francisco Pizarro. His bronze equestrian statue dominates the beautiful **Plaza Mayor**, and palaces built with wealth from Inca treasures are sprinkled throughout the city.

The **Palacio del Marqués de la Conquista**, built by Pizarro's brother, Hernando, stands across the plaza from the statue, though disappointingly, it is not open to the public. On the ornate facade are busts of Francisco Pizarro and his wife Inés Yupanqui,

sister of the Inca emperor Atahualpa. Above them is the coat of arms ceded to them by Carlos I. Behind the equestrian statue is the 15th-century church of **San Martín**, whose bell and clock towers provide ample nesting ground for several storks.

Trujillo's sights

Across the street from the church is the **Palacio de los Duques de San Carlos** (Mon–Sat 9.30am–1pm and 4.30–6.30pm, Sun 10am–12.30pm), also known as **Palacio de los Vargas-Carvajal**. The 16th-century palace has a striking Baroque facade and chimneys inspired by Inca temples. The house is now inhabited by nuns, who are more than willing to give a tour of the patio and splendid staircase.

A few steps outside the plaza's southwest corner is the **Palacio Pizarro de Orellana**, also run by nuns, which has an exquisite Plateresque patio. Francisco de Orellana was a Pizarro cousin, and the first European to navigate the Amazon. He claimed the river for Spain, and eventually perished along its banks.

FACT

Discovered in 1978 near Zalamea de la Serena in southeastern Extremadura are the remains of a 6th-century BC temple-palace, Cancho Ruano, the world's only known Tartessian monument. More information is to be found at the interpretation centre opposite the excavation site (www.canchoroano.iam.csic.es; Mon–Sun 10am–2pm, winter Mon–Sat 4–6pm,summer 5–8pm).

Statue of Pizarro in front of the church of San Martín, Trujillo.

Each step uphill in Trujillo is a step further back into the past. Follow **Cuesta de Santiago** past the **Torre del Alfiler** (Needle Tower; daily 10am–2pm and 4.30–7.30pm), now the town's interpretation centre, up to the Muslim *castillo*. Pause for breath at **Santa María la Mayor**, a 15th-century church containing the tomb of Diego Paredes, the 'Samson of Spain'. As a young child he was said to have carried the stone baptismal font from the church to his mother's bedside, and Cervantes wrote that as an adult soldier, Diego 'defeated the entire French army and held them at the end of a bridge'.

Further up is the **Casa-Museo de Pizarro** (daily 10am–2pm and 5–8pm), with exhibits documenting the exploits of the Pizarro family.

From the castle walls there is a panoramic view of the surrounding countryside, while inside are the Muslim cisterns. Upstairs is a chapel dedicated to the Virgin who enabled the Christian armies to take the castle from the Muslims by illuminating a dark fog that had enveloped them. A coin-operated machine allows the visitor to illuminate the granite statue of the Virgin; her bright light can be seen from the Plaza Mayor below.

Plasencia

An attractive town on the banks of the Río Jerte, **Plasencia** ❻ is 43km (27 miles) north of Trujillo by the EX-208. Settled by the Berbers, it was conquered by Alfonso VIII, who in 1189 granted it a coat of arms with the title *Placeat Deo et hominibus* (May it please God and Man). Until 1492 the city continued to have large Jewish and Arab populations, reflected by the narrow, winding streets in which they lived, as well as by street names, such as **Calle de las Morenas** (Street of the Dark Women). On Tuesdays, a market takes place in the **Plaza Mayor**, as it has for 800 years.

Plasencia has an impressive **Catedral** (www.catedralesdeplasencia.org; Tue–Sun 9am–1pm and Apr–Sept 5–8pm, Nov–Mar 4–7pm), which is actually parts of two cathedrals joined together. The first is 13th- to 14th-century Romanesque, with some touches of Gothic, while the second is 15th- to 16th-century Gothic with a Plateresque facade. The older cathedral, reached via a cloister with stone carving, houses an exceptional collection of religious art including the 2,000 kg (2-ton) stone Virgin of Perdón.

The choir stalls are some of the most beautiful in Spain; the carving represents both sacred and profane subjects. The sculptor, Rodrigo Alemán, declared that even God couldn't have made such a masterpiece, a blasphemy that got him locked into a nearby castle tower. According to legend, he ended his days by falling from the tower, flapping home-made wings.

Aristocratic homes

There are several palaces in Plasencia. The **Convento de los Dominicos** has been converted into a magnificent Parador (www.paradores.es), and the 14th-century Provincial Hospital on

Historical bible on display in the Catedral, Plasencia.

Plazuela Marqués de la Puebla now houses the excellent **Museo Etnográfico-Textil** (www.brocense.com; July–mid-Sept Mon–Sat 9.30am–2.30pm, mid-Sept–June Wed–Sat 11am–2pm and 5–8pm, Sun am only; free), with some vivid exhibits including regional costumes and traditional local crafts.

To the south of Plasencia is the **Parque de Monfragüe** ❼, a 500 sq km (200 sq mile) national park (www.parquedemonfrague.com or www.magrama.gob.es/es/red-parques-nacionales/nuestros-parques/monfrague). The name comes from the Roman 'Mons Fragorum', and its Mediterranean woodland and scrub protects a wealth of wildlife, including over three-quarters of Spain's protected bird species. The information centre at **Villareal de San Carlos** (tel: 927-199 134; daily), on the EX-208 between Plasencia and Trujillo, makes a good starting point, and has information (in English) on walking trails and lookout points.

Coria, 33km (20 miles) west of Plasencia, was one of Spain's earliest bishoprics (AD 589). The splendid cathedral quarter – surrounded by the best-preserved medieval walls in Europe – dwarfs today's town. A good time to visit is during the June fiestas when the gates in the wall are kept shut to allow the after-dark bull-running to take place.

Southwest of Coria is **Alcántara**, where the **Puente Romano** (Roman Bridge) soars high above the River Tagus to avoid flood water. By contrast, the once magnificent **Convento de San Benito**, sacked by Napoleon in 1807, is an atmospheric ruin. Legend has it that the monks' recipe book was stolen by General Junot, and became the source of some elements of French haute cuisine. Further south are the attractive frontier towns of Valencia de Alcántara and Albuquerque.

Cherry blossom

Extremadura's northern sierras and valleys offer an unexpected mosaic of contrasting landscapes. To the north of Coria, the **Sierra de Gata**'s hamlets and green fields border on **Las Hurdes**' ❽ slate-black slopes and beehives, caught by Luis Buñuel in his classic documentary *Tierra Sin Pan (Land*

Cherry and olive cultivation on terraces, Las Hurdes.

SIGHTINGS OF STORKS

White storks (*cigüeña* in Spanish, *Ciconia ciconia* to naturalists) are an extremely common sight in much of central Spain but particularly in Extremadura. They arrive in February and depart again in the middle of summer. Between those two times, they build large nests of sticks, mud, straw and anything else they can scavenge on church steeples, towers, rooftops, electricity pylons and other man-made structures. Apparently, far from feeling threatened by the close proximity of human beings, they feel a certain sense of protection. The relationship has benefits both ways because it is rare that people get a chance to get so close to wild animals. As they come and go about the business of raising their young, these large birds are hard to miss and easy to watch without binoculars.

Without Bread, 1932). The cramped stone dwellings built into the hillsides give a sense of the terrible poverty endured in the villages of this region. Approaching on the CV-55 from the west, you'll cross the Río Hurdano at Vegas de Coria where a road turns off, following the river valley to some of the most atmospheric 'black villages' of the region.

To the east rise the peaks of the **Sierra de Francia** and **Sierra de Gredos**, sliced through by the lush green Ambroz, Vera and Jerte river valleys. Tobacco, asparagus, paprika peppers and cherries all flourish in the region's gentle climate. In spring the sight of the snowy cherry blossom in the Jerte valley is unforgettable.

Hervás ❾, a mountain village in the Ambroz valley, has one of the best-preserved Jewish quarters in Spain. It is thought that Hervás became a predominantly Jewish settlement in the early Middle Ages, as the Jews fled Christian and Muslim persecution in the larger cities. Intricate, maze-like streets make this village an intimate and atmospheric one. A plaque marks the house thought to be the old synagogue in Calle Sinagoga.

An interesting side trip from Hervás, approximately 22km (14 miles) west on the other side of the A66, is the restored village of **Granadilla** (Tue–Sun 10am–1.30pm and 4–8pm, Nov–Mar until 6pm; free). It has been uninhabited since the 1960s, when the Embalse de Gabriel y Galán Reservoir was created on its doorstep.

Over the pass

Leading out of Hervás, there is a narrow but spectacular road, which should not be attempted in poor weather, that crosses the treeless Honduras Pass, and then plunges into the **Jerte valley**. The villages here, including Cabezuela del Valle and Jerte itself, are becoming increasingly well-liked by travellers. The area is especially popular during the March cherry blossom season. The Holy Roman Emperor Charles V (Spain's Carlos I) passed through here in 1556, on his way to the valley of La Vera, on the southern side of the Tormantos mountain range. There is now a 28km (17-mile) walking trail from the pass of Tornavacas, at the tip of the Jerte valley, crossing through the nature reserve of Garganta de los Infiernos to the village of **Jarandilla de la Vera**. The palace where the king rested on his journey, the Castillo de los Condes Oropesa, has been converted into a modern Parador (www.paradores.es).

Carlos I soon had his own lodgings built at the **Monasterio de Yuste** ❿ (www.patrimonionacional.es; Tue–Sun, Apr–Sept 10am–8pm, Oct–Mar until 6pm; free for EU citizens Wed–Thu Oct–Mar 3–6pm, Apr–Sept 5–8pm), 10km (6 miles) to the southwest of Jarandilla. Here he tended to his clock-mending and observed Mass from his bed until he died in 1558. It is the unforgettable setting – above a small lake and the picturesque village of **Cuacos de Yuste** – and the monastery's simplicity that make it so beautiful today.

Storks nesting on Torre del Alfiler, Trujillo.

The wooden Metropol Parasol on Plaza de la Encarnación.

SEVILLE

Aside from Seville's immense cultural heritage, its convivial, fun-loving atmosphere makes the city an ideal place to experience Andalusia's sultry nightlife.

eville isn't just about oranges, flamenco and bullfighting. The atmospheric capital of Andalucia, on the banks of the River Guadalquivir, is of major historical importance. The Archivo General de Indias was the centre of trade with the New World and contains important historical documents. It was in the Alcázar that Christopher Columbus met with King Ferdinand and Queen Isabel; the Moorish building is today Europe's oldest royal palace still in use. The cathedral is the largest Gothic cathedral in the world. Enjoy a tapas crawl through the old Jewish quarter, Barrio Santa Cruz, and some fun rides in the Isla Mágica theme park.

Seville. Córdoba. Granada. A resounding triumvirate of southern (Andalusian) Spanish cities whose very names roll off the tongue with a hint of arrogance. Flashy, flamboyant, proud. Balmy of weather, attractive of scenery and easily accessible by sea, Andalusia proved vulnerable to the successive settlements of the Phoenicians, Greeks, Romans, Visigoths and Muslims. But it was the Arab and Berber presence that bequeathed Andalusia the richly sensuous medieval culture of silver filigree and ornate mosques that bewitches visitors to the region today.

Under Islamic dominion, Andalusia was the centre of the most highly developed civilisation of the Middle Ages. But its reputation for riches and flair for hospitality hark back to an even earlier incarnation as the Roman province of Baetica, when Andalusia purveyed all make and manner of luxuries to the connoisseurs and cognoscenti of imperial Rome.

Such eminent 19th-century visitors as the American author Washington Irving and the English writers George Borrow and Richard Ford were inspired to record its charms in their various travel chronicles, and thus helped to

Main Attractions

Catedral and Giralda
Alcázar
Barrio de Santa Cruz
Parque de María Luisa
Plaza de Toros de la
  Maestranza
Casa de Pilatos
Museo de Bellas Artes
Museo del Baile Flamenco

The tiled alcoves in Plaza de España each represent a Spanish province.

convert the salient features of Andalusia into the universal Spanish stereotype.

Sherry wines, well-disciplined horses, brave bulls and flamboyant flamenco were the stuff of Andalusia. And who from a colder and soggier climate could easily resist the promise of 3,000 hours of sunshine annually and a mere 30cm (12ins) of rain? Generally, Andalusia's winters are mild and its summers scorching. Throughout, the climatic catchword is 'arid', as evidenced by the number of bridges spanning parched river beds, some of which are being cultivated.

Fellow Andaluces

Until the Reconquest of Granada by the Catholic Monarchs Fernando and Isabel in 1492, Andalusia had rarely been united under one ruler. Internecine strife among the *emirs* and *taifas* (principalities) of Córdoba, Jaén, Granada and Seville undermined Islamic domination until the increasing pressure of Spain's northern Christian kingdoms vanquished it.

Today Andalusia is Spain's most populous region, tallying 87,270 sq km (33,695 sq miles), 8.4 million inhabitants and comprising Spain's eight southernmost provinces. Comparable in size to Portugal, it stretches from that country in the west to Murcia in the east. Its northern reaches are marked by the Sierra Morena and its southern boundaries by the Atlantic Ocean and Mediterranean Sea.

The people of the provinces of Almería, Granada, Jaén, Córdoba, Málaga, Cádiz, Seville and Huelva, each with a provincial capital of the same name, are at once fellow *andaluces* and individual *almerienses*, *granadinos*, *cordobeses* and *sevillanos*.

Says one Seville taxi driver: 'Seville is different from the rest. Here we are more *simpático* (genial) and more polite in everything. We all call ourselves *andaluces* because we share the same flag. Of course, Cádiz is somewhat similar to Seville, but the *granadinos* are coarse fellows, as if they weren't even *andaluces*.' These provincial rivalries have their roots in a not-so-playful past of seesawing fortunes among the former Muslim kingdoms of Granada, Seville and Córdoba.

Patio de las Doncellas, Alcázar.

Southern outlook

For a long time outsiders have characterised the *andaluces* as lethargic and fond of their afternoon siesta. But at the same time all consider them to be spontaneous and witty, balancing an exaggerated sense of tragedy with a robust sense of humour.

'Here are two classes of people to whom life seems one long holiday, the very rich, and the very poor,' writes Washington Irving in *Tales of the Alhambra*, 'one, because they need do nothing, the other, because they have nothing to do; but there are none who understand the art of doing nothing and living upon nothing better than the poor classes of Spain. Climate does one half and temperament the rest… Talk of poverty! With (a Spaniard) it has no disgrace. It sits upon him with a grandiose style, like his ragged cloak. He is an *hidalgo* (nobleman) even when in rags.'

Ever since the Christians eclipsed the Muslims in Andalusia, the south has been largely poor. Not the overt, searing poverty of the developing world, but rather an undercurrent of rural poverty not readily detected by the casual tourist. Andalusia's reputation as 'a rich land inhabited by poor men' was declining until the economic crisis of 2008. There was a thriving underground economy, an increase in tourism, and rural workers, long neglected, enjoyed a range of social services. Now the region has Spain's highest level of unemployment – 29 percent in 2016.

The 1980s boom years

The 1980s brought unprecedented prosperity to Andalusia. Spain's entry into the EU in 1986 spurred development, which was further boosted by the investment in infrastructure for Expo '92, the World Fair in Seville celebrating Columbus's voyage to the New World. Four-lane highways now connect Andalusia with Madrid and the rest of Europe, and the AVE high-speed train has halved travelling time from Madrid to Seville. A direct line has also been introduced from Málaga to Seville, which takes just over two hours; approximately the same as the driving time – without the hassle of finding somewhere to park.

Café life in the Barrio de Santa Cruz.

Abundant sunshine and fertile farmland are two enduring resources. The sunshine has converted the coast, particularly the Costa del Sol, into a favourite holiday and residential area for Northern Europeans, but efforts are under way to open up lesser-known areas inland to attract hikers and wildlife aficionados.

Modern methods are being applied to farming, and thousands of hectares of what once was desert in Almería province have been transformed into plastic-covered greenhouses, where export crops, from melons to carnations, flourish all year.

Flirtatious Seville

Seville, Spain's fourth-largest city and Andalusia's capital, is the most coquettish of the three grand cities of the south. An old Spanish refrain says: *Quien no ha visto Sevilla, no ha visto maravilla* (He who has not seen Seville, has not known wonderment). George Borrow, author of *The Bible in Spain*, considered it 'the most interesting town in all Spain (beneath) the most glorious heaven...'

Even through a veil of fine December rain Seville is pretty. In the bright Andalusian sunshine, she is dazzling. A fitting setting for Byron's Don Juan, Bizet's Carmen and Rossini's barber to play out their fictional lives.

Some of the real lives that got their start here are those of the poets Gustavo Adolfo Bécquer (1836–70) and Antonio Machado (1875–1939), and the painters Diego de Velázquez (1599–1660) and Bartolomé Esteban Murillo (1618–82). Romance has apparently always coursed through the city's veins. The Muslim historian Al-Saqundi, captivated by its charm, once proclaimed: 'If one asked for the milk of birds in Seville, it would be found.' St Teresa was so taken with its beauty and boldness that she confessed she felt that anyone who could somehow avoid committing sin in Seville would be doing very well indeed.

Roman rule

'Hercules built me; Caesar surrounded me with walls and towers; the King Saint took me.' This terse recapitulation of Seville's multi-tiered history was carved long ago on the Jerez Gate. Later, Seville's port would bustle with New World activity as Spain built a lustrous but short-lived overseas empire.

In the era of discoverers, when the Netherlands, England and Spain were fighting for supremacy at sea and in the New World colonies, Seville was one of the richest cities in the world. But it had already known previous fame and fortune. Founded by the Iberians, it was usurped by Julius Caesar for Rome in 45 BC. Made an assize town and named *Hispalis*, it was given the title of *Colonia Julia Romula* and became one of the leading towns of the flourishing Roman province of Baetica, roughly corresponding to present-day Andalusia. There followed several lacklustre centuries under the Vandals and Visigoths, the latter having Seville report to their capital at Toledo.

Old mosaic tiles advertising coffee in Barrio de Santa Cruz.

Cyclists along the riverside.

Glory days

Then in 712 came the Muslims, who renamed it *Ishbiliya*. Later, as part of the Caliphate of Córdoba, Seville rivalled that capital in material prosperity and as a seat of learning. When the Caliphate broke up in the 11th century, Seville pursued an independent course. Beginning in 1023, it saw the successive rule of the Abbadites, Almoravids (1091) and Almohads (1147). Under this last dynasty a new period of prosperity reigned that left behind many of Seville's fine buildings, including the Giralda.

In 1248, Seville was reconquered for Christianity by Fernando III, the King Saint, who died and was buried here.

The wave of New World discoveries that raised Seville to the crest of its fortunes in the 16th century also dashed it in its wake when the empire ebbed a century later. In 1519, Magellan set sail from here to circumnavigate the globe. But Seville's moment of glory was all too fleeting, and decline set in again in the early 17th century, subsequently hastened by maritime competition from Cádiz, the snowballing

Stone carvings adorn the Catedral.

loss of the Spanish colonies that had brought so much trade, the troubled state of 19th-century Spain and a brief French occupation lasting from 1808 to 1812.

Its historic momentum lost, Seville strolled into the 20th century trailing a tarnished heritage that nevertheless stirred great feelings of pride among *sevillanos*. Seized early in the Civil War by the Nationalists, Seville served as a base for attacks on the rest of Andalusia. Emerging from the war physically starving and spiritually spent, the city gradually regained its legendary *alegría* (happiness) under the entrenched Franco dictatorship. But for a long time its Gypsy bravado resounded with a tragic note.

Since 1940, Seville's population has almost doubled to the current 693,000. With the granting of regional autonomy, Seville – as capital – received a boost in importance. But Expo '92, a world fair, brought an influx of professionals from other regions and countries to shake up the status quo in a community where class barriers and conservative attitudes

ISLA DE LA CARTUJA

The site of Expo '92, on the west bank of the Río Guadalquivir, was once a boggy wasteland with one building, the 15th-century **Monasterio de Santa María de las Cuevas**. Part of the monastery houses the **Centro Andaluz de Arte Contemporáneo**, with a permanent exhibition of modern Andalusian artists (www.caac.es; Tue–Sat 11am–9pm, Sun 10–3.30pm; free Tue–Fri 7–9pm, all day Sat). The western part of the island was developed into a high-tech research area. Visitors are still able to view the Expo '92 pavilions but, since most are now privately owned, they are not open to the public. However, in 2012 one reopened as **El Pabellón de la Navegación** (Tue–Sat 11am–7.30pm, Sun and Jul–Aug until 3pm; www.pabellondelanavegacion.com), a futuristic museum which charts Seville's maritime history. La Cartuja is also home to the 35-hectare (88-acre) **Isla Mágica** theme park (www.islamagica.es; Apr–Oct, times vary), with rides, outdoor entertainment, multimedia shows, bars and restaurants.

Other attractions include the oval-shaped bridge **Puente de la Barqueta** and lyre-shaped bridge **Puente del Alamillo**, the **Auditorio** (a large open-air theatre) and the **Teatro Central**, with regular performances of drama, dance and music. Also here is the Torre Cajasol, Andalucia's tallest building. The northern third of the island is occupied by Seville's largest park, the **Parque del Alamillo** (daily dawn–dusk).

seemed immovable. They brought new money and fresh ideas to a city frozen in its ritualistic ways. The Expo also transformed Seville physically, as scores of old buildings were restored and fine walkways were built along the riverside. The *Feria de Abril* (April Fair – see page 87) keeps the city on the world's radar.

The cathedral and Giralda

Virtually everything in Andalusia is of a human scale – with the exception of Seville's **Catedral** Ⓐ (Mon 11am–3.30pm; pre-booked self-guided visits 4.30–6pm; Tue–Sat 11am–5pm, Sun 2.30–6pm; www.catedraldesevilla.es). Built between 1402 and 1506, the cathedral contains five spacious aisles, a large main chapel with a wrought-iron screen and vaulting that towers 56 metres (184ft) above the transept.

Allegedly it was the chapter's aim in 1401 'to construct a church such and as good that it never should have its equal. Let Posterity, when it admires it complete, say that those who dared to devise such a work must have been mad.'

You enter the cathedral through the **Patio de los Naranjos** (Patio of the Orange Trees) – the courtyard of the city's main mosque – a shaded oasis of trees and sparkling fountains used for the ritual ablutions of Islam. From this bright courtyard, the **Puerto del Lagarto** (Gate of the Lizard) leads into the cathedral interior.

Hidden in its sombre shadows are many relics and treasures, such as paintings by Murillo, Zurbarán and Goya; a cross said to be made from the first gold brought from America by Columbus; and a funerary monument claimed to hold the explorer's remains. In fact, he almost certainly reposes in Santo Domingo, capital of the Dominican Republic.

His leaden tomb was taken from Seville to Santo Domingo cathedral in 1544, and was supposedly returned over three centuries later. But somewhere there was a mix-up, and it is believed that the bones in Seville are those of his son, Diego.

A doorway at the northeastern corner of the cathedral, between the Puerta del Lagarto and the Capilla

TIP

To enjoy a panoramic view of the city, visit the Torre de los Perdigones (Resolana, s/n; tel: 679-091 073; open daily 10,30am–5pm), a former munitions factory which includes a giant periscope that presents an intriguing image of the city projected onto a giant three-dimensional concave disc.

The huge Catedral.

TIP

If you plan to do a lot of sightseeing, invest in a Sevilla Card (www. sevillacard.es), which is valid for 72 hours, and gives free or reduced entry to museums and activities including a boat trip, the tourist bus and Isla Mágica theme park.

Real, leads to the base of Seville's trademark **Giralda**, a 93-metre (305ft) rectangular tower, erected between 1184 and 1196. It is the remaining minaret of the mosque, which was destroyed a century later. Climb to the top by a series of ramps for splendid views of the city.

The Alcázar palace

Across the **Plaza del Triunfo** from the cathedral stands a Moorish fantasy in filigree: the **Alcázar ᛒ** (www. alcazarsevilla.org; daily, 9.30am–5pm, Apr–Sept until 7pm). Built between 1350 and 1369, it is a *Mudéjar* elaboration of an original Islamic citadel and palace.

For nearly seven centuries, it was the palace of the Spanish monarchy. The most notorious inhabitant was Pedro the Cruel, who had his half-brother Fadrique assassinated in 1358 and murdered his guest, Abu Said of Granada, for his jewels. The skulls painted over Pedro's bedroom door supposedly suggest the fate of five unjust judges who crossed him during his reign.

Though less grandiose than Granada's Alhambra, Seville's Alcázar has a special cosiness and charm derived from its sense of intimacy and its attention to polychrome detail. Its fanciful floors, ceilings and walls are intricate works of art, reaching heights of richness in Carlos I's room and the **Salón de Embajadores** (Ambassadors' Room). The **Patio de las Doncellas** (Maidens' Patio) is noted for its friezes, *azulejos* (tiles) and stucco work. Well-manicured gardens and orange groves contribute to the sense of a summer sanctuary.

Between the cathedral and the Alcázar, the shelves of the **Archivo General de Indias ᛯ** (Mon–Sat 9.30am–5pm, Sun 10am–2pm; free) sag with the weight of history. Since 1785, it has been accumulating the heavy tomes that contain 36,000 files of documents chronicling the adventure of discovery, trails of colonisation, colonial administration and minutiae of trade that recall a 16th-century Seville that was the headquarters for New World trade and, as a result, one of the richest cities in the Old World.

The Jewish quarter

Stretching beyond the walls of the Alcázar is the **Barrio de Santa Cruz**, the former Jewish quarter turned fashionable neighbourhood. The walls are so white, the flowers so bright and the ironwork everywhere so exquisitely wrought that you quite expect a *señorita* in full flounce to come around the corner any minute, castanets clicking. The atmosphere is further enhanced by guitar-wielding Gypsies, who regularly play in the plazas and bars.

Amid the chic shops and rustic restaurants of this barrio (neighbourhood), you can see many traditional Andalusian homes. Wrought-iron gates mark the entrance porch and iron grilles the windows. An inner courtyard, cool and inviting with its abundant greenery, Moorish tiles

Salón de Embajadores in the Alcázar.

and central fountain, is covered with thick vines or an awning in the summer and used as the living room.

Worth a look is the **Hospital de los Venerables Sacerdotes** (Plaza de los Venerables, 8; daily 10am–2pm and 4–8pm; charge but free Sun pm), whose church is home to *Santa Rufina* by Diego Velázquez, which was acquired in 2007 for €12.5 million (£8.4 million).

Park and plaza

The **Parque de María Luisa** ⓓ (daily dawn–dusk) and the **Plaza de España** to the south of the centre have the feel of a bygone Seville. The Plaza de España is marked by a long semicircular series of arches bearing ceramic crests of all the Spanish provinces. Several ceramic-and-brick bridges span the small, concentric stream that flows through this expansive plaza. You can hire a rowing boat and putter around on the stream. The park itself is dotted with buildings left over from the Spanish-American exhibition of 1929.

One of these now houses the **Museo Arqueológico** (Sun 9am–3.30pm, Tue–Sat 9am–7.30pm, mid-June–mid-Sept Tue–Sun 9am–3.30pm; free for EU nationals). Artefacts from the Moorish palace at Medina Azahara (see page 226) are on display here. The museum also has a collection of mosaics and statuary from the well-preserved ruins of Itálica, 12km (7 miles) north of Seville.

The river

Seville straddles the banks of the **Río Guadalquivir**. Known to the Romans as 'Baetis' and the Muslims as the 'Wadi el Kebir' ('the great river'), frequent droughts render this river less than impressive, but to citizens of Seville it is every bit as revered as the Nile. Once upon a time you could be born on the 'wrong side of the river'. Over there, across the river from the cathedral,

the bullring and the up-and-coming barrio of Santa Cruz was the nefarious **Triana** neighbourhood, haven of violence and vice. Long known as the Gypsy quarter, with many flamenco movers and shakers originating from the area, today it is better-known for its atmospheric bars and as a centre for manufacturing the distinctive Seville tiles and ceramics.

Back on the other side of the river, situated along the Paseo de Cristóbal Colón, is the early 13th-century, 12-sided, battlemented **Torre del Oro** ⓔ ('Golden Tower'). If the city and port were threatened by invaders a huge chain connected this tower to a companion tower, now vanished, on the other side. Over the years the tower has housed a prison, a chapel and a gunpowder store. It now houses a small **Maritime Museum** (Mon–Fri 9.30am–6.45pm, Sat–Sun from 10.30am).

Further along the river bank is Seville's famous bullring, the **Plaza de Toros de la Maestranza** ⓕ, which can be visited on a guided tour.

The 13th-century Torre del Oro.

Neighbourhood bar in Barrio de Santa Cruz.

TIP

For a sense of authentic flamenco, check out the **Museo del Baile Flamenco** in the heart of the Barrio de Santa Cruz (Manuel Rojas Marcos, 3; tel: 954-340 311; daily 10am–10pm; www.museo flamenco.com), which was opened in 2007 by the legendary flamenco dancer Cristina Hoyos. It includes audiovisual and multimedia displays explaining the history, culture and soul of Spanish flamenco.

Paddling along the stream that flows through the Plaza de España.

Pilate's house

The 16th-century **Casa de Pilatos** (daily, 9am–6pm, until 7pm in summer; free Wed 3–7pm for EU citizens), just north of the Barrio de Santa Cruz, was named after the famous biblical magistrate whose house in Jerusalem inspired some of its features. Incorporated in this mansion of the first Marquess of Tarifa are *Mudéjar* and Renaissance elements rendered in remarkable *azulejos* and moulded stucco. In the west of the Centro area is the **Museo de Bellas Artes** (Tue–Sun mid-June–mid-Sept 9am–3.30pm, mid-Sept–mid-June Tue–Sun 9am–8.30pm, Sun 9am–3.30pm; free for EU citizens), housed in a former convent that includes a Baroque chapel with a fabulous frescoed vaulting and dome, and works by greats such as Murillo, Zurbarán, Velázquez and El Greco.

It is only in the late morning that Seville begins to stir and gradually transmutes into a vibrant city. Along **Calle Sierpes**, a stylish pedestrian thoroughfare winding from **La Campana** to the **Plaza de San Francisco**, friends meet to do business and shop. At No. 85 there once stood a prison that quartered the not-yet-prominent Miguel de Cervantes, author of *Don Quijote*.

After dinner, which is usually served between 9pm and 11pm, the bars of both Santa Cruz and Triana across the river burst explosively into life.

Metropol Parasol

In 2011 a new piece of architecture was unveiled in Plaza de la Encarnación, one of Seville's main squares. Designed by German architect Jürgen Mayer-Hermann, **Metropol Parasol** is instantly recognisable by its raised undulating form which looks like a giant wooden space ship; although locals have nicknamed it '*las setas*' (the mushrooms). Believe it or not, inside is a shopping centre, including a daily market, restaurants, and also a viewing terrace (charge) offering great views over the city. In the basement the Antiquarium (Tue–Sat 10am–8pm, Sun until 2pm) allows visitors to see the Roman remains uncovered during the building work.

Holy Week

The biggest celebration in Spain is Semana Santa, a week-long emotional build-up to the climax of Good Friday.

The week preceding Easter is Semana Santa, a time of national ritual in Spain. In every corner of the country processions snake their way, day and night, from the local parishes to the main cathedrals and back again. In the larger cities there may be more than 30 different processions in any 24-hour period. Depending on the size of the municipality and its economic means, each day is marked by regalia of varying colour, elaborate floats showing scenes from the Passion and centuries-old music. Since the 16th century, this has been the Spanish way of commemorating Holy Week. These celebrations attain a feverish pitch of pageantry and colour in the South: it has often been alleged that the *andaluces* are more demonstrative in their faith because of a need to live down the Islamic (specifically Moorish) legacy.

Celebrations

In Seville, a fervent 'thunder' fills the cathedral on Wednesday with the rending of the veil of the temple and resounds again on Saturday just before all join in singing 'Gloria in Excelsis' and ringing every bell. In Córdoba, on the afternoon of Good Friday, Mass is celebrated in the church within the mosque with a full symphony orchestra and a massive chorus. In Granada, ladies in mantillas dressed all in black and dripping with jewellery and rosaries walk through the city among the floats. In Málaga, bemused tourists from the Costa del Sol arrive at dusk to watch the Semana Santa parades along the central Alameda main street to the historic narrow streets surrounding the cathedral. Each church in the city sends out one float that weighs up to 6 tonnes and which is carried on the backs, necks and shoulders of hundreds of robed *penitentes* (penitents).

These *pasos*, or floats, are a fixed feature of Semana Santa. They bear life-size and extremely lifelike polychrome and gilded figures depicting every Passion scene from the Last Supper and the Garden of Olives to the Descent from the Cross. The figures wear wigs and real costumes that can cost thousands of euros.

As the proud parishioners watch their particular Virgin pass by they may weep, applaud, sing or even throw her some saucy compliments. Some admirers are so moved by a particular *paso* that they spontaneously sing the traditional, melancholy *saeta*. Penitents wear robes gathered with belts of esparto grass and tall, pointed hoods covering their faces except for two slits for the eyes. Called *capuchones*, these are the hoods of the Spanish Inquisition and the equally insidious Ku Klux Klan.

Party time

But the strong Andalusian sense of fun cannot be long suppressed. The processional ranks are constantly broken as people cross through the parade to greet friends and share a beer or a *boccadillo* (sandwich). In the side streets off the parade route tables and chairs are set up to provide rest and sustenance. *Torrijas*, a fried, milk-soaked confection, and *flamenquines*, deep-fried slices of veal wrapped around snow-cured ham and cheese, are traditional snacks.

Almost everywhere in Spain, the end of Semana Santa signals the beginning of the bullfighting season. In Arcos de la Frontera a local version of the 'running of the bulls' takes place on Easter Sunday, and in Málaga you can go straight from the last Easter Mass to the season's first *corrida*.

Penitents, with long red candles to light at twilight, during Seville's Holy Week.

Backstreets in the Judería (Jewish Quarter).

CÓRDOBA

The walls of the Mezquita dominate the town, while the cobbled alleyways of Córdoba's old Jewish and Muslim quarters, flanked by overflowing pots of geraniums, are a delight to explore.

The main reason to visit Córdoba is to see its spectacular mosque. Then, take a walk through the atmospheric streets of the Judería, stopping en route in a bustling bar for tapas. If you can, come in May, when the patios are in full bloom and open to the public. The Museo Arqueológico contains important finds from the local area and the Museo Provincial de Bellas Artes has works by Murillo, Zurbarán and Goya. The Moorish Alcázar has an impressive evening sound and light show in summer. And don't leave without taking to the waters in the Hammam Baños Arabes.

Handsome, honourable and forthright, Córdoba is harsher than Seville and without the benefit of a marked Gypsy grace note to soften its keen masculine edge. In its no-nonsense streets there is an absence of the benign chaos that chokes rush-hour Seville, nor is there in the town centre a subtle layering of eras as in Granada.

There are just the old and the new, clearly demarcated by an intermittent, well-tended Moorish wall. To one side are the twisted ancient alleys, to the other wide, straight streets with a contemporary purpose.

Visitors are advised to leave their cars outside the old quarter and go on foot, with good reason. Most of the roads are barely wide enough to

accommodate even the smallest of vehicles, and you might well find yourself suddenly backing a hasty retreat down a one-way street under the reproachful gaze of an impatient horse, tourists in tow, eager to return its carriage to the shaded queue outside the Roman walls.

Patrician colony

Looking at Córdoba today, it is hard to imagine the truly heady heights this city achieved in earlier epochs. The history of Córdoba, like that of

Main Attractions

Mezquita
Judería
Sinagoga
Museo Arqueológico
Hammam Baños Árabes
Alcázar
Palacio de Viana

Puerta de Almodóvar (Almodóvar Gate).

TIP

To see Córdoba at its loveliest and liveliest, visit during the Patio Festival, held in the second week of May, or the Feria, in the last week of May. Ask at the tourist office about guided tours of the patios during the rest of the year or visit the Palacio de Viana (see page 204).

Inside the Mezquita.

Granada and Seville, is a dizzying account of soaring success and dismal failure.

Like Seville, Córdoba was an important Iberian town. In 152 BC its fate passed to Roman hands when the consul Marcus Marcellus made it a colony favoured with the title *Colonia Patricia*. As the Roman 'Corduba', it became the capital of *Hispania Ulterior*; and under Augustus, it came into its own as the prosperous capital of Baetica province and Spain's largest city at the time. At this stage in its life it sired Seneca the Elder (55 BC–AD 39) and his son, Lucius Seneca (4 BC–AD 65), noted philosopher and preceptor to Nero. His statue now stands by the **Puerta de Almodóvar**, the principal entrance to the old town.

After the fall of the Roman Empire Córdoba was ruled by the Visigoths until the conquest of Iberia by the Muslims at the beginning of the 8th century. With the help of the city's disaffected Jewish residents, harassed by the Visigoths, the invaders quickly established their supremacy and ultimately raised Córdoba to the pinnacle of prestige and prosperity.

The Caliphate

At the beginning of the 8th century, *emirs* from the Damascus Caliphate had already established themselves in the city; but with the arrival of Abd-al-Rahman I in 756, a discernible dynasty was founded, capable of consolidating the power to rule over all of Muslim Spain, which the Moors called *al-Andalus*. Under Abd-al-Rahman III (912–61) and his successor Hakam II (961–76), the blessings of the Caliphate of Córdoba rained down on the city. Its overstuffed coffers, luxurious appointments and richly brocaded cultural achievements defied even the hyperbole that was second nature to the Muslims and is a lingering trait among their present-day Andalusian offspring.

Córdoba was then possibly Europe's most civilised city. In the 10th century it founded a university of great renown. Literature and science were encouraged, schools of philosophy and medicine were strongly promoted and libraries were established.

The city's inhabitants, numbering around half a million, were served by 3,000 mosques, 300 public baths and 28 suburbs. At its supreme moment of glory Córdoba was surpassed only by the city of Baghdad.

Disintegration and decline

But bad news was just around the corner. At the beginning of the 11th century internal dissent and revolt laid a foundation for its downfall. In 1031, the powerful Caliphate split up into petty kingdoms called *taifas* (principalities), and some 40 years later Córdoba itself was subsumed by the kingdom of Seville until its recapture by Fernando III in 1236. Many inhabitants fled, and the Christians were indifferent to the industry, trade and agriculture that fed the city's affluence. For centuries Córdoba wallowed in the doldrums, but over the

past 50 years its spirit has been steadily reviving. Since 1950 its population has grown by over 60 percent to more than 300,000.

Córdoba's mosque

Whether seen as a travesty or a triumph, the **Mezquita Ⓐ** (mosque; Mon–Sat Mar–Oct 10am–7pm, Sun 8.30–11.30am, 3–7pm,Nov–Feb until 6pm) is a product and a symbol of the grafting of Christianity onto Muslim Spain. As the great mosque of the Umayyad caliphs, it enjoyed such profound artistic and religious stature that it saved the city's inhabitants the arduous pilgrimage to Mecca, whose mosque was the only one of greater size and importance. Begun in 785, the mosque took two centuries to complete, expanding with the city's population before reaching its full size.

Inside, a forest of about 850 columns produces a repetitive motif of crisscrossing alleys not unlike the effect of a hall of mirrors. Uneven in height and varying in material and style, these pillars support an architectural innovation of the time: two tiers of candy-striped arches that lend added height and spaciousness. Most notable and memorable among the Islamic flourishes is the mihrab, or prayer recess, along the wall facing Mecca. The workmanship is a masterpiece of Moorish mosaic art. Interlaced arches sprout from the marble columns surrounding the vestibule; and more exquisitely decorated still is the octagonal mihrab itself, topped by a shell-shaped dome.

Newly Christian Córdoba soon claimed the mosque as its own church of the Virgin of the Assumption, building chapels against the interior walls and closing up the open northern facade to allow access only through the **Puerta de las Palmas** (Gate of the Palms). Construction of the cruciform church in the centre of the mosque began in 1523, and massive as the church is, you are not immediately aware of its looming presence upon entering the mosque. Only after considerable slaloming beneath the arches do you suddenly stumble upon a 55-metre (180ft)-long Renaissance structure with a choir, a **Capilla Mayor**, a 15-metre (50ft)-wide transept and a lavishly adorned ceiling. Its mixture of styles (Gothic, Renaissance, Italian and Baroque) required nearly a century of construction.

Outside the mosque but within its surrounding battlemented walls is the **Patio de los Naranjos**, entered through the **Puerta del Perdón** (Gate of Forgiveness) at the base of the Christian belfry that replaced the Islamic minaret. From nearby **Calleja de las Flores** (Alley of the Flowers), you can see the belfry framed in postcard splendour between the flower-studded walls of this narrow street.

Religious persecution

The site and size of Córdoba's **Judería** (Jewish Quarter) indicates that here, as elsewhere, the Jews were long considered a race apart. And like elsewhere, they were a learned, accomplished and wealthy breed that seemed never to be

Bronze statue of Moses Maimonides, a rabbi and philosopher born in Córdoba.

Patio de los Naranjos within the Mezquita's walls.

On the outskirts of the city is a Zoo and Wildlife Centre (Avenida de Linneo; tel: 957-200 807; Tue–Sun 9.30am–4.30pm), which has around 300 animals. The visitor centre has an interesting collection of animal bones.

allowed to prosper between periods of persecution. Disgruntled with their lot under the Visigoths, the Jews of Córdoba aided and abetted the Muslim victory; they subsequently enjoyed a welcome period of peace and prosperity under the tolerant Caliphate.

Córdoba was at one time home to the distinguished Muslim physicist, astrologer, mathematician, doctor and philosopher Averroës (who lived here from 1126 to 1198) and to Moses Maimonides (1135–1204), noted Jewish physician and philosopher. In Calle Maimonides today stands his monument, along with the remains of a 14th-century **Sinagoga** Ⓑ (Tue–Sun 9.30am–3.30pm; charge for non-EU citizens). Next to the synagogue is the Casa Andalusí (daily 10am–7.30pm; www.lacasaandalusi.com), a traditional Moorish house dating from the 12th century with a beautiful interior and patios. Just across from here, the **Casa de Sefarad** (www.casadesefarad.es; Mon–Fri 11am–6pm, Sat–Sun until 7pm) has a permanent exhibition about the Sephardic community in Córdoba, spread over five thematic rooms.

More Córdoba sights

Heirlooms deposited in the environs of Córdoba by the various tiers of its history are beautifully displayed in the **Museo Arqueológico** Ⓒ (Tue–Sat 9am–8.30pm, Sun until 3.30pm; charge for non-EU citizens) in the Plaza de Jerónimo Páez. Housed in a Renaissance palace of the same name, the extensive collection contains prehistoric, Roman, Visigothic, Islamic and Gothic remains. Particularly striking among them are a bronze stag from nearby Medina Azahara (see page 226), Iberian sculptures reminiscent of Chinese temple dogs and an original Roman foundation upon which the building rests. The museum also contains the world's largest collections of lead sarcophagi and Arabic capitals.

The 17th-century **Plaza de la Corredera** a little to the north is so named because of its earlier use for bullfights. The four-square, three-tiered structures house a lively morning food market, as well as a Saturday flea market. In contrast, the **Plaza del Potro** has remained vigorous since the

days when Cervantes allegedly stayed at the 15th-century *posada* in this square and wrote part of *Don Quijote*. The square's fountain-statue of a colt (*potro*) is mentioned in the book.

The **Museo Provincial de Bellas Artes ❶** (Tue–Sat 9am–8.30pm, Sun until 3.30pm), in an old hospital on the plaza, has a large collection of paintings, including several by Murillo, Zurbarán and Goya. Just across the courtyard is the **Museo Julio Romero de Torres** (Tue–Sat 8.30am–8.30pm, Sun until 2.30pm), which is devoted to the Córdoban-born artist (1874–1930). The large collection here includes many sensual studies of Córdoban women. For a spot of pampering, take a break from sightseeing at the **Hammam Baños Árabes** (Calle Corregidor Luis de la Cerda, 51; www.hammamalandalus.com; daily 10am–midnight), authentic Moorish-style steam baths a short stroll from the museum, where you can also enjoy an aromatherapy massage, followed by mint tea in the *tetería*.

Everywhere in the town you'll notice shops offering Córdoba's prime crafts in trade: silver filigree and stamped leather. Since the time of the Muslims these crafts have flourished here, but in the 16th and 17th centuries the latter in particular flourished through a prevailing fashion dictating that all walls and seats should be covered with leather, properly embossed, tooled, tinted and gilded. Just north of the Mezquita, the **Museo Arte Sobre Piel** (www.artesobrepiel.com, Mon–Sat 10.30am–2pm and 4.30–8pm) displays magnificent embossed and decorated leather pictures and artefacts in the style of the 10th-century Omeyan period.

A new addition to the Córdoban art scene is the concrete-heavy Espacio Andaluz de Creación Contemporánea, which houses artists' workshops and exhibition spaces.

The Alcázar

Just west of the Mezquita, near the much-restored **Puente Romano** (Roman Bridge) spanning the Río Guadalquivir, is the old **Alcázar de los Reyes Cristianos ❺** (Tue–Sat 8.30am–8.45pm, Sun until 2.30pm).

Calleja de las Flores (Alley of the Flowers).

Torahs inside Casa de Sefarad.

MAIMOINIDES

The most important figure of medieval Judaism was the philosopher and physician Moses ben Maimon (1135–1204), or Maimonides. He was born in Córdoba but forced into exile with his family when he was only 13, along with their co-religionists in the city. His best-known work is the *Dalalat al-Ha'irin (1190, Moreh Nebukim* in Hebrew and *Guide to the Perplexed* in English), which reconciles Judaism with Aristotelian thought. According to Maimonides, there is no contradiction between the truths of religion and the principles of metaphysics, as discovered by the human mind.

This proposition caused great arguments between Spain's liberal and conservative Jews but also influenced the development of Christian philosophy in the Middle Ages.

Built under Alfonso XI in 1328, it was the residence of Fernando and Isabel during their campaign against the Muslims in Andalusia. Islamic patios and extensive Arabic terraced gardens, with pools shaded by cypress trees, offer a respite from the summer heat; there are evening sound and light shows here in summer. Inside is a museum housing impressive Roman mosaics.

The original Roman bridge has in fact been rebuilt many times but retains its Roman foundations. At its southern end is the 14th-century **Torre de la Calahorra**. Inside the tower is the Museo Roger Garaudy (daily 10am–2.30pm and 4.30–8.30pm), with interesting sound and light displays that explain how Christians, Jews and Muslims coexisted in 10th-century Córdoba.

To the northeast of the city centre, on Plaza de Don Gome, is the **Palacio de Viana** (Tue–Sat 10am–7pm, Sun until 3pm, Jul–Aug 9am–3pm; www.palaciodeviana.com), an elegant 17th-century aristocratic home that is now a museum. It is packed with

artworks and antiques, porcelain and tapestries, but perhaps the most pleasing aspects are the 12 flower-filled interior courtyards and the delightful garden stocked with a variety of plants, including citrus and roses. On entering the first patio, note that the corner column has been deliberately omitted to facilitate the entrance of horse-drawn carriages.

Nearby is the **Plaza Santa Marina** and its monument to Manolete. Born Manuel Rodríguez in 1917, Manolete was a local boy who found fame and fortune in the bullrings. Unfortunately, he encountered an untimely death in 1947, by goring. Córdoba is famous for turning out the best bullfighters in Spain.

If you walk a little further west from Plaza Santa Marina, crossing Calle Alfaros, you will see the well-known crucifix **El Cristo de los Faroles**. It stands starkly in a hidden plaza surrounded by wrought-iron lanterns. A return visit at night is highly recommended, when the lanterns are alight and the crucifix can be seen in all its glory.

Gardens of the Alcázar de los Reyes Cristianos.

The Alhambra's Palacio Generalife.

GRANADA

'There is no pain in life so cruel as to be blind in Granada' is inscribed on the ramparts of the Alhambra. These words underline the city's unique beauty.

Granada is home to the world's finest Moorish monument: the Alhambra; walking through the Nasrid palaces and Generalife gardens is like taking a step back in time. In the grounds is one of Spain's finest hotels, the Parador de Granada. On the opposite hill to the Alhambra is the Albaicín, the oldest part of town, with narrow streets, Arab tearooms and great views, while back in the centre, the Capilla Real is the burial place of the Catholic Monarchs, King Ferdinand and Queen Isabel. Granada is forever associated with the writer Federico García Lorca, who was born in the village of Fuente Vaqueros.

Nature was generous in Granada, endowing the city with much greenery and placing it at the foot of three mountain spurs, from which it gracefully stretches up towards luminous blue skies against the blue-green backdrop of the Sierra Nevada to the southeast. To the west of the city is a broad, fertile *vega* (plain). To the north, the dainty Darro, a mountain stream, flows through the city between two of its three picturesque hills, those of the **Alhambra** and the **Albaicín**. The third hill, **Sacromonte**, is due north of the Alhambra. After the relative flatness of Seville and Córdoba, Granada's hills are a welcome change of scenic pace. For much of the year you can see snow on the Sierra Nevada, a popular winter retreat for skiers.

While Seville sprawls open-ended under the abundant Andalusian sunshine and Córdoba goes about its business with a minimum of fuss, Granada savours in its municipal valleys the romantic promise of the three hills that are the pillars of its tourism trade and the core of its own unique character.

Early history

Granada, the last stronghold and longest-running kingdom of the Muslims in Spain, began life as the obscure Iberian settlement of Elibyrge in the 5th

Main Attractions

Alhambra
Generalife
Capilla Real
Catedral
Albaicín
Sacromonte

Moroccan souk in the Albaicín quarter.

Moorish motifs decorate the pillars of Patio de los Leones.

century BC. From there it went on to become the equally obscure Illiberis of the Romans and Visigoths.

It is to the Muslims, then, that it owes a debt of gratitude for its current national and international stature. Its name derives from the Islamic 'Karnattah' and not from the Spanish word for pomegranate (*granada*), which it has nevertheless adopted as the city arms. While Seville and Córdoba both tasted wealth and glory under the Romans, Granada first knew grandeur as a provincial capital during the time of the caliphs of Córdoba. As Córdoba's prominence waned with the fall there of the Umayyads in 1031, Granada's political stock began to rise. For some 60 years the city was the capital of an independent kingdom, but inroads by the Almoravids eventually resulted in its integration into the kingdom of Seville.

When Jaén fell to the Christians in 1246 under the relentless assaults of Ferdinand III, Ibn al-Ahmar moved his capital to Granada and, as Mohammed I, founded the Nasrid dynasty that ruled for 250 years.

A golden age of prosperity

During this 'golden age' under the Muslims, the Jewish presence in Granada was important and strong. In fact, for a time Granada was known as the 'City of the Jews'. Here, as elsewhere in Muslim Spain, the Jews were doctors and philosophers and even diplomats and generals. Politically, however, Mohammed I found it expedient to remain on friendly terms with Christian Castile, and even went so far as to help Fernando III capture Seville, which little helped the *granadinos* ingratiate themselves thereafter with the *sevillanos*.

For the first time in its life, Granada was indisputably on top. In the wake of successive Christian victories in Córdoba, Seville and elsewhere throughout *al-Andalus*, Muslim refugees flocked to Granada, contributing to the trade and commerce of this up-and-coming kingdom. As surrounding Muslim kingdoms failed, Granada reaped an unprecedented prosperity. The fertile *vega* to the west enjoyed elaborate irrigation. Science, arts and the humanities flourished. Out of this impressive synergy of material, intellectual and

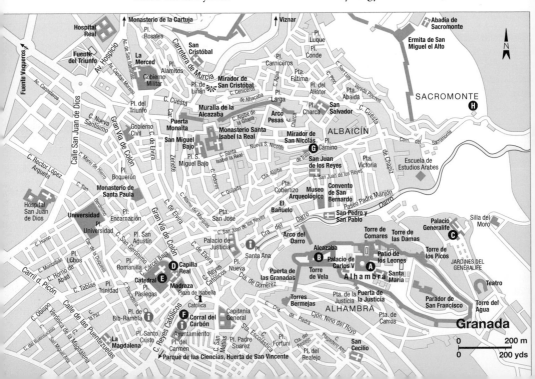

spiritual wellbeing was born the greatest triumph of Moorish art, the Alhambra During this period Granada's population swelled to 200,000, over four times that of the London of its day and just shy of its current head count.

The last Moorish stronghold

Then under Muley Hassan (1462–85) it all started to unravel over a family affair. Hassan fell in love with a Christian and entertained thoughts of repudiating his queen Ayesha, mother of his son Boabdil, for the beautiful Zoraya. Conjugal jealousy and concern for the regal inheritance of her son caused Ayesha to flee the city, which was already torn by feuds between the Abencerrajes, in support of her, and the Zegris, in support of Zoraya.

Mother and son soon returned, however, to dethrone Hassan and his brother, weakening the kingdom. Preying upon this weakness, Fernando V of Aragón captured Boabdil, the Boy King (El Rey Chico), offering him liberty at the price of remaining passive while the Catholic Monarchs gobbled up more and more of the Muslim territory. When in late 1491 Fernando and Isabel beat down the door of Granada, the city's spirit had already been broken and Boabdil put up only a token resistance. By 2 January 1492, the capture of the sole remaining stronghold of Muslim Spain was complete.

As the cross and banner of Castile cast their first Christian shadows across the 9th-century Alcazaba, Boabdil and his followers retired to the Alpujarras mountains. As Boabdil turned for a final look at the flickering glory of Granada, his mother allegedly reproved him, saying: 'You weep like a woman for what you could not hold as a man.' To this day that very spot is known as the Suspiro del Moro, the Moor's Sigh.

The resounding Godspeed that reverberated throughout Christendom with the fall of Granada never came to fruition. Religious intolerance culminating with the expulsion of the *moriscos* in 1609 drained the city of its most enterprising citizens and the glory they had wrought. By 1800, its population had dropped to just 40,000.

Today, like the rest of Andalusia, Granada is struggling following the economic crisis of 2008 but millions of tourists still come to enthuse over the artistic legacy that, after almost eight centuries of rule, was the swansong of the Muslims.

The Alhambra

The **Alhambra** Ⓐ (www.alhambra-patronato.es; daily, mid-Mar–mid-Oct 8.30am–8pm and Tue–Sat 8–9.30pm, mid-Oct–mid-Mar until 6pm and Fri–Sat 8–9.30pm; combined charge for the Nasrid Palaces, Alcazaba and Palacio Generalife; for ticket reservations see margin), the only surviving monument of Islamic Granada's great artistic outpouring, sits on a scarped ridge crowning a wooded hill. No amount of description can prepare you for its great playfulness or do justice to its exquisite delicacy and proportions. It is also Spain's most visited monument. Proclaimed one of the unofficial wonders of the world, it is the epitome of

View of the Alhambra from Mirador de San Nicolás.

TIP

Tickets to the Alhambra can sell out quickly, so purchase in advance: tel: 902-888 001 (from Spain) or 34-934-923 750 (from abroad), www.alhambra-tickets.es. Tickets have three parts: the Alcazaba, the Generalife and the Nasrid Palaces. The last can only be visited during the half-hour slot shown on the ticket: structure your visit accordingly, saving the Nasrid Palaces to the end if possible.

Patio de los Leones in the Alhambra.

Islamic imagination and artistry, the consummate expression of a sophisticated culture. Its pleasing splendour resides not in the architectural structures themselves, but in the masterful ornamentation that makes them seem almost an apparition, in the intricate delicacy of its carved wooden ceilings, the lace-like reliefs of its plaster walls, the repeated motifs of interlaced arabesques and the finely perforated tracery of the arched arcades on slender columns of white marble.

The Nasrid Palaces

Knowing a good thing when they saw it, the Catholic Monarchs had the Alhambra repaired and strengthened after their 1492 conquest and used it whenever they were in town. Subsequently, Carlos I (known as Charles V outside Spain), who had given the uninformed nod to the construction of the church inside Córdoba's mosque, deemed it insufficiently magnificent for him and had a section demolished to make way for his own palace in the 16th century. Beautiful in its own right as an example of the Italian Renaissance style, the **Palacio de**

Carlos V is nevertheless incongruous in its Aladdin's lamp setting.

The **Nasrid Palaces**, royal residence of the Muslims, lie at the heart of the Alhambra and are highlighted by the **Patio de los Arráyanes** (Patio of the Myrtles) and the **Patio de los Leones** (Patio of the Lions). The former is an open court measuring 37 metres x 23 metres (121ft x 75ft), bisected by a narrow fishpond tucked between hedges of myrtle. At either end, within the arcaded alcoves, you can see fine stalactite vaulting.

Off the northern end of this court is the lofty **Salón de los Embajadores**, the audience chamber of the Muslim kings. A dado of *azulejos* underscores the intertwining polychrome patterns and inscriptions stamped upon the stucco. Pairs of horseshoe windows admit enchanting views of Granada. And topping it all off is a domed ceiling of cedarwood.

Leading off the southern end is the Patio of the Lions (measuring 28 metres x 15 metres/90ft x 50ft), built around a massive antique fountain resting on the backs of 12 diminutive grey marble lions. Off its northern end is the **Sala de las Dos Hermanas** (Hall of the Two Sisters), containing the most elaborate of the Alhambra's honeycomb cupolas, said to comprise over 5,000 cells.

East of the Nasrid Palaces are the terraced **Partal Gardens** and charming **Torre de las Damas**.

Washington Irving

Some 19th-century writers were fortunate enough to spend some time in the Alhambra. During his three-month stay in 1829, Washington Irving began his *Tales of the Alhambra*, a collection of romantic sketches of the Muslims and Spaniards that still sells well in Granada's souvenir shops. Richard Ford, author of the *Hand-Book for Travellers in Spain*, paid the palace a visit in the summers of 1831 and 1833; and George Borrow, author of *The Bible in Spain*, visited in 1836.

The **Alcazaba** ❸ at the western extremity of Alhambra Hill was a 9th-century Islamic citadel. Today, its vista takes in the palace, the Generalife, the

Albaicín and Sacromonte sections of Granada, and the Sierra Nevada.

Gardens of seduction

Adjoining the Alhambra and overlooking both it and the city are the grounds of the former summer palace of the sultans, the **Palacio Generalife** **C** (same ticket as the Alhambra), dating from 1250. Blessed with gardens that far outclass the sparse beauty of its restored buildings, this palace is cool and green and full of restful pools and murmuring fountains.

Known in Arabic as *Jennat al-Arif*, meaning 'garden of the architect' (who remains unknown), it is filled with statuesque cypresses, diminutive shrubs, orange trees, hedges and flowers. Rumour has it that Boabdil's sultana kept trysts with her lover Hamet in the enclosed **Patio de los Cipreses**. Who can blame them? This garden is an invitation to indiscretion.

The **Patio de la Acequia** (Court of the Long Pond), within the gardens, has pretty pavilions at either end linked on one side by a gallery and on the other by the palace apartments. At some point be sure to pass along the **Camino de las Cascadas**, where runnels of water cascade down a series of conduits. Every summer from mid-June to the first week in July, the International Music and Dance Festival is staged in the grounds of the Generalife.

City sights

Away from the Alhambra, Granada has plenty more to offer. A decorative royal mausoleum, the exquisite **Capilla Real** **D** (www.capillarealgranada.com; Mon–Sat 10.15am–1.30pm and 3.30–6.30pm, Sun 11am–1.30pm and 2.30–5.30pm) was built when the Catholic Monarchs, proud of their conclusive victory over the Muslims, wished to be buried in the city where Muslim Spain met its final demise. Construction was commissioned by Fernando and Isabel, and took place between 1506 and 1521.

Many royal accessories, such as Isabel's sceptre and crown (a circle of gold embellished with acanthus scrolls) and Fernando's sword, are on display, and hanging in the sacristy are works from Isabel's own art collection, featuring 15th-century Flemish, Spanish and Italian paintings.

The stunning symmetry of the Patio de los Arrayánes (Patio of the Myrtles).

FEDERICO GARCÍA LORCA

Born in 1898 to wealthy landowners in the *vega* and raised in the city, poet and dramatist Lorca portrayed the Gypsy as exemplifying the most profound elements in the Andalusian psyche. *Gypsy Ballads*, published in 1928, brought him national fame. His plays, such as *Blood Wedding and Yerma*, were often based on folk themes and tended towards surrealism. But his political views – and his homosexuality – made him many enemies. He was in Granada in 1936 at the start of the Spanish Civil War and was arrested with hundreds of others and summarily executed by the Nationalists. A granite block in a memorial park near Viznar, 8km (5 miles) northeast of the city, marks the spot where he is believed to have been killed; his body was never found, although the supposed burial site was excavated in 2009.

TIP

To get your bearings,
consider taking a guided
tour of Granada.
Cicerone Culturo y Ocio
(tel: 607-691 676;
www.ciceronegranada.com)
regularly runs two-hour
walking tours of the
centre and Albaicín as
well as tours of the
Alhambra.

The **Catedral** (Mon–Sat 10am–6.30pm, Sun 3–6pm; http://catedralde granada.com) adjoins the Royal Chapel. Begun in 1523 in the Gothic style and continued in 1528 in the early Renaissance style, it has been described as 'one of the world's architectural tragedies, one of the saddest of wasted opportunities'. Not finished until 1714, it is a rather awkward structure.

Another interesting sight is the **Corral del Carbón**, a 14th-century market and inn later used as a coal store.

Taking a break

Sightseeing in Granada always seems to be more intense, more all-consuming than the other grand cities of the south. Perhaps it's the desire to drink in every last detail of the Alhambra, or to spend an afternoon just smelling the flowers of the Generalife. Whatever it is, there just doesn't seem to be enough time left to give the cafés and bars of Granada their proper due. In the heart of the city are cafés outfitted with marble columns and counters that evoke images of handlebar moustaches and pomaded hair, but in reality they are frequented by little old ladies in floral-print dresses and youths sipping their *café con leche*.

In the evening, crowds congregate at the **Plaza Bib-Rambla**, which was once the site of medieval jousts and bullfights. Just off the square is the maze-like **Alcaicería**, a colourful reproduction of the old Islamic souk that once stood here (it was destroyed by fire), and is now crammed with souvenir shops.

Albaicín and Sacromonte

The Albaicín quarter, the oldest part of Granada, covers a slope facing the Alhambra on the north side of the Río Darro. It was home to the first fortress of the Muslims and the haven to which they fled when the Christians reconquered the city. Today it offers the typical tangle of Andalusian alleys and simple whitewashed houses. It is home to tapas bars and Moroccan-style tea shops. Often the area's long walls signal luxuriant gardens discreetly enclosed. If you climb up the hill, the **Mirador de San Nicolás** offers a postcard view of the Alhambra. Further up, beyond the ruins of the Muslim walls, is the **Mirador de San Cristóbal**.

The **Sacromonte hill**, packed with picturesque cave dwellings, was at one time a Gypsy enclave. Most of the Gypsy families moved out decades ago, but the spirit survives in a handful of cave *zambras*, where flamenco shows are staged. It is strictly tourist fare, but among the performers there could be one destined for international fame, as more than one flamenco great has started their career here.

Fuente Vaqueros, 16km (10 miles) west of the city, was the birthplace of Federico García Lorca, one of the 20th century's greatest Spanish poets and dramatists (see page 211). The house where he lived is now the **Museo Casa Natal** (www.patronatogarcialorca.org; Tue–Sun tours at 10am, 11am, noon, 1pm, other times vary so check website).

The **Huerta de San Vincente**, an old farmhouse on Granada's southern outskirts where he wrote many famous works, is also open to the public (www. huertadesanvicente.com; Tue–Sun, times vary) and is surrounded by a lovely park.

Moroccan slippers on sale in the souk.

Dining room inside Federico García Lorca's native home in Fuente Vaqueros.

GRANADA'S GARDENS

From the intimacy of the patios to the spectacular gardens of the Generalife in Granada, Andalusia is a magnet for serious gardeners from all over the world.

Fertile soil and abundant sunshine make Andalusia a gardener's paradise, and the region is home to some outstanding gardens, including Seville's María Luisa Park and the gardens of the Generalife in Granada. But not everything is on a grand scale: peek into the *carmenes* (traditional Albaicín houses) in Granada and the patios in Córdoba.

For the Muslims, gardens were intimate places that aimed to appeal to all the senses. Aromatic plants such as mint and basil were key elements, as was the soothing sound of running water. Islamic homes were arranged around interior courtyards that provided a scented refuge from the heat, of which the patios of Córdoba are a living example. After the Muslims departed, the reigning style was the Italian garden of the Renaissance, designed to impress with proportioned layout, manicured aspect, statues and fountains. The Generalife gardens we see now owe more to this style than to the Islamic.

Each subsequent lot of settlers brought with them their preferred plants. The Phoenicians, Greeks and Romans introduced olive trees, date palms and grape vines. The Muslims brought orange trees and a great many herbs and flowers native to Asia. Explorations of new continents added to this botanical wealth. Geraniums came from southern Africa, while mimosas are originally from Australia, wisteria from Asia and bougainvillea from South America.

The Generalife in Granada is Spain's most famous garden. Originally an Islamic royal summer residence, its present layout owes more to Italian influences.

The gardens of Alcázar de los Reyes Christianos, in Córdoba, which combine Islamic patios with Arabic terraced gardens and pools of water. Muslim gardens were designed to appeal t all the senses.

Pigeons congregate around a tiled fountain in the Parque de María Luisa's Plaza de América. This Seville park was donate to the city by Princess María Luisa de Orleans in 1893.

Pools and fountains in the former summer palace, the Palacio Generalife, in Granada.

THE WONDER OF WATER

Thanks to their talent as engineers, the Romans tapped Andalusia's water resources, and their canals and aqueducts turned the region into the breadbasket of the empire. But it was the Muslims who, adapting and improving on the Roman irrigation system, regarded water as an aesthetic element as well. Fountains, pools and elaborate channels, such as the 'water stairway' in the Generalife gardens, filled the air with soothing sound and helped keep summer temperatures down. The water staircase was also used as a means of amusement: it was possible to turn the water on or increase the flow without being seen and wetting the feet of whomever was there. Water had a symbolic significance for the Muslims. Gardens were divided into four sections separated by channels of water representing the four Rivers of Life. Fountains symbolised the source of life. Taking a leaf from the Muslims' gardening book, Christian landscapers capitalised on water's use for dramatic visual effect, especially with exquisite fountains, such as in the Patio de la Madama in the 17th-century Palacio de Viana in Córdoba.

e pretty gardens of the Alcázar in Jerez de la Frontera.

batio in Córdoba. These cool, intimate spaces are a legacy of amic times. The Muslims, coming as they did from the desert, re especially fond of shady patios and gardens.

Geraniums are often considered the quintessential Andalusian flower. Yet, like so many of Andalusia's plants, it is an introduced variety; it was originally from South Africa.

ANDALUSIA

There is an extraordinary diversity of landscape, lifestyle and culture that sets Andalusia apart from the rest of Spain. From the tourist-driven costas to the simple, unspoiled *pueblos blancos* (white villages), this region has plenty to explore.

Main Attractions

Doñana National Park
Cádiz
Jerez de la Frontera
Gibraltar
Ronda
Museo Picasso, Málaga
Medina Azahara
Baeza and Úbeda

Andalusia has much to offer visitors, from the beaches of the Costa del Sol to Spain's largest national park, Parc Nacional de Doñana. Columbus set sail to the New World from the small town of Huelva and it was thanks to him that Cádiz rose to become one of the wealthiest ports in Western Europe. Inland are the famous 'white towns', including Ronda, famed for its bullfighting, and picture-perfect Arcos de la Frontera. Jerez is the place to sample sherry while Tarifa is the capital of water sports. Finally, no visit to Andalucia would be complete without seeing Málaga, birthplace of Pablo Picasso.

Within the area defined by Seville, Córdoba, Granada and the Mediterranean Sea there lies much to be seen and enjoyed. This is Andalusia, where life means simplicity, peace and hospitality. Whether you spend your holiday vagabonding from village to village or simply make inland excursions from the coast, you will marvel at the spontaneous beauty and variety of Spain's landscape. Like set changes in the theatre, Andalusia's villages and vistas seem to spring suddenly out of thin, dry air. The only constant in this ever-shifting scene is the ubiquitous olive tree.

Dunes and wetland

The **Parque Nacional de Doñana ①** (www.donanavisitas.es; tel: 959-430 432;

book guided tours in advance; June–Sept no tour on Sundays) is Spain's biggest national park, straddling more than 50,000 hectares (125,000 acres) of the Huelva and Seville provinces.

Most of the park is a special reserve, but organised tours in four-wheel-drive vehicles, starting from the visitors' centre (daily, June–Sept 8am–9pm, Oct–May 8am–7pm) at **El Acebuche**, leave twice a day for a four-hour journey through the inner areas of the reserve. The route follows the beach, where oystercatchers and dunlins scurry among

The Andalusian horse is an ancient breed.

FACT

A little to the south of Huelva at Punta del Sebo by the Rio Tinto, is the Monumento a Colón. This 34-metre (112ft) statue sculpted by Gertrude Vanderbilt Whitney was a gift from the US in honour of the 'discoverers' of America. Underneath is a small chapel.

the broken waves, and sandwich terns and black-eyed gulls swoop low across the sand. Once at the Guadalquivir estuary, the convoy swings towards the centre of the park, through pine forest and Mediterranean brush.

As you travel, guides helpfully point out red stag deer, fallow deer and boars. At the edge of the lakes and marshes you may see flocks of pink flamingos, greylags and spoonbills. The rare imperial eagle may also be spotted, surveying his empire from the topmost branches of a pine. The vehicles then turn back towards the ocean, through more pines to the dunes; these moving mountains of sand are slowly burying part of the pine wood.

The outskirts of the park may be explored on foot via a choice of self-guided paths. **El Rocío**, located on the northern fringe, makes a good base; the village is more famous for its annual *romería* (pilgrimage) 40 days after Easter Sunday (www.rocio.com).

On the Columbus trail

The small provincial city of **Huelva** ❷ lies 80km (48 miles) west of **Seville**

(see page 187) along the A-49. It has been somewhat spoilt by industrial development, but nevertheless retains a refreshingly innocent, small-town atmosphere, especially along its Gran Via. The **Museo Provincial** (www.museosdeandalucia.es; Alameda Sundheim, 13; Tue–Sun Junc–mid-Sept 9am–3.30pm, mid-Sep–May 9.30am–7.30pm, Sun am only; no charge for EU citizens) has exhibits celebrating Columbus's voyage to the New World in 1492; he set sail from Palos de la Frontera, just across the Odiel estuary, on 3 August that year.

The 13th-century **Monasterio de la Rábida** (www.monasteriodelarabida.com; Tue–Sat 10am–1pm and 4–6.15pm, Sun from 10.45am, summer until 7pm), 4km (2.5 miles) north of Palos, is a complete contrast to the industry around it. This is where Columbus met the friars Antonio de Marchena and Juan Pérez, who took his case to Queen Isabela and persuaded her to back the venture. Inside are the Columbus murals painted by Vázquez Díaz in 1930.

The coast of light

Andalusia's breezy Atlantic coast, the **Costa de la Luz**, stretches south from Huelva all the way to Cádiz and **Tarifa**, famous throughout Europe for its wind- and kitesurfing; the white sandy beaches along this coastline are relatively unspoilt, especially when compared to the adjacent Costa del Sol.

Sanlúcar de Barrameda ❸, best known for its production of manzanilla, a light, dry sherry, is a flourishing resort and fishing port less than an hour's drive from Seville on the A-4 and A-480. The town looks across the mouth of the Guadalquivir to the Doñana Park's marshlands. Sanlúcar is one of the three towns that comprise the 'Sherry Triangle' where the legendary aperitif wine is made. The others are Jerez (see page 219) and **Puerto de Santa María**, a crusty port on the Cádiz Bay. Aside from its sherry, Puerto is known for its shellfish, sold

Cádiz Cathedral.

at numerous establishments along the seafront promenade, known as Ribera del Marisco ('shellfish row').

Cádiz ❹, whose safe inner harbour first attracted the Phoenicians in 1100 BC, is on the other side of the bay. The Carthaginians arrived in 501 BC, followed by the Romans under whom 'Gades', as it was known, prospered. However, its importance declined under the succeeding Visigoths and Muslims. With the 'discovery' of America, Cádiz rose again to become the wealthiest port in Western Europe and, as a result, the target of attack for the Barbary corsairs and the envious English naval fleet. Sir Francis Drake burned ships at anchor here in 1587, delaying the sending of the Armada and boasting afterwards that he 'had singed the King of Spain's beard.'

The long history of Cádiz can be traced at the **Museo de las Cortes** (Santa Inés, 9; Tue–Fri 9am–6pm, Sat–Sun until 2pm; free), which contains a remarkable model of Cádiz as it was in 1777, and the **Museo de Cádiz** (www. museosdeandalucia.es; mid Jun–mid-Sept Tue–Sun 9am–3.30pm, mid-Sep–mid-June Tue–Sat 9am–8.30pm, Sun 9am–3.30pm; free for EU citizens) on Plaza Mina, with its two Phoenician sarcophagi.

The narrow streets of the old city are dotted with churches and monuments, the most notable being the **Catedral** (cathedral; www.catedralde cadiz.com; Mon–Sat 10am–8pm, Sun 1.30–8pm). It is a grandiose 18th-century structure capped by a Byzantine-style dome of golden tiles. In the crypt lies the tomb of composer Manuel de Falla, whose music is evocative of the magic of Andalusia.

The cathedral also houses an ecclesiastical museum (daily 10am–4pm), and you can climb the Torre de Poniente (Western Tower; daily 10am–8pm) to enjoy panoramic views of the old city. Despite its vacillating fortunes and the somewhat ramshackle appearance of some quarters, the *gaditanos* love their town and have a reputation

for being among the liveliest of Andalusians. Many leading flamenco artists hail from the Bay of Cádiz and the city runs wild every year during the crazy days of Carnival.

Sherry country

The rolling landscape between **Jerez de la Frontera ❺** and the Atlantic, known as the 'Sherry Triangle', is ideally suited to raising the grapes that the wineries of Jerez convert into extraordinary sherries and brandies. Tours and tastings are informative and readily intoxicating.

The city's annual Feria del Caballo (Horse Show) is held at the start of May. Proud of its pure-bred line of Carthusian horses, Jerez shows them off in racing, dressage and carriage competitions.

All year round these handsome Arabian animals can also be seen at the **Real Escuela Andaluza del Arte Ecuestre** (visit www.realescuela.org for show times).

Also in Jerez are the remains of an 11th-century **Alcázar**, or Moorish fortified palace (Sat–Sun 9.30am–2.30pm,

The Tourist Office publishes a useful map of the pueblos blancos (white villages). If you need a room for the night, enquire at the respective local tourist office or even at the local bar.

Training at the Royal Andalusian School of Equestrian Art, Jerez.

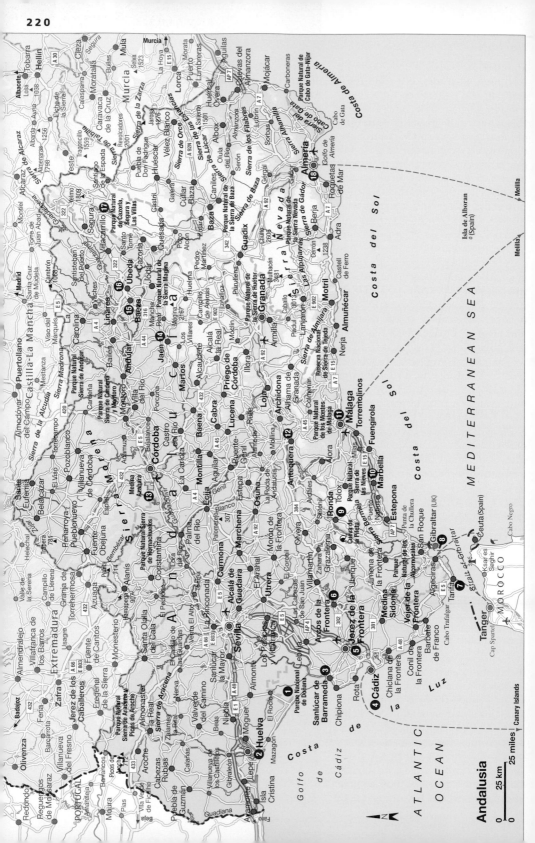

Andalusia

0   25 km

0   25 miles

Mon–Fri July–mid-Sept until 7.30pm, Apr–June and mid-Sept–Oct until 5.30pm, Nov–Mar until 2.30pm), enclosing a small chapel, and the lovely Palacio Villavicencio, built on the site of a former mosque and Moorish palace respectively and surrounded by pretty gardens. Climb to the top of the tower for stunning panoramic views accompanied by a multilingual commentary.

Arcos de la Frontera 6 (pop. over 31,000) sits on a sharp ridge above a loop of the Río Guadalete. Steep streets lead up to the panoramic Parador looking out across the mottled browns and greens of Andalusia's farmland and the blue of a large reservoir (Embalse de Arcos). This is considered the archetypal *pueblo blanco* (white village) – the term used to describe the innumerable small villages of the Andalusian hinterland whose sparkling whitewashed houses cap the mountaintops or tumble down their slopes. In common with Arcos, many of the white towns share the tag *de la frontera* ('of the border'), a reminder of their location on the contentious frontier between Christianity and Islam.

North of the Arcos–Grazalema road is **Prado del Rey** (the King's Field). Founded by King Carlos III in 1768 in an attempt to stimulate agricultural reform in Andalusia, this town is something of an early Spanish garden city, with wide streets and leafy squares.

Back on the coast road (A-48/N-340) south from Cádiz, past the white hilltop town of **Vejer de la Frontera** are the remains of the Roman city of **Baelo Claudia** (follow signs for Bolonia), founded in 171 BC. Today you can see remains of an amphitheatre, paved forum and streets. There is also a visitors' centre (www.museosdeandalucia.es; Sun 9am–3.30pm, Tue–Sat June–mid-Sept 9am–3.30pm, Apr–June until 8.30pm, mid-Sept–Mar until 6.30pm; free for EU citizens).

The road eventually arrives at **Tarifa 7**. This Moorish walled town is at the southernmost point of Europe, just 13km (8 miles) and a 35-minute boat ride from Tangier across the Strait of Gibraltar. It is on the cusp of the Atlantic and Mediterranean and a mecca for wind- and kitesurfing. The surrounding unspoilt countryside and vast sandy beaches are becoming increasingly fashionable among those seeking a change from package holidays and rampant development.

The ugly industrial chaos around **Algeciras** can be seen from the motorway on the main route to Gibraltar and the Costa del Sol. Algeciras is the main Spanish ferry port for the North African destinations of Ceuta and Tangier.

The Rock

The unmistakable profile of the limestone Rock of **Gibraltar 8** stands at the very tip of the Iberian peninsula, across the bay from Algeciras. Peaking at 425 metres (1,396ft), the territory measures less than 7 sq km (3 sq miles), yet it is home to around 32,000 people.

To enter Gibraltar, you need to possess a valid passport or identity card. It is a good idea to leave your car behind in the Spanish border town of La Linea,

On a sherry tour.

ANDALUSIA'S FINE WINE

Abroad, the name sherry may conjure up images of a sweet, creamy aperitif but Jerez is better known in Andalusia for an entirely different style of fortified wine, *fino*. Pale straw-yellow and usually around 15 percent alcohol by volume, *fino* is the drink of choice served during fiestas and is often drunk at other times accompanied by a choice of savoury tapas, particularly olives, fish and shellfish and cured ham. It is described officially as having 'a sharp, delicate bouquet slightly reminiscent of almonds with a hint of fresh dough and wild herbs'. The important thing is that it must be served chilled, at been 7 and 9°C. *Fino* is made from palomino grapes and the key is in the development by the yeast of a film of flor which protects the wine from oxidations during fermentation and gives it distinctive characteristics. Jerez de la Frontera is the best-known production area but good *fino* also comes from the Montilla-Moriles wine region of Córdoba province. Try some for yourself at one of the many bodegas in Jerez such as Bodegas Tradición (www.bodegastradicion.es), Bodegas Sandeman (www.sandeman.eu) or Bodegas Tio Pepe (www.bodegastiopepe.com), which offers a variety of themed visits including cooking with sherry and tastings accompanied by classical music or a horse show.

and take a taxi or bus from the border into Gibraltar town, as the colony's maze of narrow streets is invariably congested, and most sights can be reached easily on foot, or by minibus or cable car.

Since 1704 Gibraltar, one of the ancient Pillars of Hercules, has been a bone of contention between Britain and Spain. Before that it had been passed back and forth between the Spaniards and the Muslims, who first took it in 711 under the Berber leadership of Tariq ibn Zeyad and gave it its name 'Gebel Tarik', the mountain of Tariq. The Moorish castle, now in ruins, was his legacy. In 1462, the Spanish regained it one last time before the British seized it in 1704. It has been a bone of contention on and off between the two countries since then. In 1969 Franco closed the border during a particularly tense dispute; then in 2013 trouble started brewing again after Gibraltar constructed an artificial reef in the Bay of Algeciras, interfering – according to the Spanish government – with the local fishing fleet. The UK's eventual departure from the EU is likely to reignite conflict.

Puente Nuevo spans El Tajo gorge in Ronda.

Wildlife

This seemingly barren rock enjoys some fame for its wildlife. The origin of its distinctive Barbary apes is not known, but they are not found on the Spanish mainland. Among the variety of birds that stop here on their annual migrations to Europe are honey buzzards, griffon vultures, black storks and short-toed eagles. A good place to see them is the **Upper Rock Nature Reserve** (daily 9.30am–7.15pm, winter until 6.45pm).

A curious military feat is the Great Siege Tunnels or **Upper Galleries** (same hours as above) tunnelled into the rock at the time of the Great Siege by France and Spain between 1779 and 1783. By the end of this war the tunnel measured 113 metres (370ft). Curious, too, is the evident cultural mixture on the Rock. Arab women in full-length dress and modified *chador* cross paths with British officers, Spanish-speaking merchants and dark-skinned descendants of the Muslims.

Equally mixed are the linguistics. In a local bar the TV plays in Spanish and the radio in English, while the bartender speaks with a hybrid accent.

Bandido country

Heading inland from the coast on the A-405/A-369 towards Ronda, the countryside gradually grows wilder. In the 19th century, travelling here meant taking your life in your hands, as the hills were full of highwaymen. During and after the Civil War, the more remote of these villages harboured Republican refugees.

To reach **Castellar** (bypassing the 'new' Castellar, built in the 1960s), a road signposted 'Castillo de Castellar' climbs a rocky hillside. The archetypal castle stands like a lone sentinel on top of a craggy outcrop, enclosing an entire village. The inconvenient location meant it was abandoned and crumbled for years, until new residents moved in. Some houses in the castle grounds were restored as self-catering holiday accommodation (Hotel Rural Castillo Castellar). The next castle, too, sits on its own hilltop, crumbling. At its feet, the town of **Jimena de la Frontera** spills like white paint down the hillside where mules graze below on the steep, grassy slopes. Between Jimena and Ronda, a distance of about 56km (35 miles), stop somewhere by the roadside and indulge your senses. The scent of herbs perfumes a silence smooth as silk.

Whether you approach **Ronda** ❾ from the north or south, you are given no clues that you are about to enter a bustling town of almost 37,000 perched on a rocky bluff with sheer walls falling away a dramatic 180 metres (600ft) on three sides. A deep ravine some 90 metres (300ft) wide divides the old and new sections.

Near the **Puente Nuevo** (New Bridge) that links the old and new towns a path leads down to a fine view of this bridge that spans the vertiginous gorge. It is beautifully unobtrusive in design, allowing the magnificent scenery to shine through. Begun in 1755, after a previous effort collapsed, it seems to have been first opened for transit in 1784; its architect, José Martín de Aldehuela, fell

to his death inspecting the structure shortly before its completion. Once it was open, tightly corseted Ronda spilled out onto the tableland known as the Mercadillo, which until then had been used mainly for markets and fairs. Thanks to its auspicious position, Ronda was virtually impregnable, remaining the capital of an isolated Islamic kingdom until 1485.

The 18th-century **Plaza de Toros** (www.rmcr.org; daily, Apr–Sept 10am–8pm, Mar and Oct until 7pm, Nov–Feb until 6pm) is one of the oldest bullrings in Spain and contains a museum displaying *trajes de luces* (bullfighters' suits), documents, photos, posters and Goya prints pertaining to this uniquely Spanish art.

The sierra around Ronda

Throughout the **Serranía de Ronda**, the mountain range surrounding the city, are more storybook white towns. **Grazalema**, 32km (20 miles) west of Ronda, boasts that it gets more rain than anywhere else in Spain. Long a haunt of smugglers and brigands, it was described by Ford as a 'cut-throat

Legend has it that the British will remain in Gibraltar as long as the Barbary apes survive. When extinction threatened them in 1944, Churchill ordered reinforcements.

Ronda's old town.

FACT

It was in Ronda that bullfighting on foot first began early in the 18th century, when a noble and his horse were upended by a bull's charge. A bystander leapt into the ring and, using his hat as a lure, managed to draw the bull away from the hapless rider.

den'. These days it is more welcoming, with several hotels and a thriving artists' community. It is also the gateway to the nature reserve bearing its name. Set up in 1984, the reserve extends from **El Bosque**, where there is a small information centre, to Benaoján in the east and Cortes de la Frontera to the south. Much of the Mediterranean forest of holm oak and Montpelier maple still survives, but some areas have been converted to open ranges or brush. Here mountain goats and a superb range of birds of prey can be seen, including buzzards, griffon vultures, and Bonelli's, booted and short-toed eagles.

The **Cueva de la Pileta** (www.cueva delapileta.org; guided tours daily Apr–Sept 10am–1pm and 4–6pm, Oct–Mar until 5pm), with some remarkable prehistoric animal paintings, is signposted from the MA-8401 about 4km (2.5 miles) south of Benaoján. The paintings were discovered by a local farmer in 1905 while he was out looking for *guano* (bird droppings) to manure his fields. Perhaps the most impressive painting is one depicting a huge fish that seems to have swallowed a seal.

Not far away, through wild, pine-clad sierras, at the foot of a mountain, lies **Ubrique**, specially noted for its leatherwork. Most of these villages have spectacular settings, but that of **Zahara** ('de la Sierra' to distinguish it from Zahara de los Atunes on the Costa de la Luz) is truly breathtaking. A brilliant beacon of white, it stands on a steep crag northwest of Ronda. It offers another ancient castle and superb views. In contrast, much of the village of picturesque **Setenil** huddles in a chasm, its houses built right under dramatic lips of rock.

Costa del Sol

Most of the Sunshine Coast is in Málaga province, running from east of Gibraltar to the province of Granada. Development has been heavy – often excessive – all along the coast. However, there are still some nooks and crannies where you can avoid the crowds, as in the western section between Gibraltar and San Pedro.

Estepona, the most westerly of the Costa's swollen fishing villages and now a large town, has so far avoided too many high-rises and remains Spanish, with an old quarter of narrow streets and bars. From here on the pace quickens and the crowds thicken, with lush green golf courses interspersed with luxury villas.

The area between the flashy marina Puerto Banus and **Marbella** ⑩ is known as the Golden Mile and is the playground of celebrities, sheikhs, millionaires, royalty and bullfighters. Expensive restaurants, a casino, signs in Arabic and a mosque testify to the presence of Middle Eastern oil money. In the centre of Marbella, the old town remains picturesque, with the Plaza de los Naranjos as its showpiece. On a hot summer night this plaza becomes one vast open-air restaurant, and it can delight even hardened Costa-watchers.

The coast goes downmarket approaching **Fuengirola**. From there

Puerto Banus marina.

to Málaga tourist traffic is intense. Poor old **Torremolinos** has long suffered from a serious image problem as an apparent haven for beer-swilling youths, the spam-and-chips crowd, coach tours of grannies and a dazzling transvestite scene. These days stricter building regulations are in place, the discos have moved to Benalmádena Costa and lush landscaping has vastly improved the town centre.

Picasso's birthplace

Málaga ⓫ (pop. 569,000) is the capital of the Costa del Sol. However, it is not a resort but a bustling port founded by the Phoenicians. Its citizens sided briefly with Carthage before becoming a Roman *municipium* (a town governed by its own laws). In 711 it fell to the Muslims within a year of their invasion of Spain and was the port of the kingdom of Granada until 1487, when it was taken by the Christians after a four-month siege.

Málaga's historical ruins can be found mainly at the eastern end of the city. The 11th-century Islamic **Alcazaba** (daily summer 9am–8pm, winter 8.30am–6pm) is a maze of pretty gardens and courtyards. It is connected to the ruined 14th-century Islamic **Castillo de Gibralfaro** (opening times as Alcazaba) by a formidable double-walled rampart, while a rocky path climbs beside it. A *mirador* gives a view over the harbour and down to Málaga's bullring.

The **Catedral** (Mon–Fri 10am–6pm, Sat until 5pm; night visits possible; roof: only guided tours every hour from 11am), designed by Pedro de Mena in the 16th century, is further west on Calle Molina Lario, towards the dry river bed of the Río Guadalmedina. The grandiose cathedral's east tower was never completed, giving it the nickname La Manquita – 'the one-armed one'.

Between the Alcazaba and cathedral, at Calle San Agustín, 8, is the Palacio de Buenavista, housing the **Museo Picasso** (www.museopicassomalaga.org;

daily Jul–Aug 10am–8pm, Mar–June and Sep–Oct until 7pm, Nov–Feb 6pm; free last two hours on Sun), with a collection that spans Picasso's entire career; the majority of works were donated by his daughter-in-law Cristina. A short walk north from here is the **Casa Natal de Picasso** (http://fundacionpicasso.malaga.eu; daily 9.30am–8pm; free Sun from 4pm) at Plaza de la Merced, 15, where the artist spent his first years. The house is now a small museum containing some early sketches, ceramics, and family memorabilia, including photographs and Picasso's christening robe.

In recent years Málaga has reinvented itself as more than just Picasso's birthplace but as an arts hub with four other great museums. West of Plaza de la Constitución on Calle Compañia is the **Museo Carmen Thyssen** (www.carmen thyssenmalaga.org; Tue–Sun 10am–8pm; free Sun from 5pm). Housed in a renovated 16th-century palace, this museum focuses on Spanish and Andalusian art in the 19th century and includes works by Sorolla and Zurbarán. The colourful cubic building of the **Centre**

Plaza de la Constitución, Málaga.

Plaza de la Merced, Málaga.

TIP

Learn about Málaga's
gastronomy on one of
the daily guided
'gourmet' tours of the
city's best food shops
and markets run by We
Love Málaga (tel:
646-543 566; www.we
lovemalaga.com). They also
offer 'tapas' tours,
'flamenco and tapas'
tours and regular
walking tours of the city.
Book well in advance.

Pompidou Málaga (http://centrepompi
dou-malaga.eu; Wed–Sun 9.30am–8pm;
free Sun from 4pm) showcases contemporary works from the original Centre
Pompidou in Paris, in rotation every
five semesters, as well as two or three
temporary exhibitions. The **Centro de
Arte Contemporáneo de Málaga CAC**
(http://cacmalaga.eu, Tue–Sun 10am–8pm,
summer 10am–2pm, 5–9pm; free) promotes visual arts, and the **Colección del
Museo Ruso** (www.coleccionmuseoruso.
es; Tue–Sun 10am–8pm; free Sun from
4pm) is the Spanish branch of the State
Russian Museum presenting a vast Russian art collection.

Also worth a look is the **Museo
Automovilistico y de la Moda** (Fashion and Automobile Museum; www.
museoautomovilmalaga.com; Tue–Sun
10am–7pm), with its vintage car and
fashion displays.

For a peaceful and thought-provoking haven from Málaga's careering
traffic, visit the **Jardín Botánico La
Concepción** (www.laconcepcion.malaga.
eu; Tue–Sun, Apr–Sept 9.30am–7.30pm,
Oct–Mar until 4.30pm), located 4km
(2.5 miles) north of the city centre.

*View from the
Alcazaba over the
bullring, Málaga.*

This fabulous botanical garden dates
back to the mid-19th century and is
lushly planted with hundreds of palms
and tropical plants, with ponds, water
features and evocative statues.

Dolmens and caves

About 50km (32 miles) north of Málaga
on the A-45, **Antequera** ⑫ is an attractive town with innumerable churches
and convents. Seek out the Islamic **Castillo**, near the 16th-century Iglesia de
Santa María la Mayor, for a fine view.
To the east, a curiously shaped rock, the
Peña de los Enamorados, gets its name
from a legend of two thwarted lovers
who hurled themselves off the top.

Antequera's most unusual attractions are three dolmens which were
constructed with huge slabs of rock
in around 2000 BC. The **Cuevas de
Menga** and **Viera** (www.museosean
dalucia.es; Sun 10am–5pm, Tue–Sat
June–mid-Sept 9am–3.30pm, Apr–
June until 7.30pm, mid-Sept–Mar
until 5.30pm; free) are close together
on the edge of town, while the **Cueva
de Romeral** (same opening times) is
down the road near a defunct sugar
factory, where a guardian is on duty.

Back on the coast, east of Málaga,
Nerja is one of the larger resorts on this
part of the coast and offers some vast
caves nearby (www.cuevadenerja.com; daily
9am–4pm, July–Aug 9am–6.30pm). A
2km (1.2-mile) path leads through the
colourfully lit caverns. As yet, the full
extent of this underground wonder-
land remains unknown. But what there
is, is wonder enough. It is like an underground cathedral in an abstract Gaudí
style with stalactite pipe organs and sta-
lagmite spires. Every July these bizarre
natural sculptures are the backdrop for
a festival of music and ballet.

Some finds from the caves are on
display in the **Museo de Nerja** (Plaza
de España; www.cuevadenerja.es; daily,
same opening times as caves).

Medina Azahara

Eight kilometres (5 miles) northwest
of **Córdoba** (see page 199) stand the

emerging remains of **Medina Aza-hara** ⑬ (www.medinaazahara.org; Sun 9am–3.30pm, Tue–Sat mid-June–mid-Sept 9am–3.30pm, Apr–mid-June until 8.30pm, mid-Sep–Mar until 6.30pm; free for EU citizens), an extensive palace complex begun around 936 by Abd-al-Rahman III to satisfy the caprices of his favourite wife Zahara.

The new city stretched up the Sierra de Córdoba, the foothills of the Sierra Morena, adapting itself gracefully to the three-level terraced terrain. The highest level contains the **Alcázar**; the middle, the gardens and orchards; and the lowest, the mosque and city proper. The account of its construction, as rendered by Arab historian El-Makkari, gives some impression of its scale. Ten thousand men, 2,600 mules and 400 camels worked for 25 years, he reports, to erect the palace, gardens, fishponds, mosque, baths and schools. The royal entourage included some 12,000 men, 4,000 servants and 2,000 horses. There were hanging gardens, aviaries, zoos, streams, courts, gold fountains and a quicksilver pool.

But the life of the city was as fleeting as its very being was fantastic. In 1010, just 74 years after its conception, the Berbers attacked and burnt it. Find out about its history in the excellent new on-site museum.

Two historical towns lie between Córdoba and Seville. **Carmona**, on the main A-4 route, was an important Roman centre. Its well-laid-out **Necrópolis Romana** (www.museosde andalucia.es; Sun 9am–3.30pm, Tue–Sat mid-Jun–mid-Sept 9am–3.30pm, Apr–mid-June until 8.30pm, mid-Sep–Mar until 6.30pm; free for EU citizens) on the western extremity of the town shows the walls of the crematorium still discoloured by the heat of the fire.

Écija, 56km (34 miles) east, is built in a valley bowl with no summer breeze to relieve the heat. The ancient town is littered with (crumbling) Baroque church towers, the most notable being that of the **Iglesia de Santa María** (daily). The covered market is colourful, and Calle Caballeros (north of the main square) has several rambling and ornate merchants' houses, including the **Palacio de Peñaflor**

Ruins of Medina Azahara, on the outskirts of Córdoba.

(closed for renovation until the end of 2017), with its painted facade and unusual curved balcony.

Jaén province

A massive undulating area of 150 million olive trees dominating the landscape, Jaén province has always suffered from being a place to drive through rather than to stay. The north–south artery, the A-44, which brings you into the province, takes you directly to the provincial capital, **Jaén** . Perched above the western plain with its back to the sierras, the city has surprisingly few monuments. But what it lacks in quantity it makes up for in scale.

The **Catedral** (daily; www.catedral dejaen.org) is a massive pile built over three centuries, with a wonderful mixture of Gothic to Baroque styles. The 11th-century **Baños Arabes** (www. xn-baosarabesjaen-rnb.es; Tue–Sat 9am–10pm, Sun 9am–3pm; free), superbly excavated and restored, are among the largest and best-preserved in Spain. The city streets, in both the commercial zone and the old town stacked against the hillside, have an energy you find only in such self-possessed Spanish provincial cities.

Baeza ⑮, 40km (25 miles) northeast of the provincial capital, is an architectural gem, its honey-coloured palaces, churches and civic buildings dating chiefly to the 15th–17th centuries. Star features include the studded **Palacio de Jabalquinto** and nearby, on Plaza Santa María, the **Santa Iglesia Catedral** (daily), which was largely rebuilt in the 16th century.

The real focus of interest, however, is the **Plaza de los Leones** to the west of the centre, which is clustered with splendid Renaissance architecture. Overlooking the fountain in the middle of the square are the **Puerta de Jaén** and the adjoining **Arco de Villalar**. On the north side of the square you can see the **Antigua Carnicería**, a 16th-century butcher's shop.

A few steps away, on Paseo Cardenal Benavides, is the **Ayuntamiento** (town hall; Mon–Fri am only), a magnificent Plateresque building that was once a courthouse and jail.

Only 10km (6 miles) further north along the A-316 is the larger town of **Úbeda** ⑯, another Renaissance jewel. The **Plaza de Vázquez de Molina** – an architectural set piece in a class of its own – is unmissable. The rectangular plaza runs down from the stunningly rich-domed **Capilla del Salvador**, which was built as a family pantheon and is still privately owned by the Duques de Medinaceli. As it widens out, the plaza reveals a balanced, beautifully proportioned sequence of austere palaces unbroken by modern additions considered by many to be the purest architectural expression of the Renaissance in Spain. In 2006, an ancient synagogue was discovered and is open for guided tours (www.sinagogadelagua.com).

At the far end is the church of **Santa María de los Reales Alcázares**, built on the site of the old mosque. Also worth seeking out are the **Iglesia de San Pablo** for its impressive Plateresque tower, and the **Hospital de Santiago**, designed by Andrés de

Capilla del Salvador, Úbeda.

Vandelvira and now a cultural centre, which is sometimes compared to El Escorial for its severity of style.

The town of **Cazorla**, to the east of Úbeda, is a good access point for the **Parque Natural de Cazorla ⑰** (www.sierrasdecazorlaseguraylasvillas.es; information and maps at the Centro de Interpretación Torre del Vinagre, off the A-319 16km (9 miles) north of Empalme del Valle; tel: 953-713 017). Buses are scarce, so to get the best from a visit here you'll need a car or, better still, be prepared to walk – undoubtedly the best way to see the abundant wildlife and spectacular scenery the park has to offer. There is a modern Parador and several campgrounds in the park, as well as plenty of accommodation in Cazorla.

Sierra Nevada

The **Sierra Nevada** range southeast of **Granada** (see page 207) is also excellent for walking, though many visitors come here to ski at the 2,100-metre (6,890ft) ski station. More scenic, though, is the south-facing slope of the Sierra, the Alpujarras region, which provides prime walking and horse-riding country, and beautiful mountain villages, including Bubion, Capileira and Pampaneira. The autumnal landscape of ravines, streams and terraced farms is spectacular.

Almería

For much of the 20th century, Almería's harsh landscape of sun-scorched sierras and rocky plains was dismissed as a forgotten corner. But now the desert-like climate powers a massive agricultural business spreading over 20,000 hectares (50,000 acres) of the coastal plain.

At the centre of the southern coast sits the provincial capital of **Almería ⑱**, still dominated by the 11th-century **Alcazaba**, its severe Moorish architecture overlaid by the more grandiose Catholic upper courtyard. The coast to the east of Almería runs south to the volcanic headland of **Cabo de Gata**, a protected area since 1980 for its flora, fauna and underwater life. Small resorts and villages line this stretch of coast, culminating at **Mojácar**, which until the 1960s was a quiet white village but is now overrun with chintzy bars and boutiques.

The hillside town of Cazorla.

CAZORLA'S NATURE

One of Spain's most beautiful natural parks, the Parque Natural de Cazorla, Segura y Las Villas (to give it its full name) is a vast protected area in the northeast of Jaén province. It covers a region of more than 200,000 hectares (500,000 acres) of dense forests and mountain peaks. More than 500,000 people visit every year to enjoy the diverse natural attractions of the park.

The best times to visit, especially if you plan to walk a lot, are spring and early or late summer, when the Andalusian climate is not so intensely hot. In spring, hikers can see primroses and the dwarf violets unique to Cazorla. At any time of year visitors may spot several species of eagle, bearded vultures, deer, boar and ibex (mountain goats).

La Ciutat de les Arts i de les Ciències, Valencia.

VALENCIA AND MURCIA

Together, these two regions are often known as the Levant. Between them they enjoy more than half of Spain's eastern coastline, stretching from Catalonia to Almería.

Madrid

Main Attractions

Valencia
Costa Blanca
Alicante
Palm groves, Elx
Murcia
Cartagena

Valencia is best known for its *fallas* festival, its ceramics and its futuristic City of Arts and Sciences. In the surrounding area, the rolling hills of El Maestrat are home to some impressive medieval towns while on the coast are historic villages like Peñiscola. As well as high-rise Benidorm, the Costa Blanca has smaller, more attractive towns such as Dénia, and some great spots for scuba diving including the Illa de Tabarca. Inland, Alcoi is famed for its Moors and Christians festival. Murcia has a lovely Art Nouveau casino, while Cartagena's main attraction is a Roman theatre.

Standing in the middle of Spain's eastern Mediterranean coast, the city of **Valencia** ❶ has an enviable location, at the heart of one of Europe's most fertile regions. The fields surrounding the city can yield three to four crops a year. Orange and lemon trees line the roads. Rice grows alongside sweetcorn. Shimmering canals weave their way through the land, giving it life. This is the *huerta*, a cultivated and irrigated plain that was considered by the Muslims to be heaven on earth. Even the Spanish hero El Cid was taken by it. On his entry into Valencia he proclaimed: 'From the day when I saw this city I found it to my liking, and I desired it, and I asked God to make me master of it.'

The city he so desperately wanted had already seen the glories of past empires. It had been founded as Valentia Edetanorum by the Romans in 138 BC and was intended as a retirement colony for old soldiers.

Chosen for its strategic coastal position and mild year-round temperatures, the Romans took advantage of the sunshine and the run-off from the surrounding mountains to turn the rich soil into some of the most efficiently irrigated farmland in their domain.

Playa del Mal Pas, Benidorm.

FACT

Valencians are proud of their language, Valenciano. Place names are often given in Valenciano on street signs. It is a member of the Catalan group of languages and, along with Spanish, it is the official language of the Comunitat Valenciana. However, it is not one of the recognised languages of the European Union.

Santa Catalina tower, Valencia.

Earthly paradise

The Muslims quickly saw the potential here, and continued to improve the complex system of canals and channels. To the Muslims it was a paradise, and one that could effectively feed their people. They controlled the land for 500 years and built a city impressive enough to draw El Cid's attention. He conquered Valencia in 1094, but after his death it fell back under the jurisdiction of the Muslims in 1105. In 1238 the city fell definitively, through conquest and negotiation, and was incorporated into the kingdom of Aragón by Jaume I, El Conquistador.

The 15th century saw Valencia blossom into its Golden Age as it overtook Barcelona as the financial capital of this Mediterranean empire. Aside from its agricultural riches and its burgeoning port, the city held claim to a growing ceramics and silk industry and set up the nation's first printing press in 1474.

The city continued to prosper until 1609, when it was dealt a disastrous blow by Felipe III – the expulsion of the *moriscos* from Spain. No area was as hard hit as Valencia, which lost an estimated one-third of its people, most of them farm labourers. Its importance further declined in the early 18th century when the kingdom of Valencia was reduced to a province dependent on Madrid. And during the Spanish Civil War, the city was hard hit as capital of the Republic and one of its last strongholds to fall.

Valencia recovered much of its prestige when it became capital of the Comunidad Valenciana, one of the new autonomous regions of Spain, in 1982. Since then this city of 786,000 inhabitants, the third largest in Spain after Madrid and Barcelona, has been feverishly reinventing itself – laying out wide new avenues and investing in daring architectural projects.

The natural place to begin a tour of the city is the main square. Like most main squares, the **Plaça del Ajuntament** ⓐ lies in the city centre and is the location of the city hall, post office and bus stops. For some years, this triangular plaza was called the 'Plaza of the Valencian Nation.' While their separatist feelings are not as strong as the Catalans' or the Basques', Valencians do not

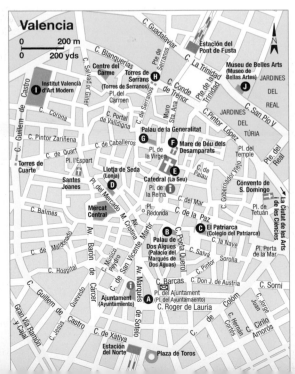

forget that the city enjoyed its Golden Age long before it was joined to Castile.

City of ceramics

Valencians are known for their individualism, sensuality, creativity, their desire to show off and their pride in their city. For evidence of this you need look no further than the splendid Art Nouveau railway station, the Estación del Norte, which is decorated on the outside with bunches of sculpted oranges and inside with stained glass and ceramic mosaics.

The craft that Valencia developed into a fine art, ceramics, is best represented in the **Palau de Dos Aïgues** ⓑ on Calle Poeta Querol, which houses the **Museu Nacional de Cerámica** (Tue–Sat 10am–2pm and 4–8pm, Sun 10am–2pm; charge except Sat pm and Sun). The industry dates back to the 13th century, when ceramic work came into use as a means of home decoration. Tapestries, which were used in colder climates to help retain heat, were never needed in Valencia, and the use of *azulejos* (coloured tiles) became popular. The oldest pieces in the museum come from two towns in the *huerta*, Paterna and Manises. Today only Manises keeps up its potteries.

Round the corner from the Ceramic Museum is the Corpus Cristi seminary, known as **El Patriarca** ⓒ (Mon–Sat, guided visits in English at 11am and 5pm; http://patriarcavalencia.es), in honour of its founder, the 16th-century archbishop and viceroy of Valencia, Juan Ribera. Grouped around its renowned two-storey Renaissance patio are a church whose walls and ceilings are covered with frescoes and a museum housing an important collection of works of art by Spanish and foreign masters (including El Greco) commissioned by Ribera.

Valencia's markets

To the north of the Plaça del Ajuntament is the Plaça del Mercat, site of the **Mercat Central** (Central Market; Mon–Sat 7.30am–2.30pm). A veritable cathedral to food, this domed building features stained-glass windows and ornate doorways and is over 8,030 sq metres (9,600 sq yards), making it one of the largest markets in Europe.

Valencia's Central Market.

Opposite stands the 15th-century **Llotja de la Seda** ● (Silk Exchange; Sun 10am–3pm, mid-Mar–mid-Oct Mon 10am–3pm, Tue–Sat until 7pm, mid-Oct–mid-Mar Tue–Sat 10am–6pm; free on Sun), built as a commodity exchange fit for a great Renaissance port. An inspiring building and World Heritage Site, it is a fine example of regional architectural style. Behind the Llotja a maze of narrow streets leads to the Plaça de la Reina. On the way, you may stumble across the charming **Plaça Redonda**, a circular covered market selling a mixture of haberdashery, clothes and crafts.

Cathedral and government

The **Catedral** ● (8.30am–8.30pm) was built on the site of a Roman temple to Diana and later a mosque. Begun in 1262 in traditional Gothic style, its interior was later covered over with a neoclassical facade, which has since been removed, revealing magnificent frescoes above the main altar. A chapel contains a small purple agate cup purported to be the Holy Grail. The south side, facing the Plaça de la

Plaça de l'Ajuntament, Valencia.

Reina, is Italian Baroque; the east door is Romanesque.

The focal point of the structure is the 15th-century octagonal bell tower known as **El Micalet** (daily 10am–1pm, 4.30–7pm), with a fine view of the glazed-tile domes of the city and the *huerta* stretching to the nearby hills. The cathedral's **Door of the Apostles**, a 14th-century portal adorned with statuary, gives on to the **Plaça de la Mare de Déu**. It is here that the ancient Water Tribunal of Valencia meets every week without fail. The proceedings are as they have been for hundreds of years (see page 236).

On the east side of the plaza and connected to the cathedral by a small bridge is the **Real Basílica de la Mare de Déu dels Desamparats** ● (Our Lady of the Abandoned; daily 7am–2pm and 4–9pm), the patron saint of the city since the 17th century. The image of the Virgin displayed above the altar was carved in 1416 for the chapel of Spain's first mental institution.

Across from the basilica is the **Palau de la Generalitat** ●, housing

FIRE AND GUNPOWDER

Look on any old building in the centre of Valencia for the small plaque which guarantees the structure is insured against fire, for in the city with Spain's most explosive fiestas, *las fallas*, insurance is essential. The fiestas celebrate the feast day of Sant Josep, patron saint of carpenters, on 19 March.

Over the centuries, street fires of wood shavings grew into large bonfires on which satirical *ninots* (guys) were burned. These, in turn, became vast Disney-style sculptures installed in the streets a week before the *cremá* (burning), on St Joseph's Day. Percussive gunpowder explosions *(mascletás)*, fireworks and crowds of visitors fill the streets in the week beforehand. At midnight on 19 March, the huge bonfire sculptures are lit and the entire city is illuminated with an orange glow. Alicante shares Valencia's passion for fire, gunpowder and fireworks, but it celebrates midsummer *fogueras* (bonfires with satirical guys) on the eve of St John's Day (23 June). To find out more about this fascinating festival visit the **Museo Fallero** (Plaza Monteolivete, 4; Mon–Sat 9.30am–7pm, Sun 9.30am–3pm). The Museo del Gremio Artistas Falleros (Avenida San José Artesano, 17; Jan–Jul and Sep–Dec Mon–Fri 10am–2pm, 4–7pm, Sat 10am–2pm; www.gremiodeartistasfalleros.com) showcases the art of making the *ninots*.

the regional government. This 15th-century Gothic palace was skilfully extended in the 1950s. Upstairs is the assembly hall of the ancient *Corts*, the Valencian parliament.

Calle Caballeros, running west from the palace, is the old main street. Its commercial importance has waned, but its former glory is seen in Gothic residences interspersed with restaurants, bars and cafés. Most of the houses here retain their beautiful patios, the sure sign of 15th-century Valencian success. Nearby is the exquisitely restored San Nicolás de Bari church (www.sannicolasvalencia.com), with beautiful Baroque frescoes.

Art museums

The maze of streets that branch off from Caballeros towards the river forms the oldest part of the city, the **Barridel Carme**. Two enormous fortified gateways are the main surviving fragments of the city's walls, which were pulled down in 1865. The oldest, **Torres de Serrans** (Tue–Sat 10am–2pm and 4.30–8.30pm, Sun 10am–3pm) ⑪ was built in the 1390s where the main road from Barcelona entered the city. The other, **Torres de Cuarte** (daily 9.30am–7pm, Sun until 3pm) on Caballeros, is still pockmarked by cannonball shots. Now, where the walls once stood, the wide avenues of Guillem de Castro and Colóm now run.

On Guillem de Castro stands the **Institut Valencià d'Art Modern** ⑪ (IVAM; www.ivam.es; Tue–Sun 11am–7.30pm, Fri until 9pm; free on Sun and Fri from 7.30pm), Spain's first and one of its most dynamic contemporary art galleries. The Valencian artists, sculptor Julio González and painter Ignacio Pinazo, are well represented, and the institute has a lively programme of temporary international exhibitions.

The Torres de Serrans looks out across the parkland in the dry bed of the River Turia to the city's largest gardens, the **Jardines del Real** (daily Nov–Mar 7.30am–8.30pm, Apr–Oct until 9.30pm; free). Beside them stands the **Museu de Belles Arts** ⑪ (Tue–Sun 10am–8pm; free). Housed in a former seminary with a blue dome, the museum's rich collection

Torres de Serrans.

includes stunning 14th- and 15th-century altarpieces by so-called Valencian 'Primitive' painters. Upstairs is a Velázquez self-portrait. There is also a fine small 19th- and 20th-century collection, which includes a handful of light-filled paintings by Sorolla and the local Impressionist school.

Towards the sea

The old watercourse of the Río Turia has been turned into a ribbon of wooded parks and sports fields crossed by old and new bridges – the most famous one being the Calatrava Bridge, one of Valencia-born architect Santiago de Calatrava's very first commissions. On the bank downstream stands the **Palau de la Música**, and beyond it a giant figure of **Gulliver** over which children clamber.

To the west stands **La Ciutat de les Arts i de les Ciències** (City of Arts and Sciences; www.cac.es), designed by Valencian architect Santiago Calatrava. This massive 21st-century complex has four main elements: the **Hemisfèric**, which houses an OMNIMAX cinema and planetarium; the **Museu de les**

Tile decoration inside Valencia's train station.

Ciències Princip Felip (daily, July–Aug 10am–9pm, 10am–6/7pm rest of year), an interactive science museum; the **Oceanogràfic** (times vary, see www.oceanografic.org) aquarium and the **Palau de les Arts** – an arts centre with a state-of-the-art opera house.

A pleasant tram ride from the Pont de Fusta station (near the Museu de Belles Arts) takes you to the city's waterfront district. The port, which handles container traffic and passenger ships, was entirely redeveloped in order to host the prestigious America's Cup yacht race, and what was only a few years ago a run-down dockside area is now a smart place to stroll on a Sunday afternoon or look for nightlife. The port area has been further redeveloped to accommodate the 5.4km (3.5-mile)-long Valencia Street Circuit, which was used for the European Grand Prix until 2012. From the port a wide flange of sandy beach extends northwards with a palm-shaded *paseo* following it all the way. Along the first stretch of this, near the port, is a line of restaurants specialising in paella.

THE WATER TRIBUNAL

Valencia's Tribunal de las Aguas (Water Tribunal) has been meeting every Thursday at noon for an estimated 1,000 years, making it one of the world's oldest functioning legal institutions but also one of the most curious.

Each of the eight elected judges represents one of the great *acequias* or irrigation canals of the *huerta* – the vast area of cultivated land surrounding the city that is under threat from the encroaching suburbs. These canals were originally built by the Romans over 2,000 years ago, and are still used to distribute water among the farmers of the area. Any questions regarding the intricate system of channels, canals and drains must be brought before the Water Tribunal. Every farmer is told precisely on which days and for exactly how long he can irrigate his fields. If he exceeds his quota he is likely to be challenged in public before the tribunal. These days, however, thanks to a reservoir topping up the water supply in summer, there are few conflicts. This means that most of the time, no sooner have the judges come together in a circle, than they retire; so visitors hoping to witness this unique event might well find themselves disappointed. In 2009, the custom was added to Unesco's list of Intangible Cultural Heritage.

The city hall's further development plans for the waterfront are controversial. They involve driving an avenue through the historic fishing quarter of the Cabanyal (www.cabanyal.com), destroying hundreds of houses in the process. Many of the houses in the Cabanyal are delightfully decorated with picturesque tiles in what is effectively a local, maritime vernacular expression of Art Nouveau. Despite the run-down state of the neighbourhood, you can still see many of these fragile details on the four streets just back from the beach and running parallel to it. As a result of widespread protests, the controversial project is now on hold. The city authorities have also agreed to invest over €12 million in the regeneration of the Cabanyal.

The Comunitat Valenciana

The 23,300 sq km (9,000 sq miles) of the Comunitat Valenciana is split into three provinces: Valencia, Castelló and Alacant (Alicante). This region approximately follows the boundaries of the old kingdom of Valencia, which was captured from the Muslims in the

13th century by an army of Aragonese, who left their language here in the form of the *valenciano* dialect.

Valencia, according to the *paso doble* that has become the region's unofficial anthem, 'is the land of flowers, light and love'. Thanks to an equable Mediterranean climate, all good things seem in abundance here. Sunshine saturates its many attractive beaches, and warm temperatures make for an active outdoor life day and night, almost all year round.

Castelló province

The Costa de Azahar (Orange Blossom Coast) was aptly named after the sea of lush green orange trees planted on Castelló province's coastal plain. Today, thanks to late development, the resorts here are less crowded than those further south. Some are particularly characterful. **Vinaròs**, for example, is still primarily a fishing port famed for its langoustines, and has a chunky fortress church in its charming old town. **Alcossebre**, further south, is modern, and backs directly onto a splendid coastal natural park,

Stunning architecture of Ciutat de les Arts i de les Ciències.

the **Serra d'Irta**, which may be explored on foot.

For independent travellers there is as much to do in the green hill country inland as on the coast, with swathes of unspoilt country preserved in natural parks. Close to the **Serra d'Espadán**'s cork woods, hardy locals swim all year round in river pools fed by warm sulphurous waters at **Montanejos**, a village in the River Mijares's steep-sided upper valley. To the north, **Penyagolosa**, a craggy peak visible from much of the province, is a favourite haunt of mountaineers and rock climbers who scale its sheer eastern rock face. (Access is via a forest track from Vistabella del Maestrat.) Silent pilgrims also walk to a sanctuary here every April to ward off drought and epidemics.

Caves and fortress towns

Further north, the beautiful rolling hills of **El Maestrat** (Maestrazgo), which straddle the border between Castelló and Teruel, are dinosaur country. Recent excavations have turned up numerous skeletons, and

there are old and new fossil museums in Morella and Sant Mateu.

Evidence of human civilisation here stretches back a long way, too. Farmers first discovered cave paintings in the **Barranc de la Valltorta**, some 25km (15 miles) inland from Vinaròs, in 1917.

Archaeologists went on to discover many more paintings up and down the gorge-like valley, and in 1998 they were protected within a large area of cultural parkland. Guided visits to four caves start from the **Museo de la Valltorta** (tel: 964-336 010; Tue–Sun, May–Sept 10am–2pm and 5–8pm, Oct–Apr 10am–2pm and 4–7pm; www.turismodecastellon.com), which stands in splendid empty countryside.

The capital of El Maestrat is **Morella** ❷, a fortress town enclosed by medieval walls over 2km (1.2 miles) long. Once every six years it hosts the Sexeni, a fiesta celebrating traditional local culture.

Other historic towns worth visiting are **Cinctorres** and **La Iglesuela del Cid** to the west and, back towards the coast, **Sant Mateu**, once the seat of the Religious Order of Montesa. In Sant Mateu there is a magnificent **Iglesia** and **Museo Arciprestal**, built in Valencian Gothic style, situated next to an arcaded village square (Tue–Sun 11am–2pm and 4–6pm, guided tours only; charge for museum).

The fortress towns of southern Spain have grown around their Muslim inheritance. The tile-making industry, centred in Alcora, Onda and Villareal, has grown into the largest industry of its kind in Europe. **Onda**'s magnificent Arab castle (Tue–Sun, June–Sept 11am–8pm, Oct–May 10am–1.30pm and 4–6pm; www.onda.es; free) possesses fragments of a plasterwork arch similar to those of the Alhambra, and its **Museu del Taulell** (Tile Museum; www.museoazulejo.org; Tue–Fri 11am–2pm and 4–8pm, Sat–Sun 11am–2pm and 5–8pm; free) is fascinating.

In **Vilafamès**, a perfectly preserved hilltop village, there are alleyways that

La Tomatina festival in Buñol.

were carved out of red rock before the Reconquest. Artists moved into the upper town here when it was left empty in the 1960s, and one of Spain's first contemporary art museums was founded here while Franco was still alive. It remains an exceptional collection of over 500 works (http://macvac.vilafames.es; Tue–Fri 10am–1.30pm and 4–7pm and Sat–Sun 10.30am–2pm, 4–7pm).

The coastal towns

By contrast with these inland towns, the province's ports and resorts are modern and stripped of their history. All were heavily battered by Franco's attacks in the last months of the Civil War, when he finally reached the coast at Vinaròs, splitting the Republic in two.

In the years that followed, most of the towns were rebuilt without much, if any, urban planning. **Castelló de la Plana** (Castellón) ❸, the provincial capital, is no exception, but it is worth getting to the centre of town to see the cathedral's bell tower, nicknamed **El Fadrí** (the Bachelor) for its solitary stance (visits by arrangement).

A short walk away is the magnificent prize-winning **Museu de Belles Arts** (www.culturalcas.com/va/museu; Tue–Sat 10am–2pm and 4–8pm, Sun 10am–2pm; free). Its painting collection is still young, but includes portraits of ten saints by Zurbarán's workshop, donated by one of the town's convents, and paintings on loan from the Prado by Ribera and Ribalta. There is also a superbly displayed ethnological collection in the basement.

Peñiscola ❹ is the most historic of the coastal towns. Here Papa Luna, who split the Catholic Church in 1421, ran a rival papacy for eight years from a castle on a tiny offshore peninsula. Today, the castle on the rocky hummock is surrounded by ugly development and the town heaves with tourists in summer, but it remains fascinating to visit (http://castillodepeniscola.dipcas.es; daily,

Valencia and Murcia

Apr–mid-Oct 9.30am–9.30pm, mid-Oct–Mar 10.30am–5.30pm). From here you can also catch a boat to the Islas Columbretes, a group of volcanic islands 60km (37 miles) off the coast. Boats have limited access here to a marine reserve designed to protect fish breeding grounds.

Further south, **Benicàssim** has a distinctive retro style lent by its curious 20th-century villas and 1960s garden estates of apartment blocks. It is packed in mid-July when its music festival, Spain's own version of Glastonbury, brings huge crowds to a festival site close to the beach. The concertgoers, known affectionately here as *fibers*, become part of the human landscape as they drift between the festival, the beach and the towns.

Valencia province: the north

Industrial and residential sprawl are fast eroding the fertile farmland which rings Valencia city, but further inland vineyards, almond groves and wheat fields provide memorable landscapes. In the valley of the Río Turia,

a good destination for hikers, you can visit the remains of a Roman aqueduct near **Chelva** , and, just to the north, **Alpuente** has a tiny town hall crammed into a tower above a 14th-century gateway.

Further south, **Requeña**, a market town crowned by a fine walled Gothic quarter, is Valencia's principal winemaking centre. The Gothic quarter, La Villa, is built on a rocky outcrop, and it looks onto vineyards planted in rusty soil around the town. Under the old town runs a network of old caves carved into the porous rock in medieval times and used variously as wartime refuges and bodega. The entrance is on Plaza de Albornoz. (Guided tours are available by arrangement with the tourist information office.)

Closer to Valencia is **Buñol**, scene of the famous Tomatina. In late August, thousands flock to join in this free-for-all tomato-throwing fight. Afterwards, the main plaza is hosed down and whitewashed for the coming year.

The province's most historic town is **Sagunt** (Sagunto) ❻, 25km (15 miles) north of Valencia. The Iberian

Sunset over Gandia.

hilltop town, which flourished here under Roman protection, was razed by the Carthaginian general Hannibal in 219 BC. This was a turning point in Spain's long colonial history, triggering the Second Punic War and the advent of Roman power in Spain. Sagunt's power shifted to Valencia, but the town was rebuilt.

Next to the whitewashed Jewish quarter, you will find the **Teatre Romà** (Roman Theatre; Sun 10am–2pm, Tue–Sat Apr–Oct 10am–8pm, Nov–Mar until 6pm; free), built in the 1st century AD and controversially restored in the 1990s.

A short but steep walk leads up to the walled site of the Iberian, Roman and later Muslim walled fortress town, misleadingly called the **Castell** or castle (Sun 10am–2pm, Tue–Sat June–Sept 10am–8pm, Oct–May until 6pm; free). It offers breathtaking views, ancient fragments of extraordinarily long walls and defensive precincts, plus a wonderful sense of wildness. From the hilltop you will also see Sagunt's seaside quarter, dominated by a vast early 20th-century iron blast-furnace, and now restored for visits.

Between Sagunt and Valencia run empty pebble beaches, now threatened by development. In **El Puig**, just off the motorway, stands the monastery where Jaume I negotiated to take Valencia city from the Muslims. Its small Virgin, kept in the chapel, is the patroness of Valencia kingdom, and various official events are held here.

South from Valencia

To the south of Valencia, **L'Albufera** ➐, a freshwater lake surrounded by marshes, is separated from the sea by a tidal sandbar. It can be reached by car or bicycle. After a major clean-up in the 1980s the lake has become a natural park. The visitors' centre is close to the turn-off to the lake's main village, El Palmar. It is a good starting point for exploring the lagoon along the paths which run through the surrounding marshes and rice fields.

El Palmar's tiny grid of streets is packed with restaurants specialising in paella and other local dishes. The odd rush-roofed *barraca* (cabin)

View over the Mediterranean from Xàbia (Jávea).

survives, and there is a makeshift quay where you can take boat-rides on flat-bottomed fishing boats for a close-up view of the lake's birdlife.

Further south, **Gandia** ⑧ is a characterful old town with good shopping. The **Palau Ducal dels Borja** (Palace of the Holy Duke; www.palauducal. com; Mon–Sat 10am–1.30pm and 4–7.30pm, Sun 10am–1.30pm only, guided tour only) was the home of St Francis of Borja (1510–72), who renounced his wealth after his wife's death and went on to become head of the Jesuit Order and a saint. Sumptuous chambers, a stunning ceramic floor and a Gothic patio are on show in the palace, which is still owned by the Jesuits. The town's golden beaches are among the province's best.

From here it is a short drive inland to **Xàtiva** (Jativa) ⑨, a lovely hill town which was an independent Muslim city state in the 12th century. It was also one of Europe's first paper-making towns. Later, it gained dubious fame as the home town of the Borja family, better known as the Borgias, two of whom became scheming popes. But

the town's privileges ended overnight, during the War of Spanish Succession, when Felipe V burnt it down for disloyalty. Rebuilt in golden stone, its old town has recovered its elegance, and is dotted with palaces, arts shops, cafés and plazas.

In the **Museu L'Álmodí** (mid-Sep–mid-June Tue–Fri 10am–2pm and 4–6pm, Sat–Sun 10am–2pm; mid-Jun–mid-Sept Tue–Fri 9.30am–2.30pm and Sat–Sun 10am–2.30pm), housed in the town's medieval granary, Felipe V receives judgement: in the excellent small art collection his portrait hangs upside down.

The Costa Blanca

Fifty years ago Alacant's beautiful, indented shoreline won fame as the **Costa Blanca**. Today, despite long stretches which are built over with whitewashed low-rise villas and high-rise blocks, there are still unspoilt sandy beaches, hidden coves, cliffs and headlands to be found. El Trenet, a local rail service that runs between Alicante and Dénia, helps give access to quieter spots.

Dénia ⑩ sits almost in the shadow of **Mount Montgó**, a humped peak with rare flora, where there is a small *parque natural*. The town, founded by the Greeks, has a largely Muslim **castle** (daily; charge), overlooking the port, which is famous for its prawns.

Just to the south, **Xàbia** (Jávea) ⑪ is built around an unusual fortified church. The town has kept a low skyline, and from here you can access the bays and beaches of **Cap de Sant Antoni** and **Cap de la Nau**, or the lush **Xaló** (Jalón) valley, where vineyards produce grapes for dessert wines.

The next resort to the south is **Calp** (Calpe), where the **Penyal d'Ifach** (Peñón de Ifach) ⑫, a huge natural limestone crag, juts into the sea above the crowded resort. As you climb and descend it, there are fine views and a glimpse of rare marine plants and birds, detailed in a visitors' centre at the base of the rock. A rocky gorge separates Calp from **Altea** ⑬ to the south. Once

High-rise buildings and beaches of Alicante.

a picturesque jumble of white houses and a well-known artists' hang-out, it is now surrounded by tightly packed villas running down to two beaches famous for their smooth, marbled grey pebbles.

Benidorm and beyond

Around the next headland looms **Benidorm ⑭**, a mini-Manhattan set beside two sweeping bays of golden sand. At night the 52-storey Gran Hotel Bali beams out above the forest of high-rise blocks. Just below the rocky promontory dividing the bays is the old centre, packed with bars and restaurants. From the Balcón del Mediterráneo you can see a long stretch of the coast, including the **Serra Gelada**, fiercely defended by nature-lovers. Here you can walk on an isolated high headland above the city. The hectic summer season, with 40,000 visitors at any time, is marked by Las Vegas-style shows and late-night opening at Tierra Mítica (www.terramiticapark. com) and Terra Natura (www.terranatura. com), the town's theme parks.

Two older resorts lie on the coast road south. At **La Vila Joiosa** (Villajoyosa) a chocolate museum tells the story of the 19th-century chocolate workshops around which the town grew. Today there are two chocolate factories here. Half an hour's drive to the south, past some excellent beaches and strings of new villas, **El Campello** is an old-fashioned resort with an excellent fish market at the end of its lively beach boulevard.

Behind the coast, winding roads make for beautiful views and slow driving to mountain villages which keep their Muslim names. **Guadalest**, spectacularly sited on a pinnacle, is the most beautiful, but horrendously crowded in summer. A quieter alternative is the road that leads north from Callosa to Pego.

Alicante

Alicante (Alacant) **⑮** grew from a small port with bathing quays into a large resort after Madrid's first direct railway line to the Mediterranean was built in 1858. A thriving provincial capital,

which has modern film studios and a university, it still holds traditional tourism close to its heart. An evening stroll along the splendid 19th-century seafront boulevard remains a classic experience.

Behind it the **Barrio de Santa Cruz**, or old town, is capped by the **Castillo de Santa Bárbara** (www.castillodesanta barbara.com; daily, Apr–Sept 10am–10pm, Oct–Mar until 8pm). At the top, you will find modern sculpture and old battlements.

Below are two very good museums: on the east side, the **Museo de Arte Contemporáneo** (www.maca-alicante.es; Tue–Sat 10am–8pm, Sun until 2pm; free), housing a 20th-century painter's outstanding contemporary art collection; on the west side, MARQ, the city's child-friendly archaeological museum (www.marqalicante.com; July–Aug Tue–Sat 11am–2pm and 6pm–midnight, Sun 11am–2pm, Sep–June Tue–Fri 10am–7pm, Sat until 8.30pm, Sun until 2pm). In the old town, two lovely churches are havens of peace. **San Nicolás**, with a peaceful Gothic cloister, and **Santa María**, Baroque fronted by a gorgeous wedding-cake facade.

FACT

Spain's best-known dish originated in the rice paddies around the Albufera lagoon. The original version, *paella valenciana*, is made with rabbit, chicken and beans from the marshes, but there are dozens of variants, many cooked with fish or shellfish.

Balcón de Mediterráneo, Benidorm.

To the north the city's high-rise blocks spill right along the beach of **Sant Joan** (San Juan), which challenges Benidorm for density, although there are more apartments than hotels here. The beach is one of the best-organised on the coast, and hums with activity in summer.

Mountains and deserts

The capital of Alicante's central mountains is **Alcoi**, built dramatically on both sides of a steep valley crisscrossed by high bridges. It may now be accessed via the fast A-7 highway, which also takes you close to **Xixona** (Jijona), where Spain's *turrón*, or almond nougat, is made. Just before arriving in Alcoi the highway narrows in a spectacular gorge snaking through thickly wooded natural park. **Penàguila**, a village inside the park, has a lovely Romantic garden with a maze, hothouse and gazebos.

Alcoi is best-known for its Moors and Christians fiesta, which features the largest mock-battles of their kind in Spain. The fiesta's exuberant costumes, some over a century old, are on show in a small museum. Close by, in the **Museu Arqueològic Municipal** (Mon–Fri 9am–2pm, Sat–Sun and public hols 11.30am–1.30pm), there is an intriguing and priceless stone tablet carved with the language of the Iberian tribes – an enigma yet to be deciphered.

From Alcoi it is just a short drive north to historic, sleepy **Cocentaina**, where you can visit a splendid palace and convent, and **Bocairent**, a charming village to its east, where you can clamber around caves carved into a limestone cliff hundreds of years ago.

The road to Madrid, which runs along the valley of the Vinalopó, was frontier territory for centuries, first between Muslims and Christians, then between Aragon and Castile. Castles are perched above towns all along the valley. The most important is **Villena**, which became capital of its own feudal territory after the Reconquest. The castle has fascinating graffiti scribbled on the walls by 18th-century prisoners held here during the War of Spanish Succession.

The Renaissance town hall holds one of Spain's great archaeological treasures, a magnificent collection

Explanada de España, Alicante.

MOORS AND CHRISTIANS

The wars of the Reconquest are ceremoniously re-enacted every year in eastern Spain's festivals of Moors and Christians. There are over 200 such celebrations, but the largest and most famous one is in the industrial city of Alcoi between 22 and 24 April. Almost a sixth of the population dresses up – sometimes at great personal expense – divides up into two armies and takes part in parades and noisy battles using blunderbusses firing blanks. The outcome is never in any doubt. The drama follows a set script until the Christian forces capture the mock castle set up in the main square with the aid of the miraculous intervention of St George. Other well-known Moors and Christians fiestas are in Onteniente (Ontinyent) at the end of August and Villena in early September.

of Iberian gold found by José María Soler, amateur archaeologist and post-office worker, in the mid-1960s. The treasure is displayed within a small **Museo Arqueológico** (www.museovillena.com; Tue–Fri 10am–2pm, Sat–Sun 11am–2pm).

South from Alicante, the inland road cuts across scrappy desert to **Elx** (Elche) ⑯, a modern oasis city. Its palm groves, with nearly a quarter of a million trees, date back to Muslim times.

One of these is unmissable: the **Hort del Cura** (Huerto del Cura), a magical 19th-century private palm garden (www.huertodelcura.com; daily from 10am, closing times vary). Less easy to find is classical Illici, now **L'Alcúdia** (on the CV-855 south; www.laalcudia.ua.es; Tue–Sun 10am–8pm,). The Dama de Elx, an Iberian bust, was dug up here by a farmer a century ago. It is kept in Madrid, against Elx's wishes, but other finds are on show in the museum here, and from here you can drive cross-country to the beach.

Further south, **Orihuela** (Oriola) ⑰ has a handsome, wealthy small **Catedral** (Mon–Fri 10.30am–2pm and 4–6.30pm, Sat am only) with a richly stocked museum. A short walk away is the **Casa-Museo Miguel Hernández**, birthplace of the poet who died imprisoned after the Civil War (www.museodeartesacro.es; Tue–Sat 10am–2pm and 4–7pm, Sun 10am–4pm). It has been left as a humble home in homage to the spirit of his poetry.

Towards Mar Menor

To the south of Alicante, the Costa Blanca resorts have sprawled, but some wonderfully unspoilt areas have been preserved in between. Just off **Santa Pola** is the **Illa de Tabarca** ⑱, a tiny island fortified against pirates, which is now a marine reserve. Ferries leave from Santa Pola (tel 680-330 422) or Alicante (tel: 686-994 538; www.cruccroskontiki.com). It is most beautiful at night, when the crowds have left. Santa Pola itself has two museums. One, aquarium-like, shows off Tabarca's wildlife, including its famous turtles; the other displays local fishing arts.

Behind Santa Pola and **Torrevieja** lie saltpans, with good birdwatching facilities at Las Matas natural park.

FACT

Murcia is rich in spa waters and has several renowned spas *(balnearios)*. Archena is the most luxurious, while Fortuna is functional but with a reputation for excellent treatments. Mula has an old-fashioned feel with communal baths and spa water piped into private flats.

Painting by Curro Gonzalez in Museo de Arte Contemporáneo, Alicante.

Exponential growth around Torrevieja has produced acres of whitewashed villas mass-marketed to Spanish and other families. Winter is the best time to visit the quayside salt museum and the gleaming modern theatre by Spanish architect Alejandro Zaero-Polo, who also designed London's 2012 Olympic stadium.

More villa-lined beaches run south to the **Costa Calida** (Warm Coast) of Murcia's coastline. A sandy spit runs north to south, enclosing the crescent-like bay to form the **Mar Menor** (literally 'Smaller Sea') ⓭. On the sheltered landward shore the old-fashioned resorts of Los Alcázares, Los Nietos and Santiago de la Ribera have quaint wooden boathouses on their beaches.

Cabo de Palos, a fishing port renowned for its scuba diving, is a great place to try local specialities such as *caldero*, a rice dish named after the cast-iron pot in which it is cooked. Just to the west are the mining landscapes of **Portman** and **La Unión**, and **Calblanque** natural park, which protects one of the best-preserved virgin stretches of the entire Mediterranean.

Murcia city

Covering just 11,317 sq km (4,369 sq miles), **Murcia** ⓴ is one of Spain's smallest regions. But it has its superlatives. One is Murcia city's Baroque architecture. The richly carved facade of the **Catedral** (daily 10am–1pm, 5–8pm; free) is a thing of wonder when the relief-work is underscored by slanting light. Close by, the **Museo Salzillo** (www.museosalzillo.es; Mon–Sat 10am–7pm, Sun 11am–2pm) houses Easter Week *pasos*, or processional floats carved by Baroque master Francisco Salzillo.

The love of ornament continues in Calle Trapería at the **Casino** (daily 10.30am–7pm). This late 19th-century caprice has original decorative details ranging from a neo-*Mudéjar* patio to a frescoed lady's cloakroom. The backdrop can be enjoyed over a leisurely lunch or dinner. Elsewhere the **Museo de Santa Clara** (Gran Vía, 1; www.museosdemurcia.com; Tue–Sat 10am–1pm and 4–6.30pm, Sun 10am–1pm; Jul–Aug Tue–Sun 10am–1pm) displays musical instruments in a convent with Muslim origins.

If you journey on up the River Segura, past spa-town **Archena**, via the villages of **Ojos** and **Ricote** to **Cieza**, you will pass through farming landscapes which keep an oriental air and see the odd *noria* (irrigation wheel) of Arab design. As water levels are falling, however, the future of the market gardens is in doubt.

Meanwhile, the region's vineyards go from strength to strength. **Jumilla**, in the north of the province, is a charming small wine town with renowned Fiestas de la Vendimia (Grape Harvest Fiestas) in mid-August, when the town's fountain runs with red wine.

Cartagena and Lorca

Two other Murcian cities keep interesting cultural heritages. **Cartagena** ㉑, a major seaport, has a raffish port quarter and defences dating back fifteen centuries. One glance at the harbour reveals why it is still an important naval base.

Dusk falls over Cartagena.

The main sights date back to this time: they include the splendid **Roman theatre** (www.teatroromanocartagena.org; Sun 10am–2pm, Tue–Sat May–Sept until 8pm, Oct–Apr until 6pm) and the **Museo Nacional de Arqueología Subacuática** (Maritime Archaeology Museum; http://museoarqua.mcu.es; Tue–Sat 10am–8pm, Sun 10am–3pm).

The old former frontier between Murcia and Andalusia is guarded by **Lorca ㉒**. High above the town its lofty **Castle** (daily mid-Mar–June and Sept 10.30am–6.30pm, until 8.30pm Jul–Aug, Oct–mid-Mar until 5.30pm) can be reached by train, or by car. It offers itineraries and a theme-park approach designed to amuse and educate children. A Parador hotel with splendid views has controversially been wedged into the castle wall during recent restoration.

In the town below, the Colegiata de San Patricio and the town hall, both in the Plaza de España, were erected at the height of Lorca's prosperity in the 17th and 18th centuries.

To the north of Lorca, the **Sierra de Espuña** is a hilly natural park with pine forests replanted in the late 19th century. Some 250 different plant species have been found there. From the park's eastern exit a road leads north to **Mula**, a small town whose innovative **Museo de El Cigarralejo** (www.museosdemurcia.com; Tue–Fri 10am–2pm, Sat–Sun 11am–2pm; free) illustrates Iberian culture through funeral trousseaux found in a nearby tumulus of ceramic burial pots.

From Mula the road rises as it leads west towards the mountains dividing it from Andalusia. It passes through **Caravaca de la Cruz ㉓**, where a septennial pilgrimage celebrates the supposedly miraculous appearance of a double cross here in 1231 inside the **Santuario de la Vera Cruz** (Sanctuary of the True Cross). Beyond this the road climbs to **Moratalla**, from where there is access to forest and the high mountains beyond.

There are more splendid wild areas on the coastline east of Lorca, between **Mazarrón** and **Aguilar** – but for how long is unsure, since constructors are eyeing the access provided by the new coastal motorway.

Murcia's Catedral.

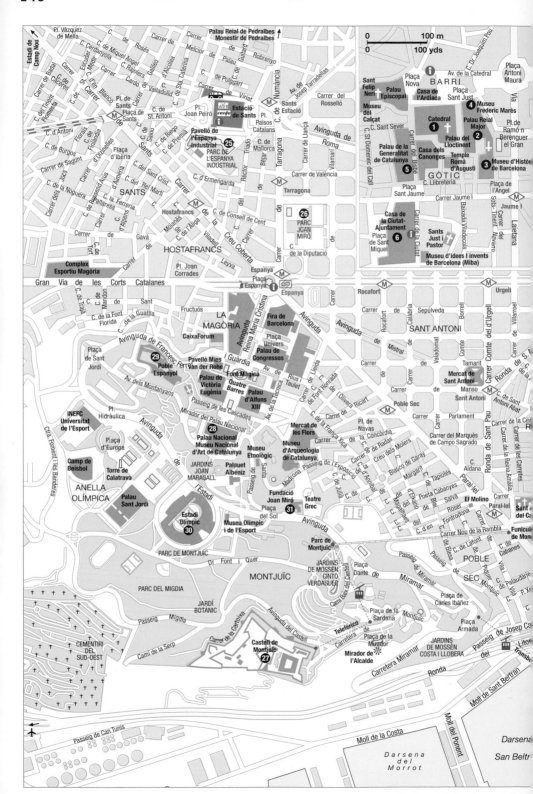

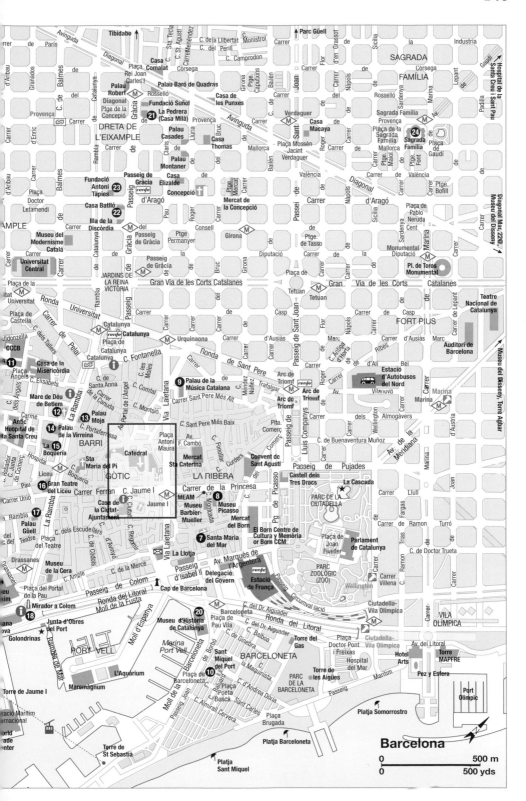

Tibidabo

Parc Güell

SAGRADA
FAMÍLIA

Hospital de la
Santa Creu i Sant Pau

Casa
Comalat

Palau Baró de Quadras

Palau
Robert
21 Fundació Suñol
La Pedrera
(Casa Milà)

Casa de
les Punxes

Sagrada Família

24 Sagrada
Família

Plaça
de
Gaudí

DRETA DE
L'EIXAMPLE

Palau
Casades

Casa
Macaya

Casa
Thomas

Plaça de la
Sagrada
Família

Palau
Montaner

23 Fundació
Antoni
Tàpies

Casa
Elizalde

Concepció

Mercat de
la Concepció

Museu del
Modernisme
Català

Casa Batlló 22
Illa de la
Discòrdia

Ptge.
Permanyer

Universitat
Central

JARDINS DE
LA REINA
VICTÒRIA

Gran Via de les Corts Catalanes

Pl. de Toros
Monumental

Teatre
Nacional de
Catalunya

Plaça de la
itat
Universitat

Tetuan

Gran Via de les Corts Catalanes

Plaça de
Castella

FORT PIUS

Auditori de
Barcelona

CCCB

Casa de la
Misericòrdia

9 Palau de la
Música Catalana

Estació
d'Autobusos
del Nord

Museu del Disseny, Torre Agbar

Mare de Déu
de Betlem

12

Arc de
Triomf

Palau
Moja

13

14 Palau
de la Virreina

BARRI

Sant Pere Més Baix

15 La
Boqueria

Sta
Maria del Pi

Plaça
Antoni
Maura

Mercat
Sta Caterina

Convent de
Sant Agustí

Castell dels
Tres Dracs

La Cascada

Catedral

GÒTIC

LA RIBERA

PARC DE LA
CIUTADELLA

16 Gran Teatre
del Liceu

Carrer Ferran

C. Jaume I

Carrer de la Princesa

Casa de
la Ciutat-
Ajuntament

MEAM
Museu
Barbier-
Mueller

8 Museu
Picasso

Mercat
del Born

Parlament
de Catalunya

17 Palau
Güell

7 Santa Maria
del Mar

El Born Centre de
Cultura y Memòria
or Born CCM

Plaça de
Joan
Fiveller

Museu
de la Cera

La Llotja

PARC
ZOOLOGIC
(ZOO)

Cap de Barcelona

Delegació
del Govern

Estació
de França

Wellington

Mirador a Colom

18

Junta d'Obres
del Port

20 Museu d'Història
de Catalunya

Barceloneta

Ciutadella-
Vila Olímpica

VILA
OLÍMPICA

Golondrinas

PORT
VELL

Marina
Port Vell

Sant
Miquel
del Port

BARCELONETA

Torre del
Gas

PARC
DE LA
CIUTADELLA

Torre de
les Aigües

Hotel
Arts

Torre
MAPFRE

L'Aquàrium

Maremàgnum

10

Pez y Esfera

Torre de Jaume I

Port
Olímpic

Torre de
St Sebastià

Platja Somorrostro

Barcelona

Platja Barceloneta

Platja
Sant Miquel

0   500 m
0   500 yds

Barceloneta beach.

BARCELONA

With its cutting-edge architecture, design, cuisine and renowned nightlife, Barcelona is one of Europe's most vibrant cities.

Barcelona is one of the world's top city break destinations and it's not difficult to see why. Aside from its buzzing nightlife and busy beaches, many visitors come to see the Sagrada Familia, Antoni Gaudí's unfinished masterpiece. The medieval Barri Gòtic makes for some atmospheric wanderings past chic boutiques and the Museu Picasso while La Rambla is the location of the spectacular Boquería market. Aside from its Modernista architecture, the city has a clutch of modern art museums including the Museu d'Art Contemporani. The Nou Camp stadium is a must see for football fans and Parc Güell is the place to escape the crowds.

The capital of Catalonia and a key Mediterranean port, Barcelona is a bilingual city, its citizens speaking both Spanish and Catalan. With one foot in France and the other in traditional Spain, in many respects the city seems almost as close to Paris as it is to Madrid, and has long been Iberia's link to the rest of Western Europe. The city most characterised by the *modernista* architect Antoni Gaudí has also produced other world figures in the arts – Miró, Tàpies, Josep Carreras, Montserrat Caballé and Jordi Savall, for instance. For the 1992 Olympic Games, it was given an enormous facelift and structural overhaul.

Chimneys of La Pedrera.

Medieval buildings were renovated, modern structures erected, a ring road created, the port and waterfront rebuilt and landscaped in a major urban regeneration programme which continues today.

Catalonian nationalism

Understanding Barcelona requires some insight into the Catalan-Spanish duality. Although about half of Greater Barcelona's 3 million inhabitants have emigrated from other parts of Spain, Barcelona is historically and

Main Attractions
Barri Gòtic
Museu Picasso
Waterfront
La Rambla
La Boqueria
Parc Güell
La Pedrera
La Sagrada Família

culturally a Catalan city, the capital of Catalonia and the seat of the Generalitat, the Catalan autonomous government. Catalonia was a self-governing principality with a parliament – the Council of the hundred – well before the formation of the Spanish state.

Catalonia became a commercial power in the Mediterranean during the 14th and 15th centuries, developing a merchant class, banking and a social structure significantly different from the feudal model that continued in most of Spain. Later, while the rest of Spain colonised, mining New World wealth, Catalonia industrialised, becoming the world's fourth manufacturing power by 1850.

Catalan, a Romance language derived from the speech of the occupying Romans, is closely related to the Provençal and Langue d'Oc French spoken in southern France. The strength of Catalan culture has fluctuated with the region's political fortunes. After uniting with the kingdom of Aragón in the 12th century, Catalonia found itself part of a new nation – Spain – when Fernando II of Aragón married Isabel I of Castile in 1469. Centuries-old privileges and institutions were suppressed by Castilian centralism over the next 300 years, most notably in 1714, when the newly installed Spanish King Felipe V, grandson of Louis XIV of France, militarily seized Barcelona and abolished all local autonomous privileges.

During the 19th century Catalonia's industrial success fostered new independence movements and a renaissance of Catalan nationalism. But in 1939 its last experiment in autonomy was crushed by Franco's victory in the Spanish Civil War.

Since Franco's death in 1975, Catalonia has undergone a spectacular cultural resurgence. Catalan, forbidden for 36 years, is the language used in state schools and universities, books and newspapers, radio and TV, theatre and cinema, the arts and sciences and official documents. It is the co-official language. The Barcelona Olympics was a high point of this new cultural golden age, with Catalan accepted as an official language, and since then it has continued to flourish.

Detail of a Nativity frieze designed by Picasso, on the exterior of the Collegi d'Arquitectes.

Bordered by the sea on one side and by the Collserola hills to the west, Barcelona is intersected by great avenues such as the **Diagonal** and the **Passeig de Gràcia**, and punctuated by open spaces that provide welcome relief from the city's human and architectural density. The two promontories of Montjuïc (by the port) and Tibidabo (behind and inland) tower over the city's chaotic sprawl.

After 1850 Barcelona broke out of the old Gothic city to create the **Eixample**, the orderly grid of wide avenues planned by Ildefons Cerdà, which occupies the middle ground between the old city and neighbourhoods like Gràcia and Sarrià, former villages set against the backdrop of hills.

The Gothic Quarter

Barcelona's old city, the **Barri Gòtic** or Gothic Quarter, is a wonderful display of solid stone, sprinkled with small shops, cafés, taverns and gourmet restaurants. Although most of the major architecture was completed between the 13th and the 15th centuries, there are traces of Roman civilisation.

Barcelona's acropolis – the highest elevation in the Barri Gòtic – was originally the Iberian village of Laia. The Romans conquered the town in 133 BC, erected the Temple of Augustus and fortified their *Mons Taber* with defensive walls in the 4th century.

The itinerary that best clarifies the city's archaeology and history begins at the **Catedral ❶** (www.catedralbcn. org; Mon–Fri 8am–12.45pm, 1.30–5pm and 5.45–7.30pm, Sat–Sun 8am–12.45pm, 2–5pm and 5.15–8pm; free entrance to cathedral and cloister, charge for choir and roof) at Plaça Nova. Known as La Seu (the 'seat' of the bishopric), construction began in 1298 and was completed over the next two centuries, with the exception of the main facade, which was not finished until the late 19th century. The two octagonal bell towers are, perhaps, the cathedral's most monumental features, while the interior cloister with its magnolias, palms, orange trees and resident geese is one of the city's most beautiful spots. The Canonja, Degà and Ardiaca houses that flank the square outside the cathedral, as well

The Barri Gòtic.

as the Capella de Santa Llúcia at the corner of Carrer del Bisbe, are also important architectural gems.

Return to Plaça Nova and cross in front of the cathedral, turning to the right down Carrer Tapineria to the Plaça de Ramón Berenguer el Gran, where you can see the eastern limit of the **Roman walls**.

After another section of Carrer Tapineria, cross through Plaça de l'Angel and along the Carrer Sots-Tinent Navarro where more sections of the walls are clearly visible. After cutting in behind the wall to Plaça Sant Just and doubling back up to Carrer Llibreteria, the Carrer Veguer leads up to the Plaça del Rei and the royal buildings of Catalonia's sovereign count-kings.

The **Palau Reial Major** ❷ (Royal Palace; Tue–Sun10am–7pm, free first Sun of the month and Sun from 3pm) and the Capella de Santa Agata are located at the foot of the tower of St Martí, worth climbing for the view over the old city. Santa Agata is an extraordinarily pure example of Catalan Gothic construction and was the chapel of the Royal Palace, the

residence of the counts of Barcelona, who became kings of Aragón in 1137.

The **Museu d'Història de Barcelona** ❸ (times vary, for details see http://museuhistoria.bcn.cat) is a part of this complex, built over Roman foundations still visible in its basement. The impressive Saló del Tinell, the early Gothic Great Hall of the Royal Palace, and the adjacent Palau del Lloctinent, complete the buildings around this regal square, widely considered the Barri Gòtic's loveliest.

Nearby, on Plaça de Sant Iu, is the **Museu Frederic Marès** ❹ (www.museumares.bcn.cat; Tue–Sat 10am–7pm, Sun 11am–8pm). The rich and eclectic collection of Spanish sculpture was donated by the sculptor Marès in 1946, with pieces dating from the Middle Ages. Its charming summer café is located in what were the royal gardens.

Seat of government

Wind through the narrow streets behind the Cathedral to Plaça Sant Jaume. The **Palau de la Generalitat de Catalunya** ❺ (pre-booked visits on 2nd and 4th weekend of each month; non-booked visits only available Apr 23rd, Sept 11th and 24th; see www.catalangovernment.eu for bookings; free) is the seat of the autonomous Catalan government. Constructed from the 15th to the 17th centuries, the main points of interest are the Gothic patio with its exterior staircase, the Sant Jordi chapel, the Patí dels Tarongers (Patio of the Orange Trees) and the Saló Daurat (Gilded Room) with its lovely murals.

The Plaça Sant Jaume, originally part of the Roman forum, is regularly a focal point for popular festivities and political demonstrations. The neoclassical facade directly across the square from the Generalitat is the **Casa de la Ciutat** ❻ or Ayuntament (town hall; Sun 10am–1.30pm; free). Inside the building, a black marble staircase leads to the main floor, the Saló de Cent (Hall of the Hundred), which was the meeting place for one of Europe's first republican parliaments.

Inside the Catedral.

The mariner's church

Across Vía Laietana is the attractive district known as the Born or La Ribera. At its heart is the superb **Santa María del Mar ❼** church (www.santamariadelmarbarcelona.org; Mon–Sat 9am–1pm, 5–8.30pm, Sun 10am–2pm and 5–8pm), a supreme example of Catalan Gothic architecture.

Begun in 1329, the basilica was the centre of Barcelona's new seafaring and merchant community and the crowning glory of Catalonia's hegemony in the Mediterranean. 'Santa María!' was a war cry of the Catalan sailors and soldiers as they stormed into Sicily, Sardinia and Greece. It is one of the city's simplest, most elegant structures: the three naves are vast and of similar height, reducing interior support to the bare minimum.

The basilica's massive stone columns, rose window, two bell towers and virtually all of the side chapels and stained-glass windows are striking, with graceful, pure lines.

The Passeig de Born behind the church, once the site of medieval jousts, is now the centre of this trendy *barri*.

The maze of streets behind it is full of boutiques, designer bars and offbeat restaurants. At the far end, the former 19th-century wrought-iron market has within it excavated remains of the old city of Barcelona. On Plaza Comercial El Born Centre de Cultura y Memòria or Born CCM (http://elbornculturaimemoria.barcelona.cat; Tue–Sun 10am–8pm, Oct–Feb Tue–Sat until 7.30pm, Sun until 8pm, market Tue–Sun 10am–midnight; free first Sun of month and Sun after 3pm) has glass walkways overlooking an archeological site and there is also an exhibit recreating everyday life in the 1700s as well as a cultural centre where literary, musical and theatrical performances are held.

Leading from the Passeig de Born is Montcada, one of Barcelona's most aristocratic streets in the 14th century and one of the most beautiful today. Some of its mansions now house museums. Five have been well restored to become the **Museu Picasso ❽** (www.museupicasso.bcn.cat; Tue–Sun 9am–7pm, Thu until 9.30pm; free Sun from 3pm); the buildings are almost as interesting as their contents.

TIP

The Museu d'Història de Barcelona has several museums under its wing. A combined entrance ticket (€7) gives access to the following sites: the Museu d'Història de Barcelona, the Museu-Monestir de Pedralbes, the Centre d'Interpretació del Parc Güell, as well as several others. See http://museuhistoria.bcn.cat for more information.

Barceloneta beach with Frank Gehry's sculpture 'Pez y Esfera' in the background.

Inside the Museu Picasso.

Palau de la Música Catalana.

The museum provides an insight into the early evolution of the artist's talent. From caricatures of his teachers in school texts to studies of anatomy as an art student and his first great paintings in the styles of the Masters – Goya, Velázquez, El Greco – Picasso's extraordinary vitality comes through.

Continue over Princesa into Corders, and turn left for the **Plaça de la Llana**, a small medieval square. From there, wind up past the **Mercat de Santa Caterina** (www.mercatsanta caterina.com), a new-generation market designed by Enric Miralles with a stunning colourful roof, part of an urban regeneration programme in the area. Cut through the backstreets to the **Palau de la Música Catalana** ➒ (www.palaumusica.org; daily guided tours Aug 9am–8pm, Jul until 6pm, Sep–June 10am–3.30pm). Erected in 1908 by the *modernista* architect Domènech i Montaner, this magnificent concert hall, flagship of Barcelona's Art Nouveau architecture, has been declared a Unesco World Heritage Site. The only concert hall in Europe to be naturally lit, it has

recently been extended by Oscar Tusquets, a leading Catalan architect.

Despite the construction of a new **Auditori**, near Glòriès, the Palau still has a full programme of concerts including occasional jazz performances. It has an attractive bar and restaurant which is a good spot to pause and admire the exuberant *modernista* details.

The waterfront

Next, you could head for **Barceloneta**, the district between the beaches and the port. The narrow alleys here have the feel of a fishing town, with brightly painted houses, laundry hanging over the pavement, and the delicious aroma of seafood from its restaurants. From the church of **Sant Miquel del Port** ➓ (daily), which stands in a lovely square just off Passeig Joan de Borbó, it's a short meander out to the beach and the start of the 4km (2.5-mile) waterfront, encompassing seven beaches. The Port Olímpic marina, lined with restaurants, music bars and cafés, is especially popular in summer. The Olympic Village, originally for athletes, has become a residential district.

The development of the waterfront, originally inspired by the Olympics, has continued due to a large-scale cultural event which took place in 2004, the Universal Forum of Cultures. Its huge exhibition site, with a state-of-the-art conference centre and a striking photovoltaic panel, marks the end of the waterfront and the city's limits.

The landscaped route running from Barceloneta to this area buzzes at weekends with cyclists, skateboarders and promenading families, and the beaches have become a fundamental part of city life. At night the *xiringuitos* (beach bars) subtly change rhythm as the DJs move in after dinner, and during city fiestas it is a focal point for celebrations and firework displays.

Ciutadella Park

Another popular weekend area is the lush Parc de la Ciutadella, named after

the citadel built by Felipe V in reply to Barcelona's long and bitter resistance in the siege of 1714. Over 1,000 houses were torn down in the Barri de la Ribera to make way for the fortress, which became a focal point of subsequent anti-centralist resentment. It was razed in 1888 and became an attractive and popular city park, home to the **Zoo** (www.zoobarcelona.cat; daily from 10am), the Zoology and Geology museums, and the Hivernacle, an elegant tropical greenhouse.

The upper Rambla

Barcelona's famous **La Rambla**, its lively, mile-long pedestrian thoroughfare, has something for everyone. Originally a seasonal river bed, the Rambla runs from Plaça de Catalunya to the Columbus monument at the port, and now extends across a wooden walkway, the Rambla del Mar, to the Maremàgnum shopping and leisure complex (http://es.club-onlyou.com), somewhat ironically called the Port Vell (Old Port).

At the top of the Rambla is Café Zurich, rebuilt in El Triangle shopping centre, a legendary place to have

coffee and meet friends. The section of the Rambla at **Font de les Canaletes**, around a cast-iron drinking fountain, is a traditional gathering point for football enthusiasts passionately debating or celebrating the fortunes of Barça, its world-famous football club.

Turning off the Rambla at Carrer Bonsuccés, you'll come to the impressive white slab of the **Museu d'Art Contemporani** ⓫ (MACBA; www. macba.cat; Mon and Wed–Fri 11am– 7.30pm, Sat 10am–9pm, Sun until 3pm), with its own collection and excellent temporary exhibitions.

Next door is the **CCCB** (Centre for Contemporary Culture; www.cccb.org; Tue–Sun 11am–8pm) in the beautifully restored Casa de la Caritat, a former orphanage. It has a full programme of exhibitions, talks, dance, music and diverse activities.

Returning to the Rambla, the next section, the **Rambla dels Estudis**, has the renovated **Mare de Déu de Betlem** ⓬ church on the right and, on the left, the **Palau Moja** ⓭, an 18th-century palace now used for exhibitions and a Generalitat bookshop.

Boating lake in Parc de la Ciutadella.

La Rambla.

Boqueria market and the central Rambla

The **Rambla de las Flors** or **Rambla de Sant Josep** is the next section of the main promenade, lined with flower stalls and overlooked by the **Palau de la Virreina** ⓮ and the **Boqueria** ⓯ market. The 18th-century Virreina Palace houses the city's cultural information centre, booking office and an exhibition space. The Boqueria is Barcelona's largest market, covered by a high-roofed, steel-girdered hangar, and is one of the city's most exhilarating places to visit.

The **Rambla del Centre** or **Rambla dels Caputxins** begins at the small square – which has a pavement mosaic by Joan Miró – in front of Barcelona's opera house, the **Gran Teatre del Liceu** ⓰ (1862), restored after a devastating fire in 1994.

The Cafè de l'Opera opposite is a popular meeting spot. Just off the Rambla on Carrer Nou de la Rambla is Gaudí's magnificent **Palau Güell** ⓱ (http://palauguell.cat; Tue–Sun, Apr–Oct 10am–8pm, Nov–Mar until 5.30pm). This palace (1890), with its mighty

Portraits by the artist Gerhard Richter, Museu d'Art Contemporani de Barcelona.

balcony, is one of the finest works that Gaudí constructed for his patron, Count Güell. Gaudí was also responsible for the interior decoration; the wooden and metal decorations are particularly impressive.

Back on the Rambla is the legendary Hotel Oriente, located in one of the few surviving former convents that once lined this side of the Rambla. The **Rambla de Santa Mònica** is the next and final part of the Rambla, extending from the entrance to Plaça Reial down to the port. The Plaça Reial, with its palm trees and uniformly porticoed 19th-century facades, is one of Barcelona's most appealing spots, sunny by day and buzzing at night.

The Maritime Museum and Port Vell

The bottom of the Rambla is flagged by one of the city's most famous landmarks, the **Monument a Colom** ⓲ (Columbus Monument; daily 8.30am–8.30pm, Oct–Feb until 7.30), designed by Gaietà Buïgas for the Universal Exhibition of 1888. A lift takes visitors up to the top of the 60-metre (200ft) column. This was the former landing point for the city; today small tour boats – called *golondrinas* (swallows) – explore the port while larger ones go along the waterfront to the Forum port. They also connect with the heliport on the quayside from which there are helicopter tours over the city. For a more peaceful bird's-eye view, take the cable car from the nearby Moll de Barcelona to the other side of the port or up to Montjuïc.

At the end of the Rambla is the excellent **Museu Marítim** ⓳ (daily 10am–8pm, free on Sun from 3pm), in the vast Gothic shipyards that once turned out 30 war galleys at a time. The exhibits include models, documents, galleon figures, maps and nautical instruments. The centrepiece is a life-size replica of the *Galera Reial*, the flagship of the Christian fleet that under Don John of Austria defeated the Turks at the Battle of Lepanto in

October 1571. The cafeteria is a pleasant spot. The *Santa Eulàlia*, a sailing vessel dating from 1918 and part of the museum, is afloat nearby in the Port Vell (daily visits, using the same ticket, closed Mon).

The Rambla continues over a walkway, so you can stroll all around the **Port Vell**, or the Maremàgnum leisure complex. Apart from its shops (daily 10am–10pm) and restaurants, **L'Aquàrium** is great for kids (www.aquariumbcn.com; daily from 10am, closing times vary, see website).

On the adjacent quay is the Palau de Mar, a handsome former warehouse, part of which has been converted into the **Museu d'Història de Catalunya ⑳** (www.en.mhcat.cat; Tue–Sat 10am–7pm, Wed until 8.30pm, Sun until 2.30pm). This state-of-the-art museum takes you from Catalan prehistory to 1980, with hands-on exhibits that will appeal especially to children. Information panels are mostly in Catalan, but this shouldn't put you off trying your hand at a medieval joust or experiencing the terror of a Civil War air raid. There are great views from the rooftop restaurant.

Gaudí's Barcelona

Few architects have marked a city as Gaudí has Barcelona. Born in nearby Reus in 1852, Antoni Gaudí i Cornet created revolutionary forms that coincided with the Art Nouveau or *modernisme* artistic movements.

The young Gaudí's work can be found in Josep Fontseré's Cascada in the Ciutadella Park where, as a student, he designed the rocks of the cascade. The Plaça Reial lampposts are also early Gaudí products. His 1889 house, **Casa Vicens**, in the **Gràcia** neighbourhood (Carrer de les Carolines, 24–26), was his first major project and the debut of totally polychromatic architecture. Gaudí's most important works in Barcelona are Parc Güell, Casa Batlló, Casa Milà (also known as La Pedrera) and, of course, his extraordinary temple of the Sagrada Família.

Parc Güell (www.parkguell.cat; daily, mid-Apr and Sept–Oct 8am–7.30pm, May–Aug until 8.30, Nov–Mar until 5.30pm) was commissioned by the Barcelona financier Eusebi Güell as a garden suburb above Gràcia. Between 1900 and 1914 Gaudí designed a covered market, a large central square, a series of paths across the side of the mountain and the plots for houses; only two were finally built, one of which houses a small museum – the **Casa-Museu Gaudí** (www.casamuseugaudi.org; daily, Apr–Sept 9am–8pm, Oct–Mar 10am–6pm); Gaudí did not design it, but lived in it for 20 years. The wall surrounding the park, decorated with a ceramic mosaic, is the first notable feature of Güell Park. One of the two lodges, with their bizarre shapes, multicoloured roofing and wild, mushroom-like towers, has opened as part of the City History museum (see page 255).

The market is known as the Sala de les Cent Columnes (Hall of the Hundred Columns). There are actually 86 Doric columns supporting an undulating ceiling decorated with mosaics.

Skateboarders take advantage of the space outside MACBA.

Mercat de la Boqueria.

The unfinished Sagrada Família.

On the rooftop of Palau Güell, designed by Gaudí for his patron, Count Güell.

The central square is surrounded by an ingeniously decorated serpentine bench which uses a wide range of found objects, tiles and rubble, all spontaneously mixed and built into the ceramic finish. A pathway winds up the mountainside, giving panoramic views of the city.

Two of Gaudí's key buildings, **La Pedrera** ㉑ (www.lapedrera.com; daily, 9am–11pm), and **Casa Batlló** ㉒ (www.casabatllo.es; daily 9am–9pm) are on the **Passeig de Gràcia** in the Eixample. Casa Batlló (at No. 43) forms part of the famous 'Illa de la Discòrdia' (Block of Discord), so named for the contrasting architectural styles of the three neighbouring buildings designed by the city's greatest 19th-century architects.

Apart from Gaudí's Casa Batlló, there is Domènech i Montaner's 1905 Casa Lleó Morera (www.casalleomorera. com) at No. 35 and Puig i Cadafalch's 1900 **Casa Amatller** at No. 41 (www. amatller.org, Mon–Fri 11am–7pm). La Pedrera, or Casa Milà, an apartment block at No. 92, is a more natural fantasy by Gaudí – repetitions of sandcastle waves and elaborate wrought-iron balustrades. A visit here includes the 'Espai Gaudí' exhibit, the spectacular rooftop and 'El Pis', a flat decorated in the style of the era.

Round the corner at Carrer d'Aragó, 255, is another astonishing building, this time designed by Domènech i Montaner between 1881 and 1886. Since 1990 it has housed the **Fundació Antoni Tàpies** ㉓ (www.funda ciotapies.org; Tue–Sun 10am–7pm), set up by the artist himself to promote modern art and culture.

Some of Tàpies's own abstract works, which are noted for their use of innovative new materials such as sand, rubbed marble and varnish as well as iron and concrete, are displayed here along with works by other modern artists. There is a shop at the entrance, selling books on Tàpies and his work.

La Sagrada Família ㉔ (www.sagrada familia.org; daily, Apr–Sept 9am–8pm, Nov–Feb until 6pm, Mar and Oct until 7pm), on the north side of the Avinguda Diagonal, was begun in 1882 as a neo-Gothic structure under the direction of Francesc P. Villar. In

MODERNISME

Modernisme is the name given to a style of architecture created in Catalonia between 1888 and 1911 and similar to France's Art Nouveau. It was heavily influenced by Catalan nationalism, its hub was Barcelona and its leading designers were Antoni Gaudí, Luis Domènech i Montaner and Josep Puig i Cadafalch. The *Modernistes* rejected society and wanted to change it through art. The movement also encompassed painting, theatre and literature, notably the violent stories by Caterina Albert and Prudenci Bertrana, who were heavily influenced by Gothic novels and Russian writers. Poetry was another of its popular forms, taking Symbolism as its muse, and its leading light was Joan Maragall. *Modernisme* ended around the time of Maragall's death – having been accepted by the bourgeoisie.

1883 Antoni Gaudí took over, completed the crypt and designed an enormous project that would reach a height of over 150 metres (500ft).

Gaudí worked on the Sagrada Família until his death in 1926. Conceived as a symbolic construction, the cathedral has three gigantic facades still being built: the Nativity facade to the east, the western side representing Christ's Passion and Death and the southern facade portraying Christ's Glory. The four spires of each facade symbolise the 12 Apostles; the tower over the apse represents the Virgin Mary; the central spire (as yet unbuilt), dedicated to Christ the Saviour, is surrounded by four lesser towers representing the Evangelists Matthew, Mark, Luke and John. The decorative sculpture and ornamentation covering the different elements of the structure are of extraordinary quality and density. Although the pace of work has been faster recently, mostly due to donations, it is still only 60 percent complete according to calculations. However, Gaudí himself said his 'client' was not in a rush.

Notable in Gaudí's buildings is the extent to which he tried to integrate the shapes and textures of nature. The influence of the peaks and heights of Montserrat (see page 279), Catalonia's holy mountain near Barcelona, is evident in the Sagrada Família. Gaudí was a deeply religious man and a mystic. His body is buried in the crypt of the unfinished temple, which continues to grow around his tomb. It is said the church will be completed in time for the 100th anniversary of the architect's death in 2026.

Just beyond the Sagrada Família is Plaça de les Glòries Catalanes, where Els Encants flea market takes place every Monday, Wednesday, Friday and Saturday morning. Nearby is the Teatre Nacional de Catalunya, designed by Barcelona architect Ricardo Bofill, Rafael Moneo's concert hall L'Auditori and the city's latest landmark, the **Torre Agbar**, Jean Nouvel's high-rise gherkin which is dazzlingly illuminated at night.

Nearby in Plaça de les Glòries is the **Museu del Disseny** (DHUB; www.dhub-bcn.cat; 10am–8pm), which

Interactive exhibits at FC Barcelona museum, Camp Nou stadium.

The terraces at Camp Nou, home of Barcelona FC.

houses the collections of the **Museu Ceràmica**, the **Museu Tèxtil I d'Indumentària and the Museu de les Arts Decoratives.**

Pedralbes

From Glòries the Diagonal traverses the city, linking the seafront to the upper part of town and the smart residential area of Pedralbes. The **Palau Reial de Pedralbes** was built for Alfonso XIII in 1925, and part of it housed the **Museu Ceràmica**, the Museu Tèxtil I d'Indumentària and the **Museu de les Arts Decoratives** until they moved to the new Museu del Disseny (see page 261) in 2014.

A spectacular dragon wrought-iron gate by Gaudí on the road up to the right of the palace is a clue that this was all once part of the Güell farm estate. Continue past it to reach the beautifully preserved **Museu Monestir de Pedralbes** (http://monestir pedralbes.bcn.cat; Apr–Sept Tue–Fri 10am–5pm, Sat until 7pm, Sun until 8pm, Oct–Mar Tue–Fri 10am–2pm, Sat–Sun until 5pm; free first Sun of the month and every Sun from 3pm),

Museu Nacional d'Art de Catalunya with four barres (columns) representing the stripes on the Catalan flag.

a haven of peace removed from the frenetic city. The bell tower, unusual three-tiered cloister and Sant Miquel chapel are perfect examples of Catalan Gothic architecture.

On the south side of the Diagonal, below Pedralbes Palace, is the home of FC Barcelona (Barça), where visitors can see the trophies and view the pitch from the Presidential box.

Designed in 1957 by Francesc Mitjans, **El Camp Nou** (www.fcbarcelona. com; opening times vary so check website) has a capacity of 120,000 and is one of the most beautiful football stadiums in the world. Fútbol Club Barcelona, for 40 years of Francoism the *only* means of expressing Catalan nationalism, is a monolithic organisation with top professional and amateur teams competing for every amateur national championship from ice hockey to baseball.

Between here and the hill of Montjuïc is **Sants**. The area around Sants was a beneficiary of the 1992 Olympic Games. The station was redesigned with the **Parc de l'Espanya Industrial** ㉕ nearby, where boats may be hired

on the small lake. Beyond it on the Carrer Aragó is another urban park, **Parc de Joan Miró** 26, dominated by the artist's colourful 22-metre (70ft) statue *Woman and Bird*.

Gràcia

Gràcia, the district above the Diagonal at the top of the Passeig de Gràcia, has a young, radical and traditionally working-class tradition and ambience. Mercé Rodoreda's moving novel, *La Plaça del Diamant* (translated as *The Time of the Doves* by David Rosenthal), gives an excellent account of life in Gràcia during the 1930s and 1940s. La Torre de Rellotge (the Clock Tower) at Plaça de Rius i Taulet is one of the centres of life in Gràcia.

This attractive neighbourhood is characterised by squares with cafés, artisan workshops, timeless grocers and boutiques, and has a lively nightlife. Its Fiesta Major is reputed to be the best local fiesta, with wild partying for two weeks mid-August.

The 1992 Olympic site

Barcelona's seafront hill overlooking the port, **Montjuïc**, was the main site of the 1992 Olympic Games and has since developed as an open, green expanse full of leisure, sports and cultural opportunities: a breath of fresh air with impressive views of the port and city.

Attractions include the **Castell de Montjuïc** 27 (http://ajuntament.barce lona.cat/castelldemontjuic/ca; daily 10am–8pm; free), which guards the harbour, the **Botanical Garden**, sports facilities, including Olympic swimming pools, the Grec (summer theatre festival) amphitheatre and some of the city's key museums.

You can get quickly to the hill by funicular from the Paral.lel metro station or gently by cable car from the port (www.telefericodebarcelona. com; 11am–7pm; charge), but to see most of what's on offer begin in Plaça d'Espanya. Walk up the hill, or take the escalator between the exhibition

pavilions towards the Palau Nacional, the enormous building which dominates the hill. Halfway up is La Font Mágica (the Magic Fountain), which surges into life in a popular *son et lumière* show (summer Thu–Sun 9–11.30pm, winter Fri–Sat 7–9pm).

The Palau Nacional is the home of the **Museu Nacional d'Art de Catalunya** 28 (MNAC; www.mnac.cat; Sun 10am–3pm, Tue–Sat May–Sept until 8pm, Oct–Apr until 6pm), which houses 1,000 years of Catalan art. Its prized Romanesque collection contains murals from churches in the Catalan Pyrenees dating from the 10th to the 12th century. The impressive 19th- and 20th-century rooms include work by Ramon Casas, Nonell, Sert and Santiago Rusiñol, as well as decorative pieces from *modernista* houses by Gaudí and his contemporaries. It also has part of the Thyssen-Bornemisza collection.

To the right of the Magic Fountain is Mies van der Rohe's restored **Pavilion** (daily 10am–8pm; charge), built originally as the German Pavilion for the International Exhibition of 1929, like the Palau Nacional and most of

Sculpture on the roof terrace at Fundació Joan Miró.

FACT

Six art museums – MNAC, the Fundació Joan Miró, the Museo Picasso, CCCB, Fundació Antoni Tàpies and MACBA – can all be visited by purchasing an Art Passport, which is valid for three months and saves around 45 percent on individual entrance fees. See http://articketbcn. org for details.

Torre de Jaume I, on Moll de la Barceloneta quay, is a stop for the cable car that carries passengers up to Montjuïc.

Montjuïc's grand edifices. The purity of its minimalism is a striking contrast to the other buildings. Opposite is the **CaixaForum**, a wonderful cultural centre in a restored *modernista* factory, with a full programme of quality exhibitions and concerts (Mon–Fri 10am–8pm, Sat–Sun until 9pm; free), as well as the Contemporary Art Collection of La Caixa Foundation.

Most popular of the 1929 exhibition projects is the **Poble Espanyol** ㉙ (www.poble-espanyol.com; Mon 9am–8pm, Tue–Thu and Sun until midnight, Fri until 3am, Sat until 4am; charge), built to show the different architectural styles of all the regions of Spain. Today it is flourishing as a tourist centre, with a good selection of bars and restaurants and a *tablao* with a flamenco show, and is popular for its late nightlife. Also here is the **Fundació Fran Daurel** (www.fundacio frandaurel.com; daily 10am–7pm; free) which has fine collection of modern art and sculpture by major artists.

Behind the Palau Nacional are the principal Olympic sites: the brown sandstone **Estadi Olímpic** ㉚, enlarged

from Pere Domènech i Roure's 1927 original; and beside it on the Plaça Europa – a wide and elegant terrace overlooking the delta of the Llobregat and the sea – the modern lines of Arata Isozaki's **Palau Sant Jordi**, one of the largest sports halls in the world. The **Museu de l'Olimpic i de l'Esport** (www.museuolimpicbcn.cat; Sun 10am–2.30pm, Tue–Sat Apr–Sept until 8pm, Oct–Mar until 6pm) traces the history of the Olympics and sport. As of 2016 the stadium also houses the state-of-the-art Open Camp (www.opencamp.info), the world's first sports theme park offering 25 experiences related to different disciplines. Blending sport and digital technology this 'sportainment' park vitually transports you to a football pitch, hockey ring, Olympic pool or athletics stadium.

On the way up to the hilltop castle is the **Fundació Joan Miró** ㉛ (www. fmirobcn.org; Sun 10am–2.30pm, Thu until 9 pm, Tue–Wed and Fri–Sat Apr–Oct until 8pm, Nov–Mar until 6pm). One of Europe's finest modern galleries, it was built in 1974 by the artist's friend Josep Lluís Sert. More than 150

POBLENOU

The latest part of the city to be redeveloped is Poblenou, along the waterfront and beyond the Olympic Village from the city centre. One way to get there is to walk down Avinguda Diagonal from the Torre Agbar and turn down Rambla de Poblenou. Once this corner of the Barcelona conurbation was a grimy neighbourhood with the thickest concentration of factories in Catalonia. In recent years, however, it has been given a facelift and its abandoned industrial premises have been renovated to make studios and workshops for artists.

Several picturesque corners, such as Plaça del Prim, and old-fashioned shops have been preserved amid the transformation. A scattering of brick chimneys and the impressive but redundant Torre de Aigües water tower serve as a reminder of Poblenou's history.

paintings, sculptures and over 5,000 drawings are on display, covering each of the artist's Surrealist creative periods. Excellent temporary exhibitions are devoted to leading modern artists.

Tibidabo

Barcelona's other hill, **Tibidabo**, the highest point of the Collserola hills behind the city, derives its name from the Devil's temptation of Christ as reported by Saint Matthew: *Haec omnia tibi dabo si cadens adoraberis me* (I will give you all this if you will fall down and worship me). Catalans say that the view from the 518-metre (1,700ft) peak, towering over the city of Barcelona on one side and looking out over the interior of Catalonia to the north and west, was the most diabolical temptation imaginable. The area provided the setting for Carlos Ruiz Zafón's evocative 2001 novel *The Shadow of the Wind*.

If you can, build in a visit to the nearby **CosmoCaixa**, the spectacular Science Museum (https://obrasocial lacaixa.org, Tue–Sun and public hols 10am–8pm) renovated and expanded into a new generation museum which enthusiastically brings science to life. It is full of interest for curious minds of all ages, from its star exhibits like the Flooded Forest, which faithfully reproduces part of the Amazon forest including its wildlife, to its broad range of temporary exhibitions.

Part of the charm of a visit to Tibidabo is the process of getting there. At the foot of Avinguda Tibidabo, take the old Tramvia Blau (Blue Tram; www.tmb.cat) to an excellent restaurant called La Venta, where the funicular to the summit departs.

The **Temple Expiatori de Sagrat Cor** (Church of the Sacred Heart), the grandly restored Hotel Florida and the Parc d'Attracions, the popular amusement park (www.tibidabo.cat; from noon, closing times vary so check website), are points of interest at the top of Tibidabo, as well as the magnificent panorama. The tremendous views of the city and the Mediterranean on one side, the fields of Catalonia and the jagged peaks of Montserrat (see page 279) on the other and, to the north, the snowcaps of the Pyrenees, are a tempting display of the city's and Catalonia's riches.

View from the Parc d'Atraccions funfair on Tibidabo hill.

ANTONI GAUDÍ'S VISION

Antoni Gaudí's amazing buildings in Barcelona established him as the most original European architect in the early years of the 20th century.

Antoni Gaudí (1852–1926) was born in Reus, Catalonia, the son of a coppersmith, and spent almost all his career in Barcelona. He was a patriotic Catalan and is said to have insisted on using the Catalan language even when talking to the King of Spain. The other major forces that shaped his life were a devotion to his work and a devout Christian faith.

In 1878 he graduated from the Escuela Superior de Arquitectura, Barcelona, and soon afterwards met Eusebi Güell (1847–1918), a wealthy industrialist and Catalan nationalist who became his main patron, commissioning the Parc Güell and other works.

Gaudí's work was influenced by various sources, including Gothic and Islamic architecture, and it has features in common with the Art Nouveau style fashionable at the time. However, his buildings have a sense of bizarre fantasy that sets them apart from anything else in the history of architecture. Walls undulate as if they were alive, towers grow like giant anthills, columns slant out of the vertical, and surfaces are encrusted with unconventional decoration, including broken bottles.

Gaudí died after being hit by a trolley bus. He cared so little for material success that – in spite of his great reputation – he was mistaken for a tramp and taken to a paupers' ward in hospital.

Richly coloured ceramic decoration in playful, abstract designs typifies Antoni Gaudí's work at Parc Güell.

Gaudí began work on his masterpiece, the Sagrada Família (Holy Family), in 1883. The huge church remains unfinished.

The dragon gate linking two entrance lodges (1884–88) for Eusebi Güell's estate in the upper part of Barcelona is one of Gaudí's finest pieces of ironwork.

Inside the curvaceous Casa Batlló on Passeig de Gràcia.

RESIDENTIAL BUILDINGS

In 1904–06 Gaudí remodelled a house for José Batlló y Casanovas, a Barcelona textiles manufacturer. The house had been built in the 1870s and was elegant but unremarkable. Gaudí completely transformed the exterior, adding an extra storey, topping it with a spectacular roof, and adorning the windows with flowing frames and balconies. Inside the house, the subtle interplay of forms continues. Immediately after the Batlló house, Gaudí designed an apartment block (1906–10) for Don Pedro Milà, Batlló's partner. The Casa Milà has been aptly nicknamed '*la pedrera*' (the quarry) because the curving facade looks like a strange cliff-face. The sense of movement and fantasy continues on the roof, where the chimneys and ventilation stacks are a riot of exuberant shapes.

On the rooftop of Casa Milà.

...ig i Cadafalch's Dutch-gabled Casa Amatller and Gaudí's scaly-...ed Casa Batlló jostle for attention on the 'Block of Discord'.

...ew from Park Güell, the park Gaudí designed and built ...tween 1900 and 1914 for his patron, Eusebi Güell, who ...tended it to be a suburban 'garden city' along the then ...hionable English lines.

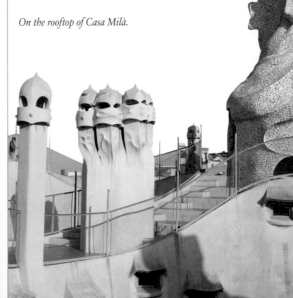

View from the castle at Tossa de Mar.

CATALONIA

Covering the area from the Pyrenees in the north to the Mediterranean in the east and the Ebro valley in the southwest, this region offers diverse scenery and attractions.

Main Attractions

Girona old town
Ruins of Empúries
Teatre-Museu Dalí, Figueres
Besalú
Tarragona
Parc Nacional de Aïguestortes
Montserrat Monastery
Poblet Monastery

atalonia is arguably the region of Spain with the strongest identity. The area is best known for three things: the ski resorts of the Pyrenees, the holiday resorts of the Costa Brava and Costa Daurada and the painter Salvador Dalí, who lived in Portlligat and whose work can be seen at the Teatre-Museu Dalí in Figueres. The charming city of Girona is home to the world's best restaurant, El Celler de Can Roca. Tarragona is noted for its Roman remains while Port Aventura is one of the largest theme parks in Europe. Montserrat is one of Spain's most spiritual sites.

Catalonia appears to have everything: rocky coasts, sandy beaches, lush plains, steppe, foothills and high sierra, all within a couple of hours of the major European metropolis of Barcelona (see page 251). There are historic cities and towns, tiny fishing villages, mountain hamlets, some 1,000 Romanesque chapels, Roman bridges, centuries-old stone farmhouses, vineyards, wheat fields, orchards, trout streams and wild boar – all in this one autonomous community. The presence of so much variety and density within such a small area, which has struggled to keep its own identity and language, is a continual surprise, even to long-time admirers of this corner of the earth.

Catalonia's 31,910 sq km (12,320 sq miles) comprise 6 percent of Spain's share of the Iberian peninsula, and are divided into four provinces, Barcelona, Girona, Lleida and Tarragona, which are subdivided into 38 *comarques*, or districts. But the most obvious components of Catalonia for the visitor are the Mediterranean, the Pyrenees and the interior.

The Costa Brava

The term *Costa Brava* (sheer, bold, rocky coast) was originally coined by the Catalan journalist Ferran Agulló in 1905 and initially only referred to part

Museu del Cinema, Girona.

of the rough coastline north of Barcelona. It is now taken to include all of the seafront that is in Girona province, from **Blanes ❶**, which has one of the Costa Brava's longest beaches, all the way up to the French border. Also at Blanes is the **Jardí Botànic Mar i Murtra** (www.marimurtra.cat; daily 9am–8pm), in a spectacular setting on the cliffs above the town, with a fantastic collection of Mediterranean and tropical plants. All along the coast, a series of *cales* or inlets, with small, intimate beaches, restaurants and hotels, punctuates rocky cliffs rising out of the blue-green Mediterranean.

Passenger boats ply their way from one inlet to another, picking up and dropping off travellers.

The hermitage of Santa Cristina, and the two beaches just below, lie between Blanes, the closest Costa Brava resort to Barcelona, and **Lloret de Mar ❷**. Above the populous and busy Lloret de Mar are the beaches at Canyelles and the Morisca inlets. Further north are the extraordinarily wild and unspoilt *cales* of Bona, Pola, Giverola, Sanlionç and Vallpregona.

Close by, **Tossa de Mar ❸**, once the haunt of artists, has a pretty old walled town, a lovely beach and a lot of charm. A little further north, **Canyet de Mar ❹** is a delicious inlet typical of this piny, rocky coastline. The coast road from Lloret de Mar to **Sant Feliu de Guíxols ❺** or the local ferry boat are the best ways to see the breathtaking coastal scenery.

An attractive small town known for its summer music festival, Sant Feliu marks the beginning of the more picturesque part of the Costa Brava, even though some of the resorts are flooded with tourists and Barcelona holidaymakers in July and August. The area is wonderful out of season under sharp winter sun, the early summer or mellow autumnal light.

Further north again are **S'Agaro**, the smart 1920s resort, and the more commercial **Platja d'Aro**, which has a big disco and shopping scene. **Palamós ❻** is the next main town along the coast. Founded in 1277, it had its heyday in the Middle Ages and is now a resort and an important cork-exporting and working fishing harbour.

Find sandy, child-friendly beaches along the Costa Brava.

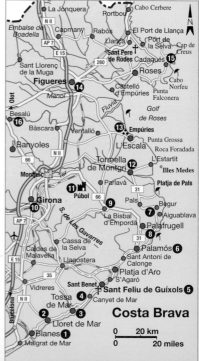

From here on a series of beaches and *cales* ranks among the simplest and most attractive stretches on the Costa Brava. S'Alguer is a tiny fishing inlet with boat houses on the sand and natural rock jetties, and Tamariu is a particularly picturesque *cala*. Aiguablava's Parador is just over the top from Tamariu, although many maps don't show this road. Aiguablava's sheer cliffs, high over the water, are among the Costa Brava's most spectacular sights, and the clear water is exquisite for snorkelling.

Begur ❼ is a trendy, pretty town full of bars and restaurants 200 metres (650ft) above the steep coastline. Distinctive features of Begur are its ruined 15th-century castle and its medieval watchtowers, which served as a defence against pirates.

About 8km (5 miles) south and a little inland, the bustling market town of **Palafrugell** ❽ is the nucleus of the pretty resorts Calella de Palafrugell and Llafranc. **La Bisbal** ❾ has held its Friday markets since 1322; earthenware products of all kinds are traditional specialities. This area, El Baix Empordà, has a wealth of medieval villages inland to explore that can only be entered on foot. Rural accommodation can often be found in or near these villages, which, despite their prettification, still have a timeless quality.

Cultured Girona

The city of **Girona** ❿, on the banks of the River Onyar, is a charming, small city. It is full of historical interest yet has a contemporary buzz with a full programme of cultural activities, gourmet restaurants, shopping and attractive hotels. A Roman settlement, it was completely surrounded by walls until modern times. It was so regularly besieged that it became known as 'the city of a thousand sieges'. In its medieval district is one of Europe's biggest and best-preserved Jewish quarters, the *Call*, with a **Museum of Jewish History** (Jul–Aug Mon–Sat 10am–8pm, Sun until 2pm, Sep–June Tue–Sat until 6pm, Mon–Sun until 2pm; free first Sun of the month). The former monastery of **Sant Pere de Galligants**, a perfect example of Catalan

Medieval castle in Tossa de Mar.

Romanesque architecture, lies to the north of the old town beside the Riu Galligants and now houses an **archaeological museum** (www.mac.cat/esl/Sedes/Girona; Sun 10am–2pm, Tue–Sat 10am–6pm).

Across the river, the **Banys Arabs** (www.banysarabs.org; Mar–Sept Mon–Sat 10am–7pm, Sun until 2pm, Oct Mon–Sat 10am–6pm, Sun until 2pm, Nov–Apr Mon–Sun until 2pm) were built in 1194, not by Muslims but by Christians.

Girona's monumental **Catedral** (www.catedraldegirona.org; daily, Apr–Oct 10am–8.30pm, Nov–Mar 10am–5.30pm), famous for its single nave, the widest Gothic nave in the world, stands impressively at the top of a long flight of stone steps. Construction of this superb basilica began in 1312 and took over four centuries to complete; several architectural styles, including Renaissance and Romanesque, have left their mark on it. The charge covers the cathedral, its cloisters and the museum, with a fine collection of ecclesiastical treasures, including medieval tapestries and manuscripts.

Girona has many interesting churches, art galleries and history museums including the **Museu del Cinema** (www.museudelcinema.cat; opening times vary, for details see website),

Catalonia

0   50 km

0   50 miles

which shows the history of cinema through a fascinating private collection There's also the **Girona Art Museum** (www.girona.cat/turisme/eng/museus_art. php; Tue–Sat 10am–6pm, Sun until 2pm), located in the old Episcopal Palace; it holds artworks dating from the Romanesque age to the early 20th century. Best of all, though, is simply to wander through history by meandering along its narrow lanes or following the stretch of 9th-century and medieval walls that skirt the eastern side of the old city.

Dalí's legacy

The northernmost section of the Costa Brava stretches from the town of **L'Escala** across the bay of Roses and north to France. Heading to the coast on the C-66 from Girona, stop at the atmospheric Castell Gala Dalí in **Púbol** ⑪ (www.salvador-dali.org; mid-June–mid-Sept daily 10am–8pm, times vary rest of year), a Gothic and Renaissance castle bought by Dalí for Gala, his adored wife. Inside, the rooms are furnished in Dalí's outlandish Surrealist style. Dalí lived here between 1982 and 1984, but a fire that broke out almost killed him and he subsequently abandoned the castle.

Heading north, **Torroella de Montgrí** ⑫, dominated by the 300-metre (985ft) rocky outcrop with the ruined Castillo de Montgrí perched on top, is known for its summer music festival. The nearby resort of **L'Estartit** is the departure point for snorkelling trips to the clear waters around the Medes Isles, a short way offshore. Just north of L'Escala, a pretty fishing port known for its anchovies, the Greek and Roman ruins at **Empúries** ⑬ (www.mac.cat; June–Sept daily 10am–8pm, Oct–mid-Nov and mid-Feb–May daily until 6pm, mid-Nov–mid-Feb Tue–Sun until 5pm) are an impressive glimpse into the area's rich history. This important site includes the Greek temples of Jupiter Serapis and Asklepios, a market place and assembly hall, as well as the remains of two Roman villas and an amphitheatre. The nearby beaches, complete with a Greek jetty, are very attractive and ideal for children. **Roses** is an important fishing port across the bay and a popular resort.

Figueres ⑭ is the area's main town, known for its 18th-century **Castell de Sant Ferrán** and its role in the development of the *sardana* – Catalonia's national dance – but mostly for its **Teatre-Museu Dalí** (www.salvador-dali. org; Jul–Sept daily 9am–8pm, Mar– June and Oct Tue–Sun 9.30am–6pm, Nov–Feb Tue–Sun 10.30am–6pm). This houses a startling collection of some of Salvador Dalí's most extraordinary creations. Born in Figueres in 1904, Dalí converted the former theatre building himself in the 1960s and early 1970s.

Among the most memorable exhibits are the Sala de Mae West and the Cadillac car awash with water on the inside, both created for the museum, and the room in which Dalí's extravagant jewellery is exhibited. The museum is understandably popular, so be prepared for a queue.

Teatre-Museu Dalí in Figueres.

Coves along the coastline between Tossa de Mar and Lloret de Mar.

Back on the coast, **Cadaqués**  is a sparkling white fishing village heavily populated with artists and literati, especially in summer, while Dalí's home in neighbouring **Portlligat** can be visited (www.salvador-dali.org; mid-June–mid-Sept daily 9.30am–9pm, times vary rest of year). **Cap de Creus**, a *parc natural* 8km (5 miles) north, makes an invigorating trip, especially if the prevailing wind, known as the *Tramuntana*, is blowing.

Nearby, the fishing town of **Port de la Selva** remains unspoilt and attractive. On the hillside above is the magnificent Romanesque monastery of **Sant Pere de Rodes** (www.en.mhcat.cat; Tue–Sat 10am–7pm, Wed until 8pm, Sun until 2.30pm), now fully restored and very striking, set against the panorama of the bright coastal towns and the sweep of the Mediterranean.

A worthwhile trip from Figueres is to the medieval village of **Besalú** ⑯, 20km (12 miles) further inland along the A-26. The village, now a national monument, is set beside the Riu Fluvià, and was once the capital of an enormous county covering present-day Barcelona and Girona provinces. It has many beautiful Romanesque buildings and a striking fortified bridge with portcullis.

The Golden Coast

With its long sandy beaches, the coast south of Barcelona is known as the **Costa Daurada** (Costa Dorada in Castilian), the 'Golden Coast'. In comparison to the rugged Costa Brava, these beaches and resorts have less personality, but there are still rewarding spots to explore.

Castelldefels is the closest beach to Barcelona, but it is worth going the extra 20 minutes to **Sitges** ⑰, a pretty town with good beaches and restaurants. Its **Museu Cau Ferrat** (www.mnac.cat; Sun 10am–3pm, May–Sept Tue–Sat 10am–8pm, Oct–Apr Tue–Fri 10am–6pm) has a fine collection of *modernista* objects donated by artist Santiago Rusiñol on his death in 1931. Also worth a look is the **Fundació Stämpfli Museu d'Art Contemporani** (www.fundacio-stampfli.org; opening times vary; charge), with its excellent collection of 1960s art.

Old City and River Onyar, Girona.

One of the high points of its busy cultural agenda is Carnival, where the gay community and locals alike party all night long and provide the best 'Rua' parada in Catalonia. The International Film Festival in October is a major event.

Tarragona

Tarragona ⑱ is rich in Roman art and archaeology. Its collection of Roman remains from the city of Tarraco were designated a Unesco World Heritage Site in 2000. It also has an impressive 12th-century **Catedral** (www.catedralde tarragona.com; opening times vary, see website for details) and a provincial freshness which, all together, create a unique blend of past and present, town and country. The impressive Roman **Aqüeducte de les Ferreres**, or Pont del Diable, is located on the city's outskirts, and the Arc de Barà is about 20km (12 miles) outside the city on the N340. The **Passeig Arqueològic** (www.tarragonaturisme.cat; Tue–Sun, mid-June–Sept 9am–9pm, Oct–mid-Jun until 7pm), a walkway through the city's ancient walls, including massive boulders set in place in the 3rd century BC, is one of Tarragona's most spectacular sights. The ruins of the **Amfiteatre** (same times as Passeig Arqueològic), built near the beach in order to use the natural incline of the shore, are also well preserved. The **Museu Nacional Arqueològic** (www.mnat.es; Sun 10am–2pm, Tue–Sat June–Sept 9.30am–8.30pm, Oct–May until 6pm) is well worth a visit.

Tarragona's **Rambla**, an elegant, broad walkway down to the sea, is a favourite spot for locals, ending in the Balcó del Mediterrani, a popular lookout point over the beaches and port.

Salou is famed for package holidays and **Port Aventura** ⑲ (www.portaven turaworld.com; opening times vary, see website for details), one of the largest theme parks in Europe.

The thrills and spills have been extended to include an aquatic park and hotels, and a golf course is planned. The park has its own train station, with several services daily from Barcelona and Tarragona.

Cambrils is an excellent fishing port and marina known for superb

TIP

Reus, inland from Tarragona, is more than a budget-airline destination. Birthplace of Spain's most famous architect, Antoni Gaudí, it has a Gaudí Centre (Plaça Mercaders, 3, www.gaudicentre.cat; daily) explaining his life and work. Follow the 'Gaudí Experience' with a walk past the town's fine *Modernista* buildings.

Dalí's house in Portlligat, near Cadaqués.

seafood. **L'Ametlla de Mar** and **L'Ampolla** are good beaches to the south, but the most interesting area is the **Delta de l'Ebre**, where even in August you can walk for miles over strands with barely a glimpse of another human – vast and empty spaces of sand, sea, sky and sun. It is a *parc natural*, known for its wildlife and rice paddies, where the traditional rice for paella is grown; El Trabucador and La Punta de la Banya are two of the wildest stretches of sand anywhere in Spain. There are plenty of routes to follow on foot or by bicycle, which can be rented in the area.

The Catalan Pyrenees

The sharp peaks and lush valleys of the Pyrenees, which form Catalonia's northern border, provide opportunities for skiing, snowboarding, climbing, adventure sports, fishing and endless walking – the outdoors experience enhanced by the region's long history of human settlement. Medieval bridges span trout streams, and gourmet restaurants welcome skiers at the foot of ski lifts.

The **Val d'Aran** is Catalonia's northwest corner. Isolated for centuries, this valley has its own language called 'L'Aranès', a linguistic branch of Gascon French with elements of Catalan and Basque. **Baquèira-Beret**, frequented by Spain's royal family, is one of the country's top ski resorts. There are mountain trails and superb views to be found on foot or horseback in the summer, or on skis in winter.

The peculiar mountain architecture of the Val d'Aran, like Alpine or Tyrolean high-country design – steep, slate roofs – reflects the stone *cordillera* that surrounds these Pyrenean dwellings. The 12th-century church at **Bossòst** is one of the most extraordinary religious monuments of the valley. The 13th-century church at **Salardú** houses the 'Sant Crist de Salardú' crucifix, one of the treasures of Pyrenean art.

The best route east from the Val d'Aran would be to start south, passing through the **Túnel de Vielha** and driving down to the **Vall de Boí**, which connects to the **Parc Nacional d'Aigüestortes i Estany de Sant**

The beach at Sitges on the Costa Daurada.

Maruici ⑳, Catalonia's only national park. The Boí valley's set of churches is the most important collection of Romanesque architecture in the Pyrenees. Aigüestortes National Park and Lake Mauricio are spectacular.

An alternative route south, equally picturesque, would be via Esport and Llavorsí, following the rushing water of the river La Noguera Pallaresa to **Sort**. The area is well charted for walking. Maps from tourist offices indicate the degrees of difficulty and *refugeos* for overnight stays. River sports are increasingly popular in this area.

East from Sort is **La Seu d'Urgell** ㉑ and its important medieval **Catedral de Santa María** and **Museu Diocesà** (Mon–Sat 10am–1.30pm and 4–7pm, until 6pm in winter, Sun 10am–1.30pm), containing sculptures, altarpieces and illuminated manuscripts. The cathedral is an outstanding example of Lombard Romanesque architecture, notable for its purity of line and proportion. The Eastern Pyrenees (Pirineus Orientales) extend almost to the Mediterranean Sea. **La Cerdanya** is an especially luminous

east–west running valley, which history has divided between France and Spain. It can be easily reached by train from Barcelona.

The Cerdanya valley

Solar energy projects, solar-powered bakeries and year-round tennis are a few results of the Cerdanya's record number of sun-hours (3,000 annually). About 45 minutes from **Puigcerdà** are a dozen ski resorts in three countries: Spain, France and Andorra. Boar, chamois and wild mushrooms are hunted in the autumn, while in spring and summer the **Riu Segre** is one of Europe's premier trout streams. The hiking and camping on the upper slopes of the Eastern Pyrenees, which reach heights over 2,900 metres (9,500ft), are superb.

Llívia ㉒, a Spanish enclave within French territory – thanks to the wording of the 1659 Treaty of the Pyrenees ceding certain 'villages' to France (Llívia was a 'town') – has ancient stone streets and buildings, Europe's oldest pharmacy, and one of the area's best restaurants, **Can Ventura**, located

Tour group outside Tarragona's cathedral.

HUMAN TOWERS

Tarragona province is known for its teams of *castellers*, who compete to build their daring human towers as high as possible during fiestas, especially the popular Santa Tecla festival in Tarragona city, on 23 September.

Three types of construction are possible: a *pilar*, with a single man on each level; a *torre*, with two men on each level; and a *castell* with three or more men per tier up to nine tiers.

The organisation of the team has to be meticulous, beginning with the formation of a tight group of strong men on the ground, *la pinya*, to take the weight of the people above. The final step is for a small boy or girl, the *anxeneta,* to scramble up all the shoulders to the top of the human tower and raise an arm to show that the structure has been completed.

in a farmhouse in the centre of town. La Cerdanya abounds in things to do: skiing, hiking, horse riding, mountain biking, golf, fishing or just browsing through tiny villages.

Guils, **Aja**, **Vilallovent** and **Bellver de Cerdanya** have retained the rustic Pyrenean flavour of the early mountain towns. La Cerdanya is open and lush, brilliant and broad compared to the Val d'Aran's steep, angular pitch.

Cradle of Catalonia

Southeast of La Cerdanya, the *cremallera* (zip) cogwheel train from Ribes de Freser up to the Vall de Núria, one of Spain's earliest winter-sports stations, is a spectacular excursion. Ribes is an easy day trip by train from Barcelona. The Vall de Núria is dominated by a sanctuary, the second most sacred place for Catalans after Montserrat.

Just to the south, **Ripoll ㉓** is an important medieval capital. A Christian stronghold and starting point of the *Reconquista*, it is considered the *bressol* (cradle) of Catalonia. The carved portal of Ripoll's **Santa María** monastery church is among the best Romanesque works in Spain.

Just east of Ripoll on the C-26 is the historic little town of **Sant Joan de les Abadesses ㉔**. The main attraction here is the **monastery** (www. monestirsantjoanabadesses.cat; daily Jul–Aug 10am–7pm, Nov–Feb Mon–Fri 10am–2pm, Sun 10am–2pm and 4–6pm, daily Mar–Apr and Oct 10am–2pm and 4–6pm, May–June and Sept until 7pm, daily Jul–Aug 10am–7pm), which was originally part of a Benedictine monastery founded in the 9th century. The highlight is the Calvary on the main altar, a masterpiece of Romanesque carving dating to 1250.

Also in this valley are the Camprodón, a ski area at Vallter, and two fine Romanesque churches at **Molló** and **Beget**.

La Garrotxa is an attractive volcanic area, good for cycling. Its capital, **Olot ㉕**, is known for its 19th-century school of landscape artists, whose work can be seen in the **Museu Comarcal** (Tue–Sun, closed lunch times). It also has the **Museu dels**

Meranges village is up in the Pyrenees.

Volcans (Volcanoes Museum; Tue–Sun, closed lunch times).

Rupit ㉖, 20km (12 miles) south of Olot in a stunning landscape, is a picturesque medieval village of stone houses. Its restaurants are famed for *patata de rupit*, potatoes stuffed with herbs, and lamb, duck and veal.

Between Olot and Girona is Banyoles, with its large lake. Here the terrain smooths out into the moist and fertile lowlands of the Empordà.

The interior

Catalans know that they have it all, an extensive coastline to spend summer weekends and an increasing range of summer activities, as well as the Pyrenees for winter skiing, but the plains and rich valleys of the interior also have plenty to offer, with smart provincial towns, medieval villages where history seems to have stood still, and a wealth of different landscapes for exploring.

Going north towards Girona from Barcelona you will find the Parc Natural de Montseny, a gentle mountain range, occasionally snowcapped in the winter, with plenty of routes mapped out for walking and excellent views of the coastal plain.

An hour north on the inland side of the Montseny, an easy day trip from Barcelona, is the thriving provincial capital of Vic ㉗, with a beautiful central square, La Plaça Major, exquisite delicatessens and a cathedral famous for the energetic murals of Catalan painter Josep María Sert. Sert's work was defaced by anticlerical vandals at the beginning of the Civil War in 1936, but was restored by the painter himself before his death in 1945. Many of the faces are said to be satirical representations of Fascist leaders, although Franco failed to catch on when he toured the cathedral.

The Museu Episcopal has a famed collection of Romanesque and Gothic art (www.museuepiscopalvic.com; Sat 10am–7pm, Sun until 2pm, Tue–Fri

Apr–Sept until 7pm, Oct–Mar 10am–1pm and 3–6pm).

Cardona ㉘, 50km (30 miles) to the west, is notable for its Parador within an ancient castle and church that overlook the Vall de Cardoner, complete with four-poster beds. The Salt Mountain, a 150-metre (500ft) hill of almost pure salt, is one of the most extraordinary geological curiosities in Catalonia; guided tours include a ride into the mountain (Tue–Sun). Solsona ㉙, further northwest, a town steeped in medieval mystery – silence, stone, tiny streets – is known for its Catedral and its Museu Diocesà (http://museusolsona.cat; Wed–Sat 11am–6.30pm, Sun until 2am, Jul–Aug open also on Tue), where you can view local archaeological finds. The two main squares are typical of early provincial architecture. Solsona's charm, however, is the *feel* of the place – the sense of time, the serenity of its antique granite world.

Black Virgin of Montserrat

Every visitor to Catalonia should see the sacred mountain of Montserrat ㉚ (tel: 938-777 701; www.montserratvisita.

Roman Aqüeducte de les Ferreres, Tarragona.

TIP

The Cistercian route links three magnificent monasteries which were a significant part of Catalan history: Poblet, Santes Creus and Vallbona de les Monges. Follow the route amidst vineyards and open countryside by foot, bike or even car. See www.larutadelcister.info for more information.

The richly decorated portico of Santa María monastery in Ripoll.

com; basilica daily 7.30am–8pm), the spiritual centre of Catalonia. The spectacular site is thrillingly reached by cable car from the Aeri de Montserrat station or by the *cremallera* (literally, 'zip': a rack railway) train from Monistrol de Montserrat station. Regular FGC trains from Plaça d'Espanya in Barcelona connect with both options. A Catalan religious shrine of great power and mystery, during the Franco regime Montserrat performed the only marriage ceremony and celebrated the only Masses in the Catalan language. *La Moreneta*, Catalonia's beloved Black Virgin (a statue said to have been made by St Luke), presides over the church nestled among the natural stone spires that rise up from the valley floor.

The boys' choir, **L'Escolania**, one of the oldest choirs in Europe, sings regularly, so it is worth timing a visit accordingly (Mon–Fri 1pm, Mon–Thu 6.45pm, Sun noon and 6.45pm; the choir are on holiday from late June–Aug and at Christmas). The museum has a valuable, wide-ranging collection, including some Impressionist paintings and one of the best collections of Catalan art (daily 10am–5.30pm).

Lleida (**Lérida** in Castilian) ㉛, 75km (45 miles) west of Montserrat, is an ancient city, perched on the edge of Spain's central plateau, capital of the province of Lleida and known for its agricultural industry, olive oil and wine production. It has a magnificent **Old Cathedral** (La Seu Vella; www.turoseuvella.cat; May–Sept Tue–Sat 10am–7.30pm, Sun until 3pm, Oct–Apr Tue–Fri 10am–1.30pm and 3–5.30pm, Sat 10am–5.30pm, Sun until 3pm), high on a hill above the old part of the city.

La Paeria (the town hall), on the Carrer Major, and the Gothic **Hospital de Santa María**, with pretty, arcaded inner courtyards, are two of Lleida's best early structures. The church of **Sant Llorenç**, in a square of the same name, represents the transition from Romanesque to Gothic. The delicate, octagonal bell tower, 76 metres (250ft) high, is particularly striking.

The town has a couple of interesting art galleries including the **Museu d'Art Jaume Morera** (http://mmorera.

paeria.es; June–mid-Sept Tue–Sun 10am–1pm and 6–8pm, Sun 10am–1pm, mid-Sep–May noon–4pm and 5–8pm, Sun 11am–2pm; free) which focuses on the work of local contemporary artists. An important commercial centre, Lleida has one of the longest shopping streets in Europe (2.2km/1.4 miles).

The **Monestir de Poblet** ㉜ (www.poblet.cat; Mon–Sat 10am–12.30pm and 3–5.25pm, Sun 10.30am–12.25pm and 3–5.25pm) is a Unesco World Heritage Site, 40km (25 miles) north of Tarragona and is the best-preserved Cistercian monastery in Europe. It was founded after the reconquest of Catalonia from the Muslims. Surrounded by a 1.8km (1-mile) wall, the complex of buildings is more reminiscent of a secular royal residence than a monastic refuge.

Ramón Berenguer IV, Count of Barcelona, completed his drive from Lleida, via the Segre and then the Ebro, to the sea and made the initial donation for the founding of the monastery in 1150 by Cistercian monks. Surrounded by rough, austere country, Poblet reflects this severity in its sober, powerful architecture. A self-sufficient unit, the monastery has always controlled vast tracts of land. It was ransacked in 1835 but subsequently rebuilt.

Penedès wine region

Vilafranca del Penedès ㉝, about 40km (25 miles) west of Barcelona, is the centre of Catalonia's largest wine-producing region, the Penedès. Its famous *cava* is a champagne-like sparkling white wine – 90 percent of it made from grapes grown in nearby **Sant Sadurní d'Anoia**. Many of the bodegas can be visited. The still wines of the region have also gained an international reputation, notably Torres, but some of the younger producers, especially of organic wines, are making their mark in conjunction with new Catalan cuisine.

Vilafranca is a town with an aristocratic architectural presence, and has plenty to offer visitors: its **Museu de les Cultures del Vi** (Sun 10am–2pm, May–Sept Tue–Sat 10am–7pm, Oct–Apr Tue–Sat 10am-2pm and 4–7pm) on Plaça Jaume I is one of the best wine museums in Europe.

Exhibit at Museu de les Cultures del Vi de Catalunya.

Plaça Santa Maria, the main square at Montserrat.

ARAGÓN

The towns and cities of this little-known region offer a feast of *Mudéjar* architecture. In sharp contrast are the dramatic landscapes of the Parque Nacional de Ordesa.

ragón is a treasure trove of Mud-éjar architecture, with fine examples in Tarazona, Catalyud and Teruel. Zaragoza is the region's capital and its main sights are the Basílica de Nuestra Señora del Pilar and the Aljafería Moorish palace. In the south, the mountains of El Maestrazgo have some spectacular gorges and historic towns. In the north, Jaca cathedral is a superb example of Romanesque architecture while the austere Monasterio de San Juan de la Peña was the inspiration for the Christian Reconquest. The Parque Nacional de Ordesa y Monte Perdido, high in the mountains, is the perfect place to get away from it all.

Aragón is known throughout Spain for the highest Pyrenees, the snowiest ski stations and as the home of the *jota*, the country's best-known folkloric music and dance. In winter, skiers race up the region's major roads in search of the perfect slopes, passing by Romanesque churches, villages that are dying from lack of attention, and walled cities that hide wonders of *Mudéjar* architecture.

Home of kings

The Romans founded Caesaraugusta, known today as Zaragoza, in 25 BC. Not much evidence of their presence remains today. Aragón was invaded along with the rest of Spain by the Muslims in AD

711; resistance to the occupation began around 100 years later.

In 1035, Ramiro I, the bastard son of Sancho III of the neighbouring kingdom of Navarre, inherited the kingdom of Aragón, which was united with Castile in 1469. At its height it included parts of France, the Balearic Islands, Naples and Sicily, and stretched as far south as the southeasterly region of Murcia.

Zaragoza was recaptured by the Christian armies at the orders of Alfonso I in 1118. But, despite the

Main Attractions

Tarazona
Zaragoza
Monasterio de Piedra
Mausoleo de los Amantes, Teruel
Albarracín
Jaca Cathedral
Monasterio de San Juan de la Peña
Ordesa National Park

Series of waterfalls in Parque Nacional de Ordesa.

Reconquest, Christians and Muslims lived alongside one another for centuries; the Muslims who remained were responsible for the *Mudéjar* architecture characteristic of the region. At the beginning of the 16th century it is estimated the *moriscos*, Muslims living under Christian domination, comprised 16 percent of the region's population. But in 1502 all Muslims were ordered to convert or leave the country, and the definitive expulsion order made in 1609 by Felipe III ended the cohabitation.

Although Fernando II was from Aragón (his marriage to Isabel of Castile marked the unification of Spain), he was not overly sensitive to the social realities of his home region. Ignoring the protests of his lords, he imposed the Inquisition, with the unpleasant result of having his Inquisitor General murdered in the Seo Cathedral in Zaragoza in 1485. The swords supposedly used to commit the crime can be seen today next to the altar.

Geographically, Aragón is divided into three areas that roughly correspond to its three provinces: the Pyrenees (Huesca), the Ebro river valley (Zaragoza) and the Iberian mountains (Teruel). It is the least densely populated of Spain's regions.

Zaragoza province

There are fine examples of *Mudéjar* architecture throughout the province of Zaragoza. **Tarazona ❶**, 72km (45 miles) northwest of the capital, is known as 'The *Mudéjar* City' and offers a spectacle of Islamic and Sephardic history. The cloisters of the 12th-century brick-domed **Catedral** (www.catedraldetarazona.es; mid-Mar–mid-Sept Tue–Sat 11am–2pm, 4–7pm, Sun until 6pm, mid-Sep–mid-Mar Tue–Sat until 6pm, Sat until 7pm, Sun am only) have some particularly fine Moorish tracery. The twisting, cobbled streets, crossed by *Mudéjar* arches, of the old Jewish district (located behind the Palacio Episcopal) are worth exploring on foot. Not to be missed are the 8th-century **Iglesia de Santa María Magdalena** and the marvellously decorated **town hall**.

The capital of the region, **Zaragoza ❷**, has a population of around 670,000. The visitor will find few monuments indicating the city's past grandeur since time, neglect and two terrible sieges suffered during the Napoleonic Wars (1808–9) destroyed a great deal. The old part of town, on the south bank of the Río Ebro, is the place to head for first – it contains most of the sights and plenty of hotels as well as lively bars.

Zaragoza has two important religious structures, the **Catedral de San Salvador**, known as **La Seo** (mid-June–mid-Sept Mon–Fri 10am–6pm, Mon–Thu 8am–8.30pm, Sat 10am–noon, 1–8.30pm, Sun 10–11.30am, 1.30–8.30pm, mid-Sept–mid-June daily 4–6.30pm, Mon–Fri 10am–2pm, Sat 10am–12.30pm, Sun 10am–noon), which was consecrated in 1119 on the site of the old mosque, and the basilica, known as **El Pilar** (www.basilicadelpilar.es; daily 6.45am–8.30pm, Sun until 9.30pm; tower: daily 10am–2pm,

Basílica de Nuestra Señora del Pilar, by the Ebro river in Zaragoza.

4–8pm, winter until 6pm, museum: Mon–Fri 10am–2pm and 4–8pm, Sat am only), built in honour of Spain's patron saint, the Virgin of Pilar, who supposedly appeared there on top of a pillar to St James in AD 40. The Parroquieta chapel's *Mudéjar* wall and ceiling, the Gothic altarpiece and the Baroque choir stalls are the cathedral's most outstanding features.

The Basílica de Nuestra Señora del Pilar, with its 11 domes, is the most distinctive feature of the city. The present building, dating from the 17th and 18th centuries, is the third on the site. Massive pillars split the church into three bays, some of the frescoes on the cupolas being the work of Goya. But the focal point is the Lady Chapel. There you will see the legendary marble pillar that supports the much-venerated Virgin, a tiny wooden image encrusted in silver, whose rich mantle is changed every day. The altarpiece in the basilica is alabaster. The day of El Pilar, 12 October, a national holiday, is attended by lavish celebrations in Zaragoza, with city processions of cardboard giants.

Moorish pleasure palace

The **Aljafería** (www.cortesaragon.es; Apr–Oct daily 10am–2pm and 4.30–8pm, Nov–Mar until 6pm and closed Sun pm; free Sun) to the west of the old town has been fully restored and is the site of the local parliament. It was first built in the 11th century by the ruling Islamic king and could well have been taken from the *Arabian Nights*, according to testimonies of the time. The Catholic Monarchs transformed part of the palace into their headquarters – later used by the Inquisition – and then it became an army barracks in the 19th century. Fernando and Isabel's throne room, with its remarkable ceiling, and the Moorish chapel are the best-preserved parts of the interior. Outside, Santa Isabel's courtyard has some splendid *Mudéjar* arches.

The **Museo Goya – Colección Ibercaja** (http://museogoya.ibercaja.es; mid-Mar–Oct Mon–Sat 10am–2pm and 4–8pm, Sun am only, Nov–mid-Mar Mon–Sat 10am–8pm, Sun 10am–2pm; free), on Calle de Espoz y Mina, has a large collection of Spanish art,

Zaragoza's central market and tram.

Aragón

0   20 km
0   20 miles

but the main draw is the fine etchings by Goya on the top floor of the building. Goya was born in the village of **Fuendetodos**, 50km (30 miles) directly south of Zaragoza. The house where he was born is a **museum** (www.fundacionfuendeto dosgoya.org; Tue–Sun 11am–2pm and 4–7pm), with rooms furnished in a simple style appropriate to the period. Nearby, a museum of Etchings (same opening times) holds the four famous series of prints by Goya: Los desastres de la guerra (the Disasters of War), La tauromaquia (Bullfighting), Los disparates (The Follies) and Los caprichos.

Calatayud ❸, 60km (35 miles) southwest of Zaragoza on the A-2, is justly famous for its ornate *Mudéjar* towers, the best example of which rises above the Colegiata de Santa María. Nearby is the **Monasterio de Piedra** ❹ (http://monasteriopiedra.com; daily 10am–1pm and 3–5pm), founded by Alfonso II in 1195 and now an oasis of gardens, lakes and waterfalls around a 12th-century Cistercian monastery (now a hotel and park complex).

Also in the southern part of Zaragoza province is the beautiful old town of **Daroca** ❺. Surrounded by nearly 3km (2 miles) of walls with more than 100 towers, Daroca appeared in the annals of the Greek voyagers.

Visitors who want to understand Spain's more recent history should visit **Belchite** ❻, 40km (25 miles) southeast of Zaragoza. This town was the site of one of the most ferocious battles of the Civil War, and its ruins have been preserved as a reminder of the horrors of war. A new town, completed in 1954, was built alongside the original devastated site.

The lovers of Teruel

Of the three Aragonese provinces, Teruel is the least known, and the capital city of **Teruel** ❼ has the smallest population of all Spain's provincial capitals. It is a province in which

Mudéjar architecture abounds, both in the capital itself and in towns so far off the beaten track that most Spaniards don't know they exist.

The **Catedral** (June–Sept Mon–Fri 11am–2pm and 4–8pm, Sat–Sun pm only, Oct–May until 7pm; free) is justly famous for its remarkable ceiling, a masterpiece of the 14th century in which daily life in the Middle Ages is depicted in portraits painted on wood. Another outstanding *Mudéjar* monument is the Gothic **Iglesia de San Pedro** on the eastern side of the former Jewish quarter.

Next to the church is the **Mausoleo de los Amantes** (www.amantesdeteruel. es; daily 10am–2pm and 4–8pm), a museum built around the funerary chapel of the Lovers of Teruel, a tragic couple immortalised in poems and plays, whose fame in Spain exceeds that of Romeo and Juliet. A relief by Juan de Avalos depicts the lovers and, if you peer into the tomb, you can see the mummified bodies. Diego Marcilla and Isabel Segura were in love, the story goes, but their parents opposed the marriage. Diego left to

TIP

Zaragoza's Roman past can be traced along the Ruta de Caesaraugusta, which takes in four sights: Museo del Foro (a reconstruction of the forum), Museo del Teatro (the ruins of the theatre), Museo del Puerto Fluvial (river port remains) and Museo de las Termas Públicas (public baths). A combined ticket costs €7.

Inside Iglesia de San Pedro, Teruel.

make his fortune and thus endear himself to his lover's father. He came home in 1217 a rich man, only to find his beloved walking down the aisle with another. He died of a broken heart the next day and Isabel kissed the cadaver and passed on to a better world with her Diego.

Visitors should also stop to admire the twin *Mudéjar* towers of San Martín and El Salvador, supposedly the result of a contest between two Muslim architects in love with the same woman. The winner won his love and the loser (who built San Martín) jumped off the tower.

Just outside Teruel is **Dinopolis** (www.dinopolis.com; Jul–Aug daily 10am–8pm, days vary the rest of the year), a palaeontological theme park.

Of all the mountain villages in Teruel, **Albarracín** ❽ is the best-preserved. Located 30km (18 miles) west of Teruel, it is a place to stroll through, admiring the town walls, the towers, the harmony between nature and man-made structures and the architectural magic of a fortified town rising high above a river.

Moving southeast of Teruel, to the harsh mountains and spectacular gorges of **El Maestrazgo** ❾, stop at **Mora de Rubielos** to see its immense castle, built between the 13th and 15th centuries, and the nearby **Rubielos de Mora** (they shouldn't be confused). The truth is that nearly any road through the mountains of Teruel will lead to *Mudéjar* towers, castles, city walls or outstanding churches.

Alcañiz ❿, to the northeast of Teruel, is famed for its castle, with murals depicting the history of the Calatrava Order, and the Colegiata de Santa María, with its great Baroque portal. North of Alcañiz, towards Zaragoza on the N-232, is **Azaila** ⓫, which has been declared a national monument due to the discovery of an ancient Iberian-Roman *castro* (hillfort).

Romanesque Huesca

If the dominant architectural or historical motif in Zaragoza and Teruel is *Mudéjar*, moving north to the province of Huesca the traveller is surrounded by Romanesque buildings.

City walls of Albarracín.

The stream of pilgrims on their way to Santiago during the Middle Ages encouraged the construction of churches from Catalonia to Galicia, of which Jaca's cathedral is one of the most important.

In addition to offering literally hundreds of well-preserved examples of the Romanesque style, this visually striking region is a paradise for hikers, skiers, walkers and climbers.

The capital of the province is **Huesca** ⓬, whose age of splendour was the 13th century. Pedro IV founded the University of Huesca in the 14th century, but it was abolished in 1845, by which time the city had been reduced to the status of an insignificant provincial capital. Huesca's **Catedral** (June–Sept Mon–Sat 10am–2pm, 4–7.30pm, Apr–May and Oct Mon–Fri 10am–1.30pm, 4–6pm, Sat am only, Nov–Mar Mon–Sat 10am–1.30pm; museum: www.museo. diocesisdehuesca.org; Mon–Fri 10am–2pm, 4–6pm, Sat am only) dates from the 15th and 16th centuries, built on the earlier foundations of the old mosque. Of particular interest is the alabaster Renaissance altarpiece by Damián Forment.

Nearby is the **Ayuntamiento** (town hall; Mon–Fri), built in 1578, with a mural depicting the story of 'The Bell of Huesca', one of the bloody legends of Spanish history: Ramiro II, a former monk who ruled Aragón in the 12th century, was disturbed by his nobles' refusal to submit to his rule. After consulting with the abbot of his former monastery, Ramiro summoned the nobles to a banquet to celebrate the casting of a new bell that the king said would be heard throughout Aragón. When they arrived Ramiro had them all decapitated, piling up their heads in the form of a large bell, and order was restored.

The other major city in the province is **Jaca** ⓭, whose **Catedral** is one of Spain's treasures of Romanesque architecture. **La Ciudadela** (www. ciudadeladejaca.es), a fortress built by Felipe II, is currently under the jurisdiction of the army but is open for guided tours in summer.

Soon after the kingdom of Aragón was established, King Sancho Ramírez

Depiction of the Lovers of Teruel in the Mausoleo de los Amantes, Teruel.

Teruel's main street.

PHILBY AT THE FRONT

The Battle of Teruel, fought between December 1937 and February 1938, in the worst winter for 20 years, was a turning point of the Spanish civil war. The Republican government hoped the capture of the city of Teruel would prove that the Nationalist advance could be stopped, but it was Franco who emerged the victor, now able to break out and reach the Mediterranean.

Among those present at the battle was Kim Philby, a British intelligence agent who was ostensibly correspondent for *The Times* newspaper but was really, as was later revealed, a Soviet spy. Philby had a miraculous escape when the car he was travelling in with two fellow journalists was hit by a shell and he was the only one to survive. He was later decorated by Franco.

TIP

If you don't have a car, or fancy a break from driving, consider taking a tour of Ordesa National Park with Ordesa Taxi (tel: 630-418 918; www.miradoresdeordesa.es). The half-day trips by minibus from Torla take in some stunning scenery as well as rare flora and fauna. Prices start at €20 per person.

founded the **Monasterio de San Juan de la Peña** ⓮ (www.monasteriosanjuan. com; daily June–Aug 10am–2pm, 3–8pm, Mar–May and Sep–Oct until 7pm, Nov–Feb Sun–Fri am only, Sat until 5pm), which became the point of religious inspiration for the Christian Reconquest campaign. Located 27km (17 miles) southwest of Jaca, the monastery is wedged between enormous boulders and under a sheer rock cliff. It contains an extraordinary Romanesque cloister and a 10th-century church, the monks' sleeping quarters and the Nobles' Pantheon, which houses the tombs of early Aragonese kings.

In the hills south of the *monasterio* is the Castillo de Loarre (www.castillo deloarre.es), one of the finest fortresses in the Pyrenees. West of Jaca are **Los Valles**, a series of valleys that eventually lead to Navarre and that maintain the old architectural, linguistic and cultural traditions of Aragón. The villages of **Hecho** and **Ansó** feature houses with odd-shaped chimneys distinguishing one town from another, and the windows are outlined in white.

Hiking in Parque Nacional de Ordesa.

Another showcase town worth a detour in northwest Aragón is **Sos del Rey Católico**, birthplace of Fernando II (the 'Catholic King') and one of the Five Towns (Cinco Villas) honoured by Felipe V for their support during the War of Spanish Succession. The entire town is a monument of grand stone mansions and flower-decked houses. The frescoed **Iglesia de San Esteban** and the Gothic **Lonja** (exchange building) are worth tracking down.

Mountaineering

In the north of Huesca province the Pyrenees are at their highest and most forbidding. Along the 150km (93-mile) frontier with France there are just three passes, and the only painless, all-year route across is the 8km (5-mile) -long **Túnel de Somport** ⓯, north of Jaca. This is magnificent country for skiing in winter: **Candanchú**, **Canfranc**, **Panticosa** and **Formigal** are all popular outdoor resorts.

The tallest peak in the range is **Aneto** (3,408 metres/11,180ft) above Benasque, followed by **Vignemale** (3,298 metres/10,820ft), just over the border in France. There are innumerable unfrequented valleys to explore (many of them dead ends), as well as pretty towns with Romanesque churches, but the geography forces a leisurely pace rather than a crammed itinerary.

By far the best introduction to the high Pyrenees is the **Parc Nacional de Ordesa y Monte Perdido** ⓰ (www. magrama.gob.es), a wilderness national park of gorges, forests, waterfalls and gigantic cliffs, inhabited by a rich flora and fauna. The town of Torla is the normal entry point and there is a visitor centre near here, a short way into the park, from which marked walking trails start. An alternative approach is to drive up to the Parador de Bielsa (www.paradores.es) in the north of Ordesa, a state-run hotel with an incomparable mountain view.

Celebrating the San Fermín festival in Pamplona.

NAVARRE AND LA RIOJA

The medieval kingdom of Navarre has an abundance of monuments, and its capital, Pamplona, hosts the world-renowned San Fermín fiesta. La Rioja's vineyards produce the best red wine in Spain.

N avarre is best known for *Los Sanfermines*, the bull-running festival in Pamplona, while La Rioja is one of the world's finest wine-producing regions, centred around the town of Haro. In Olite is the former residence of the kings of Navarre, who are buried in the Romanesque Monasterio de Leyre, while Tudela illustrates how Jews, Muslims and Christians lived in harmony. In the north of the region are lush green valleys and near the French border is the town of Roncesvalles, famous for its sheep-milk cheese and for being the start of the Camino de Santiago pilgrimage route.

In the year 778, the mighty Charlemagne, King of the Franks, made an unsuccessful attempt to conquer the lands to the south. As he headed home with his tired army, he was ambushed at Roncesvalles by Basques, who annihilated the rearguard.

There died the Frankish hero Roland, later to be immortalised in the epic poem *Chanson de Roland*, with the Basques conveniently replaced by Muslim attackers. Soon after, a group of Basque warlords declared themselves independent, and the state they founded was destined eventually to become the kingdom of Navarre. Navarre was only finally demoted to the status of province in 1841. The greatest of its kings was Sancho III, El Grande,

one of a line of Sanchos that ran from the 10th to the 13th century. Sancho III doubled Navarre's territories through astute politics, military campaigns and marriages, and introduced the beginnings of a modern legal system and a process of Church reform.

Fueros and Carlism

The period immediately following the death in 1035 of Sancho III marked an enormous advance for Navarre, as the prosperous and secure kingdom initiated the *fueros* system, or

Main Attractions

Vineyards of La Rioja
Monasterio de Santa María La Real, Nájera
Santo Domingo de la Calzada Cathedral
Pamplona and its Sanfermines fiesta
Estella
Olite Castle
Monasterio de Leyre
Roncesvalles

Olite castle, Navarre.

the guarantee by the monarchy that towns and cities could enjoy a certain autonomy with their customary laws. Beginning in the 13th century, Navarre was ruled by a succession of French dynasties. But due mainly to a series of weak rulers, the Duke of Alba was able to seize the kingdom in 1512 in the name of King Fernando.

Navarre was no longer independent but it did have its *fueros*, and the monarchs in Madrid were obliged to uphold them. This system made Navarre into a very pro-monarchist region, and it is not surprising that the new ideas of liberalism, republicanism and anti-clericalism penetrating Spain in the late 18th and 19th centuries were not well received in Navarre. The centralist tendencies these movements implied were a threat to Navarre's autonomy.

When Fernando VII died in 1833, there was bitter disagreement as to who should succeed him, his daughter Isabel or his brother Carlos. Navarre supported Carlos, in the hope that a strong ruler like him would restore its traditions. The last of the Carlist wars ended in 1876, but the Carlists resurfaced during the Civil War, when they actively sided with Franco and played a crucial role in the coup that began the war. Franco, in fact, praised Navarre after a visit in 1936 as 'the cradle of the nationalist movement'.

This set Navarre off from the neighbouring Basque Country, with which it has so many ties. Even though northern Navarre is Basque-speaking and shares a common past and many customs, the more industrial provinces of Vizcaya, Álava and Guipúzcoa sided with the Republic, and lost.

As the Basque nationalist movement began to develop in the early 20th century, there were vain attempts to unite with Navarre, but the centuries-old *Navarrismo* of the more conservative sectors has always impeded attempts at unity.

Vineyards of La Rioja

The small neighbouring region of La Rioja was ruled by Gascons, Romans, Muslims and Navarrans, before being incorporated into the crown of Castile. La Rioja only regained its name

RIOJA WINE

The wine region of Rioja is distinct from the local government region of La Rioja and extends for about 120km (75 miles) along the Ebro River. Its northern border is set by the Sierra de Cantabria and its southern one by the Sierra de la Demanda. It is divided into three parts: Rioja Alta, Rioja Baja and Rioja Alavesa (which is in the Basque province of Álava). The land slopes gently downwards from west to east, and as it does so the climate becomes gradually drier and hotter because of the influence of the Mediterranean.

The Denominación de Origen Rioja covers 57,000 hectares (142,500 acres) of vineyards, which produce 250 million litres (55 million gallons) of wine a year, 85 percent of it as reds made predominantly from tempranillo grapes. Haro is the de facto capital of the Rioja wine region and home to around a dozen bodegas which can be visited, including Bodegas Muga (Tel: 941-306 060; www.bodegasmuga.com) ; book in advance for an English-language tour. One of the best museums in the area is the **Museo de la Viña y el Vino de Navarra** (www.museodelvino denavarra.com; Mon–Sat 10am–2pm and 4–7pm, Sun am only, winter Mon–Fri 10am–5pm, Sat–Sun until 5pm) in Olite, which traces the history of wine. Rioja Trek (tel: 941-587 354; www.riojatrek.com) near Logroño offers guided tours of wineries and tasting courses. For more information about Riojan wines see www.riojawine.com.

in 1980, and was recognised as an autonomous community in 1982.

Logroño ❶, Rioja's busy capital, lies between the two zones. The old quarter, bordered by the Ebro and the medieval walls, has the most charm. Traditionally a centre for pilgrims, many monuments, such as the **Puente de Piedra** and the **Iglesia de Santiago El Real** (daily), with its equestrian statue of Saint James over the main door, are connected to the pilgrimage to Santiago de Compostela. The twin Baroque towers of Logroño's **Catedral de la Redonda** (daily) are easily distinguished among the narrow streets.

Haro ❷, 35km (22 miles) northwest of Logroño, is the undisputed wine capital of La Rioja. The flamboyant Gothic, single-naved **Iglesia de Santo Tomás** (daily), constructed in 1564, is the town's main monument. The old quarter is filled with taverns and cafés where you can sample local wines. Many of the town's manufacturers offer guided tours and tasting visits (see page 294). In nearby Briones, the fascinating private wine museum **Vivanco Museum of Wine**

Culture (http://vivancoculturadevino.es; times vary) narrates some 8,000 years of winemaking.

Leaving Logroño on the main A12 west brings you to **Nájera**, in earlier times court of the kings of Navarre. Here you will find their royal pantheon at the **Monasterio de Santa María La Real** (www.santamarialareal.net; Tue–Sun 10am–1pm and 4–7pm, winter until 5.30pm). Not to be missed are the 11th-century Gothic cloister, the Claustro de los Caballeros and the Plateresque windows over the grassy patio.

About 20km (12 miles) further west is **Santo Domingo de la Calzada ❸**, a town dedicated to the Santiago pilgrimage route. The Romanesque-Gothic **Catedral** (www.catedralsanto domingo.es) in the medieval quarter houses the 11th-century Santo Domingo's tomb.

San Millán de la Cogolla ❹, about 10km (6 miles) south of Nájera, is the site of the **Monasterio de Yuso** (www. monasteriodesanmillan.com; Easter– Sept Tue–Sun 10am–1.30pm and 4–6.30pm, closed Sun pm and Mon in winter), where a 10th-century

The grape harvest at López de Heredia winery, Haro.

manuscript on texts by Saint Augustine, the *Glosas Emilianenses*, contains the first words to have been written in Castilian Spanish.

Navarre

The Roman city of Pompaelo, **Pamplona** (Iruña) ❺ was from the 10th to the 16th century the capital of the kingdom of Navarre. Since the Civil War, the conservative, religious and hard-working Navarrans have transformed their ancient citadel into a prosperous industrial city. High-rise apartment blocks, manicured boulevards and factories form a protective ring around the lovely old city, which hovers above the **Río Arga**.

The centre of this area is the **Plaza del Castillo**, lined with outdoor cafés. Novelist Pío Baroja once said of the *paseo* in this plaza that the varying degrees of aristocracy were as evident as if they were separate floors of a building. Industry and democracy may have made a difference here, but the city's noble past is close at hand in the **Palacio de Navarra** (www.navarra.es) at the western end of the plaza.

The medieval village of Ujué.

Most of Pamplona's historical buildings are located north of the Plaza del Castillo. Near the old city walls, in the Plaza Santa María La Real, is the 14th-century **Catedral** (www.catedraldepamplona.com; mid-Mar–mid-Sept Mon–Sat 10.30am–7pm, winter until 5pm), with an 18th-century facade by the neoclassical architect Ventura Rodríguez. Inside are the lovely alabaster tombs of Carlos III of Navarre and his wife Leonor. The adjoining Gothic cloister is considered to be the best of its kind in Spain. When you've finished, stretch your legs with a walk around the city walls (www.murallasdepamplona.com).

The **Museo de Navarra** (Tue–Sat 9.30am–2pm and 5–7pm, Sun 11am–2pm; free Sat pm and Sun), situated in a 16th-century hospital in Calle Jaranta, has interesting pieces of Navarran archaeology, frescoes taken from Romanesque churches around the province and Goya's portrait of the Marquis of San Adrián.

Beginning at the south end of the Plaza del Castillo, the tree-lined **Paseo de Sarasate**, named after the native violinist, is Pamplona's main promenade.

It runs past the Monument to the Fueros and the 13th-century **Iglesia de San Nicolás**, skirting the grassy Ciudadela, a fortress built by Felipe II and now the site of outdoor concerts.

The Paseo finishes in the **Parque de la Taconera**, a park resplendent with tame deer, fountains and monuments to Navarran heroes. The **Iglesia de San Lorenzo**, located in the middle of the park, has a chapel dedicated to the city's saint, San Fermín.

The new **Museo Universidad de Navarra** (http://museo.unav.edu; Tue–Sat 10am–8pm, Sun noon–2pm, summer Tue–Sun 11am–2pm) houses contemporary art with works by Picasso, Tàpies, Rothko and Chillida as well as a vast photographic collection and a thriving cultural centre.

Pamplona's bullrun

There is a measured, stately air to Pamplona much of the time. Native *pamplonicas*, proud of their industriousness, look down upon southern Spain's legendary indolence, although the University of Navarre's student throng lead, a furious bar life. But at noon on 6 July, the Eve of San Fermín, a *chupinazo* (rocket) fired from the balcony of the 16th-century **Ayuntamiento** (town hall) puts an end to the order that has made the city flourish. For the following week, Pamplona becomes delirious. It has been said that this wildest of wild fiestas is an extension, rather than an aberration, of the Navarran personality.

The southwest countryside

Navarre province is enormously varied, ranging from the western Pyrenees to vineyards near Rioja to the desert-like Bardenas Reales north of Tudela. Pilgrims on their way to Santiago from France were obliged to travel through Navarre, with the result that Romanesque churches abound.

Southwest of Pamplona is **Estella** (Lizarra) ❻, one of Navarre's most monumental cities and the closest thing to a holy city for the Carlists. Among the splendid Romanesque churches in Estella are **Santa María Jus del Castillo** (believed to be built over a synagogue), **San Pedro** and **San Miguel**, while the 12th-century

LOS SANFERMINES

Habitually a reserved, provincial city, Pamplona becomes world-famous for one week a year between 6 and 14 July, during Los Sanfermines. The fiesta's reputation rests on an event which lasts only four or five minutes at the start of each day, the driving of bulls from a holding pen outside the city centre to the bullring for the afternoon's bullfight. Crowds of people wearing white T-shirts and red scarves around their necks run with the bulls. Don't be tempted to jump into the cordoned-off streets to join them unless you know what you are doing, as there have been many accidents and even fatal gorings.

The fiesta draws around 800,000 people from many different countries, many of whom treat it as an opportunity to spend eight inebriated and sleepless days. Few seem aware that the *encierro* is merely a detail of a traditional religious festival that gained emphasis only because of the fascination of one particular American writer. Ernest Hemingway came to Pamplona in 1923, the first of nine visits, which kick-started a life-long love of bullfighting as well as inspiring his first novel, *The Sun Also Rises*. However, not everyone is enamoured with the festival, which culminates in bullfights each evening. Animal rights group PETA has said: 'In this day and age, it's appalling that sensitive animals are still being tormented and killed in front of a screaming crowd.'

Tudela's Plaza de los Fueros, at the heart of the old town.

Path through the Irati Forest.

Palacio de los Reyes is a rare example of secular Romanesque architecture.

Not far southwest of Estella, at the foot of **Montejurra**, site of a historic Carlist victory over the republican troops in 1873, is the **Monasterio de Irache** (Wed–Sun 10am–1.15pm and 4–6pm, closed mid-Nov–mid-Jan; free), which had its own university in the 16th century. And further down the A-12 highway is **Viana**, founded in 1219 by Sancho the Strong.

The Crown Princes of Navarre held the title of Prince of Viana until they assumed the throne. In the **Iglesia de Santa María** you can see the tomb of Cesare Borgia, who died in battle here in 1507.

The NA-132 road takes you from Estella to **Tafalla**, where the Iglesia de Santa María has a beautiful Renaissance altarpiece. Before reaching Tafalla, veer to the left to visit **Artajona**, a fortified town that rises up in the distance like a ghost from the Middle Ages.

Olite

South from Tafalla is **Olite** ❼, the former residence of the kings of Navarre from the 15th century. Their castle has been restored and is used for theatre and music festivals, as well as being a government-run Parador. Two side trips from Olite are well worth the time: the village of **Ujué** has barely been touched since the Middle Ages and has miraculously survived intact. The **Monasterio de la Oliva** (daily), used today by Trappist monks, was founded in 1134 by King García Ramírez.

Tudela

South of Olite on the AP-15, **Tudela** ❽ is one of those remarkable Spanish cities that illustrate the harmony in which Christians, Muslims and Jews lived for several centuries. It was founded in 802 by the Moors, the remains of whose mosque can be seen today inside the **Catedral**, (www.palaciodecanaldetudela.com), a brilliant example of the transition from Romanesque to Gothic. The intricately carved Last Judgement doorway in the main facade is a sculpted vision of the rewards and punishments supposedly awaiting us all.

Tudela's old Jewish district (*aljama*) is one of the best-known in Spain. It is

situated between the cathedral and the junction of the Ríos Queiles and Ebro.

Northeast from Tudela, just before you reach the N-240, is the town of **Sangüesa** ⑨, located at the foot of the Navarre Pyrenees. This is another 11th-century town, founded by Alfonso I, the Warrior, with another **Iglesia de Santa María**. This one has one of Spain's most beautiful Romanesque porticoes.

Nearby, above the Yesa Reservoir and surrounded by rugged mountains, is the **Monasterio de Leyre** ⑩ (www. monasteriodeleyre.com; daily Jul–Aug 10am–7.30pm, Mar–June and Sep–Oct until 7pm, Nov–Feb 6pm), Navarre's spiritual centre in the 11th century and pantheon of Navarre kings. Consecrated in 1057, it features beautiful Romanesque architecture, including a magnificent vaulted crypt. Abandoned in the 19th century, the monastery has been restored by Benedictine monks and now includes a hotel.

Between here and Sangüesa is the fine 16th-century **Castillo de Javier**, (www.javier.es/Turismo/el-castillo.html; daily Mar–Oct 10am–7pm, Nov until 6pm, Dec–Feb until 4pm) dedicated to San Francisco Xavier, the great Jesuit missionary who was born in a house on this site.

Pilgrims still visit the castle to pay homage to San Francisco Xavier, and they say that one of the crucifixes there bled the day the saint died in 1552.

A tour of the valleys

To the north of Leyre and the N-240 highway is a series of beautiful green valleys dotted with small villages that extend west to Guipúzcoa and east to Huesca and the high Pyrenees. These valleys have few monuments per se to offer, although there are isolated Romanesque churches and hermitages, but rather stand out for their setting and traditional architecture.

Roncal and **Isaba** are two of the major villages in the Roncal valley, which is surrounded by peaks reaching as high as 2,000 metres (6,560ft).

North of Ochagavía in the Salazar valley is the **Irati Forest**, one of Europe's densest and largest beech forests, supplier of masts for the 'invincible' Armada and said to be inhabited

EAT

Roncal is best known for its semi-hard sheep's milk cheese, Queso del Roncal. It is produced between December and July, takes at least four months to mature and has a creamy, slightly spicy taste. Buy some in the village or from Quesos Larra (Parque Empresarial Valle de Roncal; www.quesoslarra. com; Mon–Sat) in Burgui.

by witches. Continuing west, you reach **Roncesvalles** ⓫ (Orreaga), where pilgrims coming from France would stop for the night at one of the most important hostelries along the road to Santiago. Today it is an Augustine monastery. Also in Roncesvalles you can see the **Colegiata Real**, an overly restored Gothic construction in whose chapterhouse lies the enormous tomb of Sancho VII, the Strong (1154–1234), and his queen.

The Baztán valley

Up the road from Orreaga at **Valcarlos** is the steep canyon where the famous ambush of 778 featured in the *Chanson de Roland* took place; you can understand how Charlemagne's men didn't stand a chance against the Basque warriors perched high on either side. This is smugglers' country, and Valcarlos has more than a few families who have made small fortunes by carrying merchandise back and forth over the French border.

The last of the valleys before entering Guipúzcoa is the beautiful **Valle de Baztán** ⓬, with its 14 villages of stone houses, many of them with noble coats of arms. There are noticeably more heraldic crests in Navarre than in most other provinces, where an estimated 20 percent of the population during the heyday of the kingdom belonged to a noble family.

The capital of the Baztán is **Elizondo**, a resort town and residence of many *indianos* – Basques who went off to the New World, made money and returned to live out their days in their villages. North of Elizondo is **Arizcun**, one of the villages partially inhabited by *cagotes*, who suffered centuries of persecution due to their supposed descent from lepers, Jews, Muslims, Visigoths or even Cathars.

Further north still is **Zugarramurdi**, where witches once gathered in caves to hold *akelarres* or covens. The caves (Jul–Sept daily 10.30am–8pm) were already inhabited in the Neolithic period, but their fame as the site of witches' gatherings arose from an Inquisition trial in Logroño in 1610, when 40 unfortunate women were accused of witchcraft and 12 of them were burnt at the stake.

Tudela.

Fishermen's quarter, Hondarribia.

Getaria's harbour.

THE BASQUE COUNTRY

Peaceful green river valleys set against forbidding peaks form the backdrop to the lively fishing ports, inviting resorts and sandy beaches of the Basque Country.

The Basque Country has a strong sense of identity and also a unique language. The main cities are San Sebastián (Donostia), famous for its Michelin-starred restaurants and beautiful beaches, and Bilbao (Bilbo), home of the futuristic Museo Guggenheim and its world-class collection of modern art; its designer, Frank O. Gehry, also designed a new hotel in Elciego. The coast here offers some of the best surfing in Europe. Inland, famously painted by Picasso, the town of Guernica (Gernika) is a reminder of the terrible tragedy of the Civil War, and Oñati has some magnificent university buildings dating back to the 16th century.

Mountain chains, like 'bones showing through skin' as one historian has described them, extend along the Bay of Biscay west of the Pyrenees, separating much of the rolling farmland of the Basque Country from the rest of Spain. In this small enclave, known locally as Euskadi, the Basques and their anthropologically mysterious ancestors have lived since the end of the last Ice Age.

A world apart

Basques live on both sides of the Pyrenees – in the French region of Pyrénées-Atlantiques, Spanish Navarre and the three Spanish provinces that have made up the autonomous Basque community since 1980: **Guipúzcoa** (Gipuzkoa) and **Vizcaya** (Bizkaia) on the coast and landlocked **Álava** (Araba) on the edge of the Iberian *meseta*. In addition to possessing physical characteristics that have led some anthropologists to believe they are directly descended from Cro-Magnon Europeans, the Basque language, Euskera, sets this people apart from their French and Spanish countrymen. This language now has equal status with Castilian for official uses. Road

Main Attractions

San Sebastián
Hondarribia old town
Basque coast
Casa de Juntas, Gernika
Bilbao and the Guggenheim Museum
San Juan de Gaztelugatxe
Vitoria
Universidad de Sancti Spiritus, Oñati

Spider sculpture 'Maman' by Louise Bourgeois outside Museo Guggenheim Bilbao.

Crème caramel pie. San Sebastián is famed for its gourmet restaurants.

signs in Basque can confuse visitors, thus Donostia stands for San Sebastián, Bilbo for Bilbao, and Gasteiz (of Visigothic origin) for Vitoria.

Basque history

Fiercely proud of their ancient past, Basques like to say they have never submitted to outside conquerors, including Muslims and Romans. Guipúzcoa and Vizcaya possess prehistoric caves and dolmens, but are notably lacking in Roman and early Christian remains. However, both the Romans and Christianity made inroads into the mountain strongholds, and the Basques' Catholicism has stood firm

ever since. They are considered the most religious people in Spain. Appropriately, Ignacio de Loyola (or Loiola), the warrior who founded the influential Society of Jesus or Jesuits, was born in this region.

To a certain extent it was religious feeling that brought the Basques into the 19th-century Carlist Wars. But, ironically, it was mainly to protect their *fueros* (local laws) that they chose what turned out to be the losing sides in both the Carlist and the Civil wars, thus losing their independence.

Repression under the Franco regime after the Civil War only stiffened resistance to domination by the

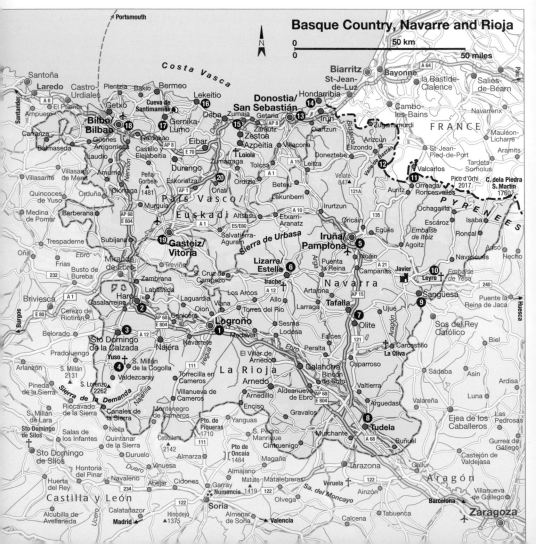

central government, and on the night of the dictator's death Basques danced in the streets. The 1979 Statute of Gernika finally gave the Basques autonomous government within the state of Spain. Political tensions continue, both between Basque politicians and central government, and between Basques themselves. Relatively few non-Basques tour the interior of the region. Visitors typically spend the summer on the mild and misty Basque coast, as Spaniards and an increasing number of French have done since the 19th century, when the point of resort life was to rest in the shade.

San Sebastián (Donostia)

The smallest province on the peninsula and one of the most densely populated corners of Europe, **Guipúzcoa** has had close cultural connections with the other side of the Pyrenees since prehistoric times. More recently, the fortified Basque ports a few kilometres from the frontier have been easy targets for the French in wartime.

Eugenie de Montijo (1826–1920), daughter of a Spanish nobleman who fought on the French side in the Peninsular War and Empress of France after her marriage to Napoleon III, is credited with setting the style for summering on the Basque coast. Once she introduced the emperor to Biarritz in the French Basque Country, other royals, including Queen Victoria, arrived. By the end of the 19th century, the Spanish and South American aristocracy had made **San Sebastián** (Donostia) **13** their chosen summer residence.

From this period date the **Casa Consistorial** (town hall), formerly the Gran Casino; the royal family's Tudor-style **Palacio Miramar**, dividing the two long curving beaches; and the high-style **Puente Zurriola** bridge over the canalised Río Urumea.

Although it is now a city of 186,000 with a diverse economy, San Sebastián is still one of the most beautiful resorts in Europe: elegant and cosmopolitan during the jazz and film festivals, favoured by the Spanish aristocracy – including the King – during the warm autumn months, but still humming with street life in the old town. In fact, along with Wroclaw in

Perusing the news.

Playa de la Concha, San Sebastián.

A UNIQUE LANGUAGE

Of Western Europe's living languages, only Euskera (Basque) does not belong to the Indo-European family. It has fascinated linguists since the Middle Ages, when scholars traced it to Tubal, the grandson of Noah who settled the peninsula after the Flood. More recently, philologists comparing the Basque words for axe, *aitzor*, and stone, *aitz*, have raised the possibility that the language dates from the Stone Age. Throughout history, Basque has been more an oral language than a written one. The first book entirely in Euskera wasn't published until the mid-16th century and the first novel only appeared in 1898, coincidental with the rise of nationalism. Basque is widely taught in schools and enjoys an equal status with Castilian. The Basques' name for their homeland, Euskadi, means 'land of Basque speakers'.

Poland, it was the European Capital of Culture in 2016.

The beaches lying beyond a windbreak of tamarisks on the elegant **Paseo de la Concha** will rarely be full and are some of the finest in Spain. This would be a good time to take the inexpensive funicular or to drive to the top of **Monte Igueldo**, the westernmost of the wooded promontories overlooking the bay of La Concha.

On 31 August, as the summer ends, a torchlight procession in the **Parte Vieja**, or Old Quarter, at the foot of Monte Urgull commemorates the virtual destruction of San Sebastián during the Peninsular War. Among the surviving structures belonging to the old walled port are the cavernous 18th-century **Basilica of Santa María del Coro**, with its apsidal portal deeply recessed to protect the sculptures from hard winters and its graceful statue of the city's namesake in a niche; and the 16th-century Dominican monastery of **San Telmo** in the Plaza de Zuloaga. This has been converted into a wonderful museum (www.santelmomuseoa.eus; Tue–Sun 10am–8pm; free on Tue), devoted mainly to Basque culture and art.

Part of the ethnographic collection is devoted to the history of the seafaring Basques. The Spanish colonisation of America depended partly on the skills of Basque navigators and shipbuilders with their long experience of deep-sea fishing. Other exhibits introduce *pelota*, the Basque national sport, and typical Basque cuisine, costume and customs. In this traditionally rainy country, the matriarchal kitchen and adjoining stable, reconstructed in the museum, became the most important rooms of the Basque farmhouse, the stone-and-timber *caserío*.

The Fine Arts collection ranges from the Hispano-Flemish to contemporary. Occupying a place of honour, the Basque painter Ignacio Zuloaga's best-known work shows three hearty Basque men enjoying a meal.

Eating clubs

Private, men-only gastronomic societies *(txokos)* were founded here in the Parte Vieja in the 1870s. Basque cookery, with its fresh vegetables, dairy products and fish from the Bay of Biscay, seasoned with subtle sauces, is generally acknowledged to be the best on the peninsula.

The neoclassical **Pescadería** (fish market), a short walk south of the Plaza de Zuloaga near the arcaded **Plaza de la Constitución**, has, appropriately, one of the grandest facades in the Parte Vieja. At the nearby market ask for Idiazabal, cheese from the long-haired Laxa sheep that has been cured and smoked, and *txakoli*, the thin white Basque wine drunk with shellfish.

The border

Northeast of San Sebastián, the fishing port and seaside resort of **Hondarribia** ⑭ (Fuenterrabía in Castilian) lies just south of the border with France and, over the centuries, has consequently suffered many attacks by the French. Its charming old town, entered through the **Puerta Santa María**, has somehow

Beach at Zumaia.

survived and still has many old houses with splendidly carved wooden balconies. The town has a fine beach and excellent fish restaurants.

The Basque coast

Going the other way from San Sebastián it's a pleasant drive west all along the hilly coast of Guipúzcoa and Vizcaya. Typical port resorts have at least one old church near the water, several good restaurants and sandy beaches. **Zarautz**, with its nice long beach, and **Getaria**, which has a smaller one, are two of the best-known producers of *txakoli*. This part of the coast may be the best place in Spain to order *chipirones en su tinta* (squid in its own ink) or *besugo* (sea bream).

In Getaria, formerly a whaling port, is a monument to Juan Sebastián Elcano, Magellan's Basque navigator, and skipper of the round-the-world voyage after Magellan was killed in the Philippines. Also born in Getaria was Cristóbal Balenciaga (1895–1972), the widely respected and highly disciplined couturier. You can learn more about him and his work at the new **Cristóbal Balenciaga Museoa** (www.cristobalbalenciagamuseoa.com; June–Sept Tue–Sun and Jul–Aug daily 10am–7pm, Mar–May and Oct Tue–Fri 10am–5pm, Sat–Sun 10am–7pm, Nov–Feb Tue–Fri 10am–3pm, Sat–Sun until 5pm; charge).

Past Getaria is the pretty resort of **Zumaia** ⓯, where the painter Ignacio Zuloaga's summer villa and studio, in a former convent, was turned into the excellent **Espacio Cultural Zuloaga** (www.espaciozuloaga.com; Thu–Sun 4–8pm) after his death. A short way inland from Zumaia, near Azpeitia, is the Santuario de Loiola (www.santuariodeloyola.org;) birthplace of the founder of the Jesuits. On his saint's day, 31 July, large crowds flock to the monastery with its basilica topped by a lofty cupola.

Although it does not look far on the map, **Lekeitio** ⓰, one of the most interesting ports on the Basque coast, is a good two-hour drive from San Sebastián. The 15th-century church at Lekcitio with its flying buttresses and baroque tower is a few metres from a pretty beach where, in the morning, you may see fishermen painting their boats, or groups of children being given swimming lessons. From Lekeitio it is only a short drive south to Gernika.

Gernika (Guernica)

The bustling modern market town of **Gernika-Lumo** ⓱ is sacred to the Basques for its associations with their ancient tradition of self-government. At least since the early Middle Ages, their representatives met here to elect a council of leaders and witness the titular monarch's oath to uphold their *fueros*. An event of enormous consequence for today's Basques, the election of José Antonio Aguirre at the **Casa de Juntas** (daily 10am–2pm and 4–7pm; free), the parliament building, in the 1936 election, revived this tradition.

Members of his government were sworn in under the **Gernikako Arbola**, the symbolic oak of Gernika.

Surfboards at Zurriola beach, San Sebastián.

(The original oak that had stood for centuries was evidently destroyed by the French in the Peninsular War. The present one, it is claimed, grew from the original tree's acorn or sapling.)

The declaration of an independent Basque state was met with swift retribution by the Nationalists under General Mola. Miraculously, the Casa de Juntas, the oak and the neighbouring **Iglesia de Santa María** (begun in the 15th century) survived the almost total destruction of Gernika on Monday 26 April 1937, one of the most infamous episodes of the 1936–9 Spanish Civil War.

Monday, then as now, was market day, and the narrow streets were crowded with farming families and refugees. A third of the civilian population was killed in the attack, and many more were wounded, when German aircraft dropped 50 tonnes of bombs then flew low to shoot at the people fleeing into the fields. *Caseríos* in the hills were also bombed. 'In the night these burned like candles', one of the dazed correspondents covering the war wrote in

The Times of London. International outrage probably discouraged the use of such air attacks again in the rest of the Civil War.

The very word 'Gernika' became synonymous with the horrors of war, symbolised in Picasso's famous painting *Guernica*, which now hangs in Madrid's Reina Sofía Museum. There is a copy of it in ceramic tiles on Calle Allende Salazar. 'General Franco's aeroplanes burned Gernika and the Basques will never forget it', predicted *The Times* correspondent. The **Museo de la Paz de Gernika** (Peace Museum; www.museodelapaz.org; Mar–Sept Tue–Sat 10am–7pm, Sun until 2pm, Oct–Feb Tue–Sat 10am–2pm, 4–6pm, Sun am only, closed Jan) recounts the event and looks at war in Spain and around the world.

The Casa de Juntas is the only other significant sight to see in Gernika, and it is mainly visited for its symbolic importance. However, the room next door to the assembly chamber has a magnificent stained-glass ceiling showing the Tree of Gernika, the various traditional economic activities of the Basque people and (round the edges) the most important monuments of Vizcaya province.

The principal attraction on the outskirts of Gernika-Lumo, to the northeast, is the **Cueva de Santimamiñe** (www.santimamiñe.com; guided tours only, mid-Apr–mid-Oct daily 11am–5.30pm, mid-Oct–mid-Apr Tue–Sun 10am–1pm), although the gallery containing its famous prehistoric wall paintings, first discovered in 1916, is closed to the public. Near the cave is the **Bosque Animado de Ibarrola**, a work of 'Land Art' by Agustín Ibarrola in which tree trunks have been painted in vibrant colours.

Bilbao and the Guggenheim

The Basque capital, **Bilbao ⓲** (Bilbo), has had its ups and downs. In 1300 the then small fishing and ironmongering village received *villa* status

Detail on Teatro Arriaga, an opera house in Bilbao.

from Diego López de Haro. His statue stands on a plinth sometimes hung with the *Ikurriña*, the red, white and green Basque flag inspired by the Union flag, at the foot of the pink-and-black Banco de Vizcaya tower in the **Plaza Circular** near the **Puente de la Victoria**. This is the main bridge joining old Bilbao on the east bank of the Río Nervión and the newer bourgeois quarter that grew up on the west bank in the 19th century.

Once you locate the Gran Vía de López de Haro, the main traffic artery running east to west from the Plaza Circular to the large **Parque de Doña Casilda Iturriza**, or one of the smart new Metro stations designed by British architect Norman Foster, it is easy to find your way around.

The spectacular **Museo Guggenheim Bilbao** (www.guggenheim-bilbao.es; Tue–Sun 10am–8pm, daily in July and Aug) has put Bilbao firmly on the cultural map and launched the entire Basque Country into a rebirth of general optimism.

If you are here in August, it is worth staying for the Semana Grande, the biggest of the week-long festivals in the three provincial capitals. The events range from heavy culture to heavy metal to bullfights, Basque folk music and traditional contests of stamina and strength.

Early Bilbao

The earliest settlements here are said to have been made near the present 15th-century Iglesia de San Antón in the Atxuri district along the Ribera east of the Siete Calles, the 'Seven Streets' of the **Casco Viejo**, or Old Town. The prosperous Casco Viejo was pillaged by the French during the Peninsular War, and much of it was destroyed in the Carlist Wars, but narrow streets and a number of pre-19th-century structures remain.

You can look over Greater Bilbao from the terrace of the **Santuario de Nuestra Señora de Begoña** (c. 1511 and later). To get there, take the lift in Calle Esperanza Ascoa behind the 15th- and 18th-century **Iglesia de San Nicolás de Bari**, the original Father Christmas and patron saint of Bilbao's children, sailors and prostitutes.

Bilbao's Ayuntamiento.

TIP

Take the weight off your feet and see Bilbao from the water with Bilboats (tel: 946-424 157; www.bilboats.com). There are hour-long trips up the River Nervión (€12) or two-hour trips along the coast past shipyards and the Bizkaia Suspension Bridge (€18). Boats leave from next to the City Hall Bridge in Plaza Pío Baroja.

Puente del Arenal, Bilbao.

Down on the waterfront is the **Museo Marítima Ría de Bilbao** (www.museomaritimobilbao.org; Tue–Sun 10am–8pm, winter until 6pm; free on Tue Sep–June), which has indoor and outdoor exhibitions of Bilbao's maritime history; the boats are usually popular with kids.

Industry and art

In the 1870s, at the end of the Second Carlist War, Bilbao began to exploit its natural iron deposits and industrialise in a big way. By the end of the century, half the Spanish merchant fleet came from Basque shipyards, much of its steel industry was located near Bilbao, and Basque bankers and businessmen wielded great financial power. The **Teatro Arriaga** (1890) on the Paseo del Arenal, the **Ayuntamiento** (1892) at the bend in the river north of the Puente de la Victoria, and the **Palacio de la Diputación** (1897) were built during this boom, and a groundswell of popular sentiment for going it alone and declaring a Basque state developed.

The wealthy, cosmopolitan aspect of Bilbao is reflected in the excellent

Museo de Bellas Artes (www.museobilbao.com; Wed–Mon 10am–8pm; free on Wed) in Iturriza Park. It contains the most important collection of paintings in northern Spain. You can visit this museum and the Guggenheim on a combined ticket called the 'Artean Pass'.

In addition to its Flemish, Catalan and classical Spanish holdings, it has a modern wing with some pieces showing the influence of various international art movements on those artists who grew up under Franco, including Isabel Baquenado, Juan José Arqueretta, Andrés Nagel and Javier Morras.

Within easy reach of Bilbao is the rugged but often beautiful coast of Vizcaya (Bizkaia) province. Mundaka, at the mouth of the Ría de Gernika, is the prettiest of the harbour towns and a Mecca for surfers. But the most impressive sight is **San Juan de Gaztelugatxe**, between Bakio and Bermeo, where a chapel is perched on a rock jutting out to sea and connected to the shore by a cobbled causeway.

The Basque interior

Vitoria (Gasteiz) **⑲** is the capital of Alava, the largest and least Bascophone of the three Basque provinces, and the seat of the autonomous Basque government. It is best-known outside Spain for the bloody battle of 1813 in which Wellington defeated the French general Jourdan.

The narrow, concentric alleyways of the old town, some named for the crafts that flourished here – Zapatería, Cuchillería, Pintorería, Herrería – underwent a certain amount of urban renewal in the mid-19th century; medieval arcades were demolished and the alleys were widened out as far as possible. But this quarter, with its three Gothic churches, town houses decorated with escutcheons and carved doorways, and shops and cafés, still imparts an authentic feeling of the prospering commercial town of the Middle Ages and Renaissance.

Vitoria (Gasteiz)

The **Feria de la Virgen Blanca** in August pays homage to the 'White Virgin', standing in her jasper niche in the porch facade of the 14th-century **Iglesia de San Miguel** (daily). The Gothic sculpture is of high quality. The city's protector, she overlooks the glassed-in balconies or *miradores* of the busy Plaza de la Virgen Blanca and the monument erected in 1917 to commemorate the Battle of Vitoria. Inside the church is a retable by Gregorio Fernández, an important Golden Age sculptor. Notice the bagpipe player in his *Adoration of the Shepherds*.

The adjacent **Plaza del Machete**, named for the large knife on which oaths to uphold the town's *fueros* (laws) were sworn, marks the southern end of the old town. Walk north from here, stopping to admire the sculpture in the porch and on the column capitals of the **Catedral de Santa María**, then retrace your steps a little way to Calle Cuchillería and Bibat, which houses the **Museo de Arqueología** (Tue–Fri 10am–2pm and 4–6.30pm, Sat am only, Sun 11am–2pm). This well-designed small museum, accommodated in a restored 15th-century merchants'

The Basques are proud of their musical traditions.

EAT

Explore San Sebastián's excellent *pintxo* scene on a foodie walking tour, Sabores de San Sebastián (tel: 943-217 717; www.sansebastian reservas.com), which runs at 11.30am on Tue and Thu in July and Aug and can be booked at the tourist office. San Sebastián Food (tel: 943-421 143; www.san sebastianfood.com) also runs culinary walking tours as well as cookery courses and wine tastings.

house, is a wonderfully sensitive adaptation of a historic structure. The tens of thousands of years of local history to which it is devoted range from the Lower Palaeolithic era through to the Middle Ages. Also here is the **Museo Fournier de Naipes** (same opening times) with its exquisite historical collection of playing cards. East of here on Calle de Francia is **Artium** (www. artium.org; Tue–Fri 11am–2pm and 5–8pm, Sat–Sun 11am–8pm), which has daring and thought-provoking displays of Basque and international contemporary art.

To the south, in a neighbourhood of large private houses between the Jardines de la Florida and the 19th-century park called El Prado, is the **Museo de Bellas Artes** (Tue–Fri 10am–2pm and 4–6.30pm, Sat 10am–2pm, 5–8pm, Sun 11am–2pm). Its varied holdings include a Crucifixion by José de Ribera and a Virgin by the irascible Sevillian painter and sculptor Alonso Cano (1601–67). There are paintings and sculptures by various Basque artists and a growing modern collection

Cathedral of Santa María, Vitoria.

featuring the work of Miró, Picasso and Antoni Tàpies, the best-known Spanish abstract painter. Opposite is the **Museo de Armería** (same times as Bellas Artes; free first Sat of the month), which has a fine collection of armour.

Seat of learning

About 30km (20 miles) from Vitoria, a short way off the GI-627, is the lovely town of **Oñati** ⑳ , where the **Universidad de Sancti Spiritus** (ask at the tourist office about guided tours) is a Renaissance gem, particularly the magnificent facade. Built in the 16th century, the university taught a range of subjects, including law and medicine, until its closure in 1902.

A stroll around the town reveals other architectural jewels, especially the Gothic **Iglesia de San Miguel**, with a cloister that spans the river, and the Baroque *ayuntamiento* (town hall).

Beyond Oñati a winding road leads into the hills and ends at the shrine of **Arantzazu** where a stark 1950s church stands in bold contrast to the stunning natural scenery.

THE GUGGENHEIM IN BILBAO

Bilbao's famous museum is the talk of the art world. This spectacular 'Metallic Flower' beside the River Nervión has become a major draw and helped reanimate the city.

The Guggenheim Museum in Bilbao opened in October 1997 to a blaze of publicity. The city's $100-million investment in the spectacular titanium 'Metallic Flower' was the keystone of the plan to redevelop the city and recover Bilbao's early 20th-century place on the international cultural map. Matched by Bilbao's other architectural triumphs – Norman Foster's designer Metro, Santiago Calatrava's La Paloma airport and his Zubizuri footbridge over the Nervión at Ubitarte – the Guggenheim reconfirmed the Basques as a people of vision and taste.

Set by the River Nervión, the 24,290-sq-metre (257,000-sq-ft) museum building was designed by Californian architect Frank Gehry. It is made up of interconnected blocks, clad in limestone and topped with a shimmering titanium roof. Light floods through glass walls and a skylight in the 50-metre (165ft)-high central atrium, and from here walkways, lifts and stairs lead through the spacious galleries set on three floors.

The Basque administration and the Solomon R. Guggenheim Foundation, based in New York, jointly administer the museum, while the Guggenheim provides curatorial expertise, as well as the core art collection and programming. While almost everyone who visits the Guggenheim marvels at the daring of the building itself, it means that the exhibitions themselves have a hard act to follow, and some people come away disappointed. What's on offer varies widely from classical and contemporary fine art to more populist subjects such as fashion design. Choose your exhibition carefully.

The building occupies a 4.2-hectare (8-acre) site on a bend in the River Nervión, by the busy Puente de la Salve. This used to be a run-down dockland and industrial area. Another renowned architect, Cesar Pelli, designed the adjacent waterfront development.

'The Matter of Time' (2005) was created by American sculptor Richard Serra. This permanent exhibit weighs about 1,200 tons and is over 430 feet long.

Anish Kapoor's 'Tall Tree & The Eye' (2009) sculpture outside the Guggenheim.

Museu d'Art Contemporani de Barcelona (MACBA).

MODERN MUSEUMS FOR MODERN ART

The Guggenheim is just one of a number of spectacular museums and galleries to open its doors in recent decades. The events of 1992 – the Seville Expo, the Barcelona Olympic Games and the naming of Madrid as cultural city of Europe – concentrated the minds of planners, architects and visionaries into turning the cities' leisure areas into modern temples for high art. There was no xenophobia: competition brought top architects from all over the world. And there was no lack of imagination: modern was set against medieval; boldness won.

Spain is not short of gallery space: vast halls and monumental buildings are dotted everywhere, and many have been enlisted for imaginative development. A prime example is the four-storey 18th-century General Hospital in Madrid, which reopened in 1992 as the magnificent Centro de Arte Reina Sofía, to house the city's 20th-century art collection. More daring is the Galician Centre of Contemporary Art, a blazingly modern building designed by Alvaro Siza Viera in the medieval centre of Santiago de Compostela in Galicia, which opened in 1997. The Museu d'Art Contemporani (MACBA) in the Raval District of Barcelona was designed by Richard Meier. This gleaming glass and stone venture opened in 1996 to general acclaim.

he titanium 'Metallic Flower' looms up in the heart of the own and is designed to have a 'sculptural presence' reflecting he waterfront, downtown buildings and surrounding hills.

The museum has a bookshop, café and restaurant, and a 300-seat auditorium with multimedia technology. Note that the Guggenheim closes on Mondays, except during July and August.

Jeff Koons's 'Puppy' (1992) is a 12-metre (40-foot) -high sculpture of a West Highland terrier made out of stainless steel and flowering plants.

Basílica de Santa María la Real de Covadonga, Asturias.

CANTABRIA AND ASTURIAS

Few parts of Spain have greater natural beauty than Cantabria and Asturias, where sandy beaches and rocky headlands are backed by the soft greens and greys of the rugged landscape.

Cantabria's main city is Santander, a sea port with several fine museums including the Museo de Bellas Artes. West of here is Altamira, where some of the finest examples of Paleolithic cave art have been found. Then there are the Picos de Europa, which offer excellent climbing and hiking opportunities. Asturias also has its fair share of cave art but is best known for its cider. The whole of the north coast is crammed with beaches and fishing villages, like Cudillero where local seafood dishes are on the menu. The Parque Natural de Somiedo is home to the few remaining European brown bears.

The autonomous regions of Cantabria and Asturias lie between the Basque Country and Galicia along the Bay of Biscay or Mar Cantábrico. A formidable mountain chain, the **Cordillera Cantábrica**, separates the coast and its narrow strip of lush, green valleys from the arid *meseta* plateau of central Spain.

There are 72 beaches in Cantabria, stretching east to west from Castro-Urdiales to San Vicente de la Barquera, and just over 200 mostly small beaches in Asturias, separated by cliffs, estuaries and promontories. From the 90-metre (300ft) **Cabo de Peñas**, north of Gijón and Avilés, you can see a large part of the coast. On rainy days you may see the tiny figure of a solitary fisherman

Playa del Camello, Santander.

on a long stretch of sand at the foot of an immense weatherbeaten cliff. On a sunny day, the same spot will be filled with bathers and beach umbrellas.

Straddling the border between the two regions are the spectacular **Picos de Europa**, which rise to over 2,640 metres (8,660ft), the highest mountains in the Cordillera.

Small nomadic bands of hunters and food-gatherers belonging to the Stone Age cultures decorated the walls and ceilings of the limestone caves in this region with pictures of the

Main Attractions

Santander
Santillana del Mar
Comillas
Altamira
Picos de Europa
Tito Bustillo cave
Covadonga
Oviedo

Gran Casino del Sardinero, Santander.

Playa Sardinero, Santander.

migratory animals they followed. The similarity between the decorated prehistoric caves in the limestone area of southern France and those of northern Spain led to the designation of a prehistoric 'Franco-Cantabrian' cultural area, which includes a number of sites in the foothills of the Pyrenees in the Basque Country and in Asturias.

Prehistory to modern times

Castro-Urdiales ❶, once an important Roman seaport, is the easternmost and one of the oldest ports on the coast of Cantabria. The Playa de Brazomar and the Playa de Oriñón at the mouth of the Ría Agüera are characteristically long, sandy Cantabrian beaches, a short walk from both summer resort facilities and an old quarter with medieval remains. From the small fortified peninsula, a ruined Templars' hostel, the 'Castle' of Santa Ana and the Gothic **Iglesia de Santa María**, with French sculptures, flying buttresses and uncompleted towers reminiscent of Notre-Dame in Paris, overlook the photogenic harbour filled with fishing boats.

At **Laredo** ❷, the long, sandy beach attracts so many summer visitors that the off-season population of over 12,000 will have multiplied by a factor of 10 by mid-August. This explains the high-rises and summer houses that follow the curve of the beautiful beach.

In the Castilian Golden Age that followed the Reconquest, this part of the coast was the administrative centre of Cantabria, and Old Castile's only outlet to the sea. The size of the Cantabrian fleet that operated here increased dramatically in the 16th century.

The ports on the Bay of Biscay were the jewels in the Spanish emperor's crown and were the basis of Spain's superior maritime capability. Ships carrying Spanish wine and wool sailed from San Sebastián, Laredo, Santander and La Coruña to Flanders and England, or into the Mediterranean through the Strait of Gibraltar.

All along this coast churches were enhanced by the massive building campaign instigated by the Catholic Monarchs. In Laredo, for example, a 16th-century doorway was added to

Cantabria and Asturias

the 13th-century Gothic **Iglesia de Nuestra Señora de la Asunción**.

In 1556 Carlos I, having abdicated in favour of his son Felipe II, sailed into Laredo from Flanders on the way to the monastery of Yuste, in Extremadura. With him arrived his sister, Mary of Hungary, ruler of the Netherlands, and the art treasures accumulated by both these great Habsburg collectors. The Spanish public collections still hold most of the priceless works of Flemish art carried across Spain from Laredo more than 400 years ago.

Across **Santoña Bay** from Laredo is the port and resort of **Santoña ❸**. There is another church, begun in the 13th century, and several beaches, including the splendid 2km (1-mile) long Playa de Nueva Berria.

Castilian summer retreat

The important modern port of **Santander ❹** has been the provincial capital of Cantabria since the 18th century, when the French plundered the coastal area to the east. The city centre, rebuilt after much of it was destroyed by a fire in 1941, looks

south across a beautiful protected bay. On a clear day in winter you can see the snowcapped peaks of the Cordillera Cantábrica from the busy quay.

There are fine beaches (El Camella, La Concha, La Primera and La Segunda, all joined at low tide) facing out to sea in the older residential and resort quarter, **El Sardinero**. Here, too, are the Gran Casino Sardinero (www.grancasino sardinero.es) and the large old-fashioned resort hotel, the Hotel Real. On the **Península de La Magdalena** is the neo-Gothic summer palace of the royal family (http://palaciomagdalena.com), an imitation of Balmoral, built by Alfonso XIII in 1912 for his English queen. It is now part of the International Menéndez Pelayo University, which offers summer courses to foreign students.

On a rainy day, visit the **Museo de Arte Moderno y Contemporáneo** (www.museosantandermas.es; Tue–Sat 10am–1.30pm and 5.30–9pm, Sun 11am–1.30pm; free) on the Calle Rubio west of the Plaza Porticada. The museum has an interesting small collection ranging from Zurbarán to contemporary Cantabrian artists, and

TIP

A good time to visit Santander is in summer for the Semana Grande (www.semanagrandesantan der.com), a week-long cultural festival in July, or the Festival Internacional de Santander (http://festival santander.com), a music festival featuring a variety of genres in August. The Baños de Ola, also in July, celebrates the first tourists who came to the city in the 19th century.

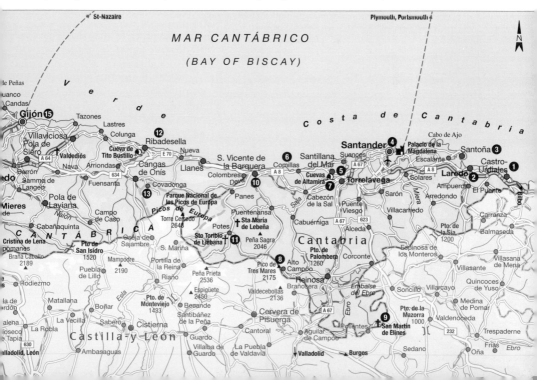

Detail on Colegiata de Santa Juliana, Santillana del Mar.

roomy galleries for temporary exhibitions. Here hang portraits of two of Spain's less-beloved rulers: Fernando VII and Isabel II, deposed in 1868 while summering in the Basque Country. The portrait of Fernando, one of several painted by Goya of this weak and cruel king, is believed to have been commissioned by the city of Santander.

Nearby, Goya's four famous series of etchings are displayed: the *Caprichos*, the *Desastres de la guerra*, the *Tauromaquía* and the *Disparates* or *Proverbios*.

The **Museo Marítímo del Cantábrico** (www.museosdecantabria.es; May–Sept daily 10am–7.30pm, Oct–Apr Tue–Sun until 6pm; free Sun from 2pm) on the waterfront is split into four sections: fishing history, maritime history, marine biology and maritime technology; the aquarium and whale skeleton are popular with kids.

Santillana del Mar and Altamira

The resorts of **Santillana del Mar** ❺ and **Comillas** ❻ on the coast west of Santander are crowded in summer with well-heeled Spaniards from further south. This is an agreeable area of first-rate beaches, pretty farms overlooking the sea, medieval and Renaissance churches and balconied, galleried and escutcheoned granite Golden Age palaces or town houses.

Santillana is an amazingly well-preserved medieval village, with fine stone mansions and cobbled streets. The 12th- to 13th-century Romanesque **La Colegiata** (Tue–Sun 10am–1.30pm and 4–7.30pm) contains the bones of one of the virgin saints, the 4th-century Santa Juliana. 'Santillana' is derived from the Latin *Sancta Juliana*. The Colegiata itself, like many other churches in the French-influenced Romanesque style, was designed to serve as a roomy reliquary entered through the elegant round-arched west portal.

Despite daily invasion by tourists, Santillana has preserved something of the character of a market town. However, it has a sinister side too: the **Museo de la Tortura** (daily 10am–8.30pm) on Calle del Escultor Jesús Otero, has a collection of torture instruments that were used in the Inquisition.

In Comillas, further along the coast, follow the signs to **El Capricho** (www.elcaprichodegaudi.com; daily, Jul–Sept 10.30am–9pm, Mar–June and Oct until 8pm, Nov–Feb until 5.30pm), the summer house built to the designs of the Catalan architect Antoní Gaudí in 1883–5. At El Capricho, Gaudí combined references to squat Romanesque columns, the minaret, *Mudéjar* brickwork, the traditional Spanish iron balcony and – most imaginatively of all – the shapes and colours of the Cantabrian countryside and seashore. Dominating Comillas is another late 19th-century building, the massive neo-Gothic **Palacio de Sobrellano** (Tue–Sun).

Unesco-listed Altamira ❼ is about 1.5km (less than 1 mile) south of Santillana del Mar. The 'Sistine Chapel' of cave art was the first, and arguably is

Medieval buildings in Santillana del Mar.

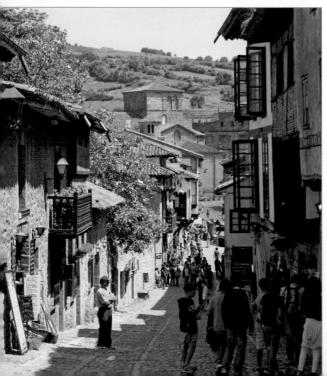

still the finest, Palaeolithic decorated cave identified. Altamira's authenticity was not generally accepted until the early 20th century, when other caves, to which the entrances had been blocked – ruling out any possibility of a hoax – were discovered.

Ironically, the quality and precise detail of figures such as the pregnant bison were the greatest impediment to the recognition of Altamira's antiquity.

Inland Cantabria

Surprisingly few visitors to Cantabria take the trouble to explore the interior of the province, but there are several unusual sights to see. The best base is Reinosa, near the end of a large reservoir, the Embalse del Ebro. From here a 20km (12-mile) drive takes you up to the mountain viewpoint (and winter-sports resort) of **Pico de Tres Mares** ❽ 'The Mountain of the Three Seas', named for three rivers which rise here and set off in different directions: the Ebro to the Mediterranean, the Pisuerga to the Atlantic (after joining the Duero) and the Nansa into the Bay of Biscay.

Deep in the hills, not far off the Santander–Burgos road, is the graceful church of **San Martín de Elines** ❾.

The Costa Verde

San Vicente de la Barquera ❿, 10km (6 miles) west of Comillas, is one of the nicest surprises on the Cantabrian coast. As you travel west, the little harbours on which the old ports were built become wider, the river valleys look greener and the mountains are higher.

The fortified walls and castle, and the 13th- to 16th-century **Iglesia de Santa María de los Angeles** (daily) on the pine-clad headland, are reflected in the inlet spanned by the 17th-century **Puente de la Maza**, a stone bridge with 28 arches. The beach, the **Sable de Merón**, is almost 3km (2 miles) long and as much as 100 metres (328ft) wide when the tide is out.

Picos de Europa

Leave the coast at San Vicente and take the road that follows the **Ría Deva** valley to **Panes**, and then up into the eastern end of the **Picos de Europa** in the direction of the town of **Potes** ⓫.

Covadonga's shrine, carved out of the mountainside.

PREHISTORY AT ALTAMIRA

In 1879, Don Marcelino de Sautuola, who lived in a villa near the site and who had seen some small engraved Palaeolithic art objects that were accepted as genuine at the Universal Exposition in Paris the year before, realised by their similarity that the paintings at Altamira were prehistoric.

The bison, hinds, wild boar, horses and other animals were painted around 12,000 years BC using several colours of pigment (ochres, manganese oxides, charcoal, iron carbonate). The three most important polychrome sites in the world are Altamira, Tito Bustillo (in Asturias) and Lascaux in Périgord, France. The actual caves are considered to be in a very delicate state of conservation and are therefore closed to the public to prevent further damage to the murals.

Most visitors are content with the only other option, which is to see a faithful replica or Neo Cueva, part of the Museo de Altamira (tel: 942-818 005; http://en.museodealtamira.mcu.es; Sun 9.30am–3pm, Tue–Sat May–Oct 9.30am–8pm, Nov–Apr until 6pm; charge but free after 2pm on Sat and all day Sun). To find out more about Spanish and European cave art head to the Parque de la Prehistoria (tel: 902-306 600; www.parquedelaprehistoria.es; opening times vary) in Teverga, which, as well as an exhibition, has replicas of Tito Bustillo cave (see page 324) and the Niaux cave in France.

'The Cubes of Memory' by the artist Agustín Ibarrola in Llanes.

Potes town in the Picos de Europa.

The narrow Desfiladero de la Hermida may be slow going, but it widens north of Potes to form the austere mountain setting for one of the jewels of Mozarabic architecture, the **Iglesia de Santa María de Lebeña** (Tue–Sun, June–Sept 10am–1.30pm and 4–7.30pm, Oct–May until 6.30pm; charge). Founded by Alfonso, Count of Liébana (924–63), and his wife Justa, possibly immigrants from Andalusia, it combines the architectural concepts of the mosque with the forms of local pre-Romanesque Asturian churches with its small agglomerative compartments and tunnel vaults. These had developed independently north of the Cordillera Cantábrica from the 8th century, based to some degree on Visigothic prototypes. Like the Asturian churches, Santa María was completely vaulted over.

Entered by a side door, the church has the feeling of a mosque, due in part to its horseshoe arches. Its 15th-century red, white and blue Virgin is now part of an 18th-century retable. A stone stele reused by a 9th-century builder is carved with Visigothic designs in roundels. A primitive human figure in the lower left corner of the stele was painted, it is said, with a mixture of blood and ashes. At the time Santa María was built, this remote area had been a centre of monastic culture for several centuries.

It was in the monastery of **Santo Toribio de Liébana** (daily, May–Oct 10am–1pm and 4–7pm, Oct–May until 6pm; free), a few kilometres south, that the 8th-century monk Beatus wrote his commentaries on the Apocalypse and the Book of Daniel. The *Beatos*, as they were called, were illuminated in the scriptoria of various monasteries in the following centuries. As examples of Mozarabic art, they are as important as Santa María. Santo Toribio also possesses what is claimed to be the entire right arm of Christ's wooden cross.

The Fuente Dé Parador west of Potes is located in the eastern part of the Picos de Europa national park at the source of the Ría Deva and surrounded by high peaks. A cable car runs from here to the **Mirador del Cable**, from which there is a view of Potes, the Deva valley, the nearby wildlife reserves and the mountains.

Asturias

Returning to the coast and entering the kingdom of Asturias, you will find yourself on an increasingly irregular shoreline. Sandy beaches and port resorts lie between high promontories. Pretty **Llanes** has a cliff walk, the **Paseo de San Pedro**, and 30 small beaches. A prehistoric menhir carved with an anthropomorphic figure called Peña Tu is at Vidiago close by; at **Colombres** is one of the more important decorated caves, El Pindal.

Ribadesella ⑫ occupies the east bank of the estuary of the Río Sella. One of the most important Franco-Cantabrian caves, **Tito Bustillo** (www.centrotitobustillo.com; tel: 902-306 600; mid-Mar–Oct Wed–Sun 10.15am–5pm, advance booking essential; free

Wed), is west of the port across the bridge over the estuary. The original entrance has been lost, so that it is uncertain whether the paintings here were exposed to daylight.

On a red ochre-painted wall overhanging the habitation site, more than 20 animals were painted in other colours and then engraved with flint tools. The size of these well-observed animals is considerable, averaging over 2 metres (6ft). They include at least one reindeer, a species rarely encountered in Cantabrian Palaeolithic art. To prevent deterioration of the paintings, the number of visitors per day is strictly limited, so be sure to book in advance, especially in high season. Also here is the **Centro de Arte Rupestre** (Wed–Sun from 10am), which has an exhibition on Tito Bustillo and its finds.

Sea and cider

An overwhelming mural painting by the Uria Aza brothers, depicting the horrors of modern war in the church at Ribadesella, is worth a sobering look, as is the view of mountains and port life from the quay.

In any of the fishing villages here, you can eat excellent *caldereta* (fish stew), hake in cider or locally caught shellfish such as sea urchins. Cider, the traditional Asturian drink, is acrated by being poured from a bottle held some distance from the glass to activate carbonation. Visitors tend to spill a lot, but it does not seem to matter.

From Ribadesella it is a pleasant excursion to **Covadonga** ⑬ in the western part of the Parque Nacional de los Picos de Europa. In a green, tree-shaded valley lies the important national shrine of Covadonga, where in the 8th century Pelayo, an Asturian warrior, crushed a Muslim force, thus becoming a symbol of Christian resistance to the invaders. A statue of Pelayo stands near a neo-Romanesque church. Continuing into the park, you reach two glacier-formed lakes, Enol and La Ercina.

Early churches of Oviedo

There are only a few sights to see in the centre of **Oviedo** ⑭, the capital of Asturias. The main one is the flamboyant Gothic cathedral, the **Catedral de San Salvador** (http://catedraldeoviedo.com; Mon–Sat), its perforated spire damaged in the 1930s and subsequently restored; the cathedral contains the Pantheon of the Asturian Kings and the Cámara Santa, their reliquary chapel.

Behind the cathedral is a burial ground for pilgrims to Santiago de Compostela and a superb **Museo Arqueológico** (www.museoarqueologico-deasturias.com; Wed–Fri 9.30am–8pm, Sat 9.30am–2pm, 5–8pm, Sun 9.30am–3pm; free) in the Monasterio de San Vicente. The museum's treasures include prehistoric artefacts, Roman mosaics and pre-Romanesque artwork.

Oviedo's best sights, however, are outside the urban area on Mount Naranco. Here stands the exquisite church of **Santa María del Naranco** (Sun–Mon 10am–12.30pm, Oct–Mar Tue–Sat 10am–2.30pm, Apr–Sept Tue–Sat 9.30am–1pm and 3.30–7pm;

View of Llanes beach from the port.

free Mon), built originally as a royal hall for Ramiro I in the mid-9th century. Up the hill is another pre-Romanesque church, San Miguel de Lillo, dating from the same period.

Fishing villages

It is only an hour's drive directly south to Puerto de Pajares (1,380 metres/4,530ft), a pass in the Picos on the border between Asturias and León. Past Mieres, and accessible only by doubling back through **Pola de Lena**, the single-naved early 10th-century pre-Romanesque **Iglesia de Santa Cristina de Lena** is perched on a hill and visible from the highway.

Heading back towards the coast, the fishing-port resorts around **Gijón** ⓯ with their folkloric festivals, and all of the pre-Romanesque churches in the area, are within easy driving distance. Gijón itself is an industrial port and the biggest Asturian city, with a population of 264,000. The old part of town is located on a narrow isthmus, centring around the arcaded **Plaza Mayor**.

Avilés ⓰, further west, also has a charming old town concealed within its industrial shell. The area around the Plaza de España is ancient and intimate, and filled with bustling bars and restaurants. The main sight here is the **Centro Cultural Internaciónal Oscar Niemeyer** (CCIA; www.niemeyercenter. org; daily guided visits June–Sept at 12.30pm and 5pm; rest of the year Wed–Fri at 5pm, Sat–Sun at 12.30 and 5pm), a stunning new cultural centre designed by Oscar Niemeyer. Continuing approximately 20km (12 miles) further west along the A-8 brings you to **Cudillero** ⓱, the most attractive Asturian fishing village, with houses hanging from steep rock walls over the ramp leading down to the harbour. Restaurants serving fresh sardines and cider line either side of the dramatic ravine. There is also a beautiful beach here, Playa del Silencio.

Luarca is a cluster of slate-roofed houses and a lively place to stay the night if you are touring this section of the Costa Verde. Beyond Luarca, the coast road continues to Navia, where a left turn up the AS-12 leads to the Celtic *castro* (hillfort) at **Coaña** ⓲ (Wed–Sun mid-Mar–mid-Sept 10.30am–5.30pm, Oct–mid-Mar until 3.30pm; free Wed), a cluster of circular stone foundations dating from the Iron Age.

The road inland from Luarca leads to the memorable old quarter of **Salas**, where the Valdés Salas castle, former residence of the Marquis of Valdés Salas, a leader of the Inquisition, is now a hotel and restaurant. From the Espinas Pass, which has a superlative 360-degree view, descend south to **Tineo** on the AS-216. Tineo is known for its ham industry and for the 14th-century García-Tineo and 16th-century Meras palaces.

Parque Natural de Somiedo ⓳, southwest of Oviedo, surrounds the Teverga and Quirós valleys, extending into the peaks of the neighbouring province of León. The park is populated by wolves, otters and shelters a few surviving European brown bears, and more than a dozen glacial lakes dot the landscape.

Cudillero.

GALICIA

Spain's green northwestern corner keeps a spectacular coastline. Inland, historic pilgrimage routes cut across empty sierras to meet at Santiago de Compostela.

I n the northwest corner of Spain, Galicia is Celtic through and through – the culture is celebrated with the Festival de Ortigueira in July. The region's main city is Santiago de Compostela, whose magnificent cathedral is the burial place of St James; it is the final destination of pilgrims on the *camino*. A Coruña's Torre de Hercules is the world's only Roman-era lighthouse while Lugo is the proud owner of some magnificently preserved town walls. The west has a wonderfully wild coastline, notably the Rías Altas and the Rías Baixas. There are some fine beaches, and octopus is usually on the menu.

Crisscrossed by myriad rivers and mountain ranges, Galicia is a green, rugged land of unforgettable vistas and ocean-chiselled coastline. Across this nature-blessed region can be found treasures left by the Celts, the Suebi, the Romans and the Visigoths who conquered and settled it. Isolated from the rest of Spain by a bulwark of mountains on the east and south and bounded to the north and west by the tumultuous North Atlantic, Galicia's natural formations include craggy mountains, long, loping valleys and distinctive *rías* or estuaries.

While mountains ring the interior, separating the region from the Spanish provinces of Asturias, León and Zamora to the east and Portugal to the south, Galicia's stormy, westernmost

point is Finisterre, or Land's End, as the Romans named it. In winter, the fishing fleet braves storms famed for their fury.

In spring and summer a striking palette of colours – deep green, yellow and orange – blooms on the inland moors, and the milder weather attracts thousands of tourists to its beaches. Lining the 380km (240 miles) of its bold, indented coastline are quaint fishing villages, busy resorts and the major ports of Vigo and A Coruña. The spectacularly wild *rías* in the north are known as the **Rías Altas**, while the

Main Attractions

Torre de Hércules, A Coruña
Betanzos
Santiago de Compostela
Roman Walls, Lugo
Rías Baixas
Pontevedra
Vigo
Baiona

Catedral, Santiago de Compostela.

TIP

Like Wales, Ireland, Brittany and several other European regions, Galicia is proud of its Celtic heritage. A good time to visit the area is during the third week of July when the International Festival of the Celtic World (www.festivaldeortigueira. com) takes place in Orgtigueira. The three-day event includes concerts by folk groups from the Celtic nations.

Cabo Finisterre, Spain's westernmost point.

gentler southwestern ones are called the **Rías Baixas**. In November 2002 the coast near Cabo Finisterre suffered Spain's worst ecological disaster when the stricken *Prestige* oil tanker released 77,000 tonnes of crude oil into the sea.

Celtic roots

Galicia and its people retain many traces of the Celts, who swept through from 900 to 600 BC and established a hold on this windswept, rain-soaked land that they did not relinquish until the arrival of the Romans in 137 BC. The region's name is derived from 'Gallaeci', the name by which the Celtic tribes were known to the Romans; they coexisted for three centuries, the golden age of Celtic culture. Hundreds of ruined hilltop *castros*, or fortified Celtic settlements, survive: those at Viladonga (Lugo), Boroña and Monte Tecla (both Pontevedra) are especially worthwhile.

Even before the Celtic centuries, the native people lived in *pallozas*, conical-shaped stone houses with thatched roofs. In isolated inland areas, such as Os Ancares in Ourense province and

parts of Lugo province, *pallozas* survived as family homes until recently, but Os Ancares (O Piornedo village) remains largely as a tourist sight. However, Galicia's population remains overwhelmingly rural; even today the population of nearly 3 million is scattered among the region's 4,000 parishes, and three out of ten Galician families still live off the land.

A regional herd of a million dairy and beef cattle provides superb-quality meat and milk. The latter is used to make farmhouse cheeses such as breast-shaped *tetilla*. Galicians are also renowned for their belief in magic, witches and superstition, although in many cases this pagan belief in the spirit world has grafted itself onto Christianity.

Pilgrims' land

Galicia remained relatively free from Muslim influence and developed a distinct cultural personality. Linguists place the beginning of the Galician language in the early 11th century, by which time it had been an independent kingdom for 500 years, albeit ruled from Asturias and León between the

8th and 11th centuries. The Galician culture showed greater affinity for Portuguese culture than for that of Spain until the final separation of the two countries in 1668.

But by the time Galicia came under the rule of the Catholic Monarchs, who established the *Junta* of the kingdom of Galicia in 1495, the region had firm economic and religious ties to the central kingdom because of the importance of Santiago de Compostela as a pilgrimage destination.

Franco's birthplace

The most famous Galician of recent times was General Francisco Franco, who was born and grew up in the port of O Ferrol, the son of a navy supply clerk. Although a native son of Galicia, Franco viewed regional loyalty as anti-Spanish, and prohibited the teaching and official use of the Galician language. Other politicians of Galician descent include the former Cuban president, Fidel Castro; the founding father of Spanish socialism, Pablo Iglesias; and the former Argentine president, Raúl Alfonsín.

Among Spaniards, Galicians are believed to make astute politicians because of their supposedly cunning nature and conservatism. It is sometimes said that if a Galician is seen on a staircase it is hard to determine whether he is going up or down.

A Coruña

A good point of departure to tour the **Rías Altas** is the port city of **A Coruña ❶**. It has been a key shipping centre for nearly 2,000 years. Julius Caesar sailed in here from Gaul (France) in AD 60 to re-establish Roman rule, and Felipe II's Armada set sail from here. The old part of the city (La Ciudad Vieja) rises from a narrow strip of land pointing out into the Atlantic, while the new section (La Pescadería) rests on the edge of the mainland and an isthmus. Because of its position near a great sea route between Northern Europe and South and Central America, A Coruña continues to play an important role as a major Atlantic port and oil refinery.

The city's showpiece is its **Torre de Hércules** (www.torredeherculesacoruna.

Torre de Hércules lighthouse near A Coruña.

Galicia

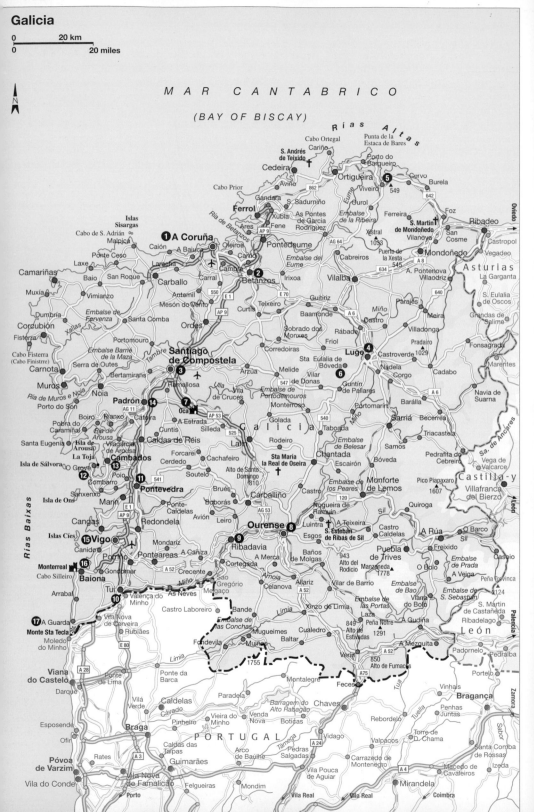

0   20 km

0   20 miles

N

MAR CANTABRICO

(BAY OF BISCAY)

com; daily, June–Sept 10am–9pm, Oct–May until 6pm; charge but free on Mon), the world's only Roman-era lighthouse, which is ten minutes by car or tram from the city centre. It dates from the time of the Celtic chieftain Breogan and was rebuilt during the reign of the Roman emperor Trajan in AD 98. It looks down on the spot where the *Mar Egeo* oil tanker ran aground on the rocks in 1992.

Back in the city centre, the characteristic enclosed glass balconies (*miradores*) of the pretty white buildings lining the seafront permit residents to admire the bay while protecting them from stiff ocean winds.

To take in the sun, cross the old town and spend some time at the downtown beach, **Riazor**, or take a short cab ride and swim at **Santa Cristina** beach on the isthmus. In the old section, pass along the gardens lining **Avenida de la Marina** and then walk over to the grandiose **Plaza de María Pita**, named after the heroine who courageously raised the alarm alerting citizens of an attack by the English admiral Sir Francis Drake in 1589.

A few streets south is the 12th-century **Castillo de San Antón**, formerly a prison and now an archaeological museum with a varied collection of Roman, Visigothic and even Egyptian artefacts (Sun 10am–2.30pm, Tue–Sat 10am–9pm Jul–Sep, until 7.30pm rest of the year; free on Sat).

The churches of **Santiago** (12th century), **María del Campo** (13th century) and **Santo Domingo** (17th century) are in the city's old section, as is the stunning **Museo de Arte Sacro da Colexiata** (Tue–Fri 9am–2pm, Sat 10am–1pm; free), with exhibits of religious silver. Just south of the old section and overlooking the harbour is the **Jardín de San Carlos**, an enclosed garden containing the granite tomb of Sir John Moore, the Englishman who died in 1809 while helping to defend the city against the French during the Peninsular War.

More modern attractions include **Domus** (http://mc2coruna.org; daily 10am–7pm, from 11am Sat–Sun), the Museum of Mankind, and the **Aquarium Finisterrae** (daily 10am–7pm), an aquarium on Paseo Alcalde Francisco.

The roads to Santiago

Betanzos ❷, a lovely unspoilt port, lies at the mouth of a *ría* a short way from A Coruña. The city reached its apogee in the 14th and 15th centuries when the nearby **Las Marinas valley** provided wheat for the entire A Coruña province. Three impressive but small Gothic churches, **Santa María del Azogue** (founded late 1300s), **San Francisco** (1387) and **Santiago**, have been well preserved and serve as an illustration of the town's best moments. The road runs north from here to the spectacular cliffs and headlands of the **Rías Altas**, Galicia's wildest coast.

Today, **Santiago de Compostela**'s ❸ horizon is still clearly identified by the distinctive sight of the twin Baroque towers of the city's **Catedral** (www.catedraldesantiago.es; daily 7am–8.30pm; free but charge for museum), which shelters the supposed tomb of St James, the patron saint of Spain.

TIP

For great views over Santiago, take a rooftop tour of the cathedral (tel: 902-557 812; daily 10am–2pm and 4–8pm). Prior to heading up, the tour also visits the 12th-century Archbishop's palace of Gelmírez, which is considered to be one of the finest Romanesque civil buildings in Spain.

Twin Baroque towers of Santiago's Catedral.

After the discovery of the tomb between AD 812 and 814, support from the Asturian king and his successors and later the offering – *voto de Santiago* – of the Spanish Monarchs created a bustling town within an otherwise turbulent province. Over the saint's tomb, King Alfonso II of Asturias ordered the erection of an earthen temple, later replaced by a stone church under the rule of Alfonso III.

In 997, al-Mansur Abu Jafar (military commander of the Caliphate of Córdoba) destroyed the entire town except for the tomb. But in 1075 work began on the present cathedral by order of King Alfonso VI of León and Castile.

The cathedral

This Romanesque building (consecrated in 1211) occupies the east end of the **Praza do Obradoiro**. Its Baroque facade by Fernando Casas y Novoa has graced the entrance to the cathedral since 1750. The interplay of curved and straight lines on the carvings appears to culminate in flickers of flame at the height of the two slender towers. Walk around the cathedral's

Town Hall, Santiago de Compostela.

contrasting four plazas, unique in Spain, for views back to the building. Inside the Baroque facade is *El Pórtico da Gloria*, the tripartite porch depicting the Last Judgement by Maestro Mateo, considered one of the greatest masterpieces in the Romanesque style.

Inside the cathedral, the high altar is dominated by a sumptuously attired 13th-century statue of St James. Some pilgrims mount the stairs behind the altar to kiss the saint's mantle. Below the altar, a crypt constructed in the foundations of the 9th-century church holds the remains of the saint (which went missing from 1589 until 1879) and two of his disciples, St Theodore and St Athanasius.

Other obligatory stops include the *Puerta das Platerías* (Silversmiths' Door), a Romanesque doorway so named because it led outside onto a plaza lined by silversmith shops, and the *Puerta Santa* (Holy Door), opened during Holy Years.

Across the spacious Praza do Obradoiro from the cathedral stairs, the **Pazo de Raxoi**, an impressive 18th-century mansion designed by French architect Charles Lemaur, serves as the City Hall. It is capped by a bronze sculpture of Santiago the Moor Slayer in battle gear, riding a charging stallion. At the plaza's south end is the **Colegio de San Jerónimo**, a 17th-century building attractive for its 15th-century-style gateway.

The north side of the plaza is occupied by the **Hostal de los Reyes Católicos**, begun in 1501 under orders of Fernando and Isabel as an inn and hospital for pilgrims. It is now a flagship Parador. The building's facade features an ornate Plateresque doorway of great beauty, and the wrought-iron work and carved columns in a chapel inside are of exceptional artistic merit.

Tourists and pilgrims

Head out of the plaza between the cathedral and the Colegio de San Jerónimo and turn into the **Rua do**

Franco, where university students, tourists and pilgrims mingle among bars, shops and colleges. The **Colegio de Fonseca** (finished in 1530) has a remarkable Renaissance doorway. Also worth visiting are the **Colegio de San Clemente** (1601), the **Convento de San Francisco**, said to have been founded by St Francis of Assisi in 1214, and the **Monasterio de San Martiño Pinario**, now a seminary, founded in the 10th century and rebuilt in the 17th century.

Just outside the Porta do Camiño in the northeast of the old city, the **Museo do Pobo Galego** (www.museodopobo.gal; Tue–Sat 10.30am–2pm and 4–7.30pm, Sun 11am–2pm; free on Sun) has a wide-ranging display of Galician trades, arts and crafts, musical instruments and traditional costumes.

In 2011, a futuristic cultural centre, Cidade da Cultura de Galicia (www.cidadedacultura.gal; guided visits Tue–Sun 11.30am and 5.30pm; charge), designed by American architect Peter Eisenman, opened on a hill southeast of the city. It houses a library, archive and the Museo Centro Gaiás (Tue–Sun 10am–8pm), which hosts temporary exhibitions.

Inland to Lugo and Ourense

Cutting across Galicia from all points of the compass are the roads that pilgrims travelled to Santiago: the original Cantabrian *camino* from the Asturian coast; the French *camino* from the Pyrenees via the Benedictine monastery at Samos and Lugo; the so-called English *camino* from A Coruña and Betanzos; the Portuguese coastal route via Tui and Pontevedra; and, finally, the route up from Central Spain via Ourense. **Lugo ❹**, the main Galician town on the French *camino*, is 95km (60 miles) east of Santiago on the N-547 highway that twists and turns through jagged mountains.

The drive is worth the effort, for circling the town is one of the best-preserved Roman walls to be found anywhere in the world. The massive schist walls, now declared a World Heritage Site, are 2km (1.2 miles) long and 10 metres (33ft) high and date from the 3rd century; the walk around the top takes just 30 minutes.

Lugo's position on the French *camino* explains the strong French influence in the Romanesque parts of its **Catedral**, begun in the 12th century (daily; free). It was expanded in the Gothic period and enlarged in the 18th century. The **Capilla de Nossa Señora dos Ollos Grandes** (Virgin of the Big Eyes), a chapel at its east end, features an exquisite Baroque rotunda, which contrasts with the Romanesque carving on the north and south doors. Across from the north door on the lovely Praza de Santa María is the 18th-century **Palacio Episcopal**, a typical *pazo*, or Galician manor house.

The **Museo Provincial** (http://redemuseisticalugo.org; Mon–Fri 9am–9pm, Sat 10.30am–2pm and 4.30–8pm, Sun 11am–2pm; free) houses a large mixed collection representing provincial

A clam shell, the sign of St James, on Santiago's Catedral.

The Santiago Legend

Since 813, pilgrims from all over Europe have travelled the Camino de Santiago across northern Spain to this remote corner of the country.

According to legend, a Spanish peasant led by a shower of stars – *campus stella* – discovered the tomb of the Apostle of Jesus in a field in the 9th century. St James (Santiago in Spanish) had been martyred in Jerusalem in ad 44, but his remains are said to have returned by boat with his followers to Spain, where he had supposedly travelled and evangelised during his life.

The discovery became a focus of unity for Christians who were separated politically and spread across a narrow strip of northern Spain. It inspired Christian efforts to carry out the Reconquest that would eventually force Muslims off the Iberian peninsula.

Whether St James ever visited Spain has always been disputed, but there is no doubt that the idea of the possession of the sacred remains of the saint aroused tremendous passion and pride. As their

Carving of a clam shell, the sign of St James on Santiago's Catedral.

battle cry, the Christian soldiers shouted '*Santiago y cierre España*' (St James, and close Spain!) to urge their brethren to defeat the Muslims. Christian fighters also gave their patron the title 'Matamoros' (Slayer of Moors).

El Camino

During the later Middle Ages, the well-travelled path of thousands of pilgrims through Navarre and Galicia became known as El Camino de Santiago (the Road to Santiago), and in the 12th century one of the world's first travel guides was written to help them on their way. The number of pilgrims increased dramatically after Pope Calixto II conceded the Roman Catholic Church's greatest privileges to the See of Santiago de Compostela and designated as Holy Years those in which the day of St James fell on a Sunday. Pilgrims who reached Santiago in those years obtained a plenary indulgence and absolution for one year. The shrine became the greatest place of Christian pilgrimage after Rome and Jerusalem, and the city itself emerged as one of Europe's most brilliant.

In reality, there are several different routes of pilgrimage to Santiago, but the principal one, known in Spanish as the *camino francés* (French route), crosses northern Spain from two points on the French border, Roncesvalles in Navarre and the Puerto de Somport in Aragón. The two branches meet at Puente La Reina, a bridge over the River Arga, and continue through Santo Domingo de la Calzada, Burgos, Fromista, León and Astorga. Along the way, the route is marked by a succession of handsome towns and cities and magnificent Romanesque and Gothic churches and cathedrals, but between these highlights are forbidding hills and stretches of bleak countryside which test the stamina of the pilgrim. After Ponferrada, the *camino* crosses the Cordillera Cantábrica at O Cebreiro to enter Galicia and continues through a succession of small towns and villages. The 800km (500 miles) from the French frontier takes a good 4–5 weeks to walk.

International pilgrims

Thousands of people make all or part of the trek each year on foot or by bicycle. Some of them begin as far away as Paris. On the way they stop at an efficient network of pilgrim hostels and get their official passports stamped as proof of their endeavour – to classify as a true pilgrim you have to walk at least 100km (62 miles). The route is marked across country and through towns by the sign of the scallop shell, the symbol of St James.

history and includes Roman mosaics discovered while building a city-centre car park.

In summer you can join the largely local crowds who flock to Lugo's coast and its relaxed fishing ports-turned-beach resorts; **Viveiro** ❺ and **Ribadeo** both have beautiful old towns that are pleasant to stroll through. Alternatively, you can explore the interior.

Santa Eulalia de Bóveda ❻, 14km (8 miles) from Lugo, is a palaeo-Christian monument that was unearthed in the early years of the 20th century, with a vestibule open to the sky and a rectangular chamber decorated with exquisite frescoes of birds and leaves (Tue–Fri 8.30am–2.30pm, Sat 10am–2pm; free).

Feudal remnants

The highways and byways of Lugo and Ourense, the two eastern inland provinces, provide an insight into Galician history.

Farming methods here are reminiscent of strip farming practised in the Middle Ages. The uneven terrain and the division of the land into small family farms, known as *minifundios*, make the mechanisation and modernisation of farming difficult. Everyone has some land and no one wants to give up their small parcels, which are usually spread apart because of the way land has been passed down through inheritance.

For a long time, a semi-feudal society persisted, with dominant *caciques* (bosses) maintaining great influence and power over peasants. One visible sign of times not so long passed is the region's weather-beaten castles and *pazos*, or manor houses, built with the rents or *foros* paid by the local aristocracy. An outstanding example of their distinctive architectural and gardening style is the **Pazo de Oca** ❼, south of Santiago on the N-525.

Ourense ❽ is said to have received its name because of the gold mined by the Romans in the Valdeorras hills of the Sil valley. Although it is now a busy commercial town, it retains the **Puente Romano** (Roman Bridge) that was rebuilt on its original foundations in the 13th century.

TIP

For hundreds of years, Ourense has attracted visitors who come to sample the mineral waters from three springs in Praza das Burgas, which emerges at a temperature of 67°C (153°F). Experience it for yourself at the Piscina Termal (www.terma sourense.com; Tue–Sun 10am–2pm, 5–9pm); tickets can be purchased at the tourist office.

A Galician granary, built on stilts to keep out vermin, by the Ría de Corcubión.

In the **Museo Arqueológico** (www. musarqourense.xunta.es; Tue–Sat 9.30am–2.30pm and 4–9pm, Sun 9.30am–2.30pm;free), just behind Praza Maior, prehistoric, pre-Roman and Roman-era specimens are kept alongside later pilgrimage art.

Close by, the **Catedral de San Martiño**'s Romanesque Pórtico del Paraíso (Paradise Door) inside the west front illustrates the 24 Old Men of the Apocalypse and still has its medieval colouring. The province's river valleys to the east are dotted with monasteries and steeply terraced vineyards along the Sol; to the west the Miño valley road is an impressive drive taking you up to **Ribadavia** ❾, a medieval wine-town, and along the Portuguese border to **Tui** ❿, with its splendid hilltop cathedral.

The Rías Baixas

You can visit most of the impressive **Rías Baixas** with relative ease by car from Pontevedra and Vigo. According to legend, **Pontevedra** ⓫ was founded by Teucer, half-brother of Ajax. But historians say the town probably dates from the Roman period, and its name from the Latin '*Pons Vetus*' (Old Bridge) that described the 11-arch span over the Río Lérez. The trading port had a brilliant life during the Middle Ages, and Columbus's *Santa María* was built in its shipyards. But after the harbour silted up, a new port built at Marín surpassed it in importance. Today the islet in the river has been converted into an open-air sculpture museum.

Pontevedra preserves the charm of an old country town, with fine examples of *cruceiros*, the stone crosses marking crossroads, in its streets. The **Santa María La Mayor** Plateresque church (daily), nestled among the alleyways in the fishermen's quarter, was built late in the 15th century by the mariners' guild. Its interior features a mix of Gothic notched arches, Isabelline twisted columns and ribbed vaulting in the Renaissance style.

Close by in Praza de la Leña is the small but stunning **Museo Provincial** (www.museo.depo.es; Tue–Sat 10am–9pm, Sun 11am–2pm; free), with Bronze Age jewellery, paintings by Zurbarán and Goya and the work of Alfonso Castaleo, a 20th-century Galician artist.

Behind Pontevedra is a lovely rolling hill country with hamlets steeped in rural traditions. In the municipality of **As Neves** in southern Pontevedra province, every year on 29 July people whose lives have been saved in one way or another during the previous year gather to thank St Marta for her saving grace; the 'saved' people dress up in funeral clothes and get inside coffins which are carried in procession setting off from the church of **Ribarteme** by their families.

From Pontevedra, the coastal highway PO-550 zigzags north around the Salnés peninsula, which has grown wealthy on tourism, intensive fish farming, smuggling and vineyards. **Combarro** is one of the picturesque fishing villages in this area.

Ourense's Puente Romano over the Minho river.

Round a cape on the southern side of the **Ría de Arousa** is the extraordinary **La Lanzada beach**. In summer hundreds camp out on this long, picturesque strand. At the far end is a nature reserve with protected dunes and marshland.

Further north is the island of **La Toja**, where Galicia's beach tourism began. A sick donkey was the first creature to benefit from the mineral waters of a spring here. Now a luxury hotel offers everything from blackjack to beauty treatments. Neighbouring **O Grove** ⑫ is a seafood-lover's paradise, with excellent restaurants, an aquarium and submarine trips in the *rías*.

In the smuggling town of **Cambados** ⑬, savour the strong Albariño varietal wine produced nearby that goes so well with seafood. A 17th-century church and the adjoining **Fefiñanes Pazo** (mansion), along with a row of arcaded houses, form the attractive **Plaza de Fefiñanes** at the town's north entrance. A little further down the highway is a lovely promenade overlooking the bay.

Costa da Morte

Padrón ⑭ is believed to be the coastal town where the boat bearing the body of St James arrived in Spain. The boat's mooring stone can be seen under the altar of the local church, beneath the bridge over the Río Sar. Galicia's most famous poet, Rosalía de Castro (1837–85; see page 339), lived for many years in a stone house near the Sar. The house is now a **museum** (Tue–Sat 10am–2pm and 4–8pm, Sun until 1.30pm). She and her husband, the historian Manuel Murguía, formed the nucleus of a group of poets and writers who were influential in stimulating the *Rexurdimento* (renaissance) in Galician letters. The *Rexurdimento* stirred latent nationalist sentiment, and by the beginning of the 20th century several nationalist parties had been formed.

The coastline to the north of Padrón is called the **Costa da Morte**, meaning the Coast of Death, so named because of the number of ships wrecked and lives lost along the rocky shoreline. The land leads out to Cabo Finisterre – literally the end of the earth to the

Loading up fishing boat with lobster pots, Combarro.

Romans – via a winding road that snakes its way through fishing villages and past a stunning 8km (5-mile) stretch of virgin beach at **Carnota**.

Vigo to the Portuguese border

Vigo ⓕ, just an hour's drive south of Pontevedra along the AP-9, is Galicia's largest and most industrialised city. It dates back to Roman times, but flourished and grew wealthier in later centuries when Carlos I authorised commercial trade with America in 1529. In 1702, a Spanish treasure convoy was intercepted and destroyed by the British navy in Vigo Bay. To this day, it is believed that tonnes of gold lie at the bottom of the bay in the hold of lost galleons.

In more recent decades, Vigo's wealth has been based on manufacturing industries such as fish-canning, car production, shipbuilding and the sleepless port, which is home to half of Spain's deep-sea fishing fleet, one of the largest in the world. Although not a traditionally beautiful city, the old quarter and Modernist buildings give it character; and the Galician art collection in the **Museo Municipal 'Quiñores de León'**, a 17th-century manor house set in the peaceful Parque de Castrelos (www.museodevigo.org; Tue–Fri 10am–2pm, Sat 5–8pm, Sun 11am–2pm; free), is unmissable.

Above all, Vigo is a city for sea-lovers. Enjoy the sun at one of several sparkling beaches, including Samil, Alcabre and Canido. Or take a ferry ride from the port to the fishing village of **Cangas** on the north side of the *ría* or to the **Islas Cíes**, small, uninhabited isles in the mouth of Vigo Bay, now protected as a natural park. Back on the mainland, an ambitious **Museo do Mar** (Tue–Sun, mid-June–mid-Sept 11am–2pm and 5–8pm, mid-Sep–mid-June 10am–2pm and 5–7pm) details the city's connection with seafaring.

To reach the port where Columbus's flagship *Pinta* docked in 1493 with news of the discovery of the New World, drive south on the AG-57 to **Baiona** ⓖ, a chic and wealthy resort with smart yachts bobbing in the bay. Castelo de Monterreal, a massive castle fortress with a long defence wall, was built on this promontory rock in about 1500. It has now been converted into a Parador hotel, which has a commanding view of the Atlantic, the Islas Estelas in the mouth of the bay and the coast south to Cabo Silleiro.

At this point, the crowds appear to drop away for the final stretch of coastline running down to Portugal. The climate in the Miño estuary has a mild, tropical quality, enabling such species as kiwis, vines and subtropical flowers to flourish. **A Guarda** ⓗ, the border town, is a beautifully unspoilt fishing port offering fine beaches and panoramic views from the Celtic **Museo Arqueológico de Santa Trega** (http://museos.xunta.gal/es/masat; Tue–Sun 10am–8pm, until 5pm in winter), located south of the town centre.

Plaza Ferreira, Pontevedra.

Vigo's busy shopping street.

Black beach and green lagoon of
El Golfo, southwest Lanzarote.

Masca village, Tenerife.

THE CANARY ISLANDS

This isolated archipelago is often forgotten in any survey of Spain. Yet 10 million tourists a year visit, and many Northern Europeans make their homes here, lured by the continuous sunshine, endless beaches and the dramatic volcanic landscapes.

O ff the west coast of Africa, the Canary Islands consist of seven islands. Tenerife, the largest, is home to the Parque Nacional de las Cañadas del Teide and high-rise resorts. Fuerteventura has some lovely beaches at Jandía and is a magnet for windsurfing enthusiasts. Gran Canaria boasts some interesting museums, including the Museu Elder. Lanzarote is noted for its volcanic landscape and the work of artist César Manrique. La Palma is the greenest island and has a beautiful capital, Santa Cruz de la Palma. La Gomera and El Hierro are the smallest islands and the perfect places to get away from it all.

The Canary Islands offer some remarkable contrasts. Here you will find one of the highest mountains in Europe, beaches of black sand and seas of still-hot volcanic lava, as well as moss-cloaked and mist-shrouded forests that have survived from the Tertiary Era. Some of the islands in this archipelago are razor-sharp, steep and volcanic, their tops hidden by cloud; a couple of them are mere slivers of sand, like slices cut from nearby mainland Africa and rolled flat by blistering sunshine.

Parts of this archipelago, marooned out in the Atlantic Ocean, are better known to Europeans escaping mid-winter blues than they are to Spaniards. At the height of the season, tourists outnumber local people by five to one. They are attracted by

a remarkably consistent climate: the average temperature of 17°C (63°F) in winter increases to 24°C (75°F) in summer, with a cooling offshore breeze.

The Canaries have been transformed by tourism from an isolated outpost of Spain into a diverse, multicultural society. The well-equipped resorts are little cities in themselves, where a babel of different languages fills the streets and bars. You can buy genuine fish and chips cooked by a man from Macclesfield and authentic sauerkraut dished up by a woman

Main Attractions

Gran Canaria
Pico de las Nieves
Puerto de Mogán
Lanzarote: Parque Nacional de Timanfaya
Fundación César Manrique
Tenerife: La Laguna
Puerto de la Cruz
Parque Nacional de las Cañadas del Teide
La Palma: Santa Cruz de La Palma

Off-roading in a dune buggy on Fuerteventura.

Playa del Inglés is the largest resort on the south coast of Gran Canaria. It has a long white-sand beach stretching for 10km (6 miles).

from Stuttgart, as well as international fast food, the ubiquitous paella and, if you look for it, genuine Canary Island cooking.

A touch of history

Despite this annual invasion, many parts of the islands are almost untouched by tourism and have retained their individuality. Elegant colonial architecture, introduced by the Spanish conquerors who arrived in the 15th century, has been lovingly restored in several cities on Tenerife and Gran Canaria. The influence of years of trade with and immigration to Latin America is evident in food, language and a certain indefinable atmosphere. World events have touched the islands at various times: Columbus stopped here for essential ship repairs on his great voyage of discovery; Nelson tried and failed to take the port of Santa Cruz in 1797 and lost his arm while trying to capture a Mexican fleet; and General Franco launched the Civil War from Tenerife in 1936.

The seven main islands are divided into two provinces: eastern Las Palmas – Gran Canaria, Fuerteventura and Lanzarote; and western Santa Cruz – Tenerife, La Palma, La Gomera and El Hierro. There are also four uninhabited islets, and countless reefs and rocks in the archipelago.

Gran Canaria

Tenerife and Gran Canaria share equal status as capital of the autonomous region of the Canary Islands, and the presidency alternates between them every four years. **Gran Canaria** is the third-largest island (1,530 sq km/590 sq miles) and has a population of 847,000. Its capital, **Las Palmas de Gran Canaria ❶** (pop. 379,000), covers the northern tip.

Las Palmas is both elegant and seedy. It has an excellent beach, **Playa de las Canteras**, a 3km (2-mile) stretch of sand, lined with cafés and restaurants, which is popular with tourists from mainland Spain; and one of the largest ports in Europe. Near the port is the Parque Santa Catalina, a bustling, palm-lined square; and the **Muelle Santa Catalina**, with a shiny new commercial centre.

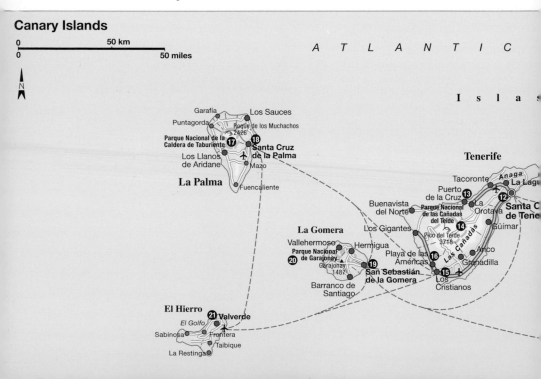

Canary Islands

0 — 50 km
0 — 50 miles

ATLANTIC

Islas

Garafía
Los Sauces
Puntagorda
Roque de los Muchachos 2426
Parque Nacional de la Caldera de Taburiente ⑰ ⑱ Santa Cruz de la Palma
Los Llanos de Aridane
Mazo
La Palma
Fuencaliente

Tenerife
Tacoronte Anaga La Lagu
Puerto de la Cruz ⑬
Buenavista del Norte La Orotava ⑫ Santa C de Tene
Parque Nacional de las Cañadas del Teide ⑭ Güímar
Los Gigantes
La Gomera Pico del Teide 3718
Vallehermoso Hermigua Las Cañadas
Parque Nacional de Garajonay ⑳ Playa de las Américas ⑯ Arico
Garajonay 1487 ⑲ Granadilla
Barranco de Santiago San Sebastián de la Gomera ⑮ Los Cristianos

El Hierro ㉑ Valverde
El Golfo
Sabinosa Frontera
Taibique
La Restinga

The star attraction here is the state-of-the-art science museum, **Museo Elder** (www.museoelder.org; Tue–Sun 10am–8pm). **Vegueta**, the old colonial quarter to the south, is the most atmospheric part of the city, centred on the broad **Plaza de Santa Ana** in which stands the mainly Gothic **Catedral de Santa Ana**, entered through the adjacent **Museo Diocesano de Arte Sacro** (Mon–Fri 10am–4.30pm, Sun until 1.30pm). The **Vegueta** daily food market (www.mercadovegueta.com; 6.30am–2pm), on Calle Medizábel, sells fruits and vegetables as well as fresh fish, local cured meats and cheeses.

Nearby, the **Museo Canario** (www.elmuseocanario.com; Mon–Fri 10am–8pm, Sat–Sun until 2pm; free on Mon and Wed from 5pm) exhibits mummies, skulls and other artefacts from the pre-Hispanic period when the aboriginal Guanches inhabited the islands. Also in Vegueta's narrow streets, the **Casa de Colón** (www.casadecolon.com; Mon–Sat 10am–6pm, Sun until 3pm), a beautiful building with latticed balconies and ornate doorways, is a museum dedicated to Columbus and the island's maritime past. It is claimed that Columbus stayed here while one of his ships was being repaired, but there is no supporting evidence. Nearby the **Centro Atlántico de Arte Moderno** (CAAM; www.caam.net; Tue–Sat 10am–9pm, Sun until 2pm; free) is a stunning modern exhibition space concealed behind a traditional facade.

Another worthy stop is the blue building of the Casa Africa (www.casafrica.es; exhibitions Mon–Fri 9am–6pm) on Calle Alfonso XIII; it promotes African culture and celebrates relations between Europe, Africa and South America. Also of note is a beautifully refurbished former 18th-century hospital, now housing the San Martín Centro de la Cultura Contemporánea (www.sanmartincontemporaneo.com; Tue–Sat 10am–9pm, Sun 10am–2pm), a modern art gallery space and concert hall.

En route to the main tourist destinations in the south, make time for some attractive old towns such as Telde, with San Juan Bautista, the oldest church on the island (begun in 1519); and **Agüimes** ❷, whose attractive Casco

FACT

Before the arrival of the Europeans, several indigenous tribes, known collectively as Guanches, lived on the Canary Islands. Examples of stone and bone implements, and other Guanche artefacts, can be seen in museums all over the islands.

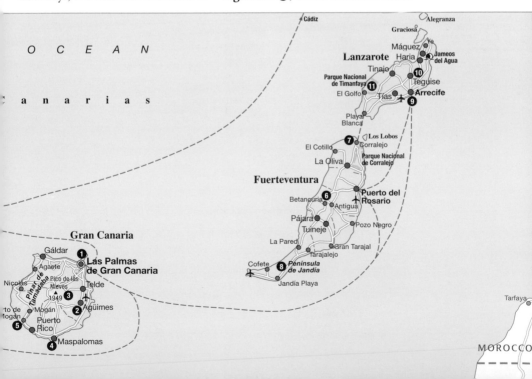

TIP

Spain's first golf club, Real Club de Golf de Las Palmas (www.realclubde golfdelaspalmas.com), opened in Gran Canaria in 1891. There are now eight other courses around the island: Las Palmeras (www.laspalmerasgolf.es) and El Cortijo (www.el cortijo.es) in the north; Maspalomas (www.maspalomasgolf.net), Meloneras (www.meloneras-golf.com), two at Salobre (www.salobregolfresort.com) and two at Anfi Tauro (www.anfi.com) in the south.

Histórico and several hotels dedicated to rural tourism, make it worth a visit. The spotless narrow streets are lined with ochre-coloured buildings, and enlivened with bronze statues depicting rural life and characters. The Iglesia de San Sebastián in the shady main square has been designated an artistic historical monument.

Nearby, the **Barranco de Guayadeque**, the island's most famous ravine, wonderful for serious walking, has some almost deserted cave villages, with bars and restaurants. The **Centro de Interpretación Arqueológica** (Tue–Sat 9am–5pm, Sun 10am–6pm) offers an interesting overview of the life of the early indigenous inhabitants. Follow the steep, winding road through the wild, scenic interior to the **Pico de las Nieves ❸** (1,950 metres/6,398ft). There is an excellent view of the central summits from the Cruz de Tejeda, which is marked by a sombre stone crucifix and a couple of busy restaurants. The view is dominated by the towering finger of the Roque Nublo, revered by the Guanches as a holy site. The lovely village of **Artenara**, reached

by a difficult but rewarding drive, has houses built into solid rock, a cave church and a renowned cave restaurant, Mesón la Silla.

Wind back to the coast (or return to the coast-hugging motorway, GC-1) to reach the huge, strident, interlinked resorts of **Playa del Inglés** and **Maspalomas ❹**, with their wonderful stretches of sandy beaches and dunes, parts of which are a designated nature reserve. Until the early 1960s the south was a remote, arid spot; now the southern shoreline is virtually a string of high-rise hotels and apartment blocks, while the 2km (1.2-mile)-long Paseo Marítimo is lined with clubs, pubs, amusement arcades, fast-food outlets and restaurants. Between the two resorts lie the dunes, a golf course, a huge amusement park, **Holiday World** (http://holidayworldmaspalomas.com; daily year round), and two water parks.

A little further along the motorway, climbing high up the hillsides, is the family-friendly resort of Puerto Rico, which is also a major sailing centre, with diving and sailing schools, and deep-sea fishing trips organised on

Folk singers in Teguise, Lanzarote.

TIMANFAYA PARK

At the entrance to Timanfaya Park, where César Manrique's famous 'fire devil' sign stands, is where you board the bus for a spectacular 40-minute tour. The park can only be visited on a coach tour or guided walk – free roaming is not allowed.

When the tour ends you will see several demonstrations on how intense the heat is. Watch park attendants throw dried brush into a hole in the ground, whereupon flames roar upwards; or pour buckets of water into a small crater, causing a cascade of boiling water to shoot into the air like a man-made geyser. Behind the glass-walled El Diablo restaurant (tel: 928-840 057), you can watch chefs officiating over a barbecue powered by natural heat emanating from just below the surface.

the harbour-side. Back on the winding coast road is the attractive, more up-market **Puerto de Mogán** ➎, where bougainvillaea-covered houses, built on a complex of seawater canals spanned by delicate bridges, surround a harbour bobbing with yachts and another from which a small fishing fleet still operates.

After this, the coast returns to its natural rugged state. You can follow a narrow, vertiginous road along the cliff top to the northwest (two viewing points have been created to allow motorists to pull off the road and enjoy magnificent views), and the attractive towns of **Agaete** and its fishing port, the **Puerto de las Nieves**, built around a picturesque rocky bay. A number of excellent fish restaurants lining the quay get busy at weekends when people from Las Palmas come for lunch. Regular ferries run from here to Santa Cruz de Tenerife and there is a linked bus service from Las Palmas. About 8km (5 miles) north of Agaete, clustered at the foot of an extinct volcano, lies **Gáldar**, ancient capital of the Guanches, which is proud of its pre-Hispanic heritage.

A cave decorated with geometric patterns, discovered in the late 19th century, was neglected for many decades, but after lengthy renovation work, the **Museo y Parque Arqueológico Cueva Pintada** (www.cuevapintada.com; June–Sept Tue–Sat 10.30am–7.30pm, Sun 11am–7pm, Oct–May Tue–Sat 10am–6pm, Sun 11am–6pm) opened to the public in 2006. Inland lies **Teror**, with some lovely colonial architecture and a famous church, the Basilica de Nuestra Señora del Pino, dedicated to the best-loved saint on the island, which is the focal point of a huge festival in the first week of September.

Fuerteventura's desert landscape.

Fuerteventura

The second largest of the Canary Islands at 1,670 sq km (645 sq miles), **Fuerteventura** also has one of the smallest populations (107,000). Like neighbouring Lanzarote and Africa only 96km (60 miles) away, Fuerteventura doesn't have the height to prod the passing clouds into releasing their water. The island is consequently barren and sandy, and its fragile economy is based on

Sands of Corralejo, Fuerteventura.

goat-rearing and, increasingly, tourism. Recent initiatives in *turismo rural* have led to the renovation of many of the island's landmark windmills and the establishment of ecological museums, such as the **Molino de Antigua Centro de Artesanía** (Tue–Sat 10am–6pm) a renovated mill on the outskirts of Antigua, and the **Ecomuseo La Alcogida** (Tue–Sat 10am–6pm) at Tefia.

The main town of **Puerto del Rosario** is straggling and not very attractive, although an extensive renovation of the harbour front has brightened it up considerably. You'll also find here the Casa Museo Unamuno (Mon–Fri 9am–2pm, Sat 10am–1pm), dedicated to Spanish philosopher, essayist, novelist and poet Miguel de Unamuno. The old capital city of **Betancuria** ❻, a pretty spot in the centre of the island, is far more interesting, with the beautiful **Iglesia de Santa María** and its attached museum (Mon–Fri 11am–5pm, Sat 11am–3pm); and a fascinating **Museo Arqueológico** (Tue–Sat 10am–6pm). Some 7km (4 miles) south of Puerto del Rosario, is the resort of **Caleta de Fuste**, a completely artificial creation, but well designed and attractive.

Fuerteventura has the Canaries' best beaches. At the northern tip lie the idyllic sands of **Corralejo** ❼, where the old part of town retains its character, although surrounded by apartment blocks and shopping malls. El Jable sand dunes, which run parallel to the coast, are now protected as the **Parque Natural de Corralejo**. On the northwestern side of the island **El Cotillo** is an attractive village with a fishing harbour, a number of good restaurants, and stretches of windswept sands. In the south the **Península de Jandía** ❽ is a region of glorious golden beaches, glittering seas with water-sports facilities, and the inevitable overdevelopment of the stretch of coast known as Costa Calma. The world's largest windsurfing centre, the Pro Centre René Egli, is located at the Hotel Los Gorriones on Playa Barca.

Lanzarote

The fourth largest of the seven islands, **Lanzarote** (810 sq km/315 sq miles)

Playa Blanca, Lanzarote.

has a population of 143,000 and a barren beauty all its own.

Arrecife ⑨, the island capital, is a modern town, although palm-lined waterfront promenades and a pleasant beach add interest, and the Charco de San Ginés, a small tidal lagoon, is surrounded by brightly shuttered buildings. As on Fuerteventura, the former capital has all the historic interest: **Teguise ⑩** has a 15th-century church, two lofty former convents, which now house occasional art exhibitions; the beautiful **Casa-Museo del Timple** (Mon–Sat 9am–4.30pm, Sun until 3.30pm), with its collection of local stringed instruments; the 16th-century **Castillo de Santa Barbara y Museo de la Piratería** (Piracy Museum; www.museodelapirateria.com; daily 10am–4pm) high on a hill, and a huge Sunday market (9am–2pm).

Lanzarote's **Parque Nacional de Timanfaya ⑪** (tel: 928-118 042; www.reservasparquesnacionales.es; guided tours only) is a massive volcanic wasteland of mangled rock and twisted lava created by early 18th-century eruptions. Bus tours around the Montañas del Fuego run throughout the day (see page 348).

Lanzarote's star resort is lively **Puerto del Carmen**, in the southeast, with sandy beaches stretching away from the original fishing harbour, and a plethora of restaurants. There are numerous other attractive spots around the southern tip, including pretty **Playa Blanca**, where the village atmosphere is being changed by a glossy marina and a lot of new building. Most of the tourist developments on the island are tastefully done, reflecting the influence of local artist César Manrique, who died in 1992 and whose sculptures can be seen all over the island (look out for them at traffic roundabouts). The **Fundación César Manrique** (http://fcmanrique.org; daily 10.30am–6pm) in Tahiche, north of the capital, is one of Lanzarote's greatest attractions; and the magical underground world Manrique created

in a volcanic tunnel system, the **Jameos de Agua** (daily 10am–6pm) in the north of the island, is another.

Tenerife

The western islands – Tenerife, La Palma, La Gomera and El Hierro – are more beautiful than the eastern group, with craggy mountains, lush valleys, deep and ancient forests and a mixture of sunshine, cloud and mist.

The largest of the islands (2,350 sq km/910 sq miles), **Tenerife** has a population of 888,000 and the highest mountain in Spain, the volcanic Pico del Teide, rising to 3,720 metres (12,200ft), with forests, green valleys and finally beaches on its lower skirts. Tenerife's capital, **Santa Cruz de Tenerife ⑫**, is a pleasant colonial town, rather smaller than Las Palmas.

The **Plaza de España** has been given an impressive makeover and now centres on a huge shallow pool, surrounded by trees. Among other sites worth visiting are the Iglesia de Nuestra Señora de la Concepción (daylight hours; free); the **Museo de la Naturaleza y el Hombre** (www.

TIP

The southwest coast of Tenerife is one of the world's most important spots for whale-watching, with pilot whales and dolphins being the most populous. Tours last from 1 to 5 hours and leave from Puerto Colón, Puerto de Los Cristianos and Puerto de Los Gigantes. Try Tenerife Dolphin (tel: 922-750 085 in the south, 922-385 116 in the north; www.tenerifedolphin.com).

Lighthouse at Punta de Teno, Tenerife.

museosdetenerife.org; Tue–Sat 9am–8pm, Mon–Sun 10am–5pm; free Fri–Sat from 4pm), with excellent collections of artefacts from the Guanche era; and the **Museu Militar** (Tue–Sat 10am–2pm; free), which exhibits the cannon reputed to have removed Admiral Nelson's arm in 1797. The elegant new concert hall, the **Auditorio**, near the port, designed by Santiago Calatrava, is eye-catching.

About 8km (5 miles) north stretch the gleaming white sands of **Las Teresitas**, one of the largest man-made beaches in the world. Santa Cruz lies in the shadow of the Anaga Mountains, which form the northern part of the island, and conceal rugged scenery and tiny villages in their green folds.

At the southern fringe lies **La Laguna**, a colonial gem that has been designated a Unesco site. One among numerous lovely buildings is the church, which has a seven-storey belfry and watchtower and, like the one in the capital, is called the Iglesia de Nuestra Señora de la Concepción.

The history of tourism in Tenerife began in 1850, with the first steamship service from Cádiz. Only the gentry could afford to travel, and they came to **Puerto de la Cruz** ⑬ and **La Orotava** in the fertile Orotava valley on the northwest coast, an area still known for its banana plantations. Both these attractive towns, with their narrow cobbled streets and elegant colonial-style mansions, flaunting ornate wooden balconies, retain some of their earlier gentility. However, because the northern coast is rough and wild, Puerto lacks one major feature that the modern tourist expects – a sandy beach. This problem has been circumvented to some extent by the landscaped **Lago Martiánez** (daily 10am–7pm, last admission 5pm), a series of swimming pools sculpted out of the rock at sea level, designed by Lanzarote architect César Manrique, and which also includes the Puerto de la Cruz Casino. Two other highlights are the Museo de Arte Contemporáneo Eduardo Westerdahl (MACEW; www.iehcan.com; Mon–Thu and Sat 10am–2pm, Fri also 5–7.30pm), with its interesting contemporary art collection, and the peaceful Jardín Botánico (Botanical Garden; daily 9am–6pm).

The **Parque Nacional de las Cañadas del Teide** ⑭ encompasses Las Cañadas, the area left by the collapse of the ancient crater around El Teide. There are good roads into the park, but because of erosion you are not allowed to climb right to the peak; instead, you can take a cable car (*teleférico*), which stops 160 metres (525ft) short of the summit. There are stunning views and some unusual rock formations. A helpful Visitors' Centre (daily 9am–4pm) at the El Portillo entrance offers advice.

Los Cristianos ⑮ and **Playa de las Américas** ⑯, the largest resorts, are in the south of the island, where the sunshine is guaranteed. Big, brash and ever busy, with 24-hour entertainment, lots of water-based activities and a huge water park, **Aqualand** (www. aqualand.es; opening times vary), they are close to the main airport, Reina

Balconies in Santa Cruz de la Palma, La Palma island.

Sofía, and are easily reached from Santa Cruz via the TF-1 motorway.

La Palma

La Palma, the greenest and fifth largest of the islands (730 sq km/282 sq miles), has retained much of its 82,000-strong population, thanks to its suitability for agriculture. The island is very steep, rising to 2,426 metres (7,960ft) at the **Roque de los Muchachos**, and falling away sharply to the sea around the rocky coast. The **Parque Nacional de la Caldera de Taburiente ⓱** (Visitors' Centre Mon–Sun 9am–6pm), with its massive volcanic crater 9km (5.5 miles) in diameter, occupies much of the northern part of La Palma. On the rim of the volcano is the Observatorio Astrofísica (tel: 922-405 500; www.iac. es; visits available; free), with one of the largest telescopes in Europe. Colonial **Santa Cruz de la Palma ⓲** is acknowledged to be the most beautiful of the Canary Islands' capitals. Among sights worth seeing are two churches with Mudéjar-style ceilings, and the lovely Casas de los Balcones – a row of houses with characteristic colourful balconies. The pretty town of **Los Llanos de Aridane**, to the west, and the bodegas in the wine-producing region of Fuencaliente in the far south should not be overlooked.

La Gomera

The second smallest of the islands (378 sq km/146 sq miles), **La Gomera** has a population of around 20,000, with tourism on the increase. The main town of **San Sebastián ⓳**, which may not have changed much since Columbus stopped here for supplies in 1492, is linked to southern Tenerife by a regular ferry service. The Parador here is one of the finest in Spain.

La Gomera's tourist areas are limited, but include the **Valle Gran Rey**, a deep, luxuriant valley in the southeast corner of the island. **Playa de Santiago**, in the south, is also popular as the site of the up-market **Jardín Tecina** hotel complex, with accommodation in

village-style houses surrounded by lush gardens. There are relatively few beaches, and the island rises steeply to its highest point (Mount Garajonay at 1,487 metres/4,878ft) in the centre of **Parc Nacional de Garajonay ⓴**, notable for its ancient Tertiary Era forest made up of moss-cloaked laurel and cedar trees.

El Hierro

The smallest of the islands at 278 sq km (107 sq miles), **El Hierro** is also the least developed and least populated, with around 10,000 inhabitants. Cattle and other livestock are the mainstay, and wines and cheeses are produced. The principal town, **Valverde ㉑**, is the only inland island capital. On the west coast, an interesting spot is the **Lagartario** (Tue, Thu and Sat 10am–2pm and 4–6pm), where some the island's giant lizards are bred. El Hierro has more volcanoes than any of the other islands (although the last eruption was two centuries ago), and there is one massive volcanic crater, of which one side has collapsed into the sea, creating **El Golfo**, a wide valley and sweeping bay, this island's most peaceful spot.

El Hierro's dramatic coastline.

Sa Creueta lookout point on Mallorca's Formentor coast, towards the Colomer rock.

THE BALEARIC ISLANDS

Writers and artists have long flocked to Mallorca, Menorca, Ibiza and Formentera, finding inspiration in the idyllic climate, the magnificent landscapes and, above all, the peace and quiet.

There are four Balearic Islands. The largest is Mallorca, which has a cosmopolitan capital, Palma, and the Serra de Tramuntana mountain range, now a Unesco World Heritage Site, as well as plenty of attractive towns and villages like Deià. Menorca is much quieter, with two towns, Maó, with its excellent Museu de Menorca, and Ciutadella; the fishing village of Fornells, is arguably the prettiest place on the island. The south of Ibiza is famed for its nightlife while the north offers a more relaxed stay and luxury rural accommodation. Formentera, the smallest island, is ideal for a quieter holiday.

The Balearic Islands are well known for their sunshine and beaches, but just a short distance away from the resorts lies a wealth of beautiful scenery and handsome old towns. On Mallorca, the largest island, the spectacular Serra de Tramuntana forms one of Europe's most dramatic coastlines, while Menorca is more gentle, with a timeless landscape and a surprising number of undeveloped little coves and beaches. Ibiza is famous for its nightlife, while tiny Formentera just about manages to retain its uncluttered simplicity.

These islands make up the autonomous region of the Balearics (Balears). Their name comes from the Greek word for sling, *ballo*. So famous were the ancient natives of the Balearics for

their skill in hurling deadly lead pellets with slings that the Romans called the two larger islands *Balear Maior* and *Balear Minor*.

Architectural remains

Skeletal remains indicate that the islands were inhabited as early as 4000 BC, but the oldest architectural ruins date from the 3rd millennium BC. On Menorca the earliest were communal ossuaries called **navetes** because they were shaped like inverted ships (*navis* is Latin for ship). The Talayotic

Main Attractions

Mallorca: Palma: Cathedral
Valldemossa: La Real
  Cartuja
Deià
Coves del Drach
Menorca: Maó: Es Port
Ciutadella
Fornells
Ibiza: Dalt Vila

Mirador on Mallorca's rugged west coast.

Age that followed – from 1000 BC to the Roman conquest – left the most archaeological testimonies on the islands, the defensive stone structures called **talayots**, believed to have been built by a people who came from the eastern Mediterranean. The Carthaginians, whose occupation dated from the mid-7th century BC, recruited Balearic mercenaries whose slings were the terror of the Romans. It was not until 20 years after the destruction of Carthage (146 BC) that Rome was able to subjugate the islands.

Conquest and reconquest

As the Roman Empire was falling apart, the Vandals swept into the islands in AD 426 and remained until they were driven out by the Byzantines 100 years later. Three centuries of Muslim domination of the Balearics, made tributary to the Emirate of Córdoba in 848, left a heritage of Moorish place names (beginning with 'Bin' or 'Al').

The Christian reconquest took place in Mallorca in 1229 under King Jaume of Aragón. The event proved decisive in the final evolution of the islands'

culture. They fell under the influence of Catalonia, and to this day each island speaks its own variant of Catalan. In the 13th century the Balearic Islands became important stops on the trade route between the north of Italy and Northern Europe. Mallorca produced great artists and craftsmen whose work may be seen in Palma's cathedral and the Castell de Bellver.

With the rise of the Turkish Empire in the 16th century, the Balearic Islands became a bastion of the expanding Spanish Empire. Watchtowers or *talaies* throughout the islands testify to the constant need to keep watch against sudden raids of Muslim corsairs in search of booty and slaves. Ibiza city's magnificent walls date from this period.

With the resurgence of Mediterranean commerce in the middle of the 17th century, Mallorcan merchants once again began to benefit from the islands' strategic location. Many of the mansions that grace the countryside date from this period, and their Italian-inspired architecture illustrates the strong links between Mallorca and

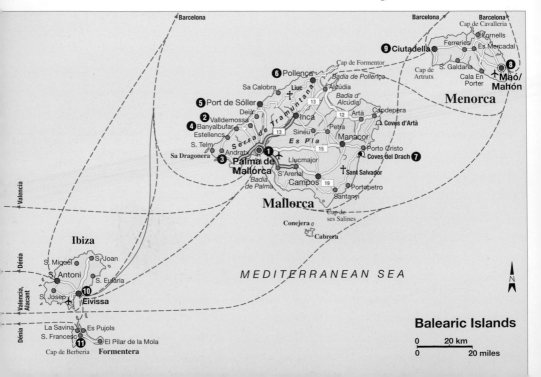

Italy. In 1708 the British seized Menorca during the War of Spanish Succession. Except for a brief occupation by the French, they remained in control until 1781.

Mallorca

Although most people arrive by air at Palma's huge Son Sant Joan airport, the most impressive way to reach Mallorca is by boat from Barcelona or Valencia to **Palma ❶**. From a distance the medieval Gothic masterpiece, the **Catedral** (www.catedraldemallorca.info; June–Sept Mon–Fri 10am–6.15pm, Apr–May and Oct until 5.15pm, Nov–Mar until 3.15pm, Sat 10am–2.15pm all year; charge for museum), known as La Seu, stands out like a huge, rose-coloured, craggy rock. Work on the cathedral began in the 13th century and was not completed until the 16th century. Its beautiful rose windows make it the most luminous of Mediterranean cathedrals. There is also an extraordinary *baldachino*, a wrought-iron crown of thorns over the high altar, added by Catalan *Moderniste* architect Antoni Gaudí, creator of Barcelona's Sagrada

Família, who worked for 10 years on the cathedral in the early 20th century. You enter through a small museum, which has splendid silver monstrances and some medieval paintings.

The 13th-century **Palau de l'Almudaina** (Tue–Sun, Apr–Sept 10am–8pm, Oct–Mar until 6pm; free last three hours Wed–Thu), beside the cathedral on the foundations of an Arab *alcàsser* or fortress, is a perfect blend of Islamic and Catalan-Gothic architecture. It has a pretty courtyard and a Gothic chapel, the Capilla de Santa Ana. The palace is still used for official functions by the royal family and has some interesting royal portraits.

The area around the cathedral was the site of the Arab city known as *Medina Mayurka*. The only architectural remnants are an arch called the Arc de la Drassana Musulmana, on Carrer Alumudaina, and the two small chambers of the **Banys Àrabs** (daily, 9am–7pm), set in tranquil gardens in Carrer Serra. This neighbourhood is especially interesting: you can peek into ancient churches, and admire the houses that once

TIP

For a lively (and loud) night out in Palma, the narrow streets immediately west of Passeig d'es Born and Avinguda Antoni Maura have the best selection of bars. The other major nightlife area is further west, around the stretch of the Passeig Marítim called Avinguda Gabriel Roca.

Palma's Gothic Cathedral.

TIP

Before leaving Valldemossa be sure to check out Costa Nord (tel: 971 612 425; www.costa nord.es; daily 9am–5pm), a cultural centre set up by Michael Douglas, who has a home nearby. Here you can watch a film about the history of the area, narrated by the Hollywood actor himself. There is also a nice restaurant.

belonged to wealthy noblemen and merchants – their lovely courtyards can be glimpsed through gates from the streets.

The nearby streets of **Almudaina, Zanglada** and **Morey** also have noble houses dating from the 16th to 18th centuries. On the **Plaça San Francesc** is a church of the same name, with an enchanting Gothic cloister; it was built during the 13th century, although its Baroque facade dates from four centuries later. One of its eight-sided chapels, all of which are decorated with Renaissance and Baroque art, contains the 15th-century sarcophagus of Ramón Llull. Outside is a statue of missionary Father Junípero Serra (see page 367).

A symbol of Palma's prosperous past is the magnificent 15th-century building known as **Sa Llotja**, one of Spain's finest civic Gothic buildings, which used to house the merchants' stock exchange; the wonderfully airy interior is used for art exhibitions. Its four crenellated, octagonal-cornered towers and galleried windows serve as a counterweight to the majestic cathedral.

The 17th-century **Consolat de Mar** next door has an impressive Renaissance-style gallery.

Almost opposite the Real Club Náutic in the nearby busy port is the prestigious **Es Baluard Museu d'Art Modern i Contemporani** (www.esbaluard.org; Tue–Sat 10am–8pm, Sun until 3pm), housed in a stunning white structure built into the city fortifications. Displays include work by Picasso, Miró and Tàpies as well as Mallorcan artists Miquel Barceló and Juli Ramis, and views of the port and the city from the museum's rooftop and terrace bar are impressive. For something different, try Palma's **Acquarium** (http://palma aquarium.com) where you can swim with sharks and rays.

About 5km (3 miles) southwest of the old town (Bus No. 3 or 46 from the Plaça d'Espanya or Plaça Rei Joan Carles) at Carrer Joan de Saridakis 29, the **Fundacío Pilar i Joan Miró** (http://miro.palmademallorca.es; Sun 10am–3pm, Tue–Sat mid-May–mid-Sept 10am–7pm, mid-Sep–mid-May until 6pm; free on Sat) is worth a visit to admire the stunning architecture of the modern building, designed by Rafael Moneo, as well as to see the changing displays of work from the Miró collection.

Not far away are two further attractions, both of which can be reached from the city centre by bus from the Plaça d'Espanya or the Turistbus. The first is the **Castell de Bellver** (http://castell debellver.palma.cat; Mon 8.30am–1pm, Apr–Sep, Tue–Sat 8.30am–8pm, Sun 10am–8pm, Oct–Mar Tue–Sat 8.30am–6pm, Sun 10am–6pm), perched on a hill to the west of the city, which has commanded the approaches to Palma since the 14th century. The second is the **Poble Espanyol** (www.puebloespanol mallorca.com; Apr–Oct 10am–7pm, Nov–Mar 9am–5pm), a walled town of replica architectural treasures from across Spain, which is kitsch but entertaining.

Scenic drives

If time is short, head straight towards the delightful little hilltop town of

Port d'Andratx.

Valldemossa ❷, about 25km (15 miles) north of the capital, to visit the former Carthusian monastery, **La Real Cartuja de Valldemossa** (www.cartuja devalldemossa.com; open from 9.30am, closing times vary), where George Sand and Chopin spent the winter of 1838–9. In spite of having a rather primitive borrowed piano to work with, Chopin composed some of his most beautiful pieces here, including the *Raindrop Prelude*. The monastery was founded in 1399, but the monks were expelled in 1835. The neoclassical chapel has frescoes on the ceiling painted by Goya's brother-in-law, Manuel Bayeu. The adjoining 16th-century palace, the **Palau del Rei Sanxo** (hours as for La Cartuja; combined ticket), was constructed on the site of one Jaume II built for his son, Sanxo, and is entered through a tranquil, plant-filled courtyard. Piano recitals of Chopin's music are held at intervals throughout the day. Valldemossa has its own saint, Santa Catalina, born here in 1531, and almost all the well-kept houses in the town have a tiled picture outside, depicting scenes from her life.

If you take the coastal route to the west of Palma (which is motorway as far as Peguera), you will come to **Andratx ❸**, which has an attractive port nearby. Despite tourist-oriented development, **Port d'Andratx** has kept its colour as a fishing village, although more yachts than fishing boats bob on the calm waters of the bay these days. Like many towns in the Balearics, the main town of Andratx was built some kilometres inland for protection from pirates and was surrounded by *talaies* or watchtowers. The fortified church, like many on the islands, was once surrounded by a moat. The somewhat isolated village of **Sant Telm** has also retained its identity and affords a striking view of the tiny nature reserve island of **Sa Dragonera**.

Nearby, the abandoned monastery of **Sa Trapa** is an excellent walk from Sant Telm. During the summer there are boat trips around Sa Dragonera,

believed to be the beach head of the Christian expedition that conquered Mallorca in 1229.

The northwest coast route

The Ma-10 coastal road from Andratx follows one of Europe's most breathtaking routes, hugging the mountainside high above the sea. The village of **Estellencs**, which straddles the steep slopes of **Mount Galatzó**, has a defensive tower used in the days when pirates were a menace. A little further along this road is the village of **Banyalbufar ❹**, set amid agricultural terraces carved out of the mountain, shored up with meticulous stone walls and irrigated by a network of canals. The town still has half of the dozen fortified towers built as a defence against the marauding Turks in the 16th and 17th centuries. North of Banyalbufar, the road turns inland, in the direction of **Esporles**, close to which you'll find the estate of **La Granja** (www.lagranja.net; daily 10am–7pm, until 6pm in winter). The estate was renowned for the purity of its water in Roman times and there are

La Real Cartuja de Valldemossa, the former Carthusian monastery.

Castell de Bellver.

Inspirational Island

Mallorca has attracted many writers and artists for almost 200 years and continues to encourage creative visitors and nurture home-grown talent.

In the mid-19th century, intellectual foreign visitors began to discover the delights of the Balearic Islands, and Mallorca in particular. Aurore Dupin-Dudevant, better-known by her pen name of George Sand, and her lover, the pianist and composer, Frédéric Chopin, spent the damp and chilly winter of 1838–9 in Valldemossa, and paved the way for many others.

Chopin completed his 24 Preludes Opus 28 while staying in the Real Cartuja de Valldemossa, although the only available piano was unfortunately not to his satisfaction.

A Chopin Festival is held in the monastery every August. Sand wrote that Mallorca was 'the most beautiful place I have ever lived' but she didn't like the people much, referring to them as 'barbarians and thieves'. Her book, *A Winter in Majorca*, was the first of what is now an extensive travel literature

Robert Graves, with his son Juan, at Deià in 1954.

on the islands. The eccentric Archduke Ludwig Salvator of Habsburg and Bourbon came to Mallorca in 1867 and fell in love with the island. He returned five years later to settle down and acquired the estate of Son Marroig, near Deià.

He maintained a large household presided over by a Mallorcan peasant girl, Catalina Homar, the great love of his life. The archduke was not an idle aristocrat: he was keenly interested in science, and wrote a total of 60 books, including his seven-volume work *The Baleares Described in Words and Images*. French artist and writer Gaston Vuillier visited in 1888 and later wrote *The Forgotten Isles*, about the Balearics, Corsica and Sardinia (1896).

An eclectic bunch

A steady stream of writers and artists looking for secluded picturesque places continued to visit Mallorca. The Catalan poet Santiago Rusinyol came here in the early years of the 20th century, and spent time in Valldemossa and Pollença. His book *The Island of Calm*, published in 1922, demonstrates his affection for the island.

The writer Anaïs Nin spent a summer in Deià in 1941 and wrote of a brief erotic encounter. Joan Miró and his Mallorcan wife, Pilar, voluntary exiles from Franco's Spain, lived in Palma from 1956 till his death in 1983. The Fundació Pilar i Joan Miró, built around his home in the city, displays much of his work (see page 360).

Robert Graves is perhaps the literary figure most closely associated with the island. He came to Deià in 1929, settled down and, apart from the Civil War years, stayed for the rest of his long life. It was here that he wrote *I, Claudius and Claudius the God*, and here that he is buried, in the hilltop cemetery. Among his many famous visitors there were some unknown ones, including the young Alan Sillitoe, who spent some time in Sóller in the mid-1950s recuperating from tuberculosis, and who Graves encouraged to write.

While here, Sillitoe commenced work on *Saturday Night and Sunday Morning*. Graves loved Deià and it is largely thanks to him that the area was designated a protected zone. His son, Tomàs, who still lives in Mallorca, has written about rural life on the island, and celebrated the traditional rustic diet in a book published in English as *Bread and Oil* (2000).

Only very prosperous writers and artists could afford to live in Deià or Valldemossa today, but Mallorca still attracts creative people looking for inspiration and tranquillity.

still numerous fountains in the leafy gardens. The interior of the house is magnificent and gives a good idea of how the landed classes once lived. The chapel and the torture chamber speak for themselves. The donkeys, pigs, wild goats and sheep in the grounds are usually a hit with children.

Continuing up the coast, about 5km (3 miles) past Valldemossa is the estate of **Miramar**, the nucleus of various properties owned by the Habsburg Archduke Ludwig Salvator. The most notable of these is **Son Marroig** (www.sonmarroig.com; Mon–Sat, Apr–Sept 10am–7pm, Oct–Mar until 5pm), on the way to Deià. This splendid mansion, built around an ancient defensive tower, has a museum of Mallorcan folklore, but is best-known for its belvedere of Carrara marble, with glorious views of the rocky promontory of Na Foradada and the coast to the west.

The honey-coloured village of **Deià** has kept much of its original architecture. It has resisted the ravages of hotel complexes and tourist shops thanks largely to the efforts of its artists' colony led by Robert Graves, who first settled here in 1929 at Gertrude Stein's suggestion. 'It's paradise, if you can stand it,' she is reported to have told him. His home, **Ca N'Alluny** (tel: 971-636 185; www.lacasaderobertgraves.com; Apr–Oct Mon–Fri 10am–5pm, Sat until 3pm, Nov–Mar Mon–Fri 9am–4pm, Sat until 2pm) on the Carretera Deià–Sóller, has been restored and opened as a museum. Narrow, winding streets lead to the top of the village and the little church of Sant Joan Bautista beside which, in a small cemetery overlooking the Mediterranean, the poet is buried. Deià is chic and very popular. Besides a luxury hotel, La Residencia, there are several less expensive alternatives, and the best selection of restaurants on the coast.

Sóller

From Deià the road wriggles its way through the hills before descending to **Sóller ❺**, a lovely little town, with interesting *moderniste* buildings, and a number of pleasant cafés, set around the main square, Plaça Sa Constitució. The town sits amid orange and lemon groves, and linked to its port (3km/2 miles to the north) by the delightful old-fashioned Orange Tram. Sóller's *moderniste* station is also the terminus for a little wooden train which has been running here from Palma on a narrow-gauge railway ever since 1912 (www.trendesoller.com; seven daily trains from Palma 8am–7.30pm). The station has an unusual attraction, too: the Sala Miró (Tue–Sun 11am–5pm; free), hung with drawings and lithographs by the artist; and a second gallery (same hours) that displays some 50 ceramic pieces by Picasso.

North through the Serra de Tramuntana

North from Sóller, towards Pollença, there are magnificent views as the road cuts through the heart of the Serra de Tramuntana, which became a Unesco World Heritage Site in 2011, over the pass of Puig Major, Mallorca's highest mountain at 1,445 metres (4,741ft). Fornalutx is an exquisite little town of

The grave of Robert Graves in Deià.

Street in picturesque Deià.

warm stone buildings that has been designated a national monument – which naturally draws in a lot of visitors, but also means building regulations are stringent. Set against the backdrop of the Tramuntana range, its steep cobbled streets are lined with cacti and palm trees. The town is set among ancient terraces of citrus fruits and gnarled olive trees, marked out with dry-stone walls. Paths run through them to pretty little Biniaraix, which is also only a half-hour walk down narrow lanes, signposted from the centre of Sóller.

A short distance past **Fornalutx** on the Ma-10, the Mirador de Ses Barques has a restaurant where you can stop for a drink while enjoying views of the coast and Port de Sóller. The route then winds past the reservoirs of Panta de Cúber and Panta de Gorg-Blau, connected by a narrow canal. Near the latter, a little road leads down to the coast. Its name, **Sa Calobra** (The Snake), is an apt one for the 12km (8 miles) of hairpin bends that loop down to sea level. The views are stunning and the road is an adventure in itself, but try to come fairly early in the morning to avoid the

streams of tourist coaches. Park where you can when the road reaches sea level and walk a short distance towards the deep gorge of Torrent de Pareis. Tunnels burrow through the rock to the river bed where the gorge widens into a huge natural theatre. The idyllic little bay, **Cala de Sa Calobra**, has a couple of restaurants and bars and a pebbly beach, but they get crowded in summer.

Around 10km (6 miles) further along the road to Pollença is the major pilgrimage site in Mallorca, the **Monestir de Lluc** (www.lluc.net; daily 10am–5pm). Located in a valley near Puig des Castellot, the massive building mainly dates from the 18th century, but pilgrims have been coming here since the 13th century to pray to a dark-stone statue of the Madonna and Child, La Moreneta. According to legend, it was discovered by an Arab boy called Lluc, whose family had converted to Christianity. People still come to venerate La Moreneta, but many also come to have lunch and admire the views, for the monastery has a restaurant, bar and barbecue area. It also offers inexpensive

Walking up Via Crucis in Pollença.

JARDINS D'ALFÀBIA

Just outside Sóller, at the exit from the tunnel that runs beneath the 496-metre (1,627ft) Coll de Sóller, are the Jardins d'Alfàbia (www.jardinesdealfabia.com; Apr–Oct daily 9.30am–6.30pm, Nov–Mar Mon–Fri 9.30am–5.30pm, Sat until 1pm), which was once the country estate of a Moorish vizier of Palma. The fountains and irrigation channels are a bit neglected, but the flowing water and shaded walks, with turkeys pecking under fig trees, and birds singing among exotic plants, are appealing. The house is full of treasures: look out for the huge, 14th-century oak chair in the print room, regarded as the most important antique in Mallorca. If you don't have a car, the Tren de Sóller (see page 363) actually makes a stop in the gardens.

accommodation (tel: 971-871 525); the rooms are fairly basic, but staying here allows you to appreciate the peace of the monastery after the tour groups have gone home. Attend Mass in the church (Mon–Sat 11.30am, Sun 11am and noon) for the experience of hearing the Lluc boys' choir, the Coro Blavets (Blue Ones), named after the colour of their cassocks. If you are staying overnight you may be able to hear the choir at 7.30pm (7pm on Sun).

Alcúdia and Pollença

On the north coast the bays of **Alcúdia** and **Pollença** ❻ are particularly attractive. The town of **Pollença**, a settlement since Roman times, lies about 5km (3 miles) inland from its port. It is a pretty town with a huge main square, the Plaça Major, surrounded by appealing cafés and restaurants and dominated by the parish church, from which the Via Crucis (Way of the Cross), a flight of 365 steps lined with cypress trees, leads to the little chapel of El Calvari. Just off the square the deconsecrated Dominican convent and church of Sant Domingo is the venue for a classical

music festival in July and August when an international line-up of orchestras and soloists performs. **Port de Pollença**, set on the wide curve of its bay, with two long beaches flanking a central marina, has been popular with English visitors for many years and retains a distinctive atmosphere.

Jutting out from the bay is the island's northernmost point, **Cap de Formentor**, a narrow headland with sheer cliffs and idyllic sandy beaches, surrounded by clear turquoise waters. The best place to appreciate the spectacular landscape is the Mirador des Colomer, a specially designed walkway with telescopes.

Heading east along the coast you reach the ancient, walled town of **Alcúdia,** where the central Plaça Constitució has some elegant Renaissance facades. A few attractive boutique hotels have opened in recent years, perhaps to cater for visitors to the Ciutat Romana (Mon–Fri 9.30–8.30, Sat–Sun until 2.30pm), the remains of the Roman city outside the town walls, and the Roman theatre on the road to Alcúdia's port, from where there are ferries to Menorca.

Cobbled streets of Fornalutx.

Cyclists on Sa Calobra.

Madonna and Child at the Monestir de Lluc.

The **Badia d'Alcúdia** to the southeast is lined with white-sand beaches, and a succession of resorts – low-key compared to those around the Bay of Palma – as far as Can Picafort, where the coast becomes rocky. Inland lies the **Parc Natural de S'Albufera** (www.balearsnatura.com; daily, Apr–Sept 9am–6pm, Oct–Mar until 5pm; free), a huge area of wetlands, where more than 200 species of birds have been spotted. It covers 800 hectares (2,000 acres), crisscrossed by a network of canals, with walking and cycling tracks running through it.

The east coast

In the northeast corner of the island, just 12km (8 miles) inland, the fortified town of **Artà** has a massive fortress, the **Santuari de Sant Salvador**, and an ancient church. The prehistoric settlement of **Ses Païsses** (Apr–Oct Tue–Fri 10am–5pm, Sat–Sun until 2pm, Nov–Mar Tue–Sun until 2pm) lies about 2km (1 mile) southeast of Artà. Set in a peaceful grove of holm oaks, the site is impressive. About 8km (5 miles) east of Artà, near the coast,

Weird and wonderful formations in the Coves d'Artà.

is **Capdepera**, with ochre-coloured buildings and another impressive walled citadel (www.castellcapdepera.com; daily, mid-Mar–mid-Oct 9am–8pm, mid-Oct–mid-Mar until 5pm). A road then runs past the Canyamel Golf Course to the **Coves d'Artà** (www.cuevasdearta.com; daily, July–Sept 10am–7pm, Apr–June and Oct until 6pm, Nov–Mar until 5pm), caves carved out of a sheer cliff face. If you take the coast road from Capdepera you come to the first resort on this coast, **Cala Ratjada**, which has an attractive seafront, a large port and a sandy beach – although better beaches can be found by following a wooded path a short distance north.

The whole of the east coast is dotted with resorts: **Cala Millor** and **Cala d'Or** are the largest and most commercialised, with lots of water sports and other facilities. **Porto Cristo** is the most old-fashioned and has a local feel; **Portocolom** is the quietest, with a working fishing port, pastel-washed houses and a pine-shaded promenade, but not much of a beach; and the prettiest is **Cala Figuera** in the southern corner, where a walkway runs alongside the fishermen's boathouses, and a number of waterside restaurants serve good fresh seafood. Many people visiting Porto Cristo are en route to the nearby **Coves del Drach** ❼ (www.cuevasdeldrach.com; daily, Apr–Oct 10am–5pm, Nov–Mar 10.45am–3.30pm, entry on the hour) where frequent tours run through 2km (1 mile) of brightly lit tunnels and chambers and a chamber-music ensemble performs beside a large subterranean lake.

You don't have to go far inland to find some small and pleasant towns. **Santanyí** is an arty little place of honey-coloured sandstone, with antiques shops and several good exhibition venues, and a friendly Plaça Major on which stand several cafés and two churches. **Felanitx**, a little further north, is a good place to buy ceramics and has a lively Sunday morning market. If you approach Felanitx from the

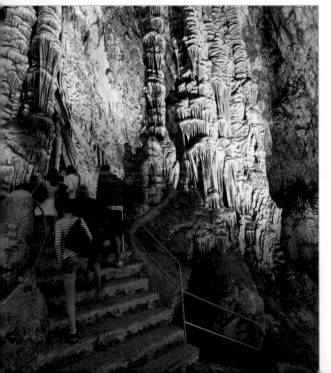

coast you could turn off the road to the **Santuari de Sant Salvador**, 509m (1,670ft) above sea level. On one side of the hill is a 14-metre (46ft) stone cross, and on the other the monument to Cristo Rei (Christ the King). There are magnificent views in all directions, and accommodation is available in the Petit Hotel Hostatgería Sant Salvador (tel: 971-515 260; www.santsalvadorhotel. com), which has a good restaurant.

If you have time to venture further into the interior of the island, there are some little jewels. **Petra** sits in the agricultural heartland, just a few kilometres from the Ma-15 running between the capital and the east coast. Father Junípero Serra, the founder of California's first missions, was born here in 1713. The **Casa Museu Fray Junípero Serra** (tel: 971-561 028; Mon–Fri 10am–1.30pm), the house in which the missionary was brought up, has been preserved and furnished much as it was, and displays scale models of Serra's missions in California and Mexico as well as maps and letters. Wall tiles on the (usually closed) monastery of Sant Bernardino, opposite, depict the Californian missions, and signs lead to Es Celler, a cavernous restaurant well known for huge plates of traditional Mallorcan food (tel: 971-561 056).

From the Ma-15 you could drop down towards Llucmajor, with a detour up the 542-metre (1,778ft) hill called the **Puig de Randa**, which is the centre of a little cluster of sanctuaries. At Llucmajor, pick up the motorway to Palma, or follow signs to **Capocorb Vell** (www.talaiotscapocorbvell.com; Fri–Wed 10am–5pm), the best-known Bronze Age site in Mallorca. The foundations of 28 enormous buildings are visible, along with two massive *talayots* (defensive towers). You are now almost on the south coast and from here the road runs along a fairly dull stretch towards the Platja de Palma. **S'Arenal**, the largest resort, merges into Les Meravelles on a 7km (4-mile) strip of packed beaches, fast-food outlets, high-rise hotels, high-octave discos, pubs, bars and beer halls. In S'Arenal, Aqualand (www.aqualand.es; July–Aug 10am–6pm, May–June and Sept until 5pm) with its mega-water slides, claims to be the biggest aquatic park in Europe. Approaching the yacht harbour of Ca'n Pastilla, the road briefly becomes pedestrianised and quieter, and before long takes you back through traffic-filled streets to Palma.

Menorca

The island of **Menorca** is much quieter than its larger neighbour, more low-key both in its man-made attractions and its landscape. It is an appealing little island, with many devotees, and has the distinction of being designated a Unesco Biosphere Reserve. It also has an abundance of prehistoric structures: the communal ossuaries called *navetes* and the defensive towers called *talayots*, of which around 200 have survived (see page 368) and *taulas* (tables, or T-shaped structures). The island, in common with the rest of the Balearics, later underwent centuries of conquest and reconquest before being

Visitors can walk the walls at Capdepera.

influenced by British occupation in the 18th century. This is most clearly seen in and around **Maó** ❽. Nowhere else in Spain are sash windows a feature of the architecture. And Menorcan Xoriguer gin, introduced by the English, has a distinctive taste and is popular throughout Spain.

Maó, which the English made the island's capital, is situated at the end of a 5km (3-mile) fjord, the only geological formation of its kind in the Balearics. **Es Port**, the large and beautiful harbour, lined by a tree-shaded promenade – with a string of mostly good restaurants and shops selling the ubiquitous Menorcan sandals called *abarcas* – is one of the liveliest areas, but there is much to see and do in the old city centre. Climb the broad steps of the Costa de Ses Voltes to visit the Plaça de Sa Constitució, dominated by the **Església de Santa Maria**, where music is played during summer morning concerts on the huge and famous organ. The excellent **Museu de Menorca** (www.museudemenorca.com; June–Sept Tue–Sat 10am–2pm and 6–8pm, Sun 10am–2pm, Oct–May Tue and Thu 10am–6pm, Wed, Fri, Sat, Sun until 2pm), in a former Franciscan monastery, is also well worth seeing.

Ciutadella

Menorca's other large town, the city of **Ciutadella** ❾, lies at the western extreme of the island. It was the capital under Muslim rule and from the time of the Christian conquest until 1722. It is a lovely town, with ochre-coloured city walls, and broad squares and stately mansions, dating from the 16th to 19th centuries, which give it a dignified air (the only one of the mansions that can be visited is the neoclassical Palau Salort). The elegant Plaça del Born is the main site of the island's most elaborate festival, the Festa de Sant Joan in late June, when prancing horses are ridden among the crowds by riders in sumptuous costumes. In the Plaça de la Catedral, lively with street entertainers in the summer months, stands the **Catedral de Santa Maria** (Mon–Sat 10.30am–1.30pm and 4–7pm; free). The main facade and splendid doorway are neoclassical, but the broad nave is Catalan Gothic,

Festa de Sant Joan, Ciutadella.

PREHISTORY IN MENORCA

Most of Menorca's prehistoric sites lie close to the two main towns – Maó and Ciutadella. At the eastern end of the island is the Talatí de Dalt, with a large central *talayot* and some burial caves. Nearby are the Navetes de Rafal Rubí, collective ossuaries shaped like upturned boats. Heading west, you reach Torre d'en Gaumés, with three *talayots*, a *taula* and a *hypostyle* (a hall with supporting columns). Not far away, the Torralba d'en Salort has the most beautiful taula of all. To the west, the Naveta d'es Tudons is believed to be the oldest roofed building in Europe, while the Torre Trencada is unusual in having medieval burial caves surrounding its *talayot.* South of Ciutadella is Son Catlar, the largest ancient monument in the Balearics, enclosed by its original 1km (0.5-mile) wall.

and it has a tower built on the foundations of a mosque. The harbour, called **Es Port** (like the one in Maó), is delightful, full of bobbing yachts and lined with fish restaurants whose tables reach almost to the water's edge.

The south coast of Menorca is dotted with resorts: one of the largest and most attractive, despite overdevelopment, is **Cala Santa Galdana**, set in a sheltered bay with sparkling turquoise waters and cut through by the beautiful limestone gorge of the Barranc d'Algendar. From the resort it is a pleasant and easy walk along pine-covered cliffs to several smaller, quieter bays.

There is no coastal road around the island; to cross from east to west, or to visit many of the coastal resorts and other places of interest, you have to return to the main road (Me-1) and make detours to left and right. However, the island's roads are relatively uncrowded and distances are not great, so this is not a problem, and it may encourage people to visit inland towns that might otherwise be missed. One of the most interesting of these, dominated by the 17th-century sandstone church of Santa Eulalia, is **Alaior**, where most of the cheese known as Queso de Mahón is made. The sleepy little town of **Es Mercadel**, some 13km (8 miles) west of Alaior, is also worth a visit, partly because it is home to several recommended restaurants specialising in Menorcan cuisine (*cuina menorquina*) and partly because it is the starting point for a drive up the sinuous but excellent road to the top of **Monte Toro**, Menorca's highest point (358 metres/1,170ft). It is topped by a still-functioning convent, a gaudy church, a restaurant and a huge statue of Christ with arms outstretched.

A road from Es Mercadel runs north to the idyllic village of **Fornells**, one of the most attractive places on the island, its whitewashed houses decked with green shutters and narrow streets brightened with flowers. There are still working fishing boats here (although there are more yachts and pleasure craft),

and some of their catch ends up in the many restaurants that line the harbour. Fornell's speciality dish is the delicious but expensive *caldereta de llagosta* (lobster stew), but there are many more economical alternatives on offer. Fornells is also the north coast's main water-sports centre, and Windsurfing Fornells (tel: 664-335 801; www.windfornells.com) offers windsurfing, sailing and water-skiing.

The northeast coast (most easily reached from Maó) is dotted with resorts, some small and quiet, some big and brash, but you can also find tranquillity in the dunes and marshes of **Parc Naturel S'Albufera des Grau** (Information Centre tel: 971-177 705), and wander along clearly marked paths to a freshwater lake where a wide variety of birds congregate, especially in the spring and autumn migratory periods.

Ibiza

Founded as *Ibosim* by the Carthaginians in the middle of the 7th century BC, **Eivissa** (**Ibiza Town**) ❿ developed a flourishing economy based on the export of salt, ceramics, glassware and agricultural products. Testimony

DRINK

Menorca is famous for its gin, which you can try – and buy – at the Xoriguer Gin Distillery (tel: 971 362 197; www.xoriguer.es) in Maó. The locals started making it in the 18th century to cater to the British soldiers who were stationed on the island. Xoriguer was the name of the windmill owned by the founding family.

Old fort in Ciutadella's harbour, Menorca.

to this prosperity are the Ibizan coins found throughout the Mediterranean.

But if Ibiza had a flourishing ancient past, its present is no less prosperous. Since the 1960s it has attracted visitors: first those in search of sophisticated nightlife as well as sun, sand and surf; later as a package-holiday destination for young travellers, whose nightlife is no longer so sophisticated, but begins in bars and discos near the port and doesn't end until well after dawn.

Dalt Vila

In contrast to the hustle and bustle around the port is the dignified serenity of the oldest part of Eivissa, **Dalt Vila** (Upper Town), enclosed within a complete ring of walls and declared a Unesco World Heritage Site in 1999. Crowning the hill of Dalt Vila, the sombre-looking **Catedral** (Apr–Oct Tue–Sun 10am–2pm and 5–8pm, Jul–Aug 6–9pm; free), begun in 1235, is built on holy ground: its predecessors on the spot were a mosque, a palaeo-Christian church, a Roman temple dedicated to Mercury and a Carthaginian temple. The basic street plan of this part of town has changed little since it was laid out by the Carthaginians.

There are archaeological relics of this period at the **Museu Arqueòlogic** (www.maef.es) in the Plaça de la Catedral and in the nearby **Museu Monogràfic** (Sun 10am–2pm, Tue–Sat, Apr–Sept 10am–2pm and 6.30–9pm, Oct–Mar 9.30am–3pm; free on Sun) at the foot of a hill called the **Puig des Molins**. Together they hold one of the world's largest and best collections of Carthaginian artefacts, including a terracotta bust of the goddess Tanit. The hill itself is a huge necropolis with more than 400 Carthaginian tombs, an open site that can be visited.

The island's second-largest town is **Santa Eulària**, on the south coast, a prosperous resort that has retained some of its original character. Go to the top of the hill called **Puig de Missa** to visit the dazzling white church and enjoy splendid views over the bay. Es Canar and Cala Llonga, excellent nearby beaches, have become resorts in their own right. One of the most popular places on the island is **Sant Antoni**, on the west coast, a fishing

Sunset over boats off Ibiza's coast.

Ibiza town and harbour.

village that is now a large-scale tourist resort. The lovely harbour, which the Romans called *Portus Magnus*, is skirted by a broad, tree-lined promenade, the Passeig Marítim.

This section of the coast has some of the finest beaches (with the best water sports) on the island, including Cala Tárida and Cala Bassa, both of which are connected to Sant Antoni by a decent bus service, as well as by water.

Formentera

The tiny island of **Formentera**, which has no airport, is separated from Ibiza by 7km (4 miles) of straits and islets. Regular hydrofoil and boat services link Eivissa to **La Savina**, Formentera's only port. This limited access is an advantage for those who want to get away from the hordes of tourists on Ibiza – nightlife here is limited to a few clubs, and the island has a low-key feel. The agricultural character of the island is reflected in its name, which is derived from *frumentum*, the Latin word for grain. You can rent a car, moped or bike in La Savina, or take a taxi, unless you are prepared to depend on the somewhat limited bus service. Mopeds are probably the best way to get around the island.

Sant Francesc ⑪, the island's capital, with a population of around 2,000, is 3km (2 miles) south of La Savina. There's a squat and sturdy church and a growing number of souvenir shops, but little of real interest to visitors.

Besides peace and quiet, Formentera offers visitors the superb, long beaches of **Illetes**, **Levant** and the glorious **Platja de Migjorn**, where most of the best hotels are located.

There is also a beach at **Es Pujols**, a package-tour-oriented resort on the north coast; and a number of small *cales* or coves, including the lovely **Cala Saona** on the west coast. Formentera has long been known as a place that welcomes naturists, and while there are no exclusively 'nude beaches', nudity is accepted on almost all of them.

If you have hired transport, take a trip to the east of the island, passing the pretty village of **Sant Ferran**, a hippie enclave in the 1960s and 1970s, where the renowned Fonda Pepe, a restaurant said to have been a Bob Dylan hang-out in those far-off days, still serves good food at reasonable prices.

Nearby, just off the main road, the **Cova d'en Xeroni** (May–Oct Mon–Sat 10am–1.30pm and 5–8pm), a huge limestone cavern full of stalagmites and stalactites. Stop farther down the road to admire the panoramic view from the *mirador* above **Es Calo**, one of the highest points on the island.

Continuing east, you reach the village of El Pilar, where there's a colourful 'hippie' market on Wednesday and Sunday afternoon; and on the island's far eastern point, presiding over sheer cliffs, is a still-working lighthouse, the **Far de sa Mola**, which affords incomparable views of the island and Ibiza, and a plaque commemorating the fact that Jules Verne chose this spot for the blast-off in his novel, *From the Earth to the Moon*.

TIP

As well as clubbing, Ibiza is also well known for its upmarket yoga retreats. These usually involve yoga classes, holistic treatments, vegetarian food and lots of free time to relax or enjoy other activities. Try Ibiza Yoga (www.ibizayoga.com) or Ibiza Retreats (www.ibiza retreats.com). Formentera Yoga (www.formenterayoga. com) is also very popular.

Plaça da Vila, Ibiza town.

Strolling down Alicante's Explanada de España.

TRAVEL TIPS

SPAIN

Transport

Getting There 374
  By Air.................................. 374
  By Rail................................. 374
  By Road 374
  By Sea................................. 374
Getting Around....................... 374
  Airport Transfer.................. 374
  Madrid Transport.............. 375
  By Air.................................. 376
  By Rail................................ 376
  By Bus................................ 376
  By Road 377
  By Sea 377

A – Z

Accommodation 378
Admission Charges 378
Budgeting for Your Trip 378
Climate................................... 378
Crime and Security 379
Customs Regulations............. 379
Disabled Travellers 379
Electricity 379
Embassies and
  Consulates 379
Entry Regulations 379
Festivals................................. 380
Gay and Lesbian Travellers 380
Health and Medical Care 380
Internet 381
Lost Property.......................... 381
Media 381
Money 381
Opening Hours....................... 382
Postal Services 382
Religious Services 382
Student Travellers.................. 382
Telephones 382

Tourist Information 382
Tour Operators 384
Websites 384
Weights and Measures 384

Language

Basic Rules............................ 385
Basic Words and Phrases 385
Greetings 385
On arrival................................ 386
In the hotel............................. 386
On the road 386
On the telephone.................... 386
Emergencies........................... 386
Shopping................................ 386
Market shopping 386
Sightseeing............................ 387
Dining Out.............................. 387
Liquid refreshment................. 387
Menu decoder 387
  Breakfast and snacks 387
Main courses 387
  Carne (Meat)...................... 387
  Aves (Fowl)........................ 388
  Pescado (Fish).................... 388
  Vegetables y cereales
   (Vegetables and cereals) . 388
  Frutas y postres (Fruit and
   desserts) 388
  Herbs and spices 388

Further Reading

History.................................... 389
Modern Spain 389
Classic Travel Writing 389
Spanish Literature.................. 389
Aspects of Spain 389
Regions.................................. 389
Other Insight Guides 389

TRANSPORT

GETTING THERE AND GETTING AROUND

GETTING THERE

By Air

Numerous charter and economy flights connect many European cities with Madrid and regional airports including Barcelona, Bilbao, Valencia, Alicante, Murcia and Málaga.

The Canary Islands are served by the main airlines; direct flights from Madrid take about two hours, and many low-cost airlines fly direct from the UK, taking just over four hours. Most flights go to Gran Canaria or Tenerife Norte (North) or Sur (South).

There is a wide range of cheap flights to the Balearic Islands, many of which are direct to Mallorca and, to a lesser extent, Eivissa (Ibiza) and Menorca, flight time around 2.5 hours.

Flights from the UK and Ireland

Airlines offering direct links between the UK and Madrid or Barcelona include **British Airways**, **Blue Air**, **Iberia**, **Vueling**, **Ryanair** and **Easyjet**. **Aer Lingus** flies to Madrid and Barcelona from Dublin.

Flights from the US

If you are visiting from North America, **Iberia** flies from Chicago, New York and Miami to Madrid and from Chicago and New York to Barcelona. From these two destinations, you can then make a connection to any of the cities in northern Spain mentioned above. **Delta**, **Air Europa** and **American Airlines** have direct flights to Barcelona and/or Madrid.

Flights from Australia

Flights from Australia to Spain generally go via Southeast Asian capitals. **Qantas Airlines** have frequent flights to the UK, from where you can catch an inexpensive flight to several Spanish cities, including Málaga, Barcelona and Madrid.

By Rail

From the UK you can get to Spain by rail by taking Eurostar to Paris and from there the TGV Dúplex/Eurodúplex (www.b-europe.com) to Barcelona. You can continue to Madrid on the AVE high-speed train (www.renfe.com). Other trains involve changing at the west Pyrenean border town of Hendaye. From here it is also possible to continue to San Sebastián, Pamplona, Barcelona and Bilbao. For information on international rail travel, see www.seat61.com and www.raileurope.co.uk.

By Road

The motorway route from Calais on France's English Channel coast to the Spanish border at Irún in the Basque Country takes about 15 hours, from where fast routes run to San Sebastián, Bilbao, Santander and Madrid. It takes slightly longer through France to get to the border at Portbou on the Mediterranean coast, to pick up the coastal motorway to Barcelona and Valencia.

By Sea

Brittany Ferries operate a year-round service from Plymouth or Portsmouth to Santander and from Portsmouth to Bilbao (both 24 hours' sailing time). Call Brittany Ferries in the UK on 0871 244 0744 for details, or visit www.brittany-ferries.com.

LD Lines run a thrice-weekly service from St-Nazaire in France to Gijón. Telephone them in the UK on 0844 576 8836 for more information, or visit www.ldlines.co.uk.

Acciona-Trasmediterránea vessels (tel: 902-454 645; www.trasmediterranea.es), carrying passengers and vehicles, travel between Almería, Málaga, Algeciras, Cádiz and ports on the African coast. They also run several services a week from Cádiz to Gran Canaria, Lanzarote and Tenerife on the Canary Islands.

There are frequent ferry services across the Strait of Gibraltar from Algeciras to Ceuta and Tangier, and from Tarifa to Tangier.

The Balearic Islands of Mallorca, Menorca and Ibiza are connected to mainland Spain by regular ferry and hydrofoil services from Barcelona and Valencia. Visitors to Formentera must make their connections from Eivissa (Ibiza town). The main service operators are Acciona-Trasmediterránea (see page 374) and Balearia, tel: 902-160 180 (www.balearia.com), which also runs a service from Dénia to Eivissa.

GETTING AROUND

Airport Transfer

Madrid's **Barajas** airport is 16km (10 miles) out of the city. The airport is at the end of **metro** line 8, with stations in Terminals 2 and 4. If you are arriving at another terminal, allow plenty of time to walk to the metro station. A suburban train links Terminal T4 with Chamartín and Atocha and several other city-centre stops.

International Airlines

International airlines operating flights to Madrid and other destinations in Spain include those listed below. All have offices or are represented at Madrid Barajas airport.
Aer Lingus tel: 902-502 737, www.aerlingus.com
Air Europa tel: 971 080 235, www.aireuropa.com
Blue Air tel: 902 570 852; www.blueairweb.com
British Airways tel: 902-111 333, www.britishairways.com
Easyjet tel: 902-599 900, www.easyjet.com
Iberia tel: 901-111 500, www.iberia.es
Ryanair tel: 807 110 182, www.ryanair.com
Vueling tel: 902 808 005; www.vueling.com

There are frequent bus services from T1, T2, T3 and T4 including the 101, 200, N27 Expres and Línea Exprés-203, which goes direct from the airport to Atocha and vice versa in about 40 minutes and costs €5. Route 200 runs from all terminals to the Avenida de América Transport Hub and Route 101 runs from T1, T2 and T3 to Canillejas Transport Hub; tickets cost €1.50 and you will need to change buses to continue to your destination. The quickest way into the city (a 20-minute journey if you are lucky) is by **taxi** from an official rank at the airport but don't even think of it during the morning or evening rush hours (€30 fixed rate).

Official Madrid taxis are white with red stripes across the doors. Several surcharges may be added to the metered fare: an airport surcharge, a small charge for each large piece of luggage, and a further surcharge for journeys on Sunday, holidays and after 11pm. All surcharges are displayed prominently inside the cab.

Barcelona airport, El Prat, 12km (7 miles) south of the city, is easily accessible by metro, train or bus. Opened in 2016, the new L9 Sud metro line has stops at T1 and T2 and goes directly from the airport to Fira Gran Via. A smooth, efficient bus service, the Aerobús, runs every 15 minutes between the airport and Plaça de Catalunya, and vice versa, stopping at Sants and other strategic places en route. It takes about 35 minutes. There are also trains to Sant Celoni, Granollers and Maçanet-

Massanes every 30 minutes, and the journey takes about 20 minutes.

Málaga airport is located 6km (3.5 miles) east of the city centre. Trains to Málaga run every half-hour from 6.30am to 11.30pm and to Fuengirola via Torremolinos and Benalmádena. The bus stop is outside Arrivals. The A Express Bus (www.emtmalaga.es) goes to Málaga Bus Station but despite its name does stop along the way, and there are direct buses to Marbella, Estepona, Algeciras, Granada, Seville, Almería and Córdoba.

For all airport information tel: 902-320 320 or see www.aena-aeropuertos.es.

Madrid Transport

Metro

The Madrid underground or Metro system is the fastest, cheapest and most efficient way of getting around the city. (If you are claustrophobic, avoid rush hours: 8–9.30am, 1.30–2.30pm and 8–9pm.) Most trains have air conditioning.

The Metro was opened by King Alfonso XIII in 1919, and today has over 300 stations, which will take you to just about every corner of the city. It operates 6am–2am and is used by over 1 million people daily. At the time of writing a single ticket costs €1.50 (€3 with airport extension).

For more detailed information on the Madrid Metro, tel: 917 796 399 or visit www.metromadrid.es. The tram network (Metro Ligero; www.meli madrid.es) comprises three lines (ML1, ML2, ML3) linking the capital with the metropolitan area.

City Buses

Single tickets cost €1.50 regardless of length of journey, and are valid

for three hours. You enter from the front and pay the driver preferably with change or small notes. Press the buzzer to tell him to let you out at the stop you want. Leave by the rear door.

Tickets must be purchased on the bus or from the bus information booths at Puerta del Sol, Plaza Callao, Plaza Cibeles, Plaza de Castilla, etc. Stamp your ticket in the slotted box behind the driver.

Buses operate 6am–midnight. There are also Night Buses called *Búhos* (owls) that operate midnight–6am, departing from Plaza Cibeles. For municipal bus information (EMT), tel: 902-507 850; www.emtmadrid.es.

If you are planning an extended period of time in Madrid and doing a lot of bus and Metro travelling, it is a good idea to purchase a Tourist Card (valid for 1,2,3,5 or 7 days) or an *Abono* (minimum period one month). This card can be applied for at any tobacconist by completing a form and providing a passport-size photograph and a photocopy of your passport or national identity document.

Taxis

Taxis in Madrid are plentiful and relatively inexpensive. They are white, bear a diagonal red stripe on the sides and the Madrid coat of arms. They are available if they are displaying a green *libre* (free) sign on the windscreen or at night have a little green light on. If a red sign with the name of a Madrid neighbourhood is displayed, it means they are on their way home and are not obliged to pick you up unless you are on their route. All taxis are metered.

Taxis can be hailed with relative ease in main thoroughfares, found at a *Parada de Taxi* (taxi stand, indicated by a large white 'T' against a dark blue

TRANSPORT

A – Z

LANGUAGE

The major railway station Estació de França, Barcelona.

background) or requested by phone from the following companies:

Radio-Teléfono Taxi (www.radio telefono-taxi.com), tel: 915-478 200; Radio-Taxi Independiente (www.radio taxiindependiente.com), tel: 914-051 213; or Teletaxi (www.tele-taxi.es), tel: 913-712 131.

By Air

Iberia is Spain's national airline, servicing national routes, and has ticket offices at the airport and Calle Velázquez, 130, Madrid, tel: 901-111 500, www.iberia.es. **Vueling**, tel: 0203 514 3971, www.vueling. com; and **Air Europa**, tel: 971 080 235, www.aireuropa.com, are carriers competing with Iberia.

A number of airlines operate flights between the Canary Islands. **Binter Canarias** (tel: 902-391 392; www. bintercanarias.com), a subsidiary of Iberia, has the most flights; others are **Air Europa** (see page 376) and Canary Fly (www.canaryfly.es).

A useful travel agent for making flight arrangements in Spain is **Halcón Viajes** (tel: 912 180 077, www.halconviajes.com. Air Europa also has flights between Mallorca and Menorca in the Balearics.

By Rail

Madrid has two main train stations: **Atocha** (www.adif.es), near the city centre, handles trains to Andalusia and the Mediterranean coast from Valencia southwards, as well as the 'suburban' Cercanías lines extending to Ávila, Sigüenza, El Escorial, Soria, Toledo, Segovia, Cercedilla and Navacerrada.

Chamartín station, in the north of Madrid, is the terminus for routes to the north and Barcelona. Trains to

A Madrid metro sign.

Trainspotting

RENFE services are divided into three kinds. **Cercanias** are local stopping trains departing from an urban nucleus. **Media distancia** (medium range) trains are organised according to regions. The most popular **larga distancia** (long-distance) routes are served by fast, comfortable trains with particular names:

Altaria: Madrid to Granada, Algeciras, and Cartagena and Murcia
Alvia: Madrid to Alicante and to Santander and Gijon
Euromed: along the Mediterranean coast; Barcelona Valencia Alicante

Extremadura and Lisbon operate from either station.

You can obtain train information about rail journeys throughout Spain from RENFE (tel: 902-320 320; www. renfe.es), the state-owned Spanish railway system. Tickets can be delivered to you for a small fee. They can also be bought at designated RENFE offices and from any travel agency displaying a RENFE sign in the window or from the stations themselves.

There are many ways to save money on rail travel in Spain. If you are going to use a lot trains, it might be worth buying an InterRail or Eurail pass before you leave home. See uk.voyages-sncf.com or, in the USA, www.raileurope.com or www.eurail.com for full details.

A high-speed rail service, the AVE, links Seville to Madrid, reducing travelling time to just over 2 hours. The fast service between Madrid and Málaga takes just over four hours.

(long-distance) trains

On other long-distance routes slower **Diurno** trains run during the day, and **Estrella** trains at night.

Almost a railway apart is the prestigious **AVE** *(alta velocidad)* network which makes key intercity connections (Madrid to Alicante, Barcelona, Burgos, Córdoba, A Coruña, Cuenca, Huesca, Lleída, Málaga, Seville, Valencia, Valladolid, Vigo and Zaragoza) and is being extended to reach Bilbao and Irún. There are also services from Barcelona to Seville and Málaga as well as Figueres on the border with France.

The special AVE track is also used on other services and links Málaga and Madrid reducing the journey time to just 2.5 hours. AVE and Talgo services are best booked in advance.

Regional trains between cities tend to be slower than the national services. The Costa del Sol between Málaga and Fuengirola is served by an efficient commuter service, every 30 minutes.

The main RENFE stations in Barcelona are **Estació de França** terminal by the port and **Sants**, west of the city centre. If you are on a train that is not terminating in Barcelona, it may be more convenient to get off at Passeig de Gràcia or Plaça de Catalunya. Barcelona also has a suburban network, run by the Ferrocarils de la Generalitat de Catalunya (FGC; www.fgc.net). Trains go from Estació Plaça d'Espanya to Montserrat, Igualada and Manresa. Get off at Santa Coloma de Cervelló to see Gaudí's Colònia Güell.

From Plaça Catalunya FGC trains go to Sabadell, Terrassa and Sant Cugat, useful for getting to the Parc Collserola just behind the city.

By Bus

Buses covering city and countrywide routes are air-conditioned, with video entertainment to pass the time, and sometimes toilets. Buses are cheaper than trains. They make frequent stops at rest areas, giving passengers a chance to eat and stretch their legs.

There are various bus companies that service specific areas of the country. Many of the main ones have offices in Madrid's **Estación Sur de Autobuses**, Méndez Álvaro. For information, tel:914-684 200; www. estacionautobusesmadrid.com.

The open road on Fuerteventura.

Among major companies covering major routes are:
Avanzabus tel: 912-722 832, www.avanzabus.com
Alsa tel: 902-422 242, www.alsa.es
For the smaller bus lines, book online with the independent operator Movelia (www.movelia.es).

By Road

Foreign motorists in Spain must have either an international driving licence or, for EU citizens, a valid licence from their country of origin, the car's registration papers and valid insurance. Those who are not EU nationals will also require a *Carta Verde* or Green Card, which can be purchased at the border.

Spain has greatly expanded its motorway network since EU funding in the mid-1990s. **Tolls** are payable on most motorways *(autopistas)*, which have rest areas, bars and service stations. Other expressways *(autovías)* are toll-free. Roadside telephones are placed at convenient intervals for assistance in case of emergency or breakdown. Madrid is inevitably the centre of the road network with arteries fanning out from it towards provincial capitals and the coasts. The A-1 (E-5) runs from Madrid to Burgos, the north coast and ultimately into France. The A-2 (E-90) goes to Barcelona via Zaragoza. Valencia is reached by the A-3 (E-901), Andalusia by the A-4 (a continuation of the E-5). The A-5 (E-90) goes through Extremadura into Portugal. The A-6 serves León, Asturias and Galicia. An important motorway follows the Mediterranean coasts: the A-7 (E-15) runs down the

Costa Brava from the French border past Barcelona, down the Costa Blanca to Almería and then along the Costa del Sol to Málaga and Algeciras and Gibraltar.

The **speed limit** is 120kph (75mph) on motorways, 100kph (60mph) on non-toll motorways; 90kph (55mph) on all other roads and 50kph (30mph) going through cities and towns. **Seat belts** must be worn by the driver and all passengers. You must also carry a reflective waistcoat, spare set of headlight bulbs and two emergency triangles or you could face a penalty fine. There are strict laws on drinking and driving and it is best to avoid drinking altogether if you are driving.

Car Rental

To rent a car in Spain you have to be at least 21 years of age with either an international licence or a valid licence from your own country. The best deals are available by reserving and paying for your car online before you leave home.

It is usually necessary to pay for the car rental with a credit card, otherwise you might have to leave a large deposit. Make sure the insurance provided in the rental agreement is adequate for your needs.

Cars can be rented on a daily basis, with an additional fee according to mileage used. Alternatively a package deal, which is available for a set number of days at unlimited mileage, is an option; consider which will be most advantageous for your journey's purpose. It is sometimes possible to pick the car up in one city and leave it in another.

There are many car-hire agencies throughout the country, including at all the major airports. These include the following:
Enterprise, tel: 912 750 995; www.enterprise.es
Avis, tel: 902-180 854; www.avis.es
Europcar, tel: 913 434 503; www.europcar.es
Hertz, tel: 902 305 230; www.hertz.es
These international chains also have branches in major cities and in the Canary and Balearic Islands. There are also numerous local companies in the Canary Islands, although generally they are specific to each island. CICAR (Canary Islands Car; tel: 928-822 900; www.cicar.com) has offices on each island and a ready availability of automatic cars. Record Rent a Car (tel: 902-123 002; www.recordrentacar.com) has offices at airports in all the main Canary and Balearic islands. Local companies are also numerous and competitive in the Balearics.

By Sea

The Balearic Islands are connected to mainland Spain by regular ferry and hydrofoil services from Barcelona and Valencia. Visitors to Formentera must make their connections from Eivissa (Ibiza town). Ferries also operate from Alicante and Dénia to Eivissa and Formentera. The main service operator is Acciona-Trasmediterránea (see page 377).

There are numerous ferry services between the Canary Islands (and some to the Spanish mainland). The main operators are **Líneas Fred Olsen** (tel: 902-100 107; www.fredolsen.es; **Acciona-Trasmediterránea** (tel: 902-454 645; www.trasmediterranea.es; and **Naviera Armas**, (tel: 902-456 500; www.navieraarmas.com).

In the Balearic Islands, the main inter-island ferry companies are Balearia (tel: 902-160 180, www.balearia.com).

City Transport

There are prominently marked taxi ranks in the central areas of cities and fares are very reasonable (a 5–10 percent tip is usual, though in no way required or expected). In general, throughout Spain public transport is good in the larger towns and cities, and the respective local tourist offices can provide you with bus and, if applicable, train timetables.

A – Z

A HANDY SUMMARY OF PRACTICAL INFORMATION

A

Accommodation

Spain may no longer be the bargain it once was, but accommodation still offers good value. Hotels are officially rated from one to five stars. Well-known hotel chains include Barceló (www.barcelo.com), Iberostar (www.iberostar.com), Melia (www.melia.com) and NH Hotels (www.nh-hotels.com). Five-star establishments are in the luxury category with all the comforts one would expect in a first-class hotel.

Bear in mind that the rating has more to do with the amenities offered than the quality of the service – small, family-run places in the lower categories can be more comfortable and friendly than large, soulless establishments with gilded fittings and marble halls.

At the bottom of the market are the *pensión* (boarding house), the *fonda* (inn) and the *casa de huéspedes* (guesthouse). These are small and spartan, but usually clean.

Paradores (www.parador.es) are state-run hotels. The service can be a little glum, but they are often located in unrivalled positions, sometimes in modern buildings but often in old castles, palaces and convents. They usually have great views and serve gourmet regional food in their restaurants.

Thousands of apartments have been built in tourist areas and if you are planning to stay more than a few days it is worth renting one. Try www.airbnb.com, www.holidaylettings.co.uk or www.secretdestinations.com.

Admission Charges

Museums and galleries normally charge a modest entrance fee of around €10. There are often reductions for senior citizens and students, and residents of EU countries will sometimes be eligible for free admission. Some churches are free to enter, but usually appreciate a donation. On Mondays, many sights are closed.

B

Budgeting for Your Trip

Allow €60 upwards per day for two persons for the least expensive accommodation, which will generally be in a *hostal*; €35 per person per day upwards for basic meals or tapas. Wine or spirits will obviously push this up. Public transport is generally inexpensive in Spain: allow around €10 for local bus and train and (where applicable) Metro travel.

C

Climate

Spain's climate ranges from the cool and rainy northwest to the hot and arid plains of Andalusia. **Central Spain** has hot, dry summers and cold winters. The rainfall is generally low, though the winter snow can be heavy on the sierras. Autumn and spring are both pleasant seasons, with afternoon temperatures ranging from around 15°C (60°F) to 25°C (77°F). Although spring can be quite wet at times, most days are dry and sunny. Summer temperatures can

rise to 38°C (100°F), although 32°C (90°F) is more typical. The air is dry, and mountain breezes make the evenings pleasantly cool. The average winter daytime temperature is 8°C (46°F), although it can drop below freezing in January and February. The wettest time is January to April. **Andalusia**'s position at the southern edge of Europe gives it hot summers and mild winters. However, there are considerable regional variations. Summers can be extremely hot in the interior, with temperatures rising to 40°C (104°F). Almería has an arid, desert-like climate. Snow covers the Sierra Nevada from November to June, and frost is common in upland areas. The Levante wind often blows hard for days on the Cádiz coast. June to October is dry, except for sporadic downpours. Heavy rain in the winter months is usually interspersed with brilliant sunshine. The best months to tour the region are in spring and autumn. In the Costa Brava winds seem to whip up from nowhere and last for days. The climate is more

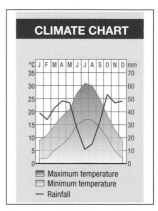

CLIMATE CHART

☐ Maximum temperature
☐ Minimum temperature
— Rainfall

reliable further south, with little rain in summer. The average temperature in coastal resorts is 25°C (77°F) in summer and 11°C (52°F) in winter. Inland it's hotter, and spring and autumn are more pleasant.

In **northern Spain**, there is much variation in climate. It rains a great deal along the Atlantic coast through Cantabria and Asturias to Galicia – even in summer – and Bilbao and Santiago are renowned for being very rainy. Winters in the north and northwest can be very wet, and it may snow. Summers, on the other hand, can be blessed with lavish amounts of sunshine everywhere. The north is, therefore, a good destination for a summer beach holiday. In **Andorra** and the **Pyrenees** the temperature can drop to below freezing in winter.

The **Canary Islands** enjoy a sunny subtropical climate with mild temperatures all year round. Daytime temperatures range from around 21°C (70°F) in January to 26°C (79°F) in August, but can be much hotter. There are some wet days in winter, particularly on north-facing coasts and in the mountains on Tenerife, La Palma and Gran Canaria. Fuerteventura and Lanzarote are drier and Fuerteventura can be very windy. The three main **Balearic Islands** enjoy similar weather conditions to each other (approximately 10°C/50°F in January to 24°C/76°F in August), with local variations caused by phenomena such as Mallorca's mountain ranges.

Crime and Security

Spain these days is no more dangerous than any other cosmopolitan community, but, as in any country, it makes sense to take a few elementary precautions.

Bag-snatching and pickpocketing are probably the worst problems, so don't allow yourself to be distracted, and take care in crowds and busy tourist areas. Avoid flashing money around. Keep valuables in the hotel safe and don't carry large sums of money or your passport (take a photocopy instead), unless you are going to exchange money. Never leave anything on display in a parked car.

If you are robbed, contact the local police station or phone the **Emergency Police** on 091. Most insurance companies require an official statement (denuncia), available from the local police station, before they will accept a claim.

Among the ruses employed by pickpockets are street-theatre artists who distract unsuspecting holiday makers, and stage accidents or fights. If confronted, do not resist, as thieves often carry knives. If you are robbed, remember that muggers usually want easily disposable cash and swiftly dispose of unwanted items, so check the nearest gutters, rubbish containers and toilets for your personal possessions.

Drivers should be cautious about accepting help from anyone other than a uniformed Spanish police officer or Civil Guard. When staying overnight, take all baggage into the hotel and, if possible, park your car in a garage or a guarded car park. On the beach, don't leave cash or valuables unattended while you are swimming.

Customs Regulations

Visitors to Spain can bring any personal effects, such as jewellery, a laptop computer, cameras, etc. If you are visiting from within the EU there are no restrictions on what you bring in for your personal consumption. If you are visiting from outside the EU, you can also bring the following items duty-free:
200 cigarettes or 100 small cigars or 50 cigars or 250g of tobacco
1 litre of alcohol of 22°
Limited amounts of perfume and eau de toilette.

If your camera, laptop computer, camcorder or other equipment is new and you do not have the purchase receipt, it would be wise to ask a customs official to certify that you brought it with you.

Pets, except birds, may be taken into Spain as long as you have a suitable health certificate for the animal signed by an officially recognised vet from the country of origin. This form should indicate the dates of the last vaccines, in particular the anti-rabies shot.

D

Disabled Travellers

Overall, facilities for disabled visitors are limited within Spain, although public transport is increasingly wheelchair-friendly, and major sights are required by law to provide wheelchair access. Restaurants are gradually introducing toilets that are disabled-friendly. Organisations that can provide more information include:

Emergency Numbers

General Emergency Number 112
Guardia Civil 062
National Police 091
Municipal Police 092
Fire Department 080
Emergency Medical Care 061

Mobility Abroad, tel: 0871 277 0888, in Spain; www.mobilityabroad. com provides support and hire of wheelchairs and disabled-friendly vehicles throughout the Costa del Sol, Costa Blanca, Costa Daurada and the Balearic and Canary islands.
Once, tel: 915-773 756, www.once. es is the Spanish association for the blind.
ECOM, tel: 934-515 550, www.ecom. cat is a federation of private Spanish organisations that provide services for disabled people.

E

Electricity

The current is 225AC or 220V, the same as most of Europe. Visitors from the US will need converters. Most plugs will require a two-pin adaptor, generally available from airport outlets or from hardware shops within Spain.

Embassies and Consulates

Australia: Torre Espacio, Paseo de la Castellana, 259D, Madrid, tel: 913-536 600, www.spain.embassy.gov.au
Canada: Torre Espacio, Paseo de la Castellana, 259D, Madrid, tel: 913-828 400, www.canadainternational. gc.ca
Ireland: Paseo de la Castellana 46-4, Madrid, tel: 914-364 093, www.embassyofireland.es
South Africa: Claudio Coello, 91, Madrid, tel: 914-363 780, www.sudafrica.com
United Kingdom: Torre Espacio,Paseo de la Castellana 259D, Madrid, tel: 917-146 300, www.gov. uk/government/world/spain
United States: Serrano, 75, Madrid, tel: 915-872 200, http://madrid. usembassy.gov

Entry Regulations

Visitors from EU countries, and from Australia, Canada, New Zealand, the US and several other specified nationalities, need only present a passport on arrival in Spain in order to stay in the country for up to 90 days. People of other nationalities must apply for a visa before travelling; it is worth contacting the Spanish consulate in your country of residence to check requirements. You should likewise check with a consulate if you are going to be staying in Spain longer than 90 days.

F

Festivals

There are a growing number of arts and music festivals in **Madrid** – the main ones include Festimad (end of April-May; http://festimad.es), **Veranos de la Villa** (music festival, July–mid-Sep; www.veranosdelavilla.com), **Festival de Otoño** (theatre and dance festival, November; www.madrid.org/fo.html) **Jazz Festival** (November; www.festivaldejazzmadrid.com) and **Suma Flamenca** (May; www.madrid.org/sumaflamenca.html).

In **Almagro** (Ciudad Real province), the 16th-century playhouse Corral de la Comedia holds an international drama festival every July, with works by playwrights from Lope de Vega to Shakespeare. See www.festivaldealmagro.com.

Highlights of the Mediterranean arts scene include a string of new summer music festivals. Among them, two are outstanding: **Benicàssim** (www.fiberfib.com), Spain's answer to Glastonbury, which takes place in July close to the beach in Castellón province, and Cartagena's **La Mar de Músicas** (www.lamardemusicas.com), a highly rated world music festival with concerts in stunning historic performance spaces (July). There are several summer jazz festivals: one in Alicante (July–Aug), one in Péñiscola (July) and the highly respected **Jazz de San Javier** (www.jazz.sanjavier.es). Other events include **Electrosplash** (www.electrosplash.com), a virtually free electronic music festival on the beaches of Valencia, and **SOS 48** (www.sos48.com), a rock music festival featuring top interntional acts in Murcia in May. The **Festival Internacional del Cante de las Minas** (http://festivalcantedelasminas.org), held in La Unión in August, celebrates the local tradition of mining flamenco, and Torrevieja's annual festival of *habaneras* focuses on songs brought back from Cuba by sailors (www.habaneras.org). Valencia's dance, theatre and cinema festivals include the **Festival Internacional de Cinema de Valencia** in June (www.cinemajove.com), which showcases films made by young directors. The area's major classical music venues, the Palau de la Música and Palau de les Artes (both with their own orchestras), are a short walk from each other in Valencia city.

There are numerous festivals throughout the year in **Barcelona**, from the **International Jazz Festival** (www.jazz.barcelona) in the autumn to the **Guitar Festival** in June (both use the Palau de la Música Catalana as a venue). There is also a **Festival of Early Music** in April and May and the **Festival of World Music**. The **Grec Festival** (http://lameva.barcelona.cat/grec) of theatre, dance and music from late June to early August uses magnificent outdoor settings like the Grec amphitheatre on Montjuïc, or the Plaça del Rei.

Elsewhere in **Catalonia** there are numerous festivals of music, theatre and dance, mostly in the summer months, like the well-established **Festival del Castell de Peralada** (www.festivalperalada.com), the **Porta Ferrada** in Sant Feliu de Guíxols, the more recent one in the exquisite setting of the botanical gardens of Cap Roig in **Calella de Palafrugell**, and the **Festival Internacional de Pau Casals** (www.auditoripaucasals.cat) in El Vendrell. Find a complete list and annual programmes on www.catalunya.com.

The San Sebastián **Jazz Festival** (www.heinekenjazzaldia.com) takes place in July, and the city also hosts an **International Film Festival** (www.sansebastianfestival.com) in September.

A number of prestigious summer music festivals are held in **Mallorca**, especially in Deià and Pollença. See www.infomallorca.net for details.

G

Gay and Lesbian Travellers

There are plenty of gay- and lesbian-friendly hotels, clubs and bars, as well as resorts, such as Torremolinos (Costa del Sol), Playa del Inglés (Gran Canaria), Playa de las Américas (Tenerife) and Sitges (Costa Brava) that cater specifically for a gay clientele. There are several gay internet sites relating to Spain, including www.gaybarcelona.com, www.gayiberia.com, www.gaymadrid4u.com, and www.benamics.com in the Balearics.

H

Health and Medical Care

No special inoculations are required for entering Spain, unless you are visiting from an area where there has been a recent outbreak of cholera or yellow fever. Tap water can be drunk without reservations, but bottled water is widely available. Food hygiene is generally good, but you should nevertheless exercise a little caution. In modest establishments avoid seafood on Sunday and Monday (it may not be as fresh as it should be), and be wary, too, of dishes containing raw egg, such as mayonnaise. In summer, come prepared with a sun hat and protective suncreams.

Medical Care

Citizens from EU countries are entitled to free medical treatment in other EU countries under a reciprocal arrangement. However, you must obtain a European Health Insurance Card (EHIC) in your home country prior to your departure. These are valid for five years and can be applied for online by logging onto www.ehic.org.uk. Although health facilities are very good you may want to take out additional cover. Private health insurance is essential for non-EU visitors.

There is a reciprocal arrangement in place with many foreign medical insurance companies. Also available is a Spanish insurance policy, ASTES, which will cover any medical or hospital care if you fall ill or have an accident during your stay in Spain. This Spanish Tourist Insurance, created and promoted by the Spanish state and backed by a group of 80 private insurance companies, covers full medical and hospital care, hotel lodging if an extension of your stay is recommended by a physician, repatriation and even lost luggage. See www.astes.org.

Pharmacies

Spain has countless pharmacies *(farmacias)*, each identifiable by a large white sign with a flashing green cross. They are usually open 9.30am–1.30pm and 4.30–8pm Mon–Fri, 9am–1.30pm Sat. In most towns an effective system of rotation operates whereby there is always one chemist open round-the-clock in each area. A sign in front of each should indicate which chemists are on duty that night, and which is closest to where you are.

Farmacias are amply stocked with over-the-counter remedies, and many drugs can be purchased without prescription; however, your particular medication may not be available, and they do not honour foreign prescriptions, so bring with you any prescription medicine you require.

Medical Emergencies

If you have a medical emergency while in Spain, your hotel should be able to recommend reliable professionals who speak several languages. The local embassy or consulate will also have a list of English-speaking doctors. You can also go to the local hospital emergency department or medical clinic to receive treatment on presentation of a European Health Insurance Card. If no help is near at hand, call the medical emergency number: 061.

Internet

Internet access is widely available throughout Spain, except in smaller villages. The respective local tourist office can provide you with a list. Most hotels offer an internet and/or Wi-fi service. Wi-fi coverage is also available at the major airports and in an increasing number of public spaces, entertainment venues and bars.

Lost Property

Lost and found in Spanish is *perdida y encontrada*, and there are offices at most major airports and bus stations.

Media

Television and Radio

There are two public nationwide television channels in Spain, TVE 1 and TVE 2, and each region has its own local stations. The better hotels have access to satellite programming, which includes a variety of channels, several of which broadcast in English.

Radio Nacional de España operates several nationwide stations, including Radio 1, a current affairs programme, Radio 5 for sports, Radio 3, a contemporary music station, and Radio Clásica, a classical music station. To listen online or find frequencies in the area you are visiting, go to www.rtve.es.

Magazines and Newspapers

The Spanish daily papers are *El País*, *ABC* and *El Mundo*. They provide full local information on cinema, theatre and TV programming. *El País* and *El Mundo* publish supplements with their Friday editions, which give listings on all the activities, exhibitions, art shows and film schedules that week, along with lists of restaurants, television, etc.

You will also be able to find the *International Herald Tribune* and *Time* and *Newsweek* magazines at news-stands in most major cities. Other papers such as *The Times*, *Financial Times*, *Guardian*, *Wall Street Journal* and the *Daily Mail* are all available.

There are a few magazines about Spain, printed in English, which you can buy. You can also pick up free English magazines with articles, events, reviews, listings and classified ads in most Irish pubs, bookshops, universities, language schools and some offices. The major newspapers have regional editions, and regions have their own dailies.

Money

The euro is Spain's official currency. It comes in coins of 1 cent of a euro, 2 cents, 5 cents, 10 cents, 20 cents, 50 cents, 1 euro and 2 euros. Bills are worth 5, 10, 20, 50, 100, 200 and 500 euros.

Best rates for foreign currency are obtained at banks, but you can also change money in cities at currency-exchange shops, *casas de cambio*. In Madrid there is one on the Puerta del Sol and at several hotels (where the rates are lower), major department stores and shops frequented by tourists – shop around.

Banks

Practically all Spanish banks will change foreign currency and traveller's cheques, for a fee. It is also possible to obtain cash at any bank against your credit card or from ATMs. Personal cheques are not used. Always carry ID with you when you go to the bank.

Banking hours vary slightly from one bank to another. Most are open 8.30am–2.30pm weekdays, and some are open Saturday until 1pm, though not usually between June and September or on Thursday afternoons. All are closed on Sunday and public holidays. Several banks open their major branches in the business districts until 6pm or later.

Unless you are importing very large sums of cash, it is best to avoid transferring money via banks. Many tourists have been left stranded for weeks waiting for cash that inexplicably gets delayed in the pipeline. Even telexed cash can take days or weeks to arrive.

Reclaiming VAT

In order to be eligible, as a tourist, for a refund of the Spanish IVA (Value Added Tax), you must come from a non-EU country and spend €90.16 or more in a single shop. Tell the shop that you intend to reclaim the

Newspaper shop in Hondarribia in the Basque country.

VAT, which is currently 21 percent in Spain. You will be given a form which you must get stamped at a duty reduction office at the airport before departure. Go to the desk of one of the companies authorised to give you a tax refund. If you leave the country other than by air, get the customs post to validate your form and then take a copy back to the shop you bought the goods from and it will make the refund. The process is explained at www.globalrefund.com.

Tipping

Service is not usually included in restaurants, so it is customary to leave the spare change (€0.30–0.60 per person) in the dish when eating at a modest restaurant and a few cents at a bar. At an averagely smart restaurant, 10 percent of the bill is appropriate, unless you're charged for service. A €0.20 tip is fine for an average taxi ride, and bathroom attendants expect around €0.10–0.20 per person.

Opening Hours

Shops are open 9.30am or 10am until 1.30 or 2pm and then reopen again in the afternoon from 4.30 or 5 until 8pm, or a little later in summer. Many close on Saturday afternoons in summer and most are closed all day Sunday.

However, the major department stores, like El Corte Inglés and FNAC, and shops in the city centres are open six days a week, 10am–9pm or 10pm, and frequently on Sunday, despite the protests of small shopkeepers. *Panaderías* (bakeries) are open every morning, including Sunday.

Although some **offices** have adopted a standard 8 or 9am–5pm work day, the general rule is still to take a long midday break for lunch and a siesta (still very much a part of Spanish life, especially in the south in summer) but then stay open until 8 or 9pm. Banks generally open Monday to Friday 8.30am to 2.30pm and 8.30am to 1pm on Saturday.

Postal Services

The district post offices are only open 9am–2.30pm on weekdays, and some open on Saturday mornings. All post offices close on Sunday. Principal post offices are open 9am–2pm and 4–7pm for general services, including preparation and postage of packages. Stamps can also be purchased at tobacconists *(estancos)* 9am–10pm every day.

Estancos are distinguishable by their brown and gold sign with the word 'Tobacos'. They are useful establishments, for in addition to selling tobacco, they can provide you with all you need for writing home – and will even weigh your letter to tell you what postage it requires.

Religious Services

The following are in Madrid:
British Embassy Church of St George, Anglican/Episcopalian, Núñez de Balboa, 43, tel: 915-765 109, www.stgeorgesmadrid.com. **Catholic masses** held in English (Sun 11am)at **Our Lady of Mercy**, Dracena, 23, tel: 917-339 409, www.ourladyofmercy.info. **Synagogue**, Balmes, 3, tel: 915-913 131, www.cjmadrid.org. The **Centro Cultural Islámico** (Mosque), tel: 913-262 610, above the M-30 highway on Calle Salvador de Madariaga, 4, is a splendid

Public Holidays

There are so many holidays, what with national and local fiestas, that it's said there is no one week in the whole year when all of Spain is working.
1 January (New Year's Day/*Año Nuevo*)
6 January (Epiphany/*Epifanía*)
Good Friday (date varies, *Viernes Santo*)
1 May (Labour Day/*Fiesta del Trabajo*)
15 August (Assumption/*La Asunción*)
12 October (Columbus Day/*Día de la Hispanidad*)
1 November (All Saints' Day/*Todos los Santos*)
6 December (Constitution/*Día de la Constitución*)
8 December (Immaculate Conception/*Inmaculada Concepción*)
25 December (Christmas Day/*Navidad*).
Each town is also entitled to two local holidays in honour of its patron saints.

example of Islamic architecture, featuring a large auditorium, library and several exhibition halls.

Student Travellers

Students generally receive a reduction on admission to museums, galleries and similar sights throughout Spain on producing a valid photo ID. Students under 26 should also pick up the European Youth Card (www.euro26.org), which offers considerable reductions on train and bus fares, as well as up to 20 percent at most youth hostels.

Telephones

All telephone numbers in Spain begin with their respective regional code for both local and international calls but these are integral to the number and you cannot leave them off for a local call. Coin and card-operated telephone booths are still relatively plentiful. Wait for the tone, deposit a coin and dial the number.

Most bars have coin-operated or meter telephones available for public use. You can also purchase Telefonica phonecards of various values at any *estanco* (tobacconist).

For **overseas calls**, it's probably better to go to privately run telephone shops *(locutorio)* where one can talk first and pay later and not have to worry about having enough coins. It is possible to call from hotels, but you will be charged much more than you would on a public phone – at least 21 percent VAT will be added to the cost of your calls. To make a direct overseas call, first dial 00 and then the country and city code without the initial '0'.

A European (but not a US) mobile phone will work in Spain. Although the most populous parts of the country and the motorways have good network coverage, you may find there is none in more remote areas. US visitors can hire a mobile phone for their stay in Spain.

Tourist Information

The official website for tourism in Spain is www.spain.info. Below is a list of the main tourist information offices *(oficinas de turismo)* and websites covering the regions and cities of Spain. Wherever you are, the local

Spanish Tourist Offices Abroad

Dublin
3 Westmoreland Street
Tel: 016 350 200
www.spain.info/en_IE/
New York
60 East 42nd Street, Suite 5300
(53rd Floor)
Tel: 212-265 8822
www.spain.info/en_US/
Chicago
845 N. Michigan Avenue, Suite 915-
E, Chicago, Illinois 60611
Tel: 312-642 1992
www.spain.info/en_US/
Los Angeles
8383 Wilshire Blvd, Suite 960,
90211 Beverly Hills, California, CA
90211

Tel: 323-658 7195
www.spain.info/us/en_US/
Miami
2655 Le Jeune Rd (Gables
International Plaza), Suite 605.
Coral Gables
Tel: 305 476 1996
www.spain.info/en_US/
Toronto
2 Bloor Street West, 34th floor,
Toronto M4W 3E2
Tel: 416-961 3131
www.spain.info/en_CA/
London
6th floor, 64 North Row, W1K 7DE
Londres
Tel: 020 731 72011
www.spain.info/en_GB/

tourist information office can help
you find accommodation and provide
information on local sights, museums
and transport.

Madrid
Madrid region: www.turismomadrid.es
Madrid city: Plaza Mayor, 27, tel:
914-544 410. www.esmadrid.com

Castilla y León
www.turismocastillayleon.com
Ávila: San Segundo, 17, tel: 920-211
387, www.turismoavila.com
Burgos: Nuño Rasura, 7, tel: 947-288
874, www.aytoburgos.es
León: Plaza de la Regla, 2, tel: 987-
237 082, www.leon.es
Palencia: Calle Mayor, 31, tel: 979-
706 523, www.palenciaturismo.es
Salamanca: Plaza Mayor, 32, tel:
923-218 342, www.salamanca.es
Segovia: Plaza Mayor, 10, tel: 921-
460 334, www.turismocastillayleon.com
Valladolid: Pabellón de Cristal Acera
de Recoletos, tel: 983-219 310, www.
info.valladolid.es
Zamora: Plaza Arias Gonzalo, 6, tel:
980-533 694, www.zamora-turismo.
com

Castilla-La Mancha
www.castillalamancha.es
Albacete: Plaza del Altozano, 1,
tel: 967-630 004, www.turismoen
albacete.com
Ciudad Real: Real Plaza Mayor 1,
tel: 926-211 044, www.ciudad-real.
es/turismo
Cuenca: Avenida Cruz Roja, 1, tel:
969-241 051, www.cuenca.es
Guadalajara: Plaza de la Aviación
Militar Española, tel: 949-887 097,
www.guadalajara.es
Toledo: Plaza del Consistorio, 1, tel:
925 265 419, www.toledo-turismo.com

Extremadura
www.turismoextremadura.com
Badajoz: Paseo de San Juan, tel:
924-224 981, www.turismobadajoz.es
Cáceres: Plaza de Santa Clara,
tel: 927 247 172, www.turismo.
caceres.es

Andalucía
www.andalucia.org
Almería: Plaza de la Constitución, tel:
950-210 538, www.turismodealmeria.
org
Cádiz: Paseo de Canalejas, tel: 956-
241 001, www.cadiz.es
Córdoba: Plaza de las Tendillas, tel:
902-201 774, www.turismodecordoba.
org
Granada: Plaza de Mariana
Pineda, tel: 958-247 128,
www.turismodegranada.org
Huelva: Calle Fernando El Católico,
14, tel: 959-257 467, www.
turismohuelva.org
Jaén: Calle Maestra, 8, tel: 953-313
281, www.turjaen.org
Málaga: Plaza Marina de la 11, tel:
952-122 020, www.malagaturismo.
com
Seville: Plaza del Triunfo, 1, tel: 954-
210 005, www.turismosevilla.org

Valencia and Murcia
Valencia region: www.
comunitatvalenciana.com
Murcia: www.murciaturistica.es
Alicante: Rambla Méndez Núñez,
41, tel: 965-200 000, www.
alicanteturismo.com
Murcia: Plaza Cardenal Belluga, tel:
968 358 749, www.turismodemurcia.
es
Valencia: Paz, 48, tel: 963 153 931,
www.visitvalencia.com
Castelló: Plaza de la Hierba, tel: 964-
358 688, www.castellonturismo.com

Catalonia
www.catalunya.com
Barcelona: Plaça Sant Jaume, 17, tel:
932-853 834, www.barcelonaturisme.
com
Girona: Rambla de la Libertat, 1,
tel: 972-226 575, www.girona.cat/
turisme
Lleida: Calle Major, 31, tel: 973
700 319, www.turismodelleida.com
Tarragona: Carrer Major, 39, tel: 977-
250 795, www.tarragonaturisme.cat
Andorra: Centro Pastor de
Andorra, tel: 978 843 164,
www.ayuntamientoandorra.es

Aragón
www.turismodearagon.com
Huesca: Plaza López Allué, tel: 974-
292 170, www.huescaturismo.com
Teruel: San Francisco, 1, tel: 978-641
461, www.teruel.es
Zaragoza: Plaza del Pilar, tel: 976-
201 200, www.zaragozaturismo.es

Basque Country
www.turismoa.euskadi.net
Bilbao: Plaza Circular, 1, tel: 944-795
760, www.bilbao.net/bilbaoturismo
San Sebastián: Boulevard 8, tel:
943-481 166, www.sansebastian
turismo.com
Vitoria: Plaza de España, 1, tel: 945-
161 598, www.vitoria-gasteiz.org/
turismo

Navarre and La Rioja
Navarra: www.turismo.navarra.es
La Rioja: www.lariojaturismo.com
Logroño: Portales, 50, tel: 941-291
260, www.lariojaturismo.org
Pamplona: Avenida Roncesvalles,
4, tel: 848-420 420, www.
turismodepamplona.es

Cantabria and Asturias
Cantabria: www.turismodecantabria.
com
Asturias: www.asturias.es
Oviedo: Marqués de Santa Cruz, tel:
985-227 586, www.turismoviedo.es

Time Zone

The UK is one hour behind
mainland Spain (and the
Balearics), along with the Canary
Islands, Portugal and Ireland.
Otherwise Spain has the same
time as most of the rest of Western
Europe, and is thus six hours
ahead of US Eastern Time and
nine hours ahead of US Pacific
Time. Daylight-saving time moves
the clocks ahead by one hour in
March and back to standard time
in October.

TRANSPORT

A – Z

LANGUAGE

Santander: Paseo Pereda, tel: 942-203 000, http://santanderspain.info

Galicia

www.turismo.gal
A Coruña: Plaza de María Pita, tel: 918-923 093, www.turismocoruna.com
Santiago de Compostela: Rúa do Vilar, 63, tel: 981-555 129, www.santiagoturismo.com
Vigo: Rúa de Cánovas del Castillo, 3, tel: 986-224 757, www.turismodevigo.org
Ourense: Progreso, 28, tel: 988-391 085, www.turismourense.com

Canary Islands

Gran Canaria: Avenida de España, Playa del Inglés, Las Palmas, tel: 928-767 848, www.grancanaria.com
Tenerife: Plaza de España, s/n, Santa Cruz, tel: 922-281 287, www.webtenerife.com
Lanzarote: Triana, 38, Arrecife, tel: 928-811 762, www.turismolanzarote.com
Fuerteventura: Almirante Lallermand, 1, Puerto del Rosario, tel: 928-530 844, www.visitfuerteventura.es
La Palma: Avenida Blas Pérez Gonzalez, s/n, Santa Cruz de La Palma, tel: 922-412 106, www.visitlapalma.es
La Gomera: Calle Real, 4, San Sebastián, tel: 922-141 512/870 281, www.lagomera.travel
El Hierro: Calle Dr Quintero, 4, Valverde, tel: 922-550 326, www.elhierro.travel

Exploring Potes in the Picos de Europa.

Balearic Islands

Mallorca: Plaça de la Reina 2, tel: 971 173 990, www.infomallorca.net
Menorca: Terminal d'Arribades, Maó, tel: 971 157 115, www.menorca.es
Ibiza: Casa de la Curia, Plaça de la Catedral, Eivissa, tel: 971-399 232, www.ibiza.travel/en
Formentera: Ferry terminal, Port de la Savina, tel: 971-322 057, www.formentera.es

Tour Operators

Explore
www.explore.co.uk
Adventure travel holidays throughout Spain.
Great Rail
Tel: 01904-521 936 (UK)
www.greatrail.com
Train tours to Spain from London.
Pullmantur
Tel: 900-838 102
www.pullmantur.es
Coach trips organised throughout Spain.
Rustic Blue
Tel: 958-763 381
www.rusticblue.com
Specialises in rural and themed holidays in Andalusia, including painting, walking and horse-trekking.
A Taste of Spain
Tel: 956-232 880
www.atasteofspain.com
Culinary holidays with courses on Basque, Mediterranean and

traditional Spanish cuisine, and gourmet activities.

Websites

There is a proliferating number of websites giving good information about Spain. Some places to start a search are:
Airports www.aena.es
Beaches www.spain.info/es/que-quieres/destinos-playa/
Flamenco http://theflamencoworld.com
Government www.lamoncloa.gob.es
Maps (of cities) http://callejero.paginasamarillas.es
National heritage www.patrimonionacional.es
Radio and television www.rtve.es
Railways www.renfe.es
Spanish language www.rae.es
Telephone info www.telefonica.com
Traffic www.dgt.es
Weather www.aemet.es
What's on/Nightlife www.guiadelocio.com
Wine www.winesfromspain.com
Yellow pages www.paginasamarillas.es

Weights and Measures

The metric system is used throughout Spain, and temperature is measured on the centigrade or Celsius scale.

LANGUAGE

UNDERSTANDING THE LANGUAGE

In addition to the national language of Spanish (Castilian), which is spoken throughout the country, some regions use another language. Catalan (spoken in Catalonia and, with variations, in the Balearics), Valenciano (Valencia) and Gallego (Galicia), like French, Italian and Portuguese, are all Romance languages derived from the Latin spoken by the Romans who conquered the Iberian peninsula more than 2,000 years ago. The exception to these linguistic origins is Euskera, the language of the Basques. Euskera is unrelated to any other Indo-European tongue, and experts are not even sure what its origins are, though some linguists now believe it may date back to the Stone Age.

The Balearic people speak Spanish, but prefer their own language, a variant of Catalan, which in Mallorca is known as *mallorquí*, in Menorca as *menorquí*, and in Eivissa (Ibiza) as *eivissenc*. These dialects differ slightly from one another in accent, local vocabulary and expressions. Their source language, Catalan, is similar to Provençal.

Following the Latin derivations that formed the basis of the Romance language of Spanish, the Muslims who settled in the peninsula centuries later contributed a great number of new words (see page 387). Following the discovery of America, Spaniards took their language with them across the globe. Today, Spanish is spoken by 250 million people in north, south and central America and parts of Africa.

Unlike English, Spanish is a phonetic language: words are pronounced exactly as they are spelt. Spanish distinguishes between the two genders, masculine and feminine. It has two entirely separate forms

of the verb 'to be' and four different ways of saying 'you'. The subjunctive verb form is another endless source of headaches for students.

The English language is one of Britain's biggest exports to Spain. Spaniards spend millions on learning aids, language academies and sending their children to study English in the UK or Ireland, and are eager to practise their linguistic skills with foreign visitors. Even so, they will be flattered and delighted if you make the effort to communicate in Spanish.

BASIC RULES

English is widely spoken in most tourist areas, but even if you speak no Spanish at all, it is worth trying to master a few simple words and phrases.

As a general rule, the accent falls on the second-to-last syllable, unless it is otherwise marked with an accent (´) or the word ends in D, L, R or Z.

Vowels in Spanish are always pronounced the same way. The double L (LL) is pronounced like the y in 'yes', the double R is rolled. The H is silent in Spanish, whereas J (and G when it precedes an E or I) is pronounced like a guttural H (similar to the end sound of Scottish *loch*).

When addressing someone you are not familiar with, use the more formal 'usted'. The informal 'tú' is reserved for relatives and friends.

BASIC WORDS AND PHRASES

yes *sí*
no *no*

thank you (very much) *(muchas) gracias*
you're welcome *de nada*
okay *bien*
please *por favor*
excuse me *perdóneme*
Can you help me? *¿Me puede ayudar?*
Do you speak English? (formal) *¿Habla inglés?*
Please speak more slowly *Hable más despacio, por favor*
I don't understand *No entiendo*
Show me the word in the book *Muéstreme la palabra en el libro*
I'm sorry *Lo siento/Perdone*
I don't know *No lo sé*
No problem *No hay problema*
Where is...? *¿Dónde está...?*
I am looking for... *Estoy buscando*
That's it *Ese es*
Here it is *Aquí está*
There it is *Allí está*
Let's go *Vámonos*
At what time? *¿A qué hora?*
When? *¿Cuándo?*
here *aquí*
there *allí*

GREETINGS

Hello!/Hi! *¡Hola!*
Hello *Buenos días*
How are you? (formal/informal) *¿Cómo está?/¿Qué tal?*
What is your name? (formal) *¿Cómo se llama usted?*
Fine thanks *Muy bien, gracias*
My name is... *Me llamo...*
Mr/Miss/Mrs *Señor/Señorita/Señora*
Pleased to meet you *¡Encantado(a)!*
I am British/American *Soy británico/norteamericano*
See you tomorrow *Hasta mañana*
See you soon *Hasta pronto*

Have a good day *Que tenga un buen día*
goodbye *adiós*
good afternoon/evening *buenas tardes*
good night *buenas noches*

ON ARRIVAL

airport *aeropuerto*
customs *aduana*
train station *estación de tren*
platform *andén*
ticket *billete*
one-way ticket *billete de ida*
return ticket *billete de ida y vuelta*
bus station *estación de autobuses*
bus *autobús*
bus stop *parada de autobús*
metro station *estación de metro*
hitch-hiking *auto-stop*
toilets *servicios*
taxi *taxi*
This is the hotel address *Ésta es la dirección del hotel*

IN THE HOTEL

I'd like a (single/double) room *Quiero una habitación (sencilla/doble)*
... with shower *con ducha*
... with bath *con baño*
... with a view *con vista*
Does that include breakfast? *¿Incluye desayuno?*
May I see the room? *¿Puedo ver la habitación?*
washbasin *lavabo*
bed *cama*
key *llave*
lift/elevator *ascensor*
air conditioning *aire acondicionado*

ON THE ROAD

Where is the spare wheel? *¿Dónde está la rueda de repuesto?*
Where is the nearest garage? *¿Dónde está el taller más cercano?*
Our car has broken down *Nuestro coche se ha averiado*
I want to have my car repaired *Quiero que reparen mi coche*
It's not your right of way *Usted no tiene prioridad*
I think I must have put diesel in my car by mistake *Me parece que he echado gasoil por error*
the road to... *la carretera a...*
left *izquierda*
right *derecha*
straight on *derecho/todo recto*
near *cerca*
far *lejos*

opposite *frente a*
beside *al lado de*
car park *aparcamiento*
over there *allí*
at the end *al final*
on foot *a pie*
by car *en coche*
town map *plano de la ciudad*
road map *plano de carreteras*
street *calle*
square *plaza*
give way *ceda el paso*
exit *salida*
dead end *calle sin salida*
wrong way *dirección prohibida*
no parking *prohibido aparcar*
motorway *autovía*
toll highway *autopista*
toll *peaje*
speed limit *límite de velocidad*
petrol *gasolina*
petrol station *gasolinera*
unleaded *sin plomo*
diesel *gasoil*
water *agua*
oil *aceite*
air *aire*
tyre *neumático*
puncture *pinchazo*
bulb *bombilla*

ON THE TELEPHONE

How do I make an outside call? *¿Cómo hago una llamada exterior?*
What is the area code? *¿Cuál es el prefijo?*
I want to make an international/local call *Quiero hacer una llamada internacional/local*
I'd like an alarm call for 8 tomorrow morning *Quiero que me despierten a las ocho de la mañana*
Hello? *¿Dígame?*
Who's calling? *¿Quién llama?*
Hold on, please *Un momento, por favor*
I can't hear you *No le oigo*
Can you hear me? *¿Me oye?*
He/she is not here *No está aquí*
The line is busy *La línea está ocupada*

EMERGENCIES

Help! *¡Socorro!*
Stop! *¡Pare!/¡Alto!*
Call a doctor *Llame a un médico*
Call an ambulance *Llame a una ambulancia*
Call the police *Llame a la policía*
Call the fire brigade *Llame a los bomberos*
Where is the nearest telephone? *¿Dónde está el teléfono más cercano?*

The Alphabet

Learning the pronunciation of the Spanish alphabet is a good idea. Spanish has three letters in its alphabet that don't exist in English: the 'ñ', the 'ch' and the 'll'.
a = *ah*, **b** = *bay*, **c** = *thay* (strong th as in 'thought'), **ch** = *chay*, **d** = *day*, **e** = *ay*, **f** = *effay*, **g** = *hay*, **h** = *ah-chay*, **i** = *ee*, **j** = *hotah*, **k** = *kah*, **l** = *ellay*, **ll** = *ell-yay*, **m** = *emmay*, **n** = *ennay*, **ñ** = *enyay*, **o** = *oh*, **p** = *pay*, **q** = *koo*, **r** = *erray*, **s** = *essay*, **t** = *tay*, **u** = *oo*, **v** = *oovay*, **w** = *oovay doe-blay*, **x** = *ek-kiss*, **y** = *ee gree-ay-gah*, **z** = *thay-tah*.

Where is the nearest hospital? *¿Dónde está el hospital más cercano?*
I am sick *Estoy enfermo*
I have lost my passport/purse *He perdido mi pasaporte/bolso*

SHOPPING

Where is the nearest bank? *¿Dónde está el banco más cercano?*
I'd like to buy *Quiero comprar*
How much is it *¿Cuánto es?*
Do you accept credit cards? *¿Aceptan tarjetas?*
I'm just looking *Sólo estoy mirando*
Have you got...? *¿Tiene...?*
I'll take it *Me lo llevo*
I'll take this one/that one *Me llevo éste/ese*
What size is it? *¿Qué talla es?*
size (clothes) *talla*
small *pequeño*
large *grande*
cheap *barato*
expensive *caro*
enough *suficiente/bastante*
too much *demasiado*
a piece *un trozo*
each *cada una/la pieza/la unidad* (eg melones, dos euros la unidad)
bill *la factura* (shop), *la cuenta* (restaurant)
bank *banco*
bookshop *librería*
chemist *farmacia*
hairdressers *peluquería*
post office *correos*
department store *grandes almacenes*

MARKET SHOPPING

Supermarkets (*supermercados*) are self service, but often the best and freshest produce is found at the town

market (mercado) or at street markets (mercadillo), where you place your order with the person in charge of each stand. Prices are usually by the kilo, sometimes by gramos (by the gram) or by unidad (by the piece).
fresh/frozen fresco/congelado
organic biológico
flavour sabor
basket cesta
bag bolsa
bakery panadería
butcher's carnicería
cake shop pastelería
fishmonger's pescadería
grocery ultramarinos
greengrocery verdulería
tobacconist estanco
market mercado
supermarket supermercado
junk shop tienda de segunda mano

SIGHTSEEING

mountain montaña
hill colina
valley valle
river río
lake lago
lookout mirador
city ciudad
small town, village pueblo
old town/quarter casco antiguo
monastery monasterio
convent convento
cathedral catedral
church iglesia
palace palacio
hospital hospital
town hall ayuntamiento
nave nave
statue estatua
fountain fuente
staircase escalera
tower torre
castle castillo
Iberian ibérico
Phoenician fenicio
Roman romano
Muslim árabe
Romanesque románico

Islamic Connections

The Muslims arrived in Spain in AD 711, and occupied parts of the peninsula for the next eight centuries. They left behind hundreds of Arabic words, many related to farming and crops, as well as place names including those of towns (often identified by the prefix Al-, meaning "the" or Ben-, meaning "son of") and rivers (the prefix Guad- means "river").

Gothic gótico
museum museo
art gallery galería de arte
exhibition exposición
tourist information office oficina de turismo
free gratis
open abierto
closed cerrado
every day diario/todos los días
all year todo el año
all day todo el día
swimming pool piscina
to book reservar

DINING OUT

In Spanish, el menú is not the main menu, but a fixed menu at a lower price. The main menu is called la carta.
breakfast desayuno
lunch comida
dinner/supper cena
meal comida
first course primer plato
main course plato principal
made to order hecho por encargo
drink included bebida incluida
wine list carta de vinos
the bill la cuenta
fork tenedor
knife cuchillo
spoon cuchara
plate plato
glass vaso
wine glass copa
napkin servilleta
waiter, please! camarero, por favor

DRINKS

coffee café
black sólo
with milk con leche/cortado
decaffeinated descafeinado
sugar azúcar
tea té
herbal tea infusión
milk leche
mineral water agua mineral
fizzy con gas
still sin gas
juice (fresh) zumo (natural)
cold fresco/frío
hot caliente
beer cerveza
bottled en botella
on tap de barril
soft drink refresco
diet drink bebida 'light'
with ice con hielo
wine vino
red tinto
white blanco
rosé rosado

dry seco
sweet dulce
house wine vino de la casa
sparkling wine vino espumoso
Where is this wine from? ¿De dónde es este vino?
pitcher jarra
half litre medio litro
quarter litre cuarto de litro
cheers! ¡salud!

MENU DECODER

Breakfast and snacks

pan **bread**
bollo **bun/roll**
mantequilla **butter**
mermelada/confitura **jam**
pimienta **pepper**
sal **salt**
azúcar **sugar**
huevos **eggs**
cocidos **boiled, cooked**
con beicon **with bacon**
con jamón **with ham**
escalfados **poached**
fritos **fried**
revueltos **scrambled**
yogur **yoghurt**
tostada **toast**
sandwich **sandwich in square slices of bread**
bocadillo **sandwich in a bread roll**

Main courses

Carne (Meat)
buey **beef**
carne picada **ground meat**
cerdo **pork**
chorizo **paprika sausage**
chuleta **chop**
cochinillo **roast pig**
conejo **rabbit**
cordero **lamb/mutton**
costilla **rib**
entrecot **beef rib steak**
filete **fillet steak**
jabalí **wild boar**
jamón **ham**
jamón cocido **cooked ham**
jamón serrano **cured ham**
lmorcilla **black pudding**
pierna **leg**
riñones **kidneys**
salchichón **sausage**
solomillo **sirloin steak**
ternera **veal or young beef**
a la brasa **charcoal grilled**
al horno **roast**
a la plancha **griddled**
asado **roast**
bien hecho **well done**
en salsa **in sauce**
en su punto **medium**

estofado **stew**
frito **fried**
pinchito **skewered snack**
poco hecho **rare**
relleno **stuffed**

Aves (Fowl)

codorniz **quail**
faisán **pheasant**
pavo **turkey**
pato **duck**
perdiz **partridge**
pintada **guinea fowl**
pollo **chicken**

Pescado (Fish)

anchoas **salted anchovies**
anguila **eel**
atún **tuna**
bacalao **salt cod**
besugo **red bream**
boquerones **fresh anchovies**
caballa **mackerel**
calamar **squid**
cangrejo **crab**
cazón **dogfish**
centollo **spider crab**
chopito **baby cuttlefish**
cigala **Dublin Bay prawn/scampi**
dorada **gilt head bream**
gamba **shrimps/prawns**
jibia/sepia **cuttlefish**
langosta bogavante **lobster**
langosta **crayfish**
langostino **large prawn**
lenguado **sole**
lubina **sea bass**
mariscada **mixed shellfish**
mariscos **shellfish**
mejillón **mussels**
merluza **hake**
ostión **Portuguese oyster**
ostra **oyster**
peregrina **scallop**
pez espada **swordfish**
pulpo **octopus**
rape **monkfish**
rodaballo **turbot**
salmón **salmon**
salmonete **red mullet**
sardina **sardine**
trucha **trout**

Vegetables y cereales (Vegetables and cereals)

verduras **vegetables**
ajo **garlic**
alcachofa **artichoke**
arroz **rice**
berenjena **aubergine/eggplant**
brocolí **broccoli**
calabacín **courgette/zuccini**
cebolla **onion**
champiñón **mushroom**
col **cabbage**
coliflor **cauliflower**
ensalada **salad**

espárrago **asparagus**
espinaca **spinach**
guisante **pea**
haba **broad bean**
judía **green bean**
lechuga **lettuce**
lenteja **lentil**
maíz **corn/maize**
menestra **cooked mixed vegetables**
patata **potato**
pepino **cucumber**
pimiento **pepper**
puerro **leek**
seta **wild mushroom**
tomate **tomato**
zanahoria **carrot**

Frutas y postres (Fruit and desserts)

fruta **fruta**
aguacate **avocado**
albaricoque **apricot**
cereza **cherry**
ciruela **plum**
frambuesa **raspberry**
fresa **strawberry**
granada **pomegranate**
higo **fig**
limón **lemon**
mandarina **tangerine**

manzana **apple**
melocotón **peach**
melón **melon**
naranja **orange**
pera **pear**
piña **pineapple**
plátano **banana**
pomelo **grapefruit**
sandía **watermelon**
uva **grape**
postre **dessert**
tarta **pie**
pastel **cake**
helado **ice cream**
natillas **custard**
queso **cheese**

Herbs and spices

albahaca **basil**
azafrán **saffron**
cilantro **coriander/cilantro**
comino **cumin**
hierbabuena **mint**
orégano **oregano**
perejil **parsley**
pimentón **paprika**
polvo de curry **curry powder**
romero **rosemary**
salvia **sage**
tomillo **thyme**

Numbers, Days and Dates

Numbers

1 *uno*
2 *dos*
3 *tres*
4 *cuatro*
5 *cinco*
6 *seis*
7 *siete*
8 *ocho*
9 *nueve*
10 *diez*
11 *once*
12 *doce*
13 *trece*
14 *catorce*
15 *quince*
16 *dieciseis*
17 *diecisiete*
18 *dieciocho*
19 *diecinueve*
20 *veinte*
21 *veintiuno*
30 *treinta*
40 *cuarenta*
50 *cincuenta*
60 *sesenta*
70 *setenta*
80 *ochenta*
90 *noventa*
100 *cien*
500 *quinientos*
1,000 *mil*
1,000,000 *un millón*

Saying the date

20 October 2017,
el veinte de octubre del dos mil diecisiete

Days of the week

Monday *lunes*
Tuesday *martes*
Wednesday *miércoles*
Thursday *jueves*
Friday *viernes*
Saturday *sábado*
Sunday *domingo*

Seasons

Spring *primavera*
Summer *verano*
Autumn *otoño*
Winter *invierno*

Months

January *enero*
February *febrero*
March *marzo*
April *abril*
May *mayo*
June *junio*
July *julio*
August *agosto*
September *septiembre*
October *octubre*
November *noviembre*
December *diciembre*

FURTHER READING

HISTORY

Moorish Spain by Richard Fletcher. The most readable short introduction to a complicated period.
Spanish Inquisition by John Edwards. A good way into the thorny issue of whether the Inquisition was as bad as it is made out to be in popular culture.
The Peninsular War 1807–1814 by Michael Glover. A helpful unravelling of the Napoleonic period in Spain, and Britain's role in driving out the French.
The Spanish Civil War by Antony Beevor. The ultimate guide to the Spanish Civil War.

MODERN SPAIN

Ghosts of Spain: Travels Through A Country's Hidden Past by Giles Tremlett. A personal exploration of how Spain's recent history casts a shadow over the present.
The New Spaniards by John Hooper. A perceptive look at the way Spain has changed since Franco's death, and is still changing.

CLASSIC TRAVEL WRITING

Face of Spain by Gerald Brenan. Foreign travellers have been traipsing through Spain for centuries and many of them have felt compelled to record their experiences and impressions. This is Brenan's informative account of his return to Spain in 1949, after the Civil War.

SPANISH LITERATURE

Don Quijote by Miguel de Cervantes. Not only the greatest work of Spanish literature but one of the greatest works of literature in any language. Much quoted, and much referred to, by the Spanish who know that there is something of both Don Quijote and Sancho Panza in all of them.

ASPECTS OF SPAIN

Death in the Afternoon by Ernest Hemingway. Although dated, this is still one of the best books to illuminate the controversial world of bullfighting.
Duende: A Journey into the Heart of Flamenco by Jason Webster. An Anglo-American man's Spanish adventure to discover the essence of flamenco.
Morbo: The Story of Spanish Football by Phil Ball. A surprisingly complex subject given an entertaining treatment.
Spanish Cinema by Rob Stone. From Buñuel's surrealist experiments to Almodóvar: the best overview of how Spain appears on the screen.
Travellers' Nature Guides Spain by Teresa Farino and Mike Lockwood. An authoritative region-by-region guide to Spain's nature reserves.
Everything is Happening: Journey into a Painting by Michael Jacobs. A fascinating story unlocking the secrets of Velázquez's greatest picture – Las Meninas.

REGIONS

Driving over Lemons by Chris Stewart. A humorous account of the author's move to the Alpujarras.
Barcelona by Robert Hughes. There is no finer book on the city than this one.
The Pilgrimage to Santiago by Edward Mullins. One of the best books about the famous route of pilgrimage across northern Spain.
Journey to the Alcarria by Camilo José Cela. A travelogue by Spain's Nobel prize-winning novelist about an area of Gudalajara province, east of Madrid.
Voices of the Old Sea by Norman Lewis. A vivid account of the three summers the master travel writer spent in a Costa Brava fishing village just after the war.
The Basque History of the World by Mark Kurlansky. Basque nationalism is frequently misunderstood by outsiders, but Kurlansky does a great job of explaining it without wasting a word or losing the reader's attention.
The Landscape of Castile by Antonio Machado. Machado was born in Seville and died in exile in France but he is often remembered for the five years he spent in the province of Soria which inspired this collection of poems.
A Winter in Mallorca by George Sand. Translated by Robert Graves. The French novelist and feminist spent the winter of 1838–9 in the monastery of Valdemossa on Mallorca with the composer Frédéric Chopin and her two children. She later published her account of their stay.

OTHER INSIGHT GUIDES

Insight Guides to Spain and the Iberian peninsula include *Insight City Guide: Barcelona, Insight Pocket Guide: Madrid* and *Insight Guide: Portugal*.
Insight Explore: Barcelona and *Insight Explore: Mallorca* offer a wealth of tailor-made routes, with easy-to-follow maps to guide you around.

Send Us Your Thoughts

We do our best to ensure the information in our books is as accurate and up-to-date as possible. The books are updated on a regular basis using local contacts, who painstakingly add, amend and correct as required. However, some details (such as telephone numbers and opening times) are liable to change, and we are ultimately reliant on our readers to put us in the picture.

We welcome your feedback, especially your experience of using the book "on the road". Maybe we recommended a hotel that you liked (or another that you didn't), or you came across a great bar or new attraction we missed.

We will acknowledge all contributions, and we'll offer an Insight Guide to the best letters received.

Please write to us at:
Insight Guides
PO Box 7910
London SE1 1WE
Or email us at:
hello@insightguides.com

TRANSPORT

A – Z

LANGUAGE

CREDITS

Insight Guide Credits

Distribution
UK, Ireland and Europe
Apa Publications (UK) Ltd;
sales@insightguides.com
United States and Canada
Ingram Publisher Services;
ips@ingramcontent.com
Australia and New Zealand
Woodslane; info@woodslane.com.au
Southeast Asia
Apa Publications (SN) Pte;
singaporeoffice@insightguides.com
Hong Kong, Taiwan and China
Apa Publications (HK) Ltd;
hongkongoffice@insightguides.com
Worldwide
Apa Publications (UK) Ltd;
sales@insightguides.com
Special Sales, Content Licensing and CoPublishing
Insight Guides can be purchased in bulk quantities at discounted prices. We can create special editions, personalised jackets and corporate imprints tailored to your needs.
sales@insightguides.com
www.insightguides.biz

Printed in China by CTPS

All Rights Reserved
© 2017 Apa Digital (CH) AG and Apa Publications (UK) Ltd

First Edition 1983
Eleventh Edition 2017

Editor: Carine Tracanelli
Author: Victoria Trott
Updater: Maciej Zglinicki
Head of Production: Rebeka Davies
Update Production: AM Services
Picture Editor: Tom Smyth
Cartography: original cartography Berndtson & Berndtson, updated by Carte

Contributors

This new edition of *Insight Guide: Spain* was commissioned by **Carine Tracanelli**, Insight's Europe editor, and updated by **Maciej Zglinicki**, a Spain specialist who has travelled extensively in the country. It is based on a previous edition written by

Insight regular **Victoria Trott**, a freelance travel journalist who studied Spanish at the universities of Leeds and Granada. Past contributors include: **Nick Inman**, **Jo Hodgson**, **Pam Barrett**, **Vicky Hayward**, **Judy Thomson** and **Peter Stone**.

About Insight Guides

Insight Guides have more than 45 years' experience of publishing high-quality, visual travel guides. We produce 400 full-colour titles, in both print and digital form, covering more than 200 destinations across the globe, in a variety of formats to meet your different needs.

Insight Guides are written by local authors, whose expertise is evident in the extensive historical and cultural background features.

Each destination is carefully researched by regional experts to ensure our guides provide the very latest information. All the reviews in **Insight Guides** are independent; we strive to maintain an impartial view. Our reviews are carefully selected to guide you to the best places to eat, go out and shop, so you can be confident that when we say a place is special, we really mean it.

Legend

City maps

	Freeway/Highway/Motorway
	Divided Highway
	Main Roads
	Minor Roads
	Pedestrian Roads
	Steps
	Footpath
	Railway
	Funicular Railway
	Cable Car
	Tunnel
	City Wall
	Important Building
	Built Up Area
	Other Land
	Transport Hub
	Park
	Pedestrian Area
	Bus Station
	Tourist Information
	Main Post Office
	Cathedral/Church
	Mosque
	Synagogue
	Statue/Monument
	Beach
	Airport

Regional maps

	Freeway/Highway/Motorway (with junction)
	Freeway/Highway/Motorway (under construction)
	Divided Highway
	Main Road
	Secondary Road
	Minor Road
	Track
	Footpath
	International Boundary
	State/Province Boundary
	National Park/Reserve
	Marine Park
	Ferry Route
	Marshland/Swamp
	Glacier / Salt Lake
	Airport/Airfield
	Ancient Site
	Border Control
	Cable Car
	Castle/Castle Ruins
	Cave
	Chateau/Stately Home
	Church/Church Ruins
	Crater
	Lighthouse
	Mountain Peak
	Place of Interest
	Viewpoint

INDEX

Main references are in bold type

A

A Coruña 331
Acquarium (Palma) 360
Acueducto (Segovia) 36, 158
A Guarda 340
Aguilar 247
Agüimes 347
Akhila 37
Alacant province 242
Alaior 369
al-Andalus 40, 100, 191, 208
Alarcón 44
Albacete 170
Albaicín (Granada) 207, 212
Albarracín 288
Alcalá de Henares 144
Alcalá del Júcar 170
Alcañiz 288
Alcántara 181
Alcaraz 170
Alcoi 244
Alcossebre 237
Alcúdia 245
Algeciras 221
Alicante (Alacant) 243
Almagro 169
Almansa 170
Almería 191, 229
Alpuente 240
Alpujarras region 229
Altamira 32, 73
Altea 242
Amfiteatre (Tarragona) 275
Andalusia 187
Andratx 361
Anfiteatro (Mérida) 176
Antequera 226
aquaparks 242
aquariums 236, 259
Aqüeducte de les Ferreres
    (Tarragona) 275
Aragón 43, 44, 283
Aranda 157
Aranjuez 144
Arantzazu 314
architecture 41
Archivo General de Indias (Seville)
    194
Arco de Trajano (Mérida) 176
Arcos de la Frontera 221
Arcos de Santa María (Burgos) 155
Argamasilla de Alba 169
Arias Navarro, Carlos 64
Arizcun 300
Arrecife 351
art 73, 78
Artà 366
Artajona 298
Artenara 348
As Neves 338
Astorga 154
Asturias 39, 40, 43, 58, 319, 324
autonomous communities 66, 69,
    232, 252, 305, 307, 357

Ávila 148
Avilés 326
Azaila 288
Aznar, José María 67

B

Badajoz 177
Badia d'Alcúdia 365
Baelo Claudia 221
Baeza 228
Balearic Islands 69, 357
Baños Arabes (Jaén) 228
Banyalbufar 361
Banyoles 279
Banys Àrabs (Girona) 272
Banys Àrabs (Palma) 359
Barranc de la Valltorta 238
Barranco de Guayadeque 348
Barri Gòtic (Barcelona) 253
Barrio de Santa Cruz (Seville) 194
Basilica de Santa Eulalia (Mérida)
    177
Basque Country 58, 61, 69, 293,
    294, 305
Begur 271
Belchite 287
Belmonte 171
Benicàssim 240
Benidorm 243
Besalú 274
Betancuria 350
Betanzos 333
Biblioteca Nacional (Madrid) 135
Bilbao 310
birds 107
Blanes 270
Bocairent 244
Bossòst 276
Bourbon dynasty 51
Brihuega 171
Buitrago del Lozoya 143
bulls 24, 204, 224
Buñol 240
Burgo de Osma 157
Burgos 155

C

Cabo de Gata 229
Cabo de Palos 246
Cabo de Peñas 319
Cabo Finisterre 339
Cáceres 178
Cadaqués 274
Cádiz 33, 35, 219
cafés 137
Cala de Sa Calobra 364
Cala d'Or 366
Cala Figuera 366
Cala Millor 366
Cala Santa Galdana 369
Calatayud 287
Caleta de Fuste 350
Calle Caballeros (Valencia) 235

Calp (Calpe) 242
Cambados 339
Cambrils 275
Camino de Santiago 336
Camp Nou (Barcelona) 262
Campo de Criptana 169
Ca N'Alluny (Deià) 363
Canary Islands 345
Cangas 340
Cantabria 35, 319
Canyet de Mar 270
Cap de Creus 274
Cap de Formentor 365
Cap de la Nau 242
Capdepera 366
Cap de Sant Antoni 242
Capocorb Vell 367
Caravaca de la Cruz 247
Cardona 279
Carlist Wars 53, 294, 306
Carmona 36, 227
Cartagena 34, 35, 36, 246
Carthaginians 34, 35, 358, 369
Casa Andalusí (Cordoba) 202
Casa Batlló (Barcelona) 260
Casa de Colón (Las Palmas) 347
Casa de la Ciutat (Barcelona) 254
Casa del Anfiteatro (Mérida) 176
Casa de las Conchas (Salamanca)
    152
Casa de los Golfines de Abajo
    (Cáceres) 179
Casa de los Picos (Segovia) 158
Casa de Pilatos (Seville) 196
Casa de Sefarad (Córdoba) 202
Casa Romana del Mithraeo
    (Mérida) 176
Casas Colgadas (Cuenca) 171
Casa Toledo-Moctezuma (Cáceres)
    179
Casa Vicens (Barcelona) 259
Castell 241
Castellar 223
Castelldefels 274
Castelló de la Plana 239
Castelló province 237
Castilla y León 43, 44, 148
castles and fortifications. *See
    also* palaces
    Alarcón 170
    Alcazaba (Almería) 229
    Alcazaba (Badajoz) 177
    Alcazaba (Granada) 211
    Alcazaba (Mérida) 177
    Alcázar (Jerez) 219
    Alcázar (Segovia) 159
    Alcázar (Toledo) 167
    Antequera 226
    Bellver (Palma) 360
    Belmonte 171
    Berlanga de Duero 160
    Calatrava la Nueva 170
    Coaña 326
    Coca 160
    Dalt Vila (Eivissa) 370

Gibralfaro (Málaga) 225
Javier 299
La Ciudadela (Jaca) 289
Loarre 290
Lorca 247
Medellín 175
Montjuïc (Barcelona) 263
Mora de Rubielos 288
Morella 238
Onda 238
San Antón (A Coruña) 333
San Servando (Toledo) 165
Santa Barbara (Teguise) 351
Sant Ferrán (Figueres) 273
Santuari de Sant Salvador (Artà)
   367
Torres de Cuarte (Valencia) 235
Torres de Serrans (Valencia)
   235
Trujillo 179, 180
Uclés 171
Upper Galleries (Gibraltar) 222
Villena 244
Castro, Rosalia de 339
Castro-Urdiales 320
Catalonia 43, 55, 56, 58, 69, 269
cathedrals
   Astorga 155
   Ávila 148
   Badajoz 177
   Barcelona 253
   Burgos 155
   Ciudad Real 169
   Ciudad Rodrigo 152
   Cuenca 171
   Eivissa 371
   Girona 272
   Granada 211
   Huesca 289
   Jaca 289
   Jaén 228
   León 73, 153
   Lleida 280
   Lugo 335
   Magistral de los Santos Justo y
      Pastor (Alcalá de Henares) 144
   Murcia 246
   Nuestra Señora de la Almudena
      (Madrid) 131
   Nueva (Salamanca) 151
   Orihuela 245
   Palencia 157
   Palma 359
   Pamplona 296
   Plasencia 180
   Primada (Toledo) 166
   Redonda (Logroño) 295
   San Martiño (Ourense) 338
   San Salvador (Oviedo) 325
   San Salvador (Zaragoza) 284
   Santa Ana (Las Palmas) 347
   Santa Maria (Ciutadella) 368
   Santa María (La Seu d'Urgell)
      277
   Santa María (Vitoria) 308
   Santiago de Compostela 333
   Santo Domingo de la Calzada
      295
   Segovia 158
   Seville 193

Sigüenza 171
Tarazona 284
Tarragona 275
Teruel 287
Tudela 298
Valencia 233, 234
Vieja (Salamanca) 152
Zamora 153
Catholic Church 21, 57, 61
caves
   Altamira 322
   Artà 366
   Drach (Mallorca) 366
   Medrano 169
   Menga y Viera (Antequera) 226
   Montesinos 169
   Nerja area 226
   Pileta 224
   Pindal (Colombres) 324
   Pintada (Gáldar) 349
   Romeral (Antequera) 226
   Santimamiñe (Gernika) 310
   Tito Bustillo 324
   Valltorta 238
Cazorla 229
Celt-Iberians 33, 34, 326, 330, 340
Celto-Iberians 35
**Centro Cultural Internaciónal
   Oscar Niemeyer (Avilés)** 326
ceramics 233
Cervantes, Miguel de 50, 144,
   163, 169
Charles V 48, 49, 75, 182
Chelva 240
Chinchilla de Monte Aragón 170
Chinchón 144
Christianity 35, 36
churches
   Capilla del Salvador (Úbeda) 228
   Capilla de Santa Bárbara
      (Salamanca) 152
   Capilla Mayor 201
   Capilla Real (Granada) 211
   Colegiata Real (Roncesvalles)
      300
   Colegiata (Santillana del Mar) 322
   El Patriarca (Valencia) 233
   El Pilar (Zaragoza) 284
   Ermita de San Antonio (Madrid)
      133
   Mare de Déu de Desamparats
      (Valencia) 234
   Mezquita Cristo de la Luz (Toledo)
      166
   Monasterio de San Juan de los
      Reyes (Toledo) 166
   Sagrada Família (Barcelona) 260
   Sagrat Cor (Barcelona) 265
   San Esteban (Segovia) 158
   San Francesc (Palma) 360
   San Francisco el Grande (Madrid)
      131
   San Isidoro (León) 154
   San Isidro (León) 73
   San Isidro (Madrid) 130
   San Martín (Segovia) 158
   San Miguel (Oñati) 313
   San Miguel (Vitoria) 314
   San Nicolás de Bari (Valencia)
      235

San Pedro (Teruel) 287
San Román (Toledo) 166
Santa Cruz del Valle de los Caídos
   143
Santa Eulalia de Bóveda 337
Santa María (Castro-Urdiales) 320
Santa María del Coro (San
   Sebastián) 308
Santa María de Lebeña 324
Santa María del Mar (Barcelona)
   255
Santa María del Naranco 325
Santa María de los Angeles (San
   Vicente de la Barquera) 323
Santa María (Écija) 227
Santa María (Gernika) 310
Santa María la Mayor (Trujillo) 179
Santa Maria (Maó) 368
Santa María (Ripoll) 278
Santa María (Sangüesa) 299
Santa María (Viana) 298
Sant Clement in Taüll, (Lérida) 74
Sant Llorenç (Lleida) 280
Sant Miquel del Port (Barcelona)
   256
Santo Tomé (Toledo) 167
Santullano (Oviedo) 73
Vera Cruz (Segovia) 159
**Cidade da Cultura de Galicia
   (Galicia)** 335
Cinctorres 238
cinema 23
Ciudad Encantada 171
Ciudad Real 169
Ciudad Rodrigo 152
climate 378
Cocentaina 244
**Colegio de San Jerónimo
   (Santiago)** 334
Columbus, Christopher 47, 66,
   193, 218, 258
Combarro 338
Comillas 322
Comunitat Valenciana 232, 237
conquistadors 173, 176, 179
Consuegra 169
convents
   Corpus Cristi (Segovia) 158
   Dominicos (Plasencia) 180
   San Benito (Alcántara) 181
   San Francisco (Santiago) 333
   San José (Ávila) 150
   San Pablo (Cáceres) 178
   Santa Teresa (Ávila) 150
Cordillera Cantábrica 319
Córdoba 199
   Caliphate 39, 42, 43, 200
Coria 181
Corralejo 350
Cortés, Hernán 48, 175
Costa Blanca 242
Costa Brava 269, 270, 273
Costa Calida 246
Costa da Morte 339
Costa Daurada 274
Costa de Azahar 237
Costa de la Luz 218
Costa del Sol 191, 224
Covadonga 39, 325
Covarrubias 156

Crusades 42, 44
Cuacos de Yuste 182
Cudillero 326
Cuenca 170

D

Dalí, Salvador 78, 273
Deià 363
Denía 242
dolmens 32, 226
Don Quijote 163, 169
Doroca 287
Drake, Sir Francis 50, 219
Duero, Río 40, 43, 153

E

Ebro, River 31, 67
Écija 227
economy 65, 67
El Acebuche 217
El Bierzo 155
El Bosque 224
El Campello 243
El Capricho (Comillas) 322
El Cid 43, 155, 231
El Cotillo 350
El Greco 75, 167
El Hierro 353
Elizondo 300
El Maestrat 238
El Maestrazgo 288
El Micalet (Valencia) 234
El Pabellón de la Navegación (Seville) 192
El Palmar 241
El Puig 241
El Rocío 218
El Toboso 169
Elx (Elche) 245
Empúries 33, 35, 273
Es Mercadel 369
Es Pujols 371
Estadi Olímpic (Barcelona) 264
Estella 297
Estellencs 361
Estepona 224
European Union 22, 63, 65
Expo '92 66, 189, 192
Extremadura 173

F

Favila 40
Felanitx 366
Felipe II 49, 75, 147, 165
Felipe IV 51, 75, 76
Fernando II of Aragón 43, 44, 47, 204, 209, 284, 290
Ferrer Bassa 74
festivals and events 86
  bullfighting 88, 224
  castellers (Tarragona) 277
  Feria de Abril (Seville) 87, 196
  Feria de la Virgen Blanca (Vitoria) 313
  flamenco festivals 83
  las fallas (Valencia) 234
  Moors and Christians 244

Santiago 333
  Tomatina (Buñol) 240
Figueres 273
flamenco 81, 85, 196, 212
Formentera 371
Fornalutx 364
Fornells 369
Franco, Francisco 58, 63, 65, 143, 331, 346
Fuendetodos 287
Fuengirola 224
Fuente Dé 324
Fuente Vaqueros 212
Fuerteventura 349
Fundació Joan Miró (Barcelona) 78

G

Gáldar 349
Galicia 69, 329
Gandia 242
García Prieto 56
Gaudí, Antoní 154, 261, 266, 322
Gernika (Guernica) 310
Getaria 309
Gibraltar 51, 221
Gijón 326
Giralda (Seville) 44, 194
Girona 271
Goya, Francisco 52, 77, 78, 127, 287
Gràcia (Barcelona) 263
Granada 44, 45
Granadilla 182
Gran Canaria 346
Greeks, ancient 33
Guadalajara 171
Guadalest 243
Guadalquivir, Río 31, 192, 195
Guadalupe 174
Gypsies 25, 82, 212

H

Habsburg dynasty 48
Hammam Baños Árabes (Córdoba) 203
Hannibal 34, 241
Haro 295
Hervás 182
Hispano-Romans 36, 37
Hondarribia 308
Hort del Cura (Elx) 245
Hospital de la Caridad (Toledo) 168
Hospital de los Venerables Sacerdotes (Seville) 195
Hospital de Santiago (Úbeda) 228
Hospital de Tavera (Toledo) 168
Hostal de los Reyes Católicos (Santiago) 334
Hostal San Marcos (León) 154
Huelva 218
Huesca 289

I

Illa de Tabarca 245
Inquisition 45, 49, 52, 151, 284
Irati Forest 299

Irving, Washington 189, 210
Isaba 299
Isabel of Castile 43, 44, 47, 151, 204, 209
Isla de la Cartuja (Seville) 192
Islam, spread of 39
Islas Cíes 340

J

Jaén 44, 228
Jameos de Agua (Lanzarote) 351
Jarandilla de la Vera 182
Jerez de la Frontera 218, 219
Jerez de los Caballeros 178
Jerte valley 182
Jesuits 52, 58
Jews 36, 41, 42, 45, 164, 165, 182, 194, 201, 208, 271
Jimena de la Frontera 223
Juan Carlos, King 61, 63, 64
Judería (Córdoba) 201
Jumilla 36, 246

L

La Alcarria 171
La Bisbal 271
La Cerdanya 277
La Ciutat de les Arts i de les Ciències (Valencia) 236
Lagartario 353
La Gomera 353
La Iglesuela del Cid 238
La Laguna (Tenerife) 352
La Mancha 163, 169
language 23, 24
  Arabic influence 41, 387
  regional 232, 330
language schools 96
Lanzarote 350
La Olmeda 157
La Orotava 352
La Palma 353
la pedrera (Barcelona) 267
La Pedrera (Barcelona) 260
La Pedriza 143
La Rambla (Barcelona) 257
Laredo 320
La Rioja 294
La Savina 371
La Seu d'Urgell 277
Las Hurdes 181
Las Marinas valley 333
Las Medulas 155
Las Navas de Tolosa, Battle of 44
Las Palmas de Gran Canaria 346
Las Teresitas (Tenerife) 352
Las Virtudes 170
La Toja 339
La Vila Joiosa 243
Lekeitio 309
León 43, 73, 153
Lerma 156
L'Escala 273
L'Estartit 273
literature 339, 362
Llanes 324
Lleida (Lérida) 43, 280
Llívia 277

Lloret de Mar 270
Llotja de la Seda (Valencia) 234
Logroño 295
Lorca 246
Lorca, Frederico García 59, 211
Los Cristianos 352
Los Llanos de Aridane 353
Los Sanfermines (Pamplona) 24
Los Valles 290
Luarca 326
Lugo 337
Lusitania Bridge (Mérida) 176

M

Madrid 123
Madrid Province 139
Madrigal de las Altas Torres 150
Maimonides 42
Málaga 225
Malasaña (Madrid) 134
Mallorca 357
Manzanares el Real 143
Manzanares, Río 123
Maó 368
Marbella 224
markets
    Boqueria (Barcelona) 258
    Central Market (Valencia) 233
    Costa del Sol 225
    hippie market (El Pilar) 371
    Mercat de Santa Caterina
        (Barcelona) 256
    Pescadería (San Sebastián) 308
    Plaça Redonda (Valencia) 234
    Rastro (Madrid) 130
Mar Menor 246
Maspalomas 348
Mausoleo de los Amantes (Teruel)
    287
Maximilian, Emperor 48
Mazarrón 247
Medellín 175
Medina Azahara 226
Menorca 357, 367
Mérida 175
Metropol Parasol (Seville) 196
Mezquita (Córdoba) 201
Mezquita Cristo de la Luz (Toledo)
    166
Milagros Aqueduct (Mérida) 177
military orders 159
Mirador del Cable (Fuente Dé) 324
Mirador de San Nicolás (Granada)
    212
Miramar 363
Miramolin 44
Miró, Joan 78, 264, 363
Mojácar 229
monasteries
    Descalzas Reales (Madrid) 125
    El Paular 143
    Encarnación (Ávila) 150
    Encarnación (Madrid) 132
    Guadalupe 175
    Irache 298
    Las Huelgas (Burgos) 155
    Leyre 299
    Lluc (Mallorca) 364
    Miraflores (Burgos) 155

Montserrat 280
Oliva (Ujué) 298
Pedralbes (Barcelona) 262
Piedra 287
Poblet 281
Rábida 218
San Juan de Duero (Soria) 157
San Martiño Pinario (Santiago)
    335
San Pedro de Cardeña (Burgos)
    155
Santa Maria de las Cuevas
    (Seville) 192
Santa María La Real (Nájera)
    295
Sant Joan de les Abadesses 278
Santo Domingo de Silos 156
Santo Tomás (Ávila) 149
Santo Toribio de Lebaña 324
Sant Pere de Galligants (Girona)
    271
Sant Pere de Rodes 274
Sant Salvador (Mallorca) 367
Valldemossa (Mallorca) 361
Yuso (San Millán de la Cogolla)
    295
Yuste 49, 182
Monasterio de San Juan de la
    Peña (Aragon) 290
Montanejos 238
Monte Igueldo (San Sebastián)
    308
Montejurra 298
Montes de Toledo 169
Monte Toro 369
Montjuïc (Barcelona) 263
Montserrat 279
Monument a Colom (Barcelona)
    258
Moratalla 247
Morella 238
Mula 247
Murcia 246
Murcia province 246
Murillo, Bartolomé Esteban 76,
    191
museums and galleries
    Álmodí (Xàtiva) 242
    América (Madrid) 136
    Arqueología (Vitoria) 313
    Arqueòlogic (Eivissa) 370
    Arqueològic Municipal (Alcoi)
        244
    Arqueológico (Badajoz) 177
    Arqueológico (Córdoba) 202
    Arqueológico Nacional (Madrid)
        135
    Arqueológico (Ourense) 338
    Arqueológico (Oviedo) 325
    Arqueológico Provincial de
        Albacete 170
    Arqueológico (Seville) 195
    Arqueológico (Villena) 245
    Art Contemporani (Barcelona) 257
    Arte Abstracto (Cuneca) 171
    Arte Contemporáneo (Alicante)
        243
    Arte Contemporáneo (León) 154
    Arte Sacro de la Colegiata (A
        Coruña) 333

Artium (Bilbao) 314
Baile Flamenco (Seville) 196
Bellas Artes (Badajoz) 177
Bellas Artes (Bilbao) 314
Bellas Artes (Santander) 321
Bellas Artes (Seville) 196
Bellas Artes (Vitoria) 312
Belles Arts (Castello de la Plana)
    239
Belles Arts (Valencia) 235
Cáceres 178
Cádiz 219
CaixaForum (Barcelona) 264
CaixaForum (Madrid) 128
Caminos (Astorga) 154
Canario (Las Palmas) 347
Casa Africa (Las Palmas) 347
Cau Ferrat (Sitges) 274
Centre Pompidou Málaga 226
Centro Andaluz de Arte
    Contemporáneo (Seville) 192
Centro Atlántico de Arte Moderno
    (Las Palmas) 347
Centro de Arte Contemporáneo de
    Málaga 225
Centro de Arte Contemporáneo de
    Málaga CAC 226
Centro de Arte Rupestre
    (Ribadesella) 325
Centro Galego de Art
    Contemporani (Santiago) 317
Cervantes (Alcalá de Henares)
    144
Ciències Princip Felip (Valencia)
    236
Colección del Museo Ruso
    (Málaga) 226
Cortes (Cádiz) 219
CosmoCaixa (Barcelona) 265
Cueva Pintada (Gáldar) 349
de Semana Santa (Zamora) 153
Diocesà (La Seu d'Urgell) 277
Diocesano de Arte Sacro (Las
    Palmas) 347
Ejèrcito (Toledo) 167
El Born Centre de Cultura y
    Memòria or Born CCM
    (Barcelona) 255
El Cigarralejo (Mula) 247
Elder (Las Palmas) 347
El Greco (Toledo) 167
Episcopal (Vic) 279
Es Baluard Museu d'Art Modern i
    Contemporani (Palma) 360
Espacio Andaluz de Creación
    Contemporánea (Córdoba)
    203
Etnográfico-Textil (Plasencia) 181
Etnográfico (Zamora) 153
Evolución Humana (Burgos) 156
Extremeno e Iberoamericano de
    Arte Contemporaneo (Badajoz)
    177
Fallero (Valencia) 234
Fray Junípero Serra (Petra) 367
Frederic Marès (Barcelona) 254
Fundació Antoni Tàpies
    (Barcelona) 260
Fundació Joan Miró (Barcelona)
    264

Fundación César Manrique (Lanzarote) 351
Fundacío Pilar i Joan Miró (Palma) 360
Fundació Stämpfli Museu d'Art Contemporani (Sitges) 274
Gaudí (Barcelona) 259
Girona Art Museum 273
Greco (Toledo) 167
Guggenheim Bilbao 77, 311
Història de Catalunya (Barcelona) 259
Història de la Ciutat (Barcelona) 254, 255
Historia (Madrid) 134
Institut Valencià de Art Moderne 235
Jewish History (Girona) 271
Julio Romero de Torres (Córdoba) 203
La Granja (Mallorca) 361
Lázaro Galdiano (Madrid) 136
León 154
Lope de Vega (Madrid) 129
Maritima Ría de Bilbao (Bilbao) 312
Marítim (Barcelona) 258
MARQ (Alicante) 243
Mar (Vigo) 340
Menorca (Maó) 367
Miguel Hernández (Orihuela) 245
Militar (Santa Cruz) 352
Modernisme Català (Barcelona) 258
Monestir de Pedralbes (Barcelona) 262
Monogràfic (Eivissa) 370
Municipal Quiñores de León (Vigo) 340
Museo Arte Sobre Piel (Córdoba) 203
Museo Fournier de Naipes (Vitoria) 314
Museo Goya – Colección Ibercaja (Zaragoza) 285
Museo Universidad de Navarra (Pampelona) 297
Museu del Cinema (Girona) 272
Museu Picasso (Barcelona) 255
Nacional Centro de Arte Reina Sofia (Madrid) 317
Nacional Centro de Arte Reina Sofía (Madrid) 128
Nacional d'Art de Catalunya (Barcelona) 263
Nacional d'Art de Catalunya(Barcelona) 74
Nacional de Arqueología Subacuática (Cartagena) 247
Nacional de Arte Romano (Mérida) 176
Nacional de Ceramica (Valencia) 233
Nacional de Escultura (Valladolid) 157
Naturaleza y el Hombre (Santa Cruz) 351
Navarra (Pamplona) 296
Nuevos Museos (El Escorial) 140

Numantino (Soria) 156
Origenes (Madrid) 130
Paz de Gernika (Gernika) 310
Picasso (Barcelona) 78
Picasso (Buitfrago del Lozoya) 143
Picasso (Málaga) 225
Pizzaro (Trujillo) 180
Pobo Galego (Santiago) 335
Prado (Madrid) 126
Prehistoria y Arqueología (Santander) 322
Provincial de Bellas Artes (Córdoba) 203
Provincial (Huelva) 218
Provincial (Lugo) 335
Provincial (Pontevedra) 338
Quijote (Ciudad Real) 169
Real Academia de Bellas Artes de San Fernando (Madrid) 125
Real Armería (Madrid) 132
Románticismo (Madrid) 134
Rosalia de Castro museum (Padrón) 339
Ruiz de Luna (Talavera de la Reina) 168
Salzillo (Murcia) 246
San Martín Centro de la Cultura Contemporánea (Las Palmas) 347
Santa Clara (Murcia) 246
Santa Cruz (Toledo) 167
San Telmo (San Sebastián) 308
Sefardi (Toledo) 166
Sorolla (Madrid) 136
Taulell (Onda) 238
Taurino (Madrid) 136
Teatre-Museu Dalí (Figueres) 78, 273
Thyssen-Bornemisza (Madrid) 127
Tortura (Santillana) 322
Valencian Institute of Modern Art (Valencia) 77
Valltorta 238
Villafamès art museum 238
Viña y el Vino de Navarra (Rioja) 294
Vino (Aranda) 157
Vi (Vilafranca del Penedès) 281
Zuloaga (Zumaia) 308
Muslim Spain 39

N

Nájera 295
Naples 51
Nationalists 58, 60
national parks 105
Aigüestortes i Estany de Sant Maruici 277
Cabañeros 169
Caldera de Taburiente 353
Cañadas del Teide 352
Doñana 67, 105, 217
Garajonay 353
Monfragüe 181
Ordesa y Monte Perdido 290
Parque Nacional de Timanfaya 351

Picos de Europa 323
Tablas de Daimiel 169
nature reserves 105
Calblanque 246
Cazorla 229
Corralejo 350
Delta de l'Ebre 276
Grazalema 223
L'Albufera 241
Las Matas 245
Montseny 279
Mount Montgó 242
Penàguila 244
Sa Dragonera 361
S'Albufera 366
S'Albufera des Grau 369
Serra d'Irta 238
Somiedo 326
Navarre 43, 44, 48, 293
Necrópolis Romana (Carmona) 227
Nerja 226
Numancia 34

O

O Ferrol 331
O Grove 339
Olite 298
Olivenza 177
Olot 278
Oñati 314
Onda 238
Orihuela (Oriola) 245
Oropesa 168
Ourense 337
Oviedo 40, 58, 325

P

Padrón 339
palaces 42
Alcazaba (Málaga) 225
Alcázar de los Reyes Cristianos (Córdoba) 203
Alcázar (Seville) 194
Alhambra (Granada) 42, 209
Aljafería (Zaragoza) 285
Almudaina (Palma) 359
Ayuntamiento (Huesca) 289
Cancho Ruano 179
Carlos V (Granada) 210
Cristal (Madrid) 128
Dos Aïgues (Valencia) 233
Ducal dels Borja (Gandia) 242
Duques del Infantado (Guadalajara) 171
Duques de San Carlos (Trujillo) 179
El Escorial 73, 139
El Pardo 143
Episcopal (Astorga) 154
Episcopal (Lugo) 335
Generalife (Granada) 211
Generalitat de Catalunya (Barcelona) 254
Generalitat (Valencia) 234
Güell (Barcelona) 258
La Granja de San Ildefonso 159
Linares (Madrid) 126

Liria (Madrid) 133
Longoria 134
Marqués de la Conquista (Trujillo) 179
Medina Azahara 195, 202, 227
Miramar (San Sebastián) 307
Moja (Barcelona) 257
Nasrid (Granada) 210
Navarra (Pamplona) 296
Nuevo (Oropesa) 168
Peñaflor (Écija) 227
Pizarro de Orellana (Trujillo) 179
Real (Madrid) 131
Reial de Pedralbes (Barcelona) 262
Reial Major (Barcelona) 254
Rei Sanxo (Valldemossa) 361
Son Marroig (Miramar) 363
Taller del Moro (Toledo) 165
Veletas (Cáceres) 178
Viana (Córdoba) 204
Virreina (Barcelona) 258
Palafrugell 271
Palamós 270
Palencia 157
Palma 358
Pamplona 296
Panteón de los Infantes (El Escorial) 141
Panteón de los Reyes (El Escorial) 141
Panteón de los Reyes (León) 73, 154
parks and gardens 214
Alcázar (Córdoba) 203
Bosque Animado de Ibarrola 310
Botanical Garden (Barcelona) 263
Campo del Moro (Madrid) 132
Casade Campo (Madrid) 134
El Parque del Retiro(Madrid) 128
Generalife (Granada) 42, 211
Jardí Botànic Mar i Murtra (Blanes) 270
Jardín Botánico La Concepción (Málaga) 226
Jardín de los Frailes (El Escorial) 140
Jardín de San Carlos (A Coruña) 333
Jardins d'Alfàbia (Mallorca) 364
Parc de Joan Miró (Barcelona) 263
Parc de la Ciutadella (Barcelona) 256
Parc de l'Espanya Industrial (Barcelona) 262
Parc Güell (Barcelona) 259
Parque de Cornalvo (Mérida) 177
Parque de Doña Casilda Iturriza (Bilbao) 311
Parque del Alamillo (Seville) 192
patios (Córdoba) 200
Real Jardín Botánico(Madrid) 129
Paseo de la Concha (San Sebastián) 308
Passeig de Gràcia (Barcelona) 260
Pastrana 171
Patio de los Naranjos (Seville) 193
Pazo de Oca 337
Pazo de Raxoi (Santiago) 334

Penàguila 244
Península de La Magdalena (Santander) 321
Peninsular War 52, 311, 333
Peñíscola 239
Penísula de Jandía 350
Penyagolosa 238
Penyal d'Ifach (Calpe) 242
Phoenicians 33, 219, 225
Picasso (Barcelona) 255
Picasso, Pablo 59, 78, 143, 225, 256, 310
Pico de las Nieves 348
Pico de Tres Mares 323
Picos de Europa 319, 323
Pizarro, Francisco 48, 176, 179
Plaça del Ajuntament (Valencia) 232
Plaça de la Mare de Déu (Valencia) 234
Plasencia 180
Platja de Migjorn 371
Playa Blanca 351
Playa de las Américas 352
Playa del Inglés 348
Playa de Santiago 353
Plaza de Colón (Madrid) 135
Plaza de España (Madrid) 133
Plaza de España (Seville) 195
Plaza de la Villa (Madrid) 130
Plaza del Castillo (Pamplona) 296
Plaza del Machete (Vitoria) 313
Plaza de los Leones (Baeza) 228
Plaza de María Pita (A Coruña) 333
Plaza de Oriente (Madrid) 132
Plaza de Toros de la Maestranza (Seville) 195
Plaza de Toros (Ronda) 223
Plaza de Vázquez de Molina (Úbeda) 228
Plaza Dos de Mayo (Madrid) 134
Plaza Mayor (Chinchon) 144
Plaza Mayor (Madrid) 129
Plaza Mayor (Salamanca) 152
Plaza Mayor (Trujillo) 179
Poble Espanyol (Barcelona) 264
Poble Espanyol (Mallorca) 360
politics 63
Pollença 365
Pontevedra 338
population 23
Port d'Andratx 361
Port de la Selva 274
Portlligat 274
Porto Colom 366
Porto Cristo 366
Portugal 44, 47, 50, 59
Potes 323
Prado del Rey 221
Praza do Obradoiro (Santiago) 334
prehistoric era 32
Primo de Rivera, José 58
Primo de Rivera, Miguel 56, 143
Púbol 273
pueblos blancos 228
Puente de Alcántara (Toledo) 165
Puente de Guadiana (Mérida) 177
Puente de la Maza (San Vicente de la Barquera) 323

Puente Nuevo (Ronda) 223
Puente Romano (Alcántara) 181
Puente Romano (Ourense) 337
Puerta de Bisagra (Toledo) 165
Puerta del Sol (Madrid) 125
Puerta del Sol (Toledo) 166
Puerto Banus 224
Puerto de la Cruz 352
Puerto del Carmen 351
Puerto del Rosario 350
Puerto de Mogán 349
Puerto de Santa María 218
Puerto Lápice 169
Puigcerdà 277
Puig des Molins (Eivissa) 370
Punta del Sebo 218
Pyrenees 31, 276, 283, 290

Q

Quintanilla de las Viñas 156

R

Real Escuela Andaluza del Arte Ecuestre (Jerez) 219
Reconquista 39, 43, 45
regionalism 21, 24, 67
Requeña 240
Rías Altas 329, 331
Rías Baixas 330, 338
Ribadavia 338
Ribadeo 337
Ribadesella 324
Ricote 246
Ripoll 278
Romans 34, 35, 36, 73, 175, 191, 195, 221, 227, 240, 247, 275, 357
Roncal 299
Roncesvalles 300
Ronda 223
Roses 273
Rupit 279

S

Sacromonte (Granada) 207, 212
Sagunt 240
Salamanca 150
Salamanca (Madrid) 135
Salardú 276
Salas 326
Sa Llotja (Palma) 360
Salou 275
Sangüesa 299
San Lorenzo de El Escorial 139
Sanlúcar de Barrameda 218
San Millán de la Cogolla 295
San Sebastián 308
San Sebastián (La Gomera) 353
Santa Cruz de la Palma 353
Santa Cruz de Tenerife 351
Santa Eulària 370
Santander 321
Sant Antoni 370
Santanyí 366
Santa Pola 245
Sant Feliu de Guíxols 270
Sant Ferran 371

Sant Francesc 371
Santiago de Compostela 73, 331, 333
Santillana del Mar 322
Sant Joan de les Abadesses 278
Sant Mateu 238
Santo Domingo de la Calzada 295
Santoña 321
Sant Sadurnì 281
Sant Telm 361
San Vicente de la Barquera 323
S'Arenal 367
Segóbriga 171
Segovia 157
Serra d'Espadán 238
Serra de Tramuntana 357, 363
Serra Gelada 243
Serranía de Cuenca 171
Serranía de Ronda 223
Ses Païsses (Mallorca) 366
Setenil 224
Seville 44, 48
sherry 218, 219, 221
Sierra de Alcaraz 170
Sierra de Atapuerca 32, 156
Sierra de España 247
Sierra de Francia 182
Sierra de Gata 181
Sierra de Gredos 150, 182
Sierra de Guadalupe 175
Sierra de Guadarrama 123, 139, 142
Sierra Nevada 229
Sigüenza 171
Sinagoga (Córdoba) 202
Sinagoga del Tránsito (Toledo) 166
Sinagoga de Santa María la Blanca (Toledo) 166
Sitges 274
Sóller 363
Solsona 279
Soria 156
Sort 277
Sos del Rey Católico 290
Spanish-American War 53, 55
Spanish Armada 49
Spanish Civil War 58, 61, 64, 68, 143, 289 , 310, 346
Spanish Empire 47, 51, 55, 147
St Ignatius Loyola 49
St James (Santiago) 35
St Paul 35
St Teresa of Ávila 150
Suárez, Adolfo 64

T

Tafalla 298
Talavera de la Reina 168
Tàpies, Antoní 78, 260

Tarazona 283
Tarifa 218, 221
Tarragona 36, 43, 275
Teguise 351
Tembleque 169
Templo de Debod (Madrid) 133
Templo de Diana (Mérida) 177
Tenerife 351
Teror 349
Teruel 60, 287
theatres and concert halls
    Auditorio (Santa Cruz) 352
    Auditorio (Seville) 192
    Corral de Comedias (Almagro) 169
    Gran Teatre del Liceu (Barcelona) 258
    Palau de la Música Catalana (Barcelona) 256
    Palau de les Arts (Valencia) 236
    Roman theatre (Cartagena) 247
    Teatre Romà (Sagunt) 241
    Teatro Arriaga (Bilbao) 312
    Teatro Central (Seville) 192
    Teatro Real (Madrid) 132
    Teatro Romano (Mérida) 36, 176
theme parks
    OAqualand (Mallorca) 367
    Dinopolis (Teruel) 288
    Isla Mágica (Seville) 192
    Port Aventura (Salou) 275
Tibidabo (Barcelona) 265
Tineo 326
Toledo 43, 164, 169
Toro 153
Torquemada, Tomás de 45
Torre Agbar (Barcelona) 261
Torre de Hércules (A Coruña) 331
Torre de la Calahorra (Córdoba) 204
Torre de las Cigüeñas (Cáceres) 178
Torre del Oro (Seville) 195
Torremolinos 225
Torrevieja 245
Torroella de Montgrí 273
Tossa de Mar 270
Trujillo 179
Tudela 298
Tui 338
Túnel de Somport 290
Turia, Río 236

U

Úbeda 228
Ubrique 224
Ujué 298
universities

Alcalá de Henares 144
Oñati 314
Salamanca 42, 150
Santiago 335

V

Valcarlos 300
Val d'Aran 276
Valdepeñas 170
Valencia 44, 69, 231
Valencia province 240
Valladolid 157
Vall de Boí 276
Valldemossa 361
Valle de Baztán 300
Valle Gran Rey 353
Valley of the Fallen 61, 143
Valverde 353
Varcía Lorca 40
Vejer de la Frontera 221
Velázquez, Diego 76, 78, 127, 141, 191, 236
Viana 298
Vic 279
Vigo 340
Vilafranca del Penedès 281
Villafranca del Bierzo 155
Villareal de San Carlos 181
Villena 244
Vinaròs 237
Vitoria 313
Viveiro 337

W

wildlife 105
Wine 103, 170, 281, 299
World War I and II 57, 60

X

Xàbia (Javea) 242
Xaló (Jalón) valley 242
Xàtiva 242
Xixona (Jijona) 244

Z

Zafra 177
Zahara de la Sierra 224
Zamora 153
Zapatero, José Luis Rodríguez 67
Zaragoza 36, 43, 283, 284
Zarautz 309
Zugarramurdi 300
Zumaia 309
Zurbarán, Francisco 76, 175